Learning from
Donald and

Learning from Mickey, Donald and Walt

Essays on Disney's Edutainment Films

Edited by
A. Bowdoin Van Riper

McFarland & Company, Inc., Publishers
Jefferson, North Carolina, and London

Library of Congress Cataloguing-in-Publication Data

Learning from Mickey, Donald and Walt : essays on Disney's edutainment films / edited by A. Bowdoin Van Riper.
p. cm.
Includes bibliographical references and index.

ISBN 978-0-7864-5957-5
softcover : 50# alkaline paper ♾

1. Walt Disney Company. 2. Walt Disney Pictures. 3. Disney, Walt — Criticism and interpretation. 4. Animated films— United States— History and criticism. 5. Documentary films— United States. 6. Motion pictures in education — United States. I. Van Riper, A. Bowdoin.
PN1999.W27L43 2011
791.43'66 — dc22 2010047490

British Library cataloguing data are available

Front cover by TG Design

Manufactured in the United States of America

McFarland & Company, Inc., Publishers
Box 611, Jefferson, North Carolina 28640
www.mcfarlandpub.com

For Cindy,
who believed

Table of Contents

Acknowledgments ix

Introduction
A. Bowdoin Van Riper 1

Section I: War and Propaganda

1. The Canadian Shorts: Establishing Disney's Wartime Style
Bella Honess Roe 15

2. "Desiring the Disney Technique": Chronicle of a Contracted Military Training Film
Douglas A. Cunningham 27

3. Cartoons Will Win the War: World War II Propaganda Shorts
Richard J. Leskosky 40

4. Cartoon Combat: World War II, Alexander de Seversky, and *Victory Through Air Power*
John D. Thomas 63

Section II: Science, Technology, Mathematics and Medicine

5. The Promise of Things to Come: *Disneyland* and the Wonders of Technology, 1954–58
A. Bowdoin Van Riper 84

6. A Nation on Wheels: Films About Cars and Driving, 1948–1970
A. Bowdoin Van Riper 103

7. "A Journey Through the Wonderland of Mathematics": *Donald in Mathmagic Land*
MARTIN F. NORDEN 113

8. Paging Doctor Disney: Health Education Films, 1922–1973
BOB CRUZ, JR. 127

Section III: Nature

9. "Nature is the Dramatist": Documentary, Entertainment, and the World According to the *True-Life Adventures*
EDDY VON MUELLER 145

10. Sex, Love, and Death: True-Life Fantasies
RONALD TOBIAS 164

11. It *Is* a Small World, After All: *Earth* and the Disneyfication of *Planet Earth*
EDDY VON MUELLER 173

Section IV: Times, Places and People

12. A Past to Make Us Proud: U. S. History According to Disney
MARIANNE HOLDZKOM 183

13. Reviving the American Dream: The World of Sports
KATHARINA BONZEL 201

14. Beyond the *Ratoncito*: Disney's Idea of Latin America
BERNICE NUHFER-HALTEN 209

15. Locating the Magic Kingdom: Spectacle and Similarity in *People and Places*
CYNTHIA J. MILLER 221

16. America's Salesman: *The USA in Circarama*
SARAH NILSEN 237

About the Contributors 255

Index 259

Acknowledgments

This project had its origins at a 2006 conference, *The Documentary Tradition*, sponsored by the Center for the Study of Film and History. For helping to bring it from there to here, I am grateful to Dan Vogel and Ron Weekes, for their contributions to the original conversation; Peter Rollins, organizer of the conference and director *emeritus* of the Center, for his encouragement; Skip Elsheimer, for his generous offer of access to his film collection; Kathy Merlock Jackson, for her astute comments and suggestions; several anonymous referees, for sharpening my ideas about the shape of the project; and my daughter Katie, for her patience with a project that I began when she was in elementary school and finished when she was in high school.

Finally, my thanks go to Cindy Miller, whose insight, enthusiasm, and willingness to be my first, best editor have been invaluable throughout this project's long life.

Introduction

A. Bowdoin Van Riper

All movie studios are in the fantasy business, but none more so than Disney. Its biggest "stars" are a plucky white-gloved mouse who keeps a pet dog, a perpetually exasperated duck in a sailor's blouse (but no pants), and a gangling, irrepressibly happy being of uncertain species. Its films have, over eight decades, shown audiences towering castles, talking animals, magic spells, and still-more exotic sights: flying elephants, ticking crocodiles, self-aware Volkswagens, and elaborate musical numbers performed by dancing tableware. The very first Mickey Mouse cartoon released, *Steamboat Willie*, set the tone with a surrealistic "concert" played entirely on barnyard animals. Pulling a cat's tail (he is not yet the upright, well-behaved citizen he will become), Mickey generates a high-pitched cry ... and immediately begins swinging the unfortunate feline by its tail to produce a siren-like wailing. He seizes first a goose and then a sow's teats, squeezing bodies and fingering extremities to transform the beasts into bagpipes. A cow's mouth gapes open before him, and he takes up a pair of mallets to play the broad, flat teeth like a xylophone. Two young trees lift their roots from the ground and dance joyously with each other in *Flowers and Trees*, the studio's first Technicolor cartoon. Mushrooms and flowers form a ring around them, cheering them on.[1]

Snow White and the Seven Dwarfs, the studio's first animated feature, provided audiences with a deeper, richer fantasy experience. The film showcased Disney's emerging "house style" of animation: soft, rounded, richly and subtly colored—"more real *than* real," in the words of Walt Disney, who had prescribed its use. The film also, through the use of a multi-plane camera, gave audiences the unprecedented sensation of moving into, not just across, the painted world.[2] *Snow White* offered audiences a chance to immerse themselves in a fully realized fantasy world, and films like *Pinocchio* (1940), *Dumbo* (1941), and *Bambi* (1944) opened the doors to others. Fantasy, rendered in a distinctively lush visual style, has remained the hallmark of Disney's animated features. The fantasy and stylization are most apparent in traditional fairy tales like *Cinderella* (1950) or *Sleeping Beauty* (1959), and in animal-centric stories like *The Jungle Book* (1967) or *The Lion King* (1994). They are equally present, however, even in nominally more realistic features, such as *The Sword in the Stone* (1963) and *Mulan* (1998). The studio's most elaborate live-action features—*Mary Poppins* (1964), *Bedknobs and Broomsticks* (1971), and *Escape to Witch Mountain* (1975) display the same qualities.[3]

Disney's close association with the fantastic has, over the years, overshadowed its long-standing interest in reality. The studio has produced and released a steady stream of films designed to educate as well as entertain: to actively convey factual information about the real world, while using it as a backdrop for comedy or drama that, in turn, leavened the educational elements of the production. Walt Disney himself coined, in 1948, the term "edutainment" to describe such productions, but Disney Studios had already been producing them for nearly a decade. The films range from eight-minute shorts through "featurettes" of varying lengths to fully-developed features.[4] They took a variety of forms: traditional live-action documentaries; dramatizations of historical events; animated illustrations of historical, scientific, and political concepts; and complex hybrids of animation, staged dramatization, and location footage. They were created for diverse audiences, and for diverse settings: movie theaters, army barracks, classrooms, television, and attractions at Disney's own theme parks. Collectively, they represent a significant portion of the studio's output.

The sheer volume of edutainment films that Disney produced, and the company's enthusiasm for recycling and repackaging them, made them an ubiquitous presence in postwar American popular culture. The *True-Life Adventures* nature documentaries, for example, were released theatrically, aired on Disney's Sunday-evening television anthology series, plundered for clips used in productions such as *Nature's Better Built Homes* (1969), and marketed to schools in 16-millimeter prints for classroom use. Animated footage depicting the early history of aviation, originally created for *Victory Through Air Power* (1943), was reused (with new narration) in the anthology-series episode *Man in Flight* (1957), and reused again in a later episode, *Fly with Von Drake* (1963). In between, they appeared as still illustrations in a *Man in Flight* comic book published by Dell. Videocassettes, laser discs, and DVDs—particularly the limited-edition "Disney Treasures" collection—gave decades-old edutainment productions a new lease on life, as did (in its early years) the Disney Channel cable television network.

Disney's edutainment films are significant, however, not simply for their ubiquity but also for the ideas they present. They are among the purest reflections of Walt Disney's worldview—a vision that continued to shape the studio's output after his death in 1966. Ideas that subtly shape Disney's narrative films—the sanctity of the patriarchal family, the moral superiority of small towns, the unmixed blessings of technology, the exceptional status of the United States, the benevolence of authority figures and the virtues of submitting to them—are preached, openly and explicitly, in Disney edutainment films. Those values, as well as the more concrete, factual content, are part of the lessons the films are designed to impart.[5] Disney's long involvement with edutainment shows that the studio, whose stock-in-trade was fantasy, was equally at home in the real world. This collection is designed to explore that dimension of the studio's films. It is a book about Disney, being serious.

Filmmaking with Intent to Educate: Disney "Edutainment" Films Defined

The distinction between "narrative" and "documentary" forms in film and television is neither crisply defined nor unproblematic.[6] A profusion of in-between terms—docudrama, biopic, pseudo-documentary, mockumentary, reality television—testify to the lack of consensus about where, or even whether, the two broad categories overlap. Documentary films concern events that actually took place, but routinely use techniques borrowed from narrative filmmaking to establish structure and create audience appeal. They emphasize certain characters and events while deemphasizing others, adjust the sequencing and tempo of events, and create, choose, or juxtapose images for the sake of visual interest. They recreate events that cameras could not or did not record, sometimes striving for perfect fidelity of detail, sometimes seeking a more impressionistic kind of truth. Narrative films tell fictional stories, but set those stories against the backdrop of the real world rather than creating wholly new worlds. They use establishing shots of buildings and landscapes that are often indistinguishable from those used in documentaries, and (particularly if set in the past) frequently use footage *from* documentaries to establish a sense of time and place. The very existence of terms (and analytical categories) like "docudrama" and "mockumentary" suggest the degree of overlap between the categories and the permeability of their boundaries.

Countless films, particularly those depicting historic figures and events, flop with unruly energy across those boundaries. Only the most openly, deliberately transgressive—Warren Beatty's *Reds*, Alex Cox's *Walker*, or Oliver Stone's *JFK*—draw more than sporadic critical commentary for their energetic blurring of lines.[7] The rest are slotted into one category or the other with little discussion and (often) for obscure reasons. War films like *Zulu*, *Tora! Tora! Tora!*, or *Gettysburg* are a particular case in point. Made with narrative-film budgets and studded with familiar actors, they eschew traditional dramatic plotlines in favor of minutely detailed recreations of well-documented historical events.[8] Frequently criticized as dull, plodding, and didactic *because* of their laser-like focus on accurately recreating past events, they are just as frequently shelved with heavily fictionalized epics like *Pearl Harbor* or wholly fictional ones like *Air Force*.

Taken as a group, the films and television programs produced by Walt

Disney Studios reflect all these complexities of definition and categorization. The vast majority fall cleanly and unambiguously into one category or the other. *Treasure Island* (1950) and *The Lion King* (1994) are narrative films. *The Living Desert* (1953) and *Roving Mars* (2006) are documentaries.

Disney documentaries are distinguished, however, by their unusually free use of narrative elements, especially fantastic or whimsical ones, in otherwise serious contexts. The Disney vault also contains films that straddle and blur the lines between categories still further. The animated featurette *Donald in Mathmagic Land* (1959), for example, uses a patently fictitious character's journey through a patently imaginary world to teach real mathematical concepts. Other Disney productions, ranging from the hallucinatory *Three Caballeros* (1945) to the sober *Mars and Beyond* (1957) intercut straightforward documentary scenes and wild flights of imagination. Television serials like *Davy Crockett* (1954–1955) or *The Swamp Fox* (1959–1961), along with feature films like *Pocahontas* (1995), take historically documented figures and make them the heroes of fictional adventures. Films such as *Ten Who Dared* (1960) and *Miracle* (2003) dramatize specific historical events, but "improve" on them (and the people involved) for dramatic purposes. Disney's willingness to use whimsical narrative elements even in the most serious of documentaries is part of what makes Disney documentaries distinctive.

Walt Disney used the term "edutainment" to describe the kind of documentaries he wanted his studio to produce: Information-rich, yet lively and engaging. This book extends it to all Disney productions that deliberately interwove documentary and narrative elements — the realistic and the fantastic — in order to educate the audience. This broader use of "edutainment" encompasses conventional documentaries like *The Living Desert* and *To The South Pole for Science*, docudramas like *Ten Who Dared* and *Miracle*, fictionalized biopics like *The Swamp Fox* and *Pocahontas*, consciously educational films like *Four Methods of Flush Riveting*, stealthily educational films like *Freewayphobia*, and hybrid works like *Magic Highway USA* and *Donald in Mathmagic Land*. The element that ties these disparate films together is their explicit intent to instruct the audience, not just about the human condition but about the details of the real world. Instructional intent — determination to convey information, or to explicitly make a point — is what distinguishes *Magic Highway USA* from *The Love Bug* and *The Swamp Fox* from *Treasure Island*. It is what separates, more broadly, the edutainment films dealt with in this book from entertainment-driven narrative films for which Disney is justly famous.

Disney Edutainment Films: A Historical Survey

Fantasia, released in 1940, was perhaps the most overtly fantastical of Disney's early animated features.[9] Its most famous segment, "The Sorcerer's

Apprentice," pitted the title character (played by Mickey Mouse) against a relentless army of marching brooms. Other segments featured cavorting centaurs, hippo ballerinas, and (in "Night on Bald Mountain") a towering demon. Squarely in the midst of these fantastical creatures, however, lay the studio's first significant experiment with realism. The fourth of the film's seven segments used Igor Stravinsky's *Rite of Spring* as an audio backdrop for the story of life on Earth, beginning with the formation of the solar system and ending with the extinction of the dinosaurs. The opening narration for the segment made the filmmakers' documentary intentions clear. The segment itself—wordless like most of the rest of the film—lived up to that promise. The art was spare and realistic, the colors deep and vibrant, but muted, and the wordless narrative consistent with the state of paleontological knowledge in the 1930s. The most memorable images from the segment—dinosaurs, first locked in mortal combat and then perishing together as the climate changes—could have come straight from Rudolph Zallinger's murals at Yale's Peabody Museum.

The outbreak of World War II broadened Disney's involvement with reality-based films. The studio turned out a steady stream of instructional cartoon shorts for the military—light-hearted in approach, but serious in intent—that were designed to educate soldiers, defense workers, and civilians on subjects ranging from recycling and personal hygiene to riveting techniques and the proper use of anti-tank weapons.[10] The studio's second line of wartime shorts was propagandistic rather than instructional. Not all the propaganda shorts were realistic—*Der Fuehrer's Face* plunged Donald Duck into a surreal, nightmarish vision of life under the Third Reich—but all sought to present reality as Walt Disney, and the country's wartime leaders, saw it. *Education for Death* purported to show how Nazi Germany indoctrinated its citizens, beginning in early childhood. The most ambitious of these wartime propaganda films was the 1943 featurette *Victory Through Air Power*. Mixing various forms of animation with stock footage and lectures by Major Alexander de Seversky, it made the case for aerial bombing as a decisive factor in modern warfare. The demands of wartime diplomacy—specifically the need to foster good relations with Central and South America—gave rise to *Saludos Amigos!* (1943) and *The Three Caballeros* (1945). Mixing animation and live action as *Victory* did, they too were designed to make a broad point: that Latin America and the United States were natural allies, and their peoples similar in culture and outlook.

The decade immediately following the end of the war brought major changes to Disney Studios. One was Walt Disney's decision to begin producing live-action features, which promised lower production costs and higher profits than costly animated features. The second was the launch of a weekly Disney anthology series on the ABC television network in the fall of 1954. The third was the opening of Disneyland, the first Disney theme park, in 1955. All three of these developments created new demand for films, and new opportunities for bringing them to a wide audience. It is no coincidence that the immediate postwar period (roughly 1945–1960) was the heyday of Disney's documentaries and docudramas.

The leading edge of this postwar wave of reality-based Disney films was the *True-Life Adventures* series of nature documentaries, which began with *Seal Island* in 1949.[11] Elaborate productions focusing on a particular animal (such as *The African Lion*) or environment (such as *The Vanishing Prairie*), they featured full color footage shot entirely on location, often in tight close-up or slow motion. Walt Disney insisted that they be factually accurate, but in practice the nuggets of fact were wrapped in layers of storyline, careful editing, and anthropromorphic narration. Designed to make the films appealing to audiences, these elements made the films more artificial than their publicity suggested. The *True-Life Adventures* series eventually encompassed 13 films, eight of which won Academy Awards, before it ended with *Islands of the Sea* in 1960. Ben Sharpsteen, who produced twelve of the thirteen, also produced a parallel *People and Places* series that began with *The Alaskan Eskimo* in 1953. As the series title suggests, these 30 minute featurettes did for geography what the *True-Life Adventures* did for natural history. Focusing on exotic areas such as *Siam* (1954), *Switzerland* (1955), and *Lapland* (1957), they combined elements of two traditional documentary forms: the travelogue, and the popular ethnography. Three of them won Academy Awards for best documentary short subject: *The Alaskan Eskimo* in 1953, *Men Against the Arctic* in 1955, and *The Ama Girls* (about life in a Japanese fishing village) in 1958.

The *Disneyland* television series, which premiered on 27 October 1954, was designed to mesh seamlessly with the studio's theatrical releases and the new Disneyland amusement park, then under construction. Old theatrical releases from the studio's vaults provided a cheap source of quality programming to fill the weekly broadcasts, and documentary shorts from the *True-Life Adventures* and *People and Places* series fit its hour-long format especially well. Short documentaries showcasing the park and its attractions also became a regular feature on *Disneyland*, as did "behind the scenes" shorts that introduced audiences to the process of movie-making. The behind-the-scenes programs fell into three broad categories. The first, like "The Story of Animated Drawing" (broadcast November 30, 1955), showed the process of animation, and used cartoon shorts from the Disney catalog as illustrations. The second, like "A Cavalcade of Songs" (broadcast February 16, 1955), featured Walt Disney discussing a particular element of the studio's cartoons, again using clips from the vault as supporting evidence. The third, like "Operation Undersea" (broadcast December 8, 1954), chronicled the elaborate efforts of Disney camera crews to shoot on location: in northern Scandinavia for the *Lapland* entry in People and Places, for example, or underwater for *20,000 Leagues Under the Sea*.

The flexible structure of the *Disneyland* program—four rotating weekly themes: Fantasyland, Frontierland, Adventureland, and Tomorrowland—meant that individual elements could be combined and recombined in different variations. The *True-Life Adventure* films, for example, were first released theatrically, then broadcast multiple times on television, and finally used as a source of footage for compilation programs like *Nature's Better-Built Homes*. Footage of the primary camera crew shot by the second-unit crew could, meanwhile, become "behind the scenes" documentary shorts of their own. Disney thus had the luxury of paying the costs of a filmmaking expedition once, then reaping the benefits multiple times.

Disneyland also featured original programming, produced for and originally aired on the television series. The most ambitious were a series of documentaries about science and technology, designed to mix animation with live-action footage and serious educational segments with comic relief.[12] Six of these hour-long programs—three about space travel and one each about highways, aviation, and nuclear energy—eventually aired, along with a three-part series of more traditional documentaries tracing the U. S. Navy's involvement in the exploration of Antarctica. Just as the *True-Life Adventures* found a second life on television, several of the made-for-television documentaries were recycled as theatrical releases. *Our Friend the Atom* was screened as a featurette in European theaters, and footage from the three Antarctica episodes was edited into a *People and Places* film titled *The Seven Cities of Antarctica*.

Impressive as they were, the science-and-technology documentaries that aired on *Disneyland* were eclipsed, in the public eye, by a simpler kind of reality-based film: the historical drama.[13] *Davy Crockett* (5 episodes; 1954–1955) was followed later in the decade by *Texas John Slaughter* (13 episodes, 1958–61), *The Nine Lives of Elfego Baca* (11 episodes, 1958–1961), and *The Swamp Fox* (6 episodes, 1959–61). All four series used conventional adventure story plots, but set them against the backdrop of real historical events. All four featured heroes based on real historical figures: Crockett, a frontiersman and member of Congress who died at the Alamo; Slaughter, a member of the Texas Rangers; Baca, a self-appointed Arizona deputy sheriff who became a frontier lawyer; and Francis "The Swamp Fox" Marion, a Revolutionary War guerrilla leader whose men harassed British forces in the Carolinas. These serialized adventures for television were complemented by a series of theatrical features based on the adventures of historical figures. These covered familiar periods from American history, such as the Revolution (*Johnny Tremain*, 1957), the Civil War (*The Great Locomotive Chase*, 1956), and the opening of the West (*Ten Who Dared*, 1960), but also the history of England (*The Sword and the Rose*, 1953), Scotland (*Rob Roy: The Highland Rogue*, 1953), Ireland (*Fighting Prince of Donegal*, 1966) and even Austria (*The Miracle of the White Stallions*, 1963).

The decade-and-a-half from the late 1950s and the first years of the 1960s were the golden age of Disney documentaries and docudramas. Noting, perhaps, the declining popularity of historical dramas at the box office and Westerns on television, the studio shifted the focus of its live-action filmmaking to family comedies like *The Absent-Minded Professor* and fictionalized animal stories like *Charlie, The Lonesome Cougar.* The output of new documentary features and shorts never entirely stopped, however. The animated *Donald in Mathmagic Land* appeared in 1959 and the historical drama *Justin Morgan Had a Horse* in 1972.

The animated shorts *Freewayphobia* and *Goofy's Freeway Troubles* (1965) and the hybrid featurette *Dad, Can I Borrow the Car?* (1970) continued an informal string of commentaries on Americans and their automobiles that had begun with *Motor Mania* in 1948. Disney's production of educational shorts for the school and corporate markets also ground onward, with titles such as 1965's *Steel and America* (made for U. S. Steel) and 1967's *Understanding Stresses and Strains* (made for Upjohn). The release of the heavily fictionalized features *Squanto: A Warriors Tale, Iron Will* (both 1994) and *Pocahontas* (1995), heralded a return to adventure stories based on real people and real events. *Pocahontas,* the first Disney animated feature to be based on real historical figures, was followed in turn by the similar *Mulan* and the direct-to-video sequel *Pocahontas II: Voyage to a New World* (both 1998) before the studio shifted its attention to based-on-a-true story sports dramas with *Remember the Titans* in 2000.

The continuation of the sports-docudrama cycle with *The Rookie* (2002), *Miracle* (2004), and *The Greatest Game Ever Played* (2005) suggests that, at the beginning of the twenty-first century, reality-based films are still an important part of the Disney Studios output. IMAX documentaries such as *Ghosts of the Abyss* (2003) and *Roving Mars* (2006) confirm it, as do recently released concert films featuring Miley Cyrus (2008) and The Jonas Brothers (2009). At this writing, nearly seventy years after the "Rite of Spring" sequence of *Fantasia* traced the history of life on our planet, the latest Disney film to reach theaters is a latter-day version of the *True-Life Adventures*: a lavish, feature-length nature documentary titled simply: *Earth.*

Why This Book?

There is no shortage of books, both scholarly and popular, about Disney's films and television programs. Many of the films treated in this volume have been treated before, and some of them (the *True-Life Adventures*) have been treated extensively. Why, then, another book on Disney films? More particularly, why *this* book?

Disney's edutainment films— documentaries, docudramas, and the rest— span seventy years and represent an extraordinary range of subject matter, narrative strategies, and visual styles. They reflect substantial investments of time, money, and equipment, and utilized the talents of a diverse group of animators, directors, cameramen, composers, and technical advisors. All of them, however, were linked by their underlying purpose: To educate the audience in the process of entertaining them. The goal of this book is to illuminate that goal, and the means used to achieve it, surveying the full range of Disney's edutainment projects. It is divided into five thematic sections, each designed to juxtapose similar films and, by doing so, to highlight both their extraordinary diversity and their surprising commonalities.

The first section, devoted to war and specifically to World War II, surveys the range and diversity of Disney's substantial contributions to the war effort. Bella Honess Roe explores the wartime training films that Disney made for the National Film Board of Canada, and Douglas A. Cunningham examines the training films that Disney made for the United States Army Air Forces. Both sets of films are edutainment in its most extreme form: They deal with topics that are serious, complex, and essential to the war effort (flush riveting, high-altitude bombing, and the proper operation of anti-tank weapons), but do so in ways designed to keep audiences of soldiers paying attention. Disney Studios' other principal contribution to the war effort was propaganda films. Richard J. Leskosky places these in context, showing how Disney pressed familiar characters into service to deliver serious wartime messages about resource conservation, diplomacy, and the evils of totalitarianism. John D. Thomas's essay on *Victory Through Air Power* rounds out the section, showing how Disney's most famous wartime production used animation to present and extend the ideas proposed in the 1942 book of the same name. *Victory*, both the book and the film, preached the value of strategic bombing as a war-winning weapon: A far cry from the gentle messages of Disney's earlier features.

Section II takes up Disney's explorations of the world-changing powers of science, technology, medicine and mathematics. A. Bowdoin Van Riper's essay focuses on the "Tomorrowland" segments from the *Disneyland* television program, which—at the height of the Cold War—celebrated the virtues of large-scale, government-funded science and technology projects. It considers the "Disney version" of subjects such as space exploration, superhighways, aviation, nuclear power, and the evolution of life, and reveals a surprising level of sophistication in Disney's attempts to inform Americans about them. The following essay considers Disney's complicated relationship with the automobile, which Walt himself saw both as an emblem of progress and American ingenuity, and a threat to the small-town way of life that Disney films and theme parks glorified. Martin F. Norden traces the complex history of a single half-hour featurette, *Donald in Mathmagic Land*, which helped to establish Disney as a major provider of educational materials for K-12 schools. Bob Cruz, Jr.'s essay on the Disney public health films rounds out the section, with in-depth looks at a different kind of educational film; so different, in fact, that it scarcely seems compatible with the Disney name. *Tommy Tucker's Tooth, The Story of Menstruation,* and *VD Attack Plan* unmistakably bear the Disney visual and narrative stamp, however, and Cruz shows how their unconventional narrative styles make potentially uncomfortable topics palatable.

Disney's nature documentaries, the subject of the third section, are perhaps the best known of all the studio's "edutainment." Eddy von Mueller first considers Disney's famous *True-Life Adventures* series of nature documentaries, still the studio's best-known and best-loved exercises in edutainment. Ronald Tobias considers a group of less-familiar "True-Life Fantasy" films that continued the *True-Life Adventures'* tradition of dramatized animal life-stories without a human presence, but shifted the balance from information to entertainment. A third essay, also by von Mueller, considers Disney's attempt to revive the *True-Life Adventure* style of film-making. It explores the continuity of *earth* with earlier Disney nature films, and the ways in which it uses twenty-first century technologies to create a larger-than-life moviegoing experience and turn nature into a form of cinematic spectacle.

Section IV considers the products of Disney Studios' fascination with telling the stories of real people and events. Marianne Holdzkom surveys the "Disney version" of American history—from the Colonial era in *Johnny Tremain* to the election of 1888 in *The One and Only, Genuine, Original Family Band*— and finds it dominated by messages about the importance of unity and common cause. Such messages were Disney's philosophical stock-in-trade, and had particular resonance during the Cold War, when most of the studio's American history epics appeared. Katharina Bonzel's essay on Disney sports films shows that, in telling the stories of essentially ordinary Americans achieving greatness on the playing field—college hockey players winning Olympic gold in *Miracle*, or coach Herman Boone achieving racial harmony in *Remember the Titans*— Disney sought to show that the American dream was alive and well as the new century began. Bernice Nuhfer-Halten considers Disney's wartime exercises in cinematic Latin American diplomacy as an effort to "sell" Latin American culture to skeptical Americans by stylizing, essentializing, and distorting it. Cynthia J. Miller's essay on the *People and Places* series (a parallel to the better-known *True-Life Adventures*) assesses its elaborately "spontaneous" glimpses of exotic lands and reduction of complex cultures to splashes of local color, while noting its enormous stylistic influence on later geographic documentaries. The final essay of the section (and the book) considers some of Disney's most technologically audacious documentaries: the Circarama films, designed to surround audiences with 360 degrees of moving images. Sarah Nilsen shows that, though best remembered as a theme-park attraction, these films actually had their roots in the Cold War, when they were deployed at world's fairs as part of a State Department effort to promote America to the world.

The diversity of subjects covered by these essays suggests the scope of Disney's engagement with the real world. Fantasy— talking animals, objects with human personalities, and a growing stable of princesses— remains the studio's stock-in-trade, but no corner of reality is truly beyond reach of the "Disney touch."

Notes

1. J. P. Telotte, *The Mouse Machine: Disney and Technology* (Urbana and Chicago: University of Illinois Press, 2008), 28–29, 48–49.

2. Telotte, *Mouse Machine*, 62–67.

3. Leonard Maltin, *The Disney Films*, 4th edition (New York: Disney Editions, 2000) surveys the studio's productions. On Disney's visual style, see: Jack Kinney, *Walt Disney and Other Assorted Characters: An Unauthorized Account of the Early Years at Disney's* (New York: Harmony Books, 1988); Ollie Johnston and Frank Thomas, *Disney Animation: The Illusion of Life* (New York: Disney Editions, 1995); John Kenworthy, *The Hand Behind the Mouse: An Intimate Biography of Ub Iwerks* (New York: Disney Editions, 2001). John Canemaker, *Walt Disney's Nine Old Men and the Art of Animation* (New York: Disney Editions, 2001). Leonard Maltin, *Of Mice and Magic: A History of American Animated Cartoons*, revised ed. (New York: Plume, 1987) and Michael Barrier, *Hollywood Cartoons: American Animation in the Golden Age* (New York: Oxford University Press, 1999) place Disney's films in the context of American animation in general. The scholarly literature on Walt Disney films is vast. Kathy Merlock Jackson, *Walt Disney: A Bio-Bibliography* (Westport, CT: Greenwood Press, 1993) is a useful guide to earlier work. For more recent studies, see "Walt Disney: A Bibliography of Materials in the UC Berkeley Library," accessed 12 May 2009 at http://www.lib.berkeley.edu/MRC/disney.html

4. Bill Cotter, *The Wonderful World of Disney Television* (New York: Disney Editions, 1997) surveys the history of the anthology series.

5. Disney's worldview is discussed in detail by his many biographers, particularly Stephen Watts, *The Magic Kingdom: Walt Disney and the American Way of Life* (Columbia: University of Missouri Press, 2001) and Neal Gabler, *Walt Disney: The Triumph of the American Imagination* (New York: Knopf, 2006).

6. Jack C. Ellis and Betsy A. McLane, *A New History of Documentary Film* (New York: Continuum, 2006), pp. 1–12 provides a basic theoretical introduction and a useful list of further readings.

7. All three films, and the larger issues they raise, are considered at length in Robert A. Rosenstone, *Visions of the Past: The Challenge of Film to Our Idea of History* (Cambridge: Harvard University Press, 1995).

8. See George MacDonald Fraser, *The Hollywood History of the World* (New York: Morrow, 1988), pp. 142–147 [on *Zulu*] and Akira Iriye, "Tora! Tora! Tora!" in Mark C. Carnes, ed., *Past Imperfect: History According to the Movies* (New York: Holt, 1995), 228–231.

9. John Culhane, *Walt Disney's Fantasia* (New York: Harry N. Abrams, 1987).

10. Richard Shale, *Donald Duck Joins Up: The Walt Disney Studio During World War II* (Ann Arbor: UMI Research Press, 1982).

11. On the history and content of the series see, for example, Cynthia Chris, *Watching Wildlife* (Minneapolis: University of Minnesota Press, 2006), pp. 28–41; Scott Hermanson, "Truer Than Life: Disney's Animal Kingdom." In *Rethinking Disney: Private Control, Public Dimensions*, ed. Mike Budd and Max H. Kirsch. (Middletown, CT: Wesleyan University Press, 2005); Gregg Mitman, *Reel Nature: America's Romance with Wildlife on Film* (Cambridge: Harvard University Press, 1999), pp. 109–130; and Margaret J. King, "The Audience in the Wilderness: The Disney Nature Films," *Journal of Popular Film and Television* 24 (1996), pp. 60–68.

12. On the three space films, see J. P. Telotte, "Disney in Science Fiction Land," *Journal of Popular Film and Television* 33 (2005), pp. 12–21; and Miek Wright, "The Disney-Von Braun Collaboration and Its Influence on Space Exploration." 1993. Accesses 28 October 2002 at http://history.msfc.nasa.gov/special/Disney.html.

13. J. G. O'Boyle, "'Be Sure You're Right, Then Go Ahead': The Early Disney West-

erns," *Journal of Popular Film and Television* 24 (1996), pp 69–82. On *Davy Crockett*, which drew the largest contemporary audiences, see Margaret J. King, "The Recycled Hero: Walt Disney's Davy Crockett," in Michael A. Lofaro, ed. *Davy Crockett: The Man, the Legend, the Legacy*, 1786–1986 (Knoxville: University of Tennessee Press, 1985).

BIBLIOGRAPHY

Barrier, Michael. *Hollywood Cartoons: American Animation in the Golden Age*. New York: Oxford University Press, 1999.

Canemaker, John. *Walt Disney's Nine Old Men and the Art of Animation*. New York: Disney Editions, 2001.

Chris, Cynthia. *Watching Wildlife*. Minneapolis: University of Minnesota Press, 2006.

Cotter, Bill. *The Wonderful World of Disney Television*. New York: Disney Editions, 1997.

Culhane, John. *Walt Disney's Fantasia*. New York: Harry N. Abrams, 1987.

Ellis, Jack C., and Betsy A. McLane, *A New History of Documentary Film*. New York: Continuum, 2006.

Fraser, George MacDonald. *The Hollywood History of the World*. New York: Morrow, 1988.

Gabler, Neal. *Walt Disney: The Triumph of the American Imagination*. New York: Knopf, 2006.

Hermanson, Scott. "Truer Than Life: Disney's Animal Kingdom." In *Rethinking Disney: Private Control, Public Dimensions*, edited by Mike Budd and Max H. Kirsch. Middletown, CT: Wesleyan University Press, 2005).

Iriye, Akira. "Tora! Tora! Tora!" In *Past Imperfect: History According to the Movies*, edited by Mark C. Carnes, 228–231. New York: Holt, 1995.

Jackson, Kathy Merlock. *Walt Disney: A Bio-Bibliography*. Westport, CT: Greenwood Press, 1993.

Johnston, Ollie and Frank Thomas, *Disney Animation: The Illusion of Life*. New York: Disney Editions, 1995.

Kenworthy, John. *The Hand Behind the Mouse: An Intimate Biography of Ub Iwerks*. New York: Disney Editions, 2001.

King, Margaret J. "The Audience in the Wilderness: The Disney Nature Films," *Journal of Popular Film and Television* 24 (1996): 60–68.

_____. "The Recycled Hero: Walt Disney's Davy Crockett." In *Davy Crockett: The Man, the Legend, the Legacy*, 1786–1986, edited by Michael A. Lofaro. Knoxville: University of Tennessee Press, 1985.

Kinney, Jack. *Walt Disney and Assorted Other Characters: An Unauthorized Account of the Early Years at Disney's*. New York: Harmony Books, 1988.

Maltin, Leonard. *The Disney Films*, 4th edition. New York: Disney Editions, 2000.

_____. *Of Mice and Magic: A History of American Animated Cartoons*, revised edition. New York: Plume, 1987.

Mitman, Gregg. *Reel Nature: America's Romance with Wildlife on Film*. Cambridge, MA: Harvard University Press, 1999.

O'Boyle, J. G. "'Be Sure You're Right, Then Go Ahead': The Early Disney Westerns," *Journal of Popular Film and Television* 24 (1996):69–82.

Rosenstone, Robert A. *Visions of the Past: The Challenge of Film to Our Idea of History*. Cambridge, MA: Harvard University Press, 1995.

Shale, Richard. *Donald Duck Joins Up: The Walt Disney Studio During World War II*. Ann Arbor, MI: UMI Research Press, 1982.

_____. "Disney in Science Fiction Land," *Journal of Popular Film and Television* 33 (2005): 12–21.

_____. *The Mouse Machine: Disney and Technology*. Urbana and Chicago: University of Illinois Press, 2008.

"Walt Disney: A Bibliography of Materials in the UC Berkeley Library" http://www.lib.berkeley.edu/MRC/disney.html

Watts, Stephen. *The Magic Kingdom: Walt Disney and the American Way of Life*. Columbia: University of Missouri Press, 2001.

Wright, Mike. "The Disney-Von Braun Collaboration and Its Influence on Space Exploration." 1993. National Aeronautics and Space Administration Marshall Spaceflight Center Website. http://history.msfc.nasa.gov/special/Disney.html

Section I: War and Propaganda

1

The Canadian Shorts

Establishing Disney's Wartime Style

Bella Honess Roe

By 1943 the United States was deeply embroiled in the Second World War and the Walt Disney Studio was nearly entirely occupied with producing films for the war effort. Ninety-four percent of the studio's output went to fulfill contracts with the government and military and these commissions effectively rescued the studio from the financial difficulties it had suffered a few years earlier.[1] These films, however, were not the studio's first foray into educational, training and promotional films. Prior to the United States' entry into the war, the Disney Studio produced five films for the National Film Board of Canada. These films demonstrate the beginnings of a "Disney style" of wartime animated film — one necessitated by expediency and economy — and introduced several narrative, stylistic and aesthetic traits that were later adopted in the studio's vast domestic wartime output as well as in its post-war educational films and television programs. In producing these training and promotional films for the Canadian government, Disney experimented with blending the factual and the entertaining and the sober and the light-hearted in order to effectively convey information and appeal to the public during a time of conflict.

Several decades before the Second World War, producers of military films recognized animation's potential advantages over live action for clarification and illustration. During the First World War, the animation pioneer and studio head John Randolph Bray received a request from the military to make training films. Bray sent along one of his top animators, Max Fleischer, to do the job. Along with draftsman Jack Leventhal, Fleischer produced many training films before peace was declared in 1918.[2] Their films, which included extensive animation, were the first army training films produced, and they covered hundred of different subjects.[3] For example, in 1917 Fleischer made a series of films (including *How to Read an Army Map* and *How to Fire a Lewis Gun*) that were used to train American soldiers heading to the battle zones of Europe. This early realization that animation could clarify and explain more effectively and efficiently than live action was shared by Walt Disney, who made two educational films about dental health at the beginning of his career in Kansas in the 1920s.[4]

Nearly two decades later, Disney showed an astute foresight for animation's wartime potential with the speculative production of a training film for the Lockheed Aircraft Corporation, which had premises close to his Burbank studio. *Four Methods of Flush Riveting* (1940) is a somewhat dry animated lecture. An authoritative voice-of-god commentary guides the viewer through four different methods of riveting (such as the "countersink method" and the "double-dimple"), designed to minimize turbulence by reducing drag on the aircraft surface. The clearly drawn and labeled images of the riveting process are animated on a plain blue background and the look of the film is akin to textbook diagrams put into simple motion. Disney screened this film for a group of guests invited to the studio in 1941 to debate the different ways animation might be used in a non-entertainment capacity.[5] John Grierson, who was by then head of the National Film Board of Canada (NFBC), was particularly enthusiastic about *Flush Riveting* and not put off by its rudimentary aesthetics. In fact, he was so impressed with the film he suggested that every time a new piece of military equipment was delivered, an animated training film should go with it.[6]

The NFBC was established in 1939, with a mandate from the government "to make and distribute films across the country that were designed to help Canadians everywhere in Canada understand the problems and way of life of Canadians in other parts of the country."[7]Previously, filmmaking in Canada had lacked direction and scarcity of funds hindered the quality of the films produced. Grierson was brought to Canada first in 1938, in the light of his stature and experience as a documentary director and producer in Great Britain, to assess the state of film in the country and report back to the government. Working within several state departments making sponsored films from the beginning of the 1930s, Grierson championed a sober, yet visually arresting type of documentary filmmaking that came to be known as the British documentary movement.[8] Grierson was also a master of using film for educational and persuasive ends and it was this potential that he saw in *Flush Riveting*.[9] Indeed, he suggested that animation challenged the assumption that documentary was the best form with which to teach and persuade audiences when he said "animation seems to have a capacity for simplifying the presentation of pedagogical problems as documentary films have not."[10] Grierson's conviction that animation could be applied to non-fictional ends led him, early in his tenure, to commission from Disney on behalf of the Canadian government one instructional film and four shorts promoting the purchase of War Savings Certificates.

The shorts were intended as an appeal to the Canadian public to buy savings certificates to support the war effort instead of spending their money on material goods or investing in traditional ways. The shorts were required to be, then, both diverting and convincing, playing on the audience's sense of patriotism and entertaining them at the same time. Character animation featuring the popular figures from the Disney stable presented in vibrant Technicolor, rather than the dry approach and limited color palette of *Flush Riveting*, was deemed the best way to achieve this goal. There were, however, time and budgetary constraints on the production of the shorts and Disney-style character animation was time consuming and costly to produce. *Snow White and the Seven Dwarfs* (1937), Disney's first feature-length animated film, had cost an astounding $1.5 million to make.[11] Disney's short subjects were less expensive, but still not cheap to make. The production cost of a *Silly Symphony*,[12] Disney's shorts animated to music made during the 1930s, ranged from around $5,000 for the early black and white shorts to nearly $70,000 for some of the last color *Symphonies* made towards the end of the decade.[13] *The Three Little Pigs* (1933), for example, had a production cost of nearly $16,000, and the cost of making prints for distribution nearly doubled this amount.[14] In the 1930s the studio was producing twenty short films a year, as determined by their distribution deal with United Artists.[15] The production process of these films was drawn-out and meticulous, with animators taking the time to test their pencil sketches on film before committing the images to celluloid in ink and paint.[16] *The Three Little Pigs* took five months to produce from the original story idea to finished film, and two months to animate, and this was not an unusually long production schedule for a *Silly Symphony*.[17] Disney had just $20,000 to produce all four Canadian shorts, about the same as the average budget of a single *Silly Symphony*, and far less than Disney had been spending on these shorts in the late 1930s.[18] Furthermore, the ongoing war was proving a drain on the national economy, creating an urgent need for bond sales. For all these reasons, Disney chose to re-use and adapt material from the studio's previous output.[19] In three of the NFBC shorts, Disney even directly re-purposed significant chunks of already successful films and shorts, playing on the popularity of the original material to encourage people to invest their money in the war effort.

Seven Wise Dwarfs (1941) opens with the diamond mine sequence from *Snow White*. But, instead of "heigh-ho"-ing themselves back to their cottage at the end of a hard day's work, the dwarfs march off to the nearest post office, singing "heigh-ho, heigh-ho, we all must help you know; we'll win the war with 5-for-4, heigh-ho, heigh-ho."[20] Disney artfully threads the idea of investing your savings and earnings in the war effort into a story with which audiences would already be familiar. The dwarfs heft their sacks of diamonds into the post office in order to put the fruits of their labor toward the national cause, encouraging the audience to make a connection between work, reward and investment in war bonds. The film also plays on already established characters to inform audiences where they can buy their bonds. The ever-hapless Dopey gets distracted from the group by a poster advertising bonds in the window of a bank and it is into this establishment that he drags his bag of gems. Having

Dopey wander off from the group fits with the behavior that viewers expect from this specific character and adds a level of humor and amusement to the film. In a light-hearted way, however, this action also fulfils the function of telling audiences they can buy bonds at both post offices and banks.

We can see that in the first half of this short subject, which runs at just under four minutes, the government's message is delivered with a light touch. In the second half, however, the tone moves from gently encouraging to overtly persuasive. As Dopey leaves the bank and rushes to catch up with the rest of the dwarfs he fumbles with his stash of bonds and several escape his clutches. These bonds float towards us as the background changes from the familiar world of the seven dwarfs and Snow White's magic kingdom to a plain gray backdrop. The escaped bonds morph into an artillery shell, onto which the words "lend your savings" are superimposed in yellow and red block capital letters that fill up the screen. In a movie theatre, where Canadian audiences would have watched these shorts, the declarative words would have loomed over them, marking a strong contrast with the highjinks of the friendly, familiar dwarfs just a few seconds earlier. The music also changes, to a dramatic orchestral score that matches this new, serious tone. In the following animated images of the arsenal of war, connections are made through graphics. Shells fired by anti-aircraft guns destroy enemy planes, forming the words "keep your money fighting" as they explode against gray skies. A printing press churning out bonds morphs into a conveyer belt of planes and shells. The final image of the film makes the message crystal clear. Several planes fly towards the audience, their guns blazing, creating bullet holes that spell out "invest in victory" and the message is emblazoned on a background of a night sky filled with fighter planes and tracing searchlights.

The other three Canadian shorts employ this same structure: a light-hearted first half, which uses characters and scenes familiar from Disney's back catalogue, and a more serious second half that literally spells out the message of the films to cinema-goers. Just as feature film success was capitalized on in *Seven Wise Dwarfs*, *Thrifty Pig* (1941) re-uses parts of the popular *Silly Symphony, The Three Little Pigs.* This film had been a huge hit on its release in 1933, in part due to the catchy song, "Who's Afraid of the Big Bad Wolf?" that had audiences whistling its tune even after the first preview.[21] The song, written by Frank Churchill, became Disney's first music hit and the film itself grossed $150,000 in its first two years and "proved to be the most popular cartoon short ever up to that time (and possibly of all time)."[22] *The Three Little Pigs was* so popular, in fact, that the distributor, United Artists, was taken by surprise by the demand for prints and in some areas resorted to shuttling copies between theatres by messengers on bicycle.[23] It was also the first Disney short to receive foreign language soundtracks and re-shot scenes for distribution in overseas territories.[24]

The original story of *The Three Little Pigs,* which is based on the classic fairytale, sees two fun-loving pigs paying the price for putting whimsy before work when the Big Bad Wolf easily destroys their homes, built quickly but flimsily out of straw and sticks.. The efforts of their third, more diligent porcine colleague, who took the time to build his house out of bricks and stone rather than having fun and singing songs, pays off when his sturdy workmanship thwarts the efforts of the Wolf. In the version re-imagined for Canadian wartime audiences, the hard-working pig is building his house out of bricks made of war bonds and flies a Union Jack proudly in his front yard. As in the original short, the Big Bad Wolf, whose raggedy top hat is replaced with a swastika-emblazoned military cap and red armband, huffs and puffs and blows away the first two houses, but only succeeds in loosening the plaster on the third house, revealing the sturdy bond-bricks underneath. These building materials, it would seem, are stronger than the gusts of the Nazi enemy. The Wolf turns tail and flees when Thrifty Pig hurls bricks that bounce off his behind. A chorus of "who's afraid of the Big Bad Wolf? The Union Jack's still flying. We'll be safe from the Big Bad Wolf, if you lend your savings" fades into the graphic portion of the film that encourages us to "spend less" and "lend our savings," written on the smoke streaming out of factory chimneys. The same "invest in victory" message, strafed out by oncoming planes, closes the four-minute short.

It has been suggested that *The Three Little Pigs* can be read as an allegory for Depression-era America. The film was released during the "first hundred days" of Franklin D. Roosevelt's presidency, when a message of consistent and decisive action was being sent out to the nation. The film can be seen, Robert Sklar argues, as celebrating this "confident, purposeful spirit of the early New Deal."[25] Richard Schickel suggests, however, that the film embodies the conservative attitudes of outgoing president Herbert Hoover, through encouraging a financially strapped nation that hard work would pull them out of the doldrums and protect them for the future.[26] Underlying both these readings is the notion that good will triumph over bad, be it through hard work or forward thinking. This message is refigured, and far less open to interpretation, in *Thrifty Pig*. Here personal thrift is advocated as a means of directly protecting oneself from the advance of Nazism. Following on from this is the suggestion that supporting the war financially will help the nation and the allies defeat a foreign enemy that threatened to mercilessly destroy the Canadian way of life. The threat is made clear, but so is the optimistic suggestion that financial self-sacrifice will equate to victory. Thus, a Depression-era allegory translates to a wartime message.

Similarly, in *Donald's Decision* (1941) the moralistic message of the original film from which material was harvested, *Donald's Better Self* (1938), is translated into a patriotic message of putting your nation's needs before one's own. In the original film, a schoolboy Donald grapples with whether to attend his lessons or go fishing. His conscience manifests in two physical forms—an angelic duck and a devilish duck, both of which try to convince him that their way is the right way. Angelic duck leads him to his lessons, whereas devilish duck tempts him away with a day of leisure and schools him in the bad habits of pipe smoking. A physical showdown between the two ducks sees Donald take the angel's side and, with a little nudging, march off to the schoolhouse with his books in hand. The remake has a grown-up Donald lazing in a hammock, sipping a drink, while a voice on the radio encourages listeners to invest in war bonds. As Donald rolls over to take a nap, the angel duck emerges from his body and urges him to take the contents of his piggy bank and buy war savings certificates. As they head off together, Donald passes a mailbox that gets his attention with a spinning red flag (which we can see forms the sign of a swastika). The devil duck emerges and tells Donald to spend his hard-earned money on himself and to have some fun. The fight sequence between the two ducks is lifted from the original film and the result is the same — Donald sides with his good conscience and dutifully follows the angel duck. This time, however, they march towards the post office, which flies the Union Jack, and Donald carries his piggy bank instead of school books.

The wartime short plays on Donald's familiar characteristics— his tendency to be led astray and to not instinctively know what the right action is. Through his character arc in this short, the audience gets to play out their own reservations about buying war bonds (immediate personal gain versus long term national good) through the moral indecision of this loveable, familiar, cartoon duck. Similarly to *Thrifty Pig, Donald's Decision* re-works the Depression era subtext of early Disney short cartoons regarding hard work to play out the wartime message that investing in war bonds is the best decision for you and your nation. Donald, furthermore, was a Disney character that was as popular with adults as he was with children.[27] In fact, he was far more popular with adults than Mickey Mouse, which perhaps explains why Disney chose to feature the duck, rather than the emblematic Mickey, in this Canadian short that was intended to appeal primarily to adult audiences.[28]

The shortest of the four promotional films, *All Together* (1942), eschews a narrative in favor of displaying a large number of familiar characters in the name of evoking a sense of camaraderie and community. It shows a parade of Disney characters marching in front of the Canadian Parliament (recognizable from its Gothic-revival style), rallying the audience to buy war bonds. Geppetto and Pinocchio lead the way, followed by Donald and his nephews. Pluto is there too, and Mickey, in his conductor role as seen in *The Band Concert* (1935), leads his band atop a float, while the seven dwarfs bring up the rear. Mickey's float is emblazoned with "win the war" and the other characters carry banners saying "all together for war savings" and "5 for 4." There is no singing or dialogue in this film, which relies instead on the image of a variety of characters marching together to evoke a sense of community and national spirit. Robert Sklar points out that this was a familiar theme from Disney's 1930s short cartoons, which advocated playing by society's rules and thinking of oneself as not as an individual, but as part of a wider community.[29] Once again, the peacetime message of Disney's cartoons is adapted to the wartime situation and the short aims to convince people that buying war savings certificates constitutes uniting with your fellow citizens in the name of winning the war. As in the other three shorts, this film concludes with a graphic, serious section that makes the message clear. Planes fly in formation, spelling out the words "all together," a tank rolls towards us, filling the screen, as the words "keep your money fighting" are emblazoned across it in vast yellow block letters. Piles of savings certificates become sails on a warship that flies the Union Jack and the words "buy more and more" are superimposed on the ocean beneath it.

While the war savings certificate promotional films were short, succinct and to the point, with an emphasis on entertainment and persuasion, the training film Disney made for the Canadian government is longer and has a more involved structure. *Stop That Tank !* (1942) does, however, take a more lighthearted approach to the instruction of the workings and use of the MK-1 anti-tank rifle than the dry informational approach of *Flush Riveting* to its subject matter. The twenty-one minute film begins with an entertaining animated section drawn in typical Disney style and produced in Technicolor. Hitler, who is caricatured as a sallow, belching figure with a protruding red nose, leads a convoy of tanks attacking a sleepy village, rallying his troops with cries that they are "being oppressed." To Hitler's surprise, the Canadian infantry pop out from under haystacks and farmyard animals and defend their territory with anti-tank guns. Hitler's forces are quickly thwarted and he gets catapulted down a crater into hell. Here he wails and whines to a round-faced red devil who translates his incomprehensible German gibberish. As Hitler rolls around on the ground, tearing off his clothes, the devil chuckles at the Fuhrer's tantrums and tells us that Hitler says, "against your anti-tank rifles, he simply can't win." The leader of the enemy is thus reduced to a non-threatening figure through the use of entertaining animation—a propaganda technique that Disney repeated in later shorts made in the U.S., such as *Der Fuehrer's Face* (1943) and *Education for Death* (1943).

This opening section then segues to a title screen that sets up the rest of the film: "The Anti-Tank Rifle (Boys Mk. 1) Characteristics and Details of Operation." The comedy overture is over and the next eighteen minutes are mostly devoted to a serious and straightforward demonstration of the workings of this piece of weaponry. The change in tone from amusing to serious is further amplified by the switch to an informative voiceover intoned by a narrator in Received Pronunciation. While there is frequent use of live-action imagery in this section, mostly footage of soldiers demonstrating how to shoot and clean the gun, animation prevails. The majority of this animation is, however, of a style and tone very different from that of the opening three minutes, but familiar from *Four Methods of Flush Riveting.*

Rather than being used to entertain, the animation in the training portion of the film is used to clarify and explain. It operates as a moving diagram of the Boys Mk. 1 rifle, through which the different functions of the gun are demonstrated and its working parts revealed. The animation had to be precise and accurate to the experience the soldiers would have working the guns in the field, so, as Richard Shale notes, the Disney animators based their drawings on a rifle that was shipped down especially to the British Consul in Los Angeles.[30] The implication that animation can reveal and explain details more clearly than live action is apparent with the narrator's invitation to observe the inner workings of the rifle "through the magic of x-ray animation." By using animated drawings, the filmmakers are able to clearly show us what happens inside the gun when it is fired, an insight that would be impossible to achieve as clearly (or at all) with live action film. Similarly, when live action footage of a soldier loading cartridges into the magazine segues into animation that shows us the inside of the magazine and its strong, loaded spring, the action and strength that is required to compress the spring in order to load the rounds into the magazine is clarified and emphasized. The use of instructional animation in *Stop That Tank!* reinforces Grierson's initial response to *Flush Riveting* regarding animation's pedagogic potential. Animation allows complete control over the construction of the image and used in this instructional way offers the chance to demonstrate and illustrate in a similar way to a diagram in a textbook.

There are, however, notable instances of light relief in the eighteen-minute training section of *Stop That Tank!* In an animated sequence on how to aim the gun the explanation of how to hit a moving object explains to would-be users that failure to properly line up a target traveling across their line of sight can cause them to hit the wrong thing. A badly aimed shot results in a cow jumping with a loud squeal from behind some bushes and complaining about poor aim. A clumsy young private, who looks remarkably similar to Dopey, crops up several times in the film. At one point he strains, to no avail, to lift up the Boys rifle, demonstrating its heavy weight and the point made by the narrator that it is best carried on a vehicle. Later, he gets whacked on the nose by the spring in the magazine, emphasizing that care should be taken when opening it to insert cartridges. At the end of the film, the narrator encourages us careful maintenance of the weapon, comparing it to a woman in its repayment of good treatment. The foolish private is then seen snuggling up in bed with his rifle, kissing and stroking its barrel, to the disapproving response of the narrator who comments, "say, that's going a little too far."

While *Stop That Tank!* ostensibly has a two-part structure similar to the first three promotional shorts, its various narrative and stylistic strategies reveal the different purpose of this film. Whereas the shorts needed to persuade the public to part with their hard-earned wages, the training film needed to clearly inform and educate military personnel. Thus, with the shorts it was essential to grab people's attention with the familiar, entertaining animated section and then persuade them of the importance of buying war bonds with the hard-hitting, dramatic graphic sections. The latter halves of the four films clearly articulated the subtextual patriotic message delivered in their opening sections. The stylistic contrast between these two sections also emphasizes the seriousness of the message of the films, something that is further backed-up by the use of dramatic, orchestral music in the graphic sections. The sudden switch from fun Disney full animation to dark tones of the graphic animation would have been a jolt to audiences familiar with Disney's shorts and would have hammered home the importance of buying war savings certificates. The shorts also show how Disney and the NFBC subscribed to the popular opinion of the time regarding successful propaganda. Eric Smoodin has pointed out that by the 1930s it was accepted that the most "effective propaganda was the most overt" and that "propaganda should state its objectives clearly," in contrast to previous opinion that working on people's unconscious was the best way to persuade.[31] This went hand-in-hand with the psychological theory that the behavior of individuals could be manipulated and directed towards goals and actions that benefited society.[32] The four shorts are squarely aimed at the Canadian audience's conscious conception of morality and patriotism in an unquestionable message that persuades them to do the right thing.

In *Stop That Tank!*, while it is easy to distinguish between moments where we are being entertained and moments where we are being educated, the differentiation is less dramatic and the humorous sections act as moments of light relief for an audience that would have been expecting the type of dull filmed lecture common in instructional films. The film is not relying on evoking a strong reaction from the audience and does not need to rally the public into action. Instead, clarity and understanding are key and the entertaining interjections in the instructional part of the film can be seen as a strategy for keeping the viewers interested in the onscreen material. Similarly, the military audience does not need to be convinced of the value of the Boys Mk. 1 rifle, rather just to understand how it functions in the field. The audio track of the latter section of *Stop That Tank!*, when compared to the shorts, further exemplifies this purpose. The rousing music is replaced with a sober, clear voice over that explains the images on screen.

Both types of film, however, use entertainment as a means to an end. The shorts and the training film use a style of animation that viewers would have associated with fun, leisure and amusement. This animation is used as a sweetener to the serious, functional parts of the films for audiences who would not yet have been familiar with the use of animation for non-fictional purposes. We can surmise, then, that the entertainment sections would have made audiences more responsive to the intended messages of these films, making them more palatable than if they had been delivered via all live action or entirely animated in the dry, pedagogic style of *Flush Riveting*.

Disney's approach to animation that was intended to have real-world results of persuasion and education was modified and honed as he produced greater and greater numbers of these types of films for the American government. There are, then, differences to be seen between these five Canadian films and the later domestic output. In the educational shorts aimed at the American cinema-going public, there was often a less clear distinction between entertainment and education as seen in the Canadian war savings certificates films. Many, such as *Out of the Frying Pan and Into the Firing Line* (1942), which featured Minnie and Pluto, seamlessly integrate the message of the film (the importance of collecting cooking fat for use in munitions) into one coherent narrative, a structure that we can see Disney experimenting with in *Stop That Tank!* with the integration of humor into the instructional part of the film. In other films that do contain a similar structure to the Canadian shorts—such as *The New Spirit* (1942), which uses Donald Duck to encourage people to pay their income tax—the graphic second half of the film is presented in as lush and rich an animation style as the first, character-based section.

This focus on quality of animation was, however, unusual for Disney during the war years. Similarly, Richard Shale has pointed out that the U.S. training films rarely included the kind of humor seen in *Stop That Tank!* and were mostly, in the name of economy, produced in black and white. In fact, Disney spent much of the war in a state of frustration regarding the types of films he had to output in order to fulfill the military and government contracts that kept his studio afloat and he "bristled at the idea of having to produce largely unimaginative training and educational films with primitive animation."[33] The speed with which the studio had to churn out films meant usual Disney procedures of trialing and testing material had to be abandoned and the famously perfectionist studio head had to dramatically lower his aesthetic standards.

It is clear, however, that the ethos of Disney's domestic wartime animation was established with the films made for the National Film Board of Canada. It was in these five films that the studio first explored educating, training and persuading through animation and the achievement of real world results through a medium better known for children's entertainment. Disney also appreciated that there are some tasks to which animation is better suited than live action. A serious message can be sweetened if delivered by a friendly, familiar character. Complex mechanical workings, military maneuvers and geographical positions are better explained in moving drawings. After the war Disney continued to explore ways to blend fun and pedagogy. The *True-Life Adventure* series of nature documentaries made by the studio between 1948 and 1960 has been described as "smoothly blending education with entertainment."[34] Likewise, the Man in Space series "blended information and humor, pedagogy and entertainment."[35] The Canadian war films form the foundation for Disney's later educational films and show how Walt Disney was a pioneer, as he was in many other ways, of the use of animation for nonfictional ends and the potential for using entertainment to educate.

Notes

1. Richard Shale, *Donald Duck Joins Up: The Walt Disney Studio During World War II* (Ann Arbor: UMI Research Press, 1976), 24.
2. Richard Fleischer, *Out of the Inkwell: Max Fleischer and the Animation Revolution* (Lexington: University Press of Kentucky, 2005), 27.
3. Ibid.
4. *Tommy Tucker's Tooth* (1922) and *Clara Cleans Her Teeth* (1926) were commissioned by Dr. McCrum of the Deener Dental Institute.
5. Shale, 16.
6. Ibid.
7. National Film Board of Canada website. Accessed 1 November 2009 at http://www.nfb.ca/history/about-the-foundation/
8. Grierson pioneered this style in his 1929 film *Drifters*, about the herring fishing industry.
9. This is also one of the reasons Grierson was recruited to head the NFBC, an appointment that occurred shortly after the film board was established.
10. Grierson, quoted in Shale, 16.
11. Leonard Maltin, *Of Mice and Magic: A History of American Animated Cartoons*. Rev. ed. (New York: New American Library, 1987), 57. This equates to approximately $7,000 per minute of screen time.
12. The negative cost is the cost to produce a film and does not include costs such as distribution or promotion.
13. See Russell Merritt, and J. B. Kaufman. *Walt Disney's Silly Symphonies: A Companion to the Classic Cartoon Series*. (Germona, Italy: La Cineteca del Friuli, 2006). The average cost of a black and white *Silly Symphony* was $10,200, or $17 per foot. The color *Symphonies* cost on average $32,400, or $36 per foot.
14. Merritt and Kaufman, 126; Neal Gabler, *Walt Disney: The Biography* (London: Aurum Press, 2006), 184.
15. Richard Schickel, *The Disney Version: The Life, Times, Art and Commerce of Walt Disney*. (London: Pavilion Books, 1986), 150.
16. Merritt and Kaufman, 36–37.
17. Merritt and Kaufman, 124. The production time of the *Silly Symphonies* ranged from around a month for the early black and white shorts to over eight months for some of the later color shorts.
18. Maltin, 42; Shale, 17.
19. This is a strategy that Disney would continue to adopt after the war when, for example, the opening sections of the 1943 film *Victory Through Air Power* would reappear in the 1957 *Man in Flight* episode of the *Disneyland* TV series and the 1963 episode *Fly with Von Drake*.
20. "5-for-4" refers to the government promotional offer selling five dollars' worth of savings certificates for four dollars.
21. Gabler, 183.
22. John Grant, *Encylopedia of Walt Disney's Animated Characters* (New York: Harper & Row, 1987), 55.
23. Gabler, 183.
24. Merritt and Kaufman, 40.
25. Robert Sklar, "The Making of Cultural Myths—Walt Disney," in *The American Animated Cartoon: A Critical Anthology*, edited by Gerald Peary and Danny Peary (New York: E. P. Dutton, 1980), 58–65, on p. 64.
26. Schickel, 154.
27. Grant, 62

28. This choice also reflects the character differences of Donald and Mickey and is indicative of the fact that by the early 1940s Mickey had developed into the kind of character that would have no internal quandaries regarding the best use for the contents of his piggy bank.

29. Sklar, 64–65.

30. Shale, 19

31. Eric Smoodin, *Animating Culture: Hollywood Cartoons from the Sound Era* (New Brunswick, NJ: Rutgers University Press, 1993), 81.

32. Ibid.

33. Gabler, 389.

34. Steven Watts,*The Magic Kingdom: Walt Disney and the American Way of Life.* Columbia: University of Missouri Press, 1997, 304.

35. Watts, 309.

Bibliography

Fleischer, Richard. *Out of the Inkwell: Max Fleischer and the Animation Revolution.* Lexington: University Press of Kentucky, 2005.

Gabler, Neal. *Walt Disney: The Biography.* London: Aurum Press, 2006.

Grant, John. *Encylopedia of Walt Disney's Animated Characters.* New York: Harper & Row, 1987.

Maltin, Leonard. *Of Mice and Magic: A History of American Animated Cartoons,* revised edition. New York: Plume, 1987.

Merritt, Russell, and J. B. Kaufman. *Walt Disney's Silly Symphonies: A Companion to the Classic Cartoon Series.* Germona, Italy: La Cineteca del Friuli, 2006.

National Film Board of Canada website. http://www.nfb.ca/history/about-the-foundation/

Schickel, Richard. *The Disney Version: The Life, Times, Art and Commerce of Walt Disney.* London: Pavilion Books, 1986.

Shale, Richard. *Donald Duck Joins Up: The Walt Disney Studio During World War II.* Ann Arbor, MI: UMI Research Press, 1982.

Sklar, Robert. "The Making of Cultural Myths—Walt Disney." In *The American Animated Cartoon: A Critical Anthology*, edited by Gerald Peary and Danny Peary, 58–65. New York: E. P. Dutton, 1980.

Smoodin, Eric. *Animating Culture: Hollywood Cartoons from the Sound Era.* New Brunswick, NJ: Rutgers University Press, 1993.

Watts, Steven. *The Magic Kingdom: Walt Disney and the American Way of Life.* Columbia: University of Missouri Press, 1997.

2

"Desiring the Disney Technique"

Chronicle of a Contracted Military Training Film

DOUGLAS A. CUNNINGHAM

Between 1942 and 1945, the Walt Disney Studio made more than a hundred contracted training films for the armed forces—mostly for the Navy, which lacked a robust internal filmmaking capability of its own.[1] Disney produced over a hundred films for the Navy, but only a few dozen for the Army. Only a handful of films were made exclusively for the Army Air Forces (AAF), which operated under the auspices of the Army during the war but became the independent United States Air Force in 1947. Despite its subordinate relation to the larger Army, the AAF boasted, by 1943, the largest training-film production capability in the U.S. Armed Forces. The AAF's First Motion Picture Unit or (FMPU) in Culver City, California—formed in the summer of 1942 and staffed in large part by Hollywood studio professionals recruited to serve as uniformed, active-duty AAF members—oversaw this prolific and remarkably self-sufficient enterprise. The FMPU produced the majority of the AAF's training films: more than 300 over the course of the war.[2]

On occasion, however, the AAF did contract the production of films from commercial vendors such as Disney, most often because the FMPU could not, for scheduling or backlog reasons, make those films itself. In such cases, too, the FMPU often worked hand-in-hand with such vendors (including Disney) to ensure the future success of the film. This essay will trace the bureaucratic trail that the Disney-made training film series *High-Level Precision Bombing* followed through AAF channels, and examine how Disney's 1943 film *Victory through Air Power* heavily influenced AAF decisions to contract with Walt Disney Productions for the two-part 1944 series.

The Ancillary Impact of a Commercial Failure

An understanding of Disney's *High-Level Precision Bombing* series and its path to production requires, first, an explanation of strategic bombing itself and the political role it played in the AAF's push toward postwar independence. In crude terms, strategic bombing is the practice of high-altitude bombing of sites of logistical significance far beyond the front lines of the ground war. Its targets included centers of industrial production, major railroad and other transportation corridors. Brigadier General William "Billy" Mitchell aggressively advocated this new and controversial doctrine throughout the 1920s, but his ideas were generally ignored — even detested — by the entrenched U.S. military establishment, which saw air power as tactical support for traditional ground and naval forces rather than as a decisive military arm in its own right.[3] Many AAF advocates— particularly those that favored a separation from the Army and the concomitant establishment of an independent air force —continued to tout the advantages of strategic bombing throughout the 1920s and 30s.[4] Among these advocates was Mitchell's admirer and fellow aviator, Russian *émigré* Alexander P. de Seversky, who championed Mitchell's ideas throughout his own career in America, and particularly in his 1942 book, *Victory through Air Power*. After America's entry into World War II, the AAF found itself in a position, both politically and technologically, to demonstrate the validity of its strategic bombing theories— an important opportunity given that the AAF had for so long based its arguments for independence on the uniqueness of its strategic bombing mission.[5]

Initiated in the summer of 1943 by the AAF's Air Staff at headquarters in Washington, D.C., the film that would later become the *High-Level Precision Bombing* series was almost certainly ordered in response to lessons learned during the AAF's first independent bombing campaigns over Europe during the first half of the year. In this respect, the films could not have been timelier. Intended to train AAF bombardiers on the most efficient methods to achieve accurate bombings of enemy targets, both films (produced simultaneously throughout the fall and early winter of 1943) went into wide distribution throughout the AAF in 1944.[6] The story of how the series came about and the related tale of the bureaucratic channels through which it passed, however, reveal much about the extent to which the AAF paid close attention to Disney's other government-funded efforts and, in particular, the studio's feature-length curiosity, *Victory through Air Power* (a hybrid of animation and live-action produced as an adaptation of de Seversky's book of the same name).

Victory through Air Power made the most direct and convincing case for strategic bombing of any film made during World War II. In fact, the case seemed so convincing at the time that the Navy Department — the AAF's longstanding rival for the military aviation spotlight — actually attempted to discourage Disney from producing it, "arguing the film would scuttle [the Navy's] search for funds and resources."[7] This anecdote typifies the fierce rivalry between the AAF's ground-based military aviation services (which took various forms under the auspices of Army control and oversight between 1907 and 1947) and the Navy's carrier-based aviation forces that characterized the first half of the century, and — in particular — the years immediately following World War II. Although *Victory through Air Power* claims no official ties to the government or its opinions, Steven Watts notes that "a high-ranking officer in the AAF encouraged [Disney] to go ahead [with production of the film] because people didn't understand air power's growing centrality to the Allied military effort."[8] The identity of this "high-ranking officer" remains vague, but the individual's opinions did not stray far from those held by a number of top AAF brass of the time. Shale reports, however, that while many AAF officials visited the Burbank studios during the film's production, "Not all of these pilgrims visiting Mecca [the Walt Disney Studio] were in accord ... and by late 1942 and early 1943 the Disney Studio had become a battleground for aviators."[9] Perhaps Disney's heavy-handed approach and de Seversky's association with the still-controversial Mitchell steered the War Department away from any direct involvement with the film during a time when interservice rivalries needed to be set aside in favor of interservice cooperation.[10] Still, *Victory through Air Power* looks official. The credits gave de Seversky (long since retired) his U.S. Army rank of major, and Disney's close partnership with the government on other collaborative, war-related projects must certainly have led some audience members to believe they were watching yet another military-sanctioned product.[11]

Traditionally regarded as a deliberate abstraction of reality, animation in *Victory through Air Power* becomes much more powerful for its glamorized semblance of reality: the depictions of warfare, machinery, and fiery ruin are packed with realistic detail. At the same time, however, these scenes seem strangely larger-than-life and dreamy, as if part of some child's fantasized version of warfare. Perhaps this fantasy accounts for oft-cited comments made by critic James Agee in his 1943 review of the film for *The Nation*: "'I noticed, uneasily, that there were no suffering and dying enemy civilians under all those proud promises of bombs; no civilians at all, in fact.... The sexless sexiness of Disney's creations have always seemed to me queasy, perhaps in an all-American sense; in strict descent from it is this victory-in-a-vacuum which is so morally simple a matter ... of machine-eat-machine.'"[12] Still, others (the *New York Times*, for example) praised Disney's fantastic approach:

> Through a brilliantly Technicolored array of maps and diagrams, Mr. Disney and his artists have animated de Seversky's ideas with a clarity which could never be achieved simply through the spoken word. The designer and former Russian flying ace of the first World War discourses at length and with warm conviction throughout the latter half of the film, but it is the remarkably lucid exposition effected by the drawings which makes his formula for "true" aerial strategy understandable even to

> upper-grade elementary school pupils. Mr. Disney has proved in one bold stroke that the motion picture has great possibilities as an educational factor.[13]

While *The Commonweal* found the film "a little heavy-going," it also remarked, "Perhaps if we had paid more attention to Mitchell in the '20s, this film would not have had to be made. But having been made, and made so well, it provides another illustration of the value of cinema as an educational medium."[14] Despite such favorable reviews as those seen in the *New York Times* and *The Commonweal*, however, the film failed miserably at the box office.[15]

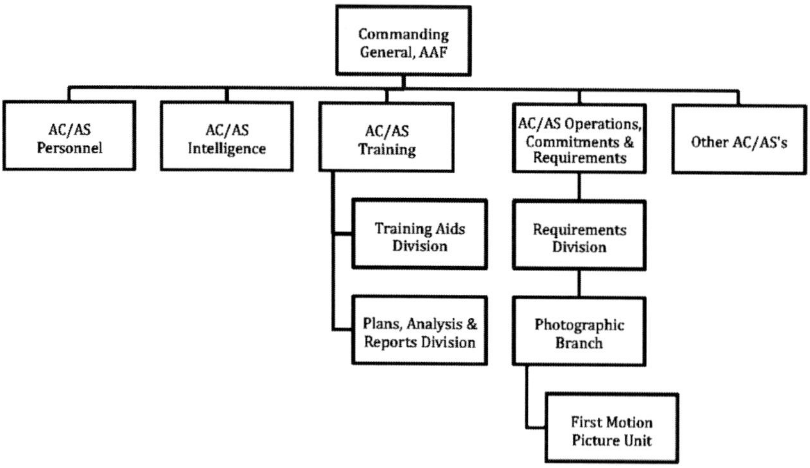

Figure 1. Abridged chart of the AAF's Air Staff organization as of the summer and fall of 1943.[16]

Although the AAF did not officially endorse *Victory through Air Power*, the film's innovative animation and Technicolor visuals seem to have made a deep impression on top AAF officials. In a July 20th, 1943, letter to Colonel Lawrence Carr, the commander of the AAF's Training Aids Division in New York City, Brigadier General Robert W. Harper, Assistant Chief of Air Staff, Training (see Figure 1), based in Washington, D.C., requested the production of a training film that would focus exclusively on the concepts inherent to strategic bombing. Harper's letter emphasized the need for the film to stress the importance of the bomber crew in the successful execution of such missions:

> The purpose of this film is to instill in our heavy bomber crews a deep sense of their individual responsibility and importance in the furtherance of the enemy's defeat through precision placement of the bombs.... [I]t is believed that a film of this nature, if its importance is to be conveyed effectively, will require *an animation technique such as appears in the recent Walt Disney film "VICTORY THROUGH AIR POWER*[.]" The proposed film, of necessity must demonstrate through animation the complex-

ities, interrelationships and [interdependence] of war industries, so that the heavy bombing crews will understand the full significance of their missions. In addition, this film must dramatize, by showing [the] effect upon industry of the over-all implications of strategic bombing and the precision placement of bombs. To accomplish this purpose, it is believed that a *treatment comparable to the recent Disney film on Air Power is required.*[17]

Harper evidently wanted a film that would motivate as well as educate: a film that would not only explain strategic bombing, but argue for its efficacy and importance. He wanted a film *like* Disney's *Victory Through Air Power* but still different in many respects. In other words, Harper was clearly looking for something very specific: a shortened, streamlined, less expensive (and less politically problematic) version of *Victory*.

Consistent with Harper's desires, a First Lieutenant Peter R. Nehemkis—of Harper's Plans, Analysis, and Reports Division (then under the leadership of Lieutenant Colonel Walt D. Merrill)—seems to have initiated preliminary negotiations in earnest with Walt Disney Productions.[18] By July 21st, in fact, Roy O. Disney had already sent a letter to Harper requesting a greenlight for the company to proceed on Disney's proposal for a project on strategic bombardment; as the letter indicates, the Disney company knew that it could effectively play on the significant aesthetic and doctrinal advocacies of *Victory through Air Power*:

[Given] ... the quality of our current production, VICTORY THROUGH AIR POWER ... [and] careful analysis of production costs on this picture, we feel that [a] per foot arrangement of between $50.00 and $75.00 would be an equitable [rate at] which to proceed with the *intent of producing the picture as inexpensively as possible, with the same quality as* VICTORY THROUGH AIR POWER*.... [Consistent] with the studio's policy on all war films, this film would be [done on a no-profit], cost basis, and would run between 18 and 30 minutes*, dependent [upon] script content.[19]

Here, Roy Disney relied on the company's extensive prior experience in producing films on behalf of the U.S. Government in order to provide cost estimates for a new production. The letter also demonstrates, however, the extent to which Walt Disney Productions actively, even aggressively, sought to secure such contracts—particularly during a period of economic insecurity at the studio following the 1941 employee strike and the disappointing box-office returns on *Fantasia* (1940) and *Pinocchio* (1940).[20] Disney Productions had, by July of 1943, produced so many films at cost for federal agencies that the proactive process for securing this new contract must have seemed like business as usual.[21]

Solidifying the Contract

Harper replied to Roy O. Disney on July 22nd, stating that a final decision as to what organization would produce the picture, whether commercial or military, had yet to be made:

> In accordance with customary procedure, a project number has been assigned for the production of the training film "Strategic Bombardment," and the project is now in the hands of the Army Air Forces Photographic Branch, Requirements Division, [Assistant Chief of Air Staff, or "AC/AS"] Operations, Commitments and Requirements, who will decide shortly whether Air Force facilities or an outside agency will be utilized to produce this film.[22]

AC/AS Operations, Commitments, and Requirements (OCR), in turn, passed the decision down three levels of management (through its Requirements Division to the Motion Picture Branch to, finally, the First Motion Picture Unit in Culver City, California) for a final decision.[23] As Nehemkis later reported, "Prior to my departure from Washington, [OCR] had advised that the [First] Motion Picture Unit alone could determine what agency would produce the film on 'Strategic Bombing' and that this determination would be made after a script had been prepared."[24] OCR dispatched Nehemkis from Washington, D.C., to Culver City on or around July 30th to meet face to face with FMPU members. On August 2nd, Nehemkis met with FMPU leadership and production staff, and at that time, "the Motion Picture Unit quickly determined that the Disney Organization was the only one capable of producing this film, and negotiations were immediately undertaken."[25]

A major reason for the AAF's decision to contract with Disney rather than produce the film internally rested with the backlog of productions at the FMPU.[26] Indeed, the FMPU's monthly Production Progress Report dated August 31st, 1943, lists over 125 projects assigned and in various stages of production at that time—many of which were slated to include complicated animation sequences to be overseen by the over-tasked Animation Department and its over-tasked (if highly qualified) leadership—Rudolf Ising and Frank Thomas, two former Disney artists turned AAF military men).[27] Among the more ambitious of such projects was *Camouflage Cartoon*—directed by Ising and written by Thomas—a fully animated, two-reel, Technicolor short designed to instruct AAF personnel on the essentials of airbase camouflage.[28] At that time only 65 percent complete, *Camouflage Cartoon* claimed a great deal of time and manpower within the FMPU's Animation Department, as did many other films requiring a heavy animation component, to include *Elementary and Pylon Eights* (slated for direction by Ising), *Fighter Combat Formations: Attacks and Escorts* (85 percent complete, but needing "additional animation"), *Advanced Formation Flying* (90 percent complete but still requiring the completion of "final animation"), *How to Fly the B-26: Loading* ("[a]nimation in work"), and *Lazy Eights* (10 percent compete, and, like *Camouflage Cartoon*, requiring the use of a complex, animated character).[29] The Animation Department was so busy, in fact, that another film, *Operation and Maintenance of the Electronic Turbo Super Charger*, was also slated in this same Production Progress Report for production by Disney.[30] In an August 7th memorandum to Brigadier General Harper, in fact, Lieutenant Colonel Merrill of AC/AS Training's Plans, Analysis, and

Reports Division concurred with the assessment that the FMPU was too overwhelmed to produce the strategic-bombing film, but he noted, too, that "a desire for the Disney technique" also played a role in the decision to outsource the film's production.[31] Although Merill did not expound on his thoughts about what might constitute the "Disney technique," we might assume that he, along with his superior, Brigadier General Harper, was impressed by the visual flair of *Victory through Air Power*. (We might also assume Merill knew Harper would understand exactly what he meant by the term "Disney technique," given that Harper had initiated the request in the first place.)

Along with deciding that Disney would produce the film that had by now come to be known through official correspondence as *Strategic Bombing*, conference calls among personnel in AC/AS, Training, and AC/AS, OCR, on or around August 6th determined initially that Perc Pearce—"the chief story writer for Disney" and the officially credited "story director" of *Victory through Air Power*—would act as the film's *de facto* writer while one of the FMPU's chief scenario writers, Captain Norman Krasna, would serve as "General Supervisor and Consultant for the film."[32] (Krasna was, in fact, the celebrated talent who had penned 1941's *The Devil and Miss Jones*, nominated for an Academy Award for Best Original Screenplay, and *Princess O'Rourke*, the film that would later win that same award for 1943.) Nehemkis, by this time in California and actively consulting with both the FMPU in Culver City and Disney in Burbank, respectively, pointed out that the film would require a different working dynamic between the AAF and Walt Disney Productions than that to which military officials had grown accustomed:

> The Disney Organization does not work along the same lines [as other] commercial producers, since animation technique requires a different approach. A script is not prepared. Rather basic ideas, in terms of individual drawings and sequences are first developed. Actual production [and the] filming is only undertaken after this procedure is thoroughly [laid] out on the boards.[33]

Accordingly, Merrill scheduled Krasna and Pearce for an immediate research visit to the Air Force School of Applied Tactics (AFSAT) in Orlando, Florida, where they would study the theories of strategic bombing and its recent successes in the North Africa campaign.[34]

In an August 5th conference among Colonel Waters and Major Zimmer of Training Aids Division, Major Cowling of the FMPU, and Lieutenant Colonel Merrill of the Plans, Analysis, and Reports Division, all parties agreed that "Captain Krasna would not be suitable for supervision, as his talents lie along the lines of scenario writing [i.e., the writing of training films structured around a dramatic narrative], consequently Captain Krasna was eliminated."[35] All AAF officials involved still wanted Pearce to visit AFSAT in Orlando "prior to setting up his 'Boards,'" however, and they also determined that although "the picture would be produced by Disney ... it would be closely supervised by Training Aids and AFSAT to assure the proper end result."[36] This supervision was to include a visit to Walt Disney Productions in Burbank "[p]rior to actual filming" by an AFSAT official of "technical ability and theater knowledge" who would perform a "final check" on Disney's plans.[37]

Additionally, all conferees determined that Disney should take no longer than three months to produced the requested film, and an initial total cost estimate of $90,000 seems to have been attached to the film at some point, "subject to change due to no [T]echnicolor being desired."[38] (The project ultimately cost only $66,958.)[39] Significantly, in an August 9th letter to Colonel Lawrence Carr of Training Aids Division, Harper noted that although he (Harper) had suggested "the use of an animated technique, either animated or live action will be satisfactory if the proper end result can be secured."[40] The point Harper made here proved important, for despite the fact that *Victory through Air Power* played an important role in priming the imaginations of AAF officials about the possibilities for their film, *Strategic Bombing*, in truth the final product(s) employed more live action than dynamic animation. Indeed, the two films eventually produced and released seem significantly different from Harper's original intent in several other ways, not the least of which proved to be their stated aims. Whereas the original concept for *Strategic Bombing* centered on convincing airmen of the absolute importance of their roles in the successful execution of a strategic-bombing mission, the two separate films ultimately released seem more like reinforcements of standardized bombing procedures.

One Series, Two Films

At some point after August 1943, the single project at one time titled *Strategic Bombing* seems to have been divided into two separate films intended as halves of an overall series titled *High-Level Precision Bombing*. The change was probably motivated by mistakes made during the Allied bombing campaigns of 1943 and, in particular, the high-level precision bombing raids on Schweinfurt and Regensberg, which, combined resulted in the loss of over 60 Allied aircraft on a single day.[41] One could assume, however, that once the partial failures of these raids and their associated "lessons learned" began to permeate the AAF's institutions of doctrinal theory and strategy development (in particular, the aforementioned Air Force School of Applied Tactics in Orlando at which Disney's Pearce had been assigned to conduct background research), additional requirements might have been levied on the film that then required a splitting of the current project into two parts that would address different aspects of the overall high-level precision bombing protocol. The first of the two films in the series—*High-Level Precision Bombing (Part 1: The Bombing Computers)*—concerns the proper use and functions of two calibration and calculation devices, the E6-B computer (which resembled and operated like a manual slide rule) and the Automated Bombing Computer (ABC), which attached as a supplement to the Norden bombsight. As the narration states, "Through the use of either the E6-B or ABC computer, pre-set sight data can be computed without any change in the ship's course." The bulk of this film consists of live-action close-ups of hands manipulating both computers to calculate drift, dropping angles, and bomb release points, although animation is occasionally employed to reiterate numbered directions, to indicate — via arrows— where parts of the computers need to be manipulated, or to capture overall conceptual ideas. In general, the film is dedicated to the idea that proper use of either device will significantly improve the accuracy of bombs dropped from high altitudes. In this respect, *The Bombing Computers* does bear some resemblance to the original intent of *Strategic Bombing*; after all, *The Bombing Computers* reflects Harper's desire to validate the practice of high-level precision bombing in that it seeks to persuade airmen that proper applications of advanced technology can help them to achieve success.

Like *The Bombing Computers*, the second film in the series, *High-Level Precision Bombing (Part 2: Combat Bombing Procedure)*, uses animation sparingly, but that use nevertheless seems more integrated with the purpose and drive of the film as whole, which explains the five-point procedure by which a bombardier is meant to properly execute a bombing mission. The film begins with the off-screen narrator relating the story of a recent bombing raid over an important Axis oil refinery (the site goes unnamed in the film), during which three successive aircraft had to be replaced as lead bomber because the bombardier in each had forgotten to follow one important element of combat-bombing procedure. The film then spends the rest of its 22 minutes reviewing the five constitutive phases of every bombing mission and the necessary actions required by the bombardier at each of these phases. Much of the film's construction also concerns the techniques used by the bombardier during Phase 5 of the procedure, during which he is expected to take evasive action at scheduled intervals while approaching the target. (The bombardier would temporarily assume piloting duties once the aircraft began its bombing run.) During this sequence, the film integrates live-action close ups and medium shots of a bombardier performing regulation procedures followed immediately by an animated aerial view of a bomber moving according to the adjustments made by the bombardier as shown in the previous two.

Disney completed the two-part *High-Level Precision Bombing* series on January 21st, 1944, after which time both films were distributed widely throughout the relevant units of the AAF.[42] While the FMPU is credited prominently as working "in cooperation" with the studio in the opening titles of both films in the series, the exact nature of this cooperation — once Krasna had been eliminated as "General Supervisor"— remains unclear. The FMPU's function in the production could have taken many forms between August of 1943 and January of 1944. One possibility is that FMPU personnel continued to act as "West Coast" liaisons between AAF representatives based on the East Coast (officials from Training Aids Division in New York and AFSAT experts from Orlando, for example) and Perc Pearce's Disney team working to assemble both pictures. Another possibility is that the FMPU provided both production and post-production assistance with the series; after all, the FMPU had ready-made mock-ups of cockpits and bombardier bays for use in shooting different types of training films, and these may have come in handy for Disney filmmakers. Additionally, the FMPU may have assisted in some aspects of post-production, a practice that was not uncommon for the FMPU given that it often performed similar services for overseas combat-camera crews that sent materials back to Culver City for final assembly.

The most likely role played by the FMPU, however, was probably that of a friendly consultant and overseer of Disney's work on the series. This does not imply that Walt Disney Productions lacked the necessary knowledge of its craft to effectively execute and complete this project; rather, the FMPU, having by this time produced dozens of training films (most often to great acclaim from the leadership that requested them) for AAF organizations worldwide, possessed a keen knowledge of the most effective ways to reach and instruct its core audience, and this knowledge about the AAF may have proved useful for Disney.

Conclusion

While the visuals and dramatic flair inherent to Disney's 1943 feature, *Victory through Air Power*, inspired high-placed AAF officials within the office of the Assistant Chief of Air Staff, Training, as they were trying to make a decision regarding what organization would produce the film on strategic bombing they desired, ultimately, the films produced for the *High-Level Precision Bombing* series bear little resemblance to *Victory through Air Power*, employing far more live action than dynamic animation. Still, the arcing arrows and their concomitant explosions—demonstrated in the "hub-and-spoke" wheel sequence of *Victory through Air Power*—would eventually resurface in an FMPU–produced film, 1945's *Air Power and Armies* (animated in-house at the FMPU, without help from Disney), which advanced many of the same arguments about strategic air power's role in combined air-ground operations that Disney had forwarded two years earlier. Still, although the AAF produced most of its training films internally during World War II, it sometimes turned to outside vendors for films when the First Motion Picture Unit could not make space within its schedule for another project. This essay has chronicled the bureaucratic processes whereby such a film came to be assigned to Walt Disney Pictures, Inc., and the ways in which that company's *Victory through Air Power* played a major role in that decision. Indeed, some of the very same talents that had helped to bring *Victory through Air Power* to life also worked to produce the project that eventually came to be known as the *High-Level Precision Bombing* series. Tracing the history of the series' production from an AAF point of view provides a unique glimpse into the kinds of demands levied on the Walt Disney Studio during this period, as well as an understanding of the extent to which Disney's independent feature products (e.g., *Victory through Air Power*) significantly influenced a desire for "the Disney technique" even in films intended strictly for military use. Although the *High-Level Precision Bombing* films differ quite noticeably in style from *Victory*'s vaulting arrows and visual metaphors, one can — after reviewing AAF correspondence — recognize in the series the fruits of seeds planted by *Victory through Air Power*'s immediate effect on high-ranking AAF officials during the summer of 1943.

Notes

1. Richard Shale, *Donald Duck Joins Up: The Walt Disney Studio During World War II* (Ann Arbor, MI: UMI Research Press, 1982), 165–170.
2. Robert B. Miller, foreword to "History of 18th AAF Base Unit (Motion Picture Unit): A Report for War Activities Committee of the Motion Picture Industry," by James Scanlan, File 262.1–1, Air Force Historical Research Institute, Maxwell Air Force Base, Alabama.
3. For a remarkable summary of Mitchell's life and work, see David Jablonsky, *Roots of Strategy*, Vol. 4 (Mechanicsburg, PA: Stackpole Books, 1999), 409–420.
4. For a comprehensive treatise on the decades-long fight to achieve an independent United States Air Force, see DeWitt S. Copp, *A Few Great Captains* (McLean, VA: EPM Publications, 1989) and R. Earl McClendon, *Autonomy of the Air Arm* (Washington, DC: U.S. Government Printing Office, 1996).
5. An early but primary example of this is assertion may be seen in William Mitchell's 1925 book, *Winged Defense*, reprinted in its entirety in Jablonsky, 421–516.
6. Scanlan, "History of 18th AAF Base Unit (Motion Picture Unit) (Formerly Designated 1st Motion Picture Unit): A Report for Historical Division, AC/AS Intelligence, Headquarters, Army Air Forces," 189.
7. Steven Watts, *The Magic Kingdom: Walt Disney and the American Way of Life* (New York: Houghton Mifflin, 1997), 235–36.
8. Watts, 236.
9. Shale, 70.
10. McClendon, 94–95.
11. Leonard Maltin, *The Disney Films*, 3rd ed. (New York: Hyperion, 1995), 64.
12. Quoted in Richard Schickel, *The Disney Version: The Life, Times, Art, and Commerce of Walt Disney* (New York: Simon & Schuster, 1985), 275.
13. "The Globe Presents 'Victory Through Airpower,' a Disney Illustration of Major de Seversky's Book," *New York Times*, 19 July 1943. Accessed 27 March 2010 at: http://movies.nytimes.com/movie/review?res=9404EFDF1738E33BBC4152DFB1668388659EDE
14. Philip T. Hartung, "Winged Victory," *The Commonweal*, 6 August 1943: 393–94.
15. Watts, 236.
16. "Organization Chart, Army Air Forces, November 15, 1943" *Air Force: The Official Service Journal of the U.S. Army Air Forces* 27, no. 1 (1944): 32–33.
17. Brigadier General Robert W. Harper to Commanding Officer, Training Aids Division, 20 July 1943, Decimal Files, October 1942–May 1944, 062.2, Training Films, July 1, 1943–September 5, 1943, RG 18 (AAF), NACP.

18. Roy O. Disney to Brigadier General Robert W. Harper, 21 July 1943, Decimal Files, October 1942–May 1944, 062.2, Training Films, July1, 1943–September 5, 1943, RG 18 (AAF), National Archives and Records Administration, College Park. Emphasis mine.
19. Ibid. Emphasis mine.
20. Shale, 20–22.
21. Shale, 168.
22. Brigadier General Robert W. Harper to Roy O. Disney, 22 July 1943, Decimal Files, October 1942–May 1944, 062.2, Training Films, July1, 1943–September 5, 1943, RG 18 (AAF), NACP.
23. First Lieutenant Peter R. Nehemkis, Jr., to Brigadier General Robert W. Harper, 4 August 1943, Decimal Files, October 1942–May 1944, 062.2, Training Films, July1, 1943–September 5, 1943, RG 18 (AAF), NACP.
24. Ibid.
25. Ibid.
26. Lieutenant Colonel Walter D. Merrill to Brigadier General Robert W. Harper, 7 August 1943, Decimal Files, October 1942–May 1944, 062.2, Training Films, July1, 1943–September 5, 1943, RG 18 (AAF), NACP.
27. First Motion Picture Unit Production Progress Report, 31 August 1943, Decimal Files, October 1942–May 1944, 062.2, Training Films, July1, 1943–September 5, 1943, RG 18 (AAF), NACP. Also, "Cartoon Hall of Fame," *ASIFA–Hollywood Animation Archive*, http://www.animationarchive.org/bio/2005/12/ising-rudolph.html (accessed 20 February 2010).
28. First Motion Picture Unit Production Progress Report, 31 August 1943.
29. Ibid.
30. Ibid. Yet another FMPU–Disney collaboration, this film was also completed in January of 1944. See Scanlan, 99, 101, 189, and 190. Also, Shale, 169.
31. Merrill to Harper, 7 August 1943.
32. Lieutenant Colonel Walter D. Merrill to Brigadier General Robert W. Harper, 6 August 1943, Decimal Files, October 1942–May 1944, 062.2, Training Films, July1, 1943–September 5, 1943, RG 18 (AAF), NACP.
33. Nehemkis to Harper, 4 August 1943.
34. Merrill to Harper, 6 August 1943.
35. Merrill to Harper, 7 August 1943.
36. Ibid.
37. Ibid.
38. Ibid. Notes about cost, Technicolor, and time deadline appear in handwriting on this document along with Merrill's initials.
39. Scanlan, 189.
40. Brigadier General Robert W. Harper to Colonel Lawrence Carr, 9 August 1943, Decimal Files, October 1942–May 1944, 062.2, Training Films, July1, 1943–September 5, 1943, RG 18 (AAF), NACP.
41. Geoffrey Perret, *Winged Victory: The Army Air Forces in World War II* (New York: Random House, 1993), 218.
42. Scanlan, 101.

Bibliography

"Cartoon Hall of Fame." *ASIFA–Hollywood Animation Archive*. http://www.animation-archive.org/bio/2005/12/ising-rudolph.html

Copp, DeWitt S. *A Few Great Captains*. McLean, VA: EPM Publications, 1989.

"The Globe Presents 'Victory Through Airpower,' a Disney Illustration of Major de Seversky's Book," *New York Times*, 19 July 1943.

Hartung, Philip T. "Winged Victory." *The Commonweal*, 6 August 1943: 393–94.
Jablonsky, David. *Roots of Strategy*, vol. 4. Mechanicsburg, PA: Stackpole Books, 1999.
Maltin, Leonard. *The Disney Films*, 3rd edition. New York: Hyperion, 1995.
McClendon, R. Earl. *Autonomy of the Air Arm.* Washington, DC: U.S. Government Printing Office, 1996.
"Organization Chart, Army Air Forces, November 15, 1943" *Air Force: The Official Service Journal of the U.S. Army Air Forces* 27, no. 1 (1944): 32–33.
Perret, Geoffrey. *Winged Victory: The Army Air Forces in World War II.* New York: Random House, 1993.
Schickel, Richard. *The Disney Version: The Life, Times, Art, and Commerce of Walt Disney.* New York: Simon & Schuster, 1985.
Shale, Richard. *Donald Duck Joins Up: The Walt Disney Studio During World War II.* Ann Arbor, MI: UMI Research Press, 1982.
United States Army Air Force papers. National Archives, College Park, MD.
Watts, Steven. *The Magic Kingdom: Walt Disney and the American Way of Life.* New York: Houghton Mifflin, 1997.

3

Cartoons Will Win the War

World War II Propaganda Shorts

RICHARD J. LESKOSKY

With the entrance of the United States into the Second World War, the Walt Disney Studio also embarked on a new period in its history. The war in Europe, even before U.S. entry, had had a profound effect on the studio since it cut Disney off from the lucrative European market he needed to recoup his investments in his feature-length productions. The day after Pearl Harbor, the studio campus took on the appearance of a military base, with soldiers stationed there to protect the nearby Lockheed Aircraft plant. That same day Disney also received his first U.S. government contract. By 1943, ninety-four per cent of the studio's output was government-funded, including classified work.[1]

The bulk of this work consisted of training films, but some films were intended for more widespread distribution, and designed to educate and influence viewers. Any theatrically released cartoon which depicted America's enemies as monsters and/or buffoons or which evoked positive feelings about America's role in the war could in some sense be considered propaganda. This discussion, however, will take a narrower focus and consider as propaganda only those cartoons, made at the government's behest which, displayed a more structured and obvious message.

Although traditional theatrical cartoon production accounted for less than ten per cent of the Disney studio's output at the height of the war, Disney images nonetheless permeated American society at that time. This chapter discusses nine short Disney cartoons commissioned by the government for largely propagandistic purposes, but those cartoons were part of a much larger body of Disney war-related images, both animated and still, which Americans in the early 1940s could readily see on a regular basis and which provided a visual context for the overtly propagandistic films discussed in this chapter.[2] This larger body of imagery included bond rally films produced for Canada, Good Neighbor health films made for Latin American distribution, training films made for various branches of the armed forces, and the educational/hortatory featurette *Victory Through Air Power*, all of which are considered elsewhere in this book. The abundance of such imagery undoubtedly made it easier for viewers to accept the more message-laden images in the nine short films discussed here.

Disney artists designed about 1,200 insignia for military units, many featuring familiar Disney characters,[3] as well as posters supporting the war effort.[4] Disney images appeared in ads in family publications such as *Collier's* and *The Saturday Evening Post.* Popular publications including *Life, Fortune,* and *Popular Science Monthly* ran articles on Disney's war-related projects along with illustrations from the films and photos of the artists at work. Wartime documentaries made to inform G.I.s and the American public about the causes and importance of the war — most notably, Frank Capra's *Why We Fight* series— relied on Disney-produced animated maps and related graphics.

Even before U.S. entry into the war, service comedies had become a recognizable Hollywood genre, casting familiar comedians as members (often unwilling or accidental) of the military, where conflicts with superiors figured more prominently than conflicts with enemy troops.[5] Once the United States entered the war, popular animated characters donned military uniforms, went through basic training, and even saw action in two dozen or so films. Donald Duck, one of the cartoon stars most commonly seen in uniform, appeared in five cartoon service comedies.[6] Goofy also appeared in uniform in *How to Be a Sailor* (1944), and even Pluto got into the act — though not, strictly speaking, into uniform — as a mascot or military watchdog in three films.[7]

Disney's animated propaganda shorts proper fell into three categories: agricultural documentaries, home front calls to action, and "psychological" films. Agricultural documentaries detailed the importance of American crops to the war effort both at home and around the world. Home front calls to action explained the necessity of paying one's taxes or conserving resources. Psychological films examined the German psyche and compared it with its American counterpart or explored other psychological aspects of the war. Education was the overt aim of each of these categories, but that education was also intended to lead to action supporting the American war effort. And even though they differed from the studio's regular theatrical releases in the manner in which they told their stories and in having obvious messages specifically related to the war, their propaganda function was supported and complemented by Disney's overriding intention to entertain his audience. Long before he had Mary Poppins sing it, Disney lived by the principle that "a spoonful of sugar helps the medicine go down."

Selling the War, Disney Style

During the early 1930s, Walt Disney's studio increasingly emphasized character animation (along with a stock company of characters) and developed certain Principles of Animation which gave its cartoons a distinctive look and tone.[8] The Silly Symphonies became testing grounds for new techniques and addressed specific animation challenges (*The Three Little Pigs*, for example, explored ways of individuating physically identical characters). At the same time, Walt Disney actively encouraged his animators to continue their art education with, among other resources, life drawing lessons at the studio. *Fantasia* (1940) carried this notion onto the screen with its explicit intent of edifying as well as entertaining. So the mix of education/indoctrination and entertainment that would make the propaganda films so effective was a natural extension of already exiting Disney traits. And that Disney used these films in turn to develop techniques that would continue to appear in certain types of productions for decades to come continued his developmental strategies of the 1930s.

Disney employed one or more of the following devices in each of the studio's propaganda films: a voice of authority imparting information or delineating proper attitudes and courses of action, the use of contrasting moral exemplars to demonstrate the consequences of different attitudes or courses of action, and a blending of different graphic styles. In each case, this represented a departure from Disney's general practice but also an elaboration of devices used only rarely in his previous films—in short, an evolution of storytelling form to serve new purposes.

Voices of authority. Disney's pre-war films relied most heavily on images and music, with minimal assistance from the dialogue, to tell their stories.[9] Virtually every Disney animator interviewed by researchers has described Walt as a peerless storyteller who would act out entire cartoons when explaining projects to his artists (or government sponsors).[10] This aptitude for, and commitment to, "showing rather than telling" manifested itself throughout Disney's purely entertainment offerings.

The rare pre-war exceptions with voiceovers had very specific justifications. The Oscar-winning *Ferdinand the Bull* (1938) adapted from the immensely popular 1936 children's book, *The Story of Ferdinand*, preserved author Munro Leaf's humorous, endearing text in voiceover (while almost completely ignoring illustrator Robert Lawson's visual style in favor of the studio's own). *Goofy's Glider* (1940), the first of a popular series of ersatz instructional films starring Goofy, relied for its comedy on the dichotomy between its voiceover narration and its visuals. Throughout the series, while the narrator's cultivated voice gave a reasonably accurate account of the proper way to go about the sport or other activity in the title, the audience saw Goofy serving as a fumbling or even contradictory example of those same principles.[11] And of course an on-screen authoritarian narrator figured prominently in *Fantasia* (1940).

Once the United States entered the war, Disney embarked in earnest on the production of serious instructional films, with *Four Methods of Flush Riveting* (1942) for neighboring Lockheed Aircraft. Here the use of voiceover came into its own, with straightforward verbal instruction to explain the simple, nearly diagrammatic animation of the flush riveting process and the reasons for its use. Educational films that were also designed to entertain, the propaganda shorts used techniques from both *Four Methods* and the Goofy comedies of instruction. Their off-screen voices of authority, often employing a more overtly oratorical delivery, explained to the audience what they were seeing and sometimes even explained to the characters within the film what they ought to be doing. Voiceover and on-screen action thus reinforced each other, driving the message home.

This technique was particularly useful in the propaganda films for presenting densely packed lists of information — a need that did not arise in the comedies of instruction, the health films, or the training films. The off-screen narrator would recite, for example, the uses to which a citizen's taxes might be put or a series of illustrative similes making more graspable such not easily visualized concepts as, say, the annual United States potato output. The verbal catalog would be matched with a montage of images so that the combined aural and visual assault had a heightened emotional impact to fix the message in the viewer's mind.

Moral Dichotomies. A teaching tool that Disney uses repeatedly in his commissioned films is the presentation of exemplars of good and bad behaviors or right and wrong choices and the consequences of those actions and choices. Disney employed this device in virtually all the health films made for the Coordinator of Inter-American Affairs as part of the Good Neighbor Policy. Improper or uneducated behavior result in sickness and death while health awareness and proper hygiene lead to a better life. In *Donald's Decision* (1942), commissioned by the National Film Board of Canada to sell War Savings Certificates, angel and devil Donald replicas clash over investing in Canada's war bonds. This film depended in large part on recycled footage from *Donald's Better Self* (1938) where angel and devil battle over Donald's decision to play hooky.

This particular teaching method had its origin in Disney's early film career in Kansas City. *Tommy Tucker's Tooth* (1922), a largely live-action Laugh-O-Gram and Disney's first educational film, contrasted the hygiene and career potentials of dentally careful Tommy Tucker and slovenly Jimmie Jones. Disney also made his points more comprehensible by relating them to phenomena with which the audience would be familiar, drawing comparisons between proper tooth care and measures taken to prevent the spoilage of food and the deterioration of clothing. A second dental hygiene film, *Clara Cleans Her Teeth* (1926), presented before and after visions of a young girl's bad and good oral cleansing habits.[12]

Blending Levels of Realism. Throughout the 1930s, Walt Disney pushed his animators to ever higher levels of artistic quality and enhanced realism.[13] Most of the studio's new ideas, processes, and inventions produced visual cues suggestive of qualities in the real world (depth of field, say, or illusions of mass in a moving figure). Disney was not striving for anything like photorealism in his cartoons, though. but rather believability in his animated characters—in effect, an emotional rather than a strictly physical realism.[14]

This process meant Disney increasingly avoided the inherently surreal aspects of the animated cartoon which other studios—most notably, the Fleischers—regularly exploited and which Disney himself had relied upon in his studio's early years. Characters no longer enjoyed the complete graphic freedom of his Oswald the Rabbit, who could detach parts of his body, stretch his limbs to any length as needed, and turn symbols from his own dialogue balloons into tools or vehicles to achieve his immediate goals. Instead, characters and objects in Disney sound films acquired a certain stability of form and did not metamorphose into other shapes, and objects generally did not come to life unless that was the whole point of a particular cartoon as in *Music Land* (1935), a Romeo and Juliet story with living musical instruments.[15]

By the time the studio began work on its propaganda films, it had developed three distinct styles or modes with different levels of verisimilitude, which I will refer to here as cartoon, realistic, and schematic.

The cartoon style, marked by caricature and exaggeration, predominated in Disney's entertainment shorts. Though it became more sophisticated and achieved greater verisimilitude through the 1930s, it remained essentially comic in tone and intent .Animal characters were anthropomorphized. Human characters were generally drawn with head to body proportions that did not match those in real humans, and their facial features were generally more rounded than in real life and displayed different proportions. Most characters, human or animal, were constructed from underlying circles and ellipses, lacked fine details, and moved more rapidly and comically than their real-life counterparts.

The realistic style covered a range of more detailed artwork and was used to tell more serious stories.. Animated characters appeared more closely modeled after real world beings. Humans displayed body proportions consistent with those of real people, and their facial features showed lines and shapes one might expect to see in life drawings. Their torsos were more likely to be built up from underlying rectangles and trapezoids. Animals tended to resemble more closely their real world counterparts, and their movements tended to have a speed more closely approximating real life. Finer detail appeared in characters, objects, and especially backgrounds. Backgrounds often looked more painterly, resembling oil paintings or watercolors rather than pencil drawings. This style appeared occasionally in the Silly Symphonies[16] and reached its acme there in the Oscar-winning *The Old Mill* (1935). The animal denizens of the mill were rendered in a more naturalistic manner which complemented the greater detail in the rendering of the mill's decrepit interior, the use of the multiplane camera to create appearance of depth, and the various special effects reflections and gleams off rain and pond. Disney employed this style more often in the feature films, especially in their more serious moments—the scene in *Snow White and the Seven Dwarfs* (1937), say, when the Queen's huntsman is supposed to kill Snow White but instead spares her life.

In the propaganda films, something of a paradox occurs with regard to realistic images. Though they are by definition more natural—that is, they look more like what they represent than the caricatures of the cartoon style—they generally have a higher symbolic content. A loaf of bread rendered in near photo-realistic style represents not a particular, single loaf of bread but all the bread produced by the United States in one year or simply the notion "Bread." The same is true of moving images of tanks, say, which may be rendered in considerable detail but do not represent a specific line of tanks invading a particular country; instead they represent war machines in general or the concepts of "Invasion," "Aggression," or "Conquest." This echoes the use of stock footage and captured footage in the live-action *Why We Fight* series to represent specific events (whether or not they were actual recordings of those events) but more often to convey simply general impressions of conflict, aggression, and Axis infamy.

The schematic style includes diagrams, maps, and highly stylized figures. Disney employed this style only sparingly in its regular entertainment shorts until introducing explanatory game diagrams as a gag in the Goofy instructional comedy *How to Play Baseball* (1942). This was perhaps inspired by the other government sponsored work the studio had begun doing, such as the animated maps for the Army Signal Corps's *Why We Fight* films. Schematic rendering may have a humorous or serious function, depending on its context, but its overt intent in either case will appear to be educational or explanatory. Generally, Disney tended to avoid noticeable mixes of these styles and levels of realism in his entertainment shorts in order not to distract viewers and thus compromise the illusion of reality the animators were manufacturing.[17] The schematic diagrams in the Goofy instructional comedies passed, however, as natural inclusions in a spoof of educational films. In the propaganda shorts, realistic and cartoon styles appeared in the same film but were usually assigned to distinct sections dealing with different aspects of the main subject, although, as will become evident in the descriptions of individual films, a realistic image might pop up in a more cartoonish section or a cartoon caricature could suddenly appear amidst an array of realistic images. Schematic illustrations could appear in either context, and several films successfully employed all three styles to significant degrees.

Although these different styles appear in all three categories of Disney propaganda shorts, the realistic and schematic styles tend to show up more often in the Agricultural Documentaries, and the cartoon style shows up to a greater degree in the Home Front Calls to Action and the Psychological Films. Presumably, in those films the propagandistic intent was more obvious and so needed to be made more palatable by being rendered in a style audiences would automatically associate with pure entertainment.

Agricultural Documentaries

The war represented a huge drain on the country's resources. Food rationing had become law. Gasoline, rubber, and scrap metal were diverted to military uses, thereby reducing the general mobility of the population. In response, Disney supplied the government with two films explaining the importance of food to the war effort and justifying the audience's sacrifices for their fighting men.[18] The films also served to link agricultural workers with the military, thereby implicitly justifying to the general populace the deferments from active service accorded to farm workers. Additionally, they furthered the sense of the whole hemisphere working together, which lay at the root of the Good Neighbor Policy.

***Food Will Win the War* (1942).** Directed by Ben Sharpsteen, the film was made with supervision by the Agricultural Marketing Administration for the Department of Agriculture. *Food Will Win the War* took its title from a phrase Secretary of Agriculture Claude Wickard coined in a nationwide radio address: "Food will win the war and write the peace." That in fact was the original full title, but it was shortened on the recommendation of the Office of the Coordinator of Information, apparently to avoid suggesting that the United States planned to take the lead in shaping the post-war world.[19]

The film opens dramatically with an image of the world on fire, followed by a primarily still image of a ruined farm. The off-screen narrator briefly explains the conflict and the plight of the Allies in charged terms and offers America as a source of hope and food. A United States map blossoms with the outlines of various European countries within its borders illustrating that American farmlands far exceed those in the countries depicted. Next, silhouettes of American farmers and their families stand astride the globe as the narrator praises their labors ("Grim farmers with sleeves rolled up, ready for sacrifices") and announces that America has twice as many farmers as Germany has soldiers. The farmer silhouettes begin to show more detail: they are wearing overalls, but faces remain blank. Next, ranks of farm equipment harvest a crop[20] while the narrator describes them in military terms, further emphasizing the farmer-soldier equivalence: "Panzer forces of food," "battalions of combines, "regiments of trucks," "divisions of corn pickers, potato diggers, planting machines."

The narrator next presents a catalog of commodities along with the amounts of each America produces. Though each commodity is illustrated with a realistic image, the narrator provides bizarre statistics for each crop. The analogies become as surreal as anything Disney has ever done: "Or should we turn this milk into butter, war-flooded fields of Holland could be reclaimed by dikes it would build." In the midst of realistic renderings of surreal images, a giant cartoon bowling ball (representing vitamins) scatters pins with the faces of Hitler, Mussolini, and Hirohito, and the planet Earth gets a pie in the face. Happy cartoon hens, recycled from *Golden Eggs* (1941), lay eggs, and the Three

Little Pigs (imitating Archibald Willard's famous painting, *The Spirit of '76*) lead a parade of pigs (presumably to the slaughterhouse). A giant farmer silhouette pours grain into the hold of a Victory ship, and the narrator launches into another litany. The ships, ships, ships ("...ships protected by the blasting fire of men of war, ships loaded with food for freedom....") cross the seas, protected by planes and warships from Axis subs with skull-shaped bows, to deliver foodstuffs to those who fight for a list of freedoms. It all ends with a close up of food crates bearing the Lend-Lease program emblem (an eagle and four stars) that Disney had designed for the Department of Agriculture.[21]

Among Disney propaganda films, *Food Will Win the War* most demonstrates a likely influence from Disney's work with Frank Capra's film unit of the Special Service Division Army Service Forces. Like, say, *Prelude to War* (1942), it tells its story in a montage of images both verbal and visual. It begins by presenting a dichotomy between the ravaged farms of Europe and the bounties of American agriculture just as *Prelude* began with a comparison between the free world and the slave world. Its language is factual but emotionally loaded. It uses specific images to make general or symbolic points. It employs maps and deploys statistics about relative strengths and resources of the opposing forces. And it uses at least some recycled footage.

The Grain That Built a Hemisphere (1943).[22] More focused in its content, *The Grain That Built a Hemisphere*, directed by Bill Roberts, concentrates specifically on the past, present, and future of corn production. Made under the auspices of the Coordinator of Inter-American Affairs (CIAA) for the Latin American market, as were the health films commissioned by the CIAA, the film was nonetheless released theatrically in the U.S. and nominated for an Oscar for Best Documentary.[23]

The film begins with a map of North and South America covered by golden grain with a stylized Indian off to the side grinding corn by rolling a cylindrical stone *mano* over a flat stone *metate*.[24] The off-screen narrator explains the theories of how modern corn evolved, accompanied by schematics of the reproductive systems of possible corn ancestors. An Indian (in silhouette with highlights along the edges of his limbs and torso like the roustabouts in the tent-raising scene in *Dumbo*) passes by one of these plants in the Andes while hunting a deer (recycled from *Bambi*). Eventually when game becomes scarce, an Indian whose features are actually shown discovers that the plant's kernels, depicted in a naturalistic style, are edible. Then follows a summary of the importance of corn to the civilizations of the Mayas, the Aztecs, and the Incas (including corn gods and Aztec human sacrifice). A map shows the spread of corn throughout South America, then North America, and finally the world. Behind an outline of the Indian's forearms working with *mano* and *metate*, an array of basic corn-based foods appears as the narrator lists them. The narrator praises the Indian discoverer and developer of corn and then goes on to explain how modern farmers grow corn with highly productive and efficient machinery.

The narrator then explains the process of in-breeding corn which leads to bigger plants. Like the preceding scenes, this is illustrated with realistic images and handled seriously except for an odd descent into the cartoonish when "two unrelated strains are joined in wedlock" accompanied by Wagner's *Bridal Chorus* as they link their leaves like arms. This produces a new, larger strain and leads to a set of statistics about the consumption of corn by farm animals, with scenes recycled from *Farmyard Symphony* (1938). The narrator next discusses the role science plays in developing food and other products from corn. A diagram of a corn kernel shows the different parts which may be used for various products illustrated realistically in another catalogue sequence.[25] The shimmering, vaguely ominous reflection of a researcher on a bubbling retort marks a shift to a catalogue of potential new (war) uses for corn products: fuel for planes, high explosives for bombs (a plane dropping bombs is recycled from *The New Spirit*), tires, "fabric for parachutes better than silk," "plastics harder than steel for cars, for tanks, men of war, ships of peace...." For its finale, the film returns to the recurring visual motif of the Indian, whom the narrator thanks again for discovering corn.

The Grain That Built a Hemisphere signals its Good Neighbor origins with its title (changed from the original, succinct *Corn and Corn Products* to suggest a link between North and South America),[26] its emphasis on the importance of South America in the history of this vital crop, its recurring visual motif of the Indian grinding corn, and its repeated verbal thanks to corn's Indian discoverers. It does eventually get around to referencing the war but with more restrained images and language than *Food Will Win the War*. The emphasis remains on furthering hemispheric harmony rather than actively denouncing European and Asian enemies.[27]

Home Front Calls to Action

More than food was needed from the home front to win the war. Money, in the form of taxes, was of course essential; but even simple items, such as cooking grease, could be recycled into war matériel. When asking viewers to make sacrifices or change common behavior (*i.e.*, save and turn in grease that might ordinarily have been used for flavoring), Disney relied on his popular cartoon characters to hook viewers, inserted a voiceover explanation of the target behavior, and followed that with a visual and verbal catalogue of the positive effects of that behavior, rendered in a generally realistic style.

On 18 December 1941, Treasury Secretary Henry J. Morgenthau and Guy Helvering, Commissioner of Internal Revenue, asked Walt Disney to produce a film which would urge the fifteen million new taxpayers created by the 1941 tax law to pay their taxes in a timely (and cheerful) manner. Walt responded with *The New Spirit* starring Donald Duck, but when Morgenthau saw the storyboards and heard Walt's description on 4 January 1942 he was unimpressed. He had hoped for an everyman sort of protagonist rather than a recognized studio character. Walt explained that putting his top cartoon star in the film was like MGM lending the Treasury Department Clark Gable. In any case, because the film had to go into production immediately for a February release to prepare viewers for the March 15 filing deadline, Morgenthau had to approve the film.

The film was generally considered a success; according to a Gallup poll, it induced 37% of its viewers to pay their taxes immediately.[28] But Walt unfortunately had only a letter of intent from Morgenthau and not an actual contract, and Congress objected to paying for a cartoon instead of bombers. Disney was not even able to recover all the production costs, let alone print costs. Nonetheless, Disney continued to make propaganda films for the government and even a sequel for the Treasury Department, *The Spirit of '43*, but with the money guaranteed by Congress up front this time.[29]

***The New Spirit* (1942).** Over the opening title credits Cliff Edwards (the voice of Jiminy Cricket) sings about the "new spirit." Multiple Donald Ducks are dancing to the tune, though these are soon revealed as reflections in a multi-paneled mirror. The song emanates from Donald's radio (although the image is rendered more realistically, the knobs and speaker nonetheless vaguely suggest a face), and when he marches up to it, one reflection remains in the mirror until it realizes that Donald has moved on (not a typical sort of sight gag for Disney at this time). Donald salutes as Edwards sings about the Yankee Doodle spirit; a close-up shows flags waving in his eyes (also not a typical Disney sight gag). An announcer speaks about the country preparing for "total war," and Donald arms himself with shotgun, sword, baseball bat, boxing gloves, axe, golf club, and a bear trap. When the announcer says that he can help and that it will mean some sacrifice but no medals, Donald begs to be told what he can do. When the announcer says it is paying his taxes on time, however, Donald grumbles and asks what's the rush. The announcer reiterates that the country is at war and launches into a taxes litany culminating in what will become a catch phrase for this and its sequel, "taxes to beat the Axis."

Inspired, Donald rushes off to return laden with a globe, calculators, math and law books, jar of paste, piggy bank, file drawer, rulers, compass, and large bottle of aspirin. The announcer tells him that he does not need all that since he made less than $3000 and can use the short form (shown in realistic close-up).[30] He just needs ink, a pen, and a blotter. These come to life on his desk to voice their encouragement and cooperation (yet another gag Disney had eschewed years earlier). The announcer instructs Donald on filling out the form, which the fountain pen does automatically, though not without comment (it also puts a question mark after "actor" on the Occupation line and notes that dependents Huey, Dewey, and Louie are "Adopted"). When the announcer encourages him to mail his check in early, Donald races out the door and past the mailbox, which calls out after him, to zip across a map of America from California to Washington.

An off-screen narrator now explains that taxes run the factories that make guns and other war machines. Tax forms for people with different income levels appear. A factory whistle with a minimal face wearing an Uncle Sam hat sounds off, and a realistic montage, in *March of Time* style, shows factory machines turning out war matériel while the narrator catalogues the weapons that taxes and factories make. A montage of weapons follows with occasional returns to factory whistles (which wear naval caps when the catalog gets to ships) and depictions of what our planes, guns, and ships do to the enemy's (Axis subs once again have ugly faces on their bows). This culminates in an assault on a terrifying Nazi war machine combining elements of tank, airplane, and artillery battery, all topped with a horned helmet. When it lies in wreckage, the first four notes of Beethoven's Fifth Symphony sound: three short notes and one long, the Morse code symbol for "V." As the narrator promises victory and a chorus sings "America the Beautiful," silhouettes of tanks and planes radiate out from the bottom of the screen as clouds and stars simulate an American flag.

The film, directed by Wilfred Jackson and Ben Sharpsteen, maintains a cartoon style while Donald is on-screen but segues through the schematic of the U.S. map to a generally realistic style for the factory/weapons montage. Moderately surreal elements appear in the Donald section (the independent reflection, the talking pen and ink) and in the realistic section (cartoonish anthropomorphic factory whistles and the realistically rendered Nazi War Machine). American planes and tanks are drawn in a straightforward, bright style which presents them realistically but without a lot of detail. Enemy machines are rendered with more detail, the impression of more weight, and an overriding darkness. They appear more solid in a sense and very menacing, but with some bizarre elements (subs with faces, planes with fangs) which simultaneously heighten their negative connotations but compromise their reality. The explanations of the tax form and the need to pay early are clear-cut and concise, though the language ratchets up to the *Why We Fight* level in the taxes/factories/weapons catalog.

The disembodied voice of authority which characterizes all the propaganda films appears here in both diegetic (radio announcer) and non-diegetic (voiceover narrator) forms.[31] In post-war films, Disney would continue to use both forms for educational entertainments but generally not within the same film.

The Spirit of '43 **(1943).** A factory whistle intones "Payday" and puffs smoke in dollar sign shapes. As the narrator announces that millions of dollars go into workers' hands, a close-up shows Donald's fingers riffling through a sheaf of greenbacks. According to the narrator, two separate personalities exist in the mind of the worker — the thrifty and the spendthrift. The thrifty personality arrives on the scene first. An older Scottish version of Donald in kilt and tam with sideburns and pince-nez glasses (the progenitor of Donald's rich uncle, Scrooge McDuck), he advises Donald to save his money. Donald puts it in his pocket, but it immediately begins literally burning a hole in it. The smoke summons the spendthrift, a sleeker version of Donald in a zoot suit, who tries to entice him into The Idle Hour Club with the promise of a couple of "good dates." But Thrifty says he has better dates— the tax deadlines. The narrator announces that, thanks to Hitler and Hirohito, taxes will be higher than ever this year and asks whether the viewer (or Donald) will have the money to pay them when they fall due. Spendthrift tears up Thrifty's calendar pages, and the "spend/save" argument quickly becomes a tug-of-war with Donald in the middle until a rip in his jacket sends the two antagonists sprawling in opposite directions. Spendthrift falls through the saloon's swinging doors, now revealed to be swastika-shaped, while Thrifty crashes into a wall, knocking off plaster to reveal a brick pattern suggesting the Stars and Stripes. The narrator asks Donald what he will do now—"spend for the Axis or save for taxes?" Donald gets swastikas in his eyes as he looks toward Spendthrift leaning on the swinging doors, with his tie and cigarette smoke now swastika-shaped and a moustache and bangs like Hitler's. With stars in his eyes, Donald looks at Thrifty standing defiant against the flag-like brick background. He walks toward Spendthrift, who now looks even more Hitler-like, and punches him back through the swinging doors which shatter into a V and a Morse Code dot-dot-dot-dash ("V") accompanied by the first four notes of Beethoven's Fifth. Donald pays his taxes, though Thrifty finds a coin Donald has hidden under his hat and adds it to his payment. The film then repeats the taxes/factories/weapons montage and voiceover of *The New Spirit.*

Director Jack King (who also did Donald's service comedies) employs the same moral strategy in *The Spirit of '43* as in his *Donald's Better Self* (1938), pitting fanciful good and bad counselors against each other in a struggle for Donald's moral compass. He eschews the religious implications of the earlier film's angel and devil ducks for secular icons, though.[32] The film essentially repositions the Allies/Axis dichotomy from the international stage to the individual's own mind, thereby giving the individual's decision global consequences. This strategy evidently struck a chord with Disney, and he employed variations of it in subsequent propaganda films.

Out of the Frying Pan and into the Firing Line **(1942).** Made for the Conservation Division of the War Production Board, *Out of the Frying Pan and into the Firing Line*, directed by Jack King, encouraged viewers to save kitchen grease for the war effort.

Minnie Mouse fries bacon and eggs (shown in realistic close-up), and Pluto looks eager to have the grease poured on his dry dog biscuits. Just as Minnie is about to do that, however, the radio (also shown in close-up in realistic detail) interrupts with an injunction not to throw away kitchen fats since they are needed to make glycerin for explosives. Statistics follow on how much is thrown away each year and how many shells that would make. The narrator and a visual montage repeatedly link grease with American weapons and their devastating effect on the enemy (with drops of grease metamorphosing into bullets and bombs). When the narrator announces "Your pound of waste fat will give some boy at the front an extra clip of cartridges," Pluto looks over at a picture of Mickey in uniform with a rifle on his back (the only time Mickey is ever seen in military uniform in a wartime cartoon).[33] Pluto salutes with his ear and declines the bacon grease. Instead, he and Minnie follow the announcer's instructions for straining and preserving the grease, and then Pluto takes it to a butcher who collects fats for the military. While an artillery battery in silhouette fires off a round, the announcer/narrator gives a final recommendation to the audience to save fats and directs viewers to look for the official recycling insignia in their butcher's window.

Shorter than the other films here, *Out of the Frying Pan* gets its simple message across quickly and with relatively less of the standard war imagery. Of course, it is also not asking anything that takes much of a sacrifice—certainly nothing like paying taxes—and viewers who participate in the program can even get cash rewards. Minnie and Pluto are drawn in their normal cartoon style while the industrial/military section looks more realistic. Disney couches the appeal to help our soldiers in more personal terms, both in the voiceover and in the picture of Mickey in uniform, as well as with the generally domestic feel of the opening scene. This strategy is entirely in keeping with a support effort that takes place largely in one's kitchen.

Once again, the voice of authority appears both in diegetic (radio announcer) and non-diegetic (voiceover) forms. The radio voice helped fortify the image of a typical day at home whereas a voiceover during that breakfast scene directing the characters' actions might have suggested the sort of government intrusion into the home dramatized in the first section of *Der Fuehrer's Face.*

Psychological Films

Disney's hardcore propaganda shorts, all commissioned by the CIAA and released theatrically in 1943, focused on regimentation and the exploitation of emotions (usually fear) in controlling people. *Education for Death* and *Reason and Emotion* are structured like documentaries, while *Der Fuehrer's Face* and *Chicken Little* could pass for a typical Donald Duck comic short or a Silly Symphony, respectively..

***Der Fuehrer's Face* (1943).** Disney changed the original title, *Donald in Nutziland*, when Spike Jones's boisterous recording of Oliver Wallace's theme song became a huge hit months before the film hit theatres. Although released on 1 January 1943, the film, directed by Jack Kinney, carries a 1942 copyright and won the Oscar as Best Animated Short of 1942.

A Nazi marching band singing the title song (voiced by Cliff Edwards) parades through a landscape suffused with swastikas. Clouds, trees, shrubs, hedges, windmill vanes, hydrants, fences, street signs, and telephone poles are all distorted into the twisted cross. A generic Japanese soldier plays the tuba. An effeminate caricature of Hermann Göring plays the flute (and gets goosed by the trombone). Mussolini pops up briefly for a verse.

They awaken Donald, who has been giving the Nazi salute in his sleep. The exterior of his house presents a caricature of Hitler's face with architectural features suggesting nose, moustache, and bangs. Inside, twisted crosses decorate wallpaper, bed, dressing screen, and window shade pull. The numerals on the clocks are swastikas, and the spring on the cuckoo, which resembles Hitler, is swastika-shaped. A soldier with bayoneted rifle marches outside his window.

Donald salutes pictures of Hitler, Hirohito, and Mussolini. His breakfast consists of coffee made from one bean, a couple of atomizer spritzes of "Aroma de Bacon & Eggs," and a slice sawed from a loaf of bread displaying an obvious wood grain.[34] A copy of *Mein Kampf* is thrust into the frame on a bayonet for his edification. The band marches in and then out again with Donald carrying the bass drum and getting kicked in the rear.

When he arrives at work prodded by bayonets, the factory whistle (with mouth and helmet) intones "Heil Hitler," and he goes to work screwing the tops onto shells and saluting whenever a Hitler portrait comes down the assembly line. After a frantic scramble with shells and portraits, Donald gets a one-minute paid vacation. This consists of a threadbare canvas mountain scene and forced calisthenics to build him up for more work. His alternating arm and head movements turn him into a living swastika. Afterwards he must work overtime at an ever increasing pace, causing him briefly to split in two and then have a nervous breakdown. He hallucinates a writhing dance of flexible shells which owes much to the pink elephants sequence in *Dumbo*. Donald appears as Hitler and also shows up moving down an assembly line being pounded by a giant living shell. Everything blows up, and it rains Donalds until he wakes up in his own bed in stars and stripes pajamas. When he sees a shadow apparently giving the Nazi salute, he begins to do the same but then realizes it's the shadow of his model Statue of Liberty, which he proceeds to hug, saying "Oh boy, am I glad to be a citizen of the United States of America!" The camera irises in and then out again for a final chorus of the title song with an image of Hitler getting a rotten tomato thrown in his face (a similar image is featured on the poster for the film and the sheet music for the song).

Donald's audience would have been familiar with rationing and overtime at defense plants from their own experience. *Der Fuehrer's Face* demonstrated humorously how much worse the situation was in Germany. Donald's dream self is obviously motivated solely by fear rather than any sort of allegiance to

Hitler, and any slight sign of resistance, such as grumbling on the assembly line, is met with instant threats of violence. Though the tone is light and made even more comic by the surreal hallucination sequence, the film nonetheless brings home its points about forced labor, shortages, and fear among those under Hitler's rule and the corollary that Americans are (or should be) happy to work for their country's war industries.

Although there is no narrator here, diegetic voices of authority appear as orders presumably from the marching band or perhaps the soldier outside Donald's window in the breakfast scene and as commands from the loudspeakers at the munitions factory. These diegetic yet disembodied voices reinforce the sense of a totalitarian environment.

Education for Death **(1943).** Based on the 1941 book by Gregor Ziemer[35] and directed by Clyde Geronimi, *Education for Death*— the most inflammatory and serious of the Disney propaganda films—follows the growth and education of a young German boy named Hans from sickly innocent to goose-stepping slave of the Third Reich. It employs cartoon, realistic, and schematic styles of rendering in telling its story and relies heavily on the narrator for explanation and commentary (including translating the characters' German dialogue).

"What makes a Nazi?" narrator Art Smith asks as a scarlet swastika occupies the screen. In a large hall in the typical overwhelming Nazi style of architecture, Hans's parents hand over his birth certificate and proof of Aryan ancestry to a faceless uniformed figure. He calls their attention to a list of unacceptable names (which include not only Franklin and Winston at the top but also lower down Elias— Walt's own middle name and his father's given name — and lower still, Clyde). He presents the parents with a copy of *Mein Kampf.*

Hitler's book dissolves to a book of Nazi-approved fairy tales (*Märchen der neuen Ordnung*) to illustrate what Hans learns in kindergarten. It opens to "Sleeping Beauty" ("Dornröschen"), and the style changes from realistic to cartoon. A witch identified as Democracy menaces Sleeping Beauty. A prince in armor arrives to send the witch crashing through a leaded glass window to escape. The prince's kiss awakens Sleeping Beauty, who turns out to be an obese, bibulous Germania (contrary to her slim silhouette in the preceding shots but in keeping with the stereotypical comic movie image of the fat Wagnerian soprano). The knight is revealed to be Hitler. They *heil,* he rants for a while, and she sings. Then he picks her up and after some slapstick gets her onto his horse and rides away as rows of trees salute. The film cuts to a reasonably accurate cartoon rendering of *The Standard Bearer (Der Bannerträger)*, Hubert Lanzinger's 1937 portrait of Hitler as a knight on horseback, which Hans and his kindergarten classmates salute.[36]

When Hans becomes ill, though, a shadowy uniformed figure bursts into his bedroom to threaten his mother that the state will take over if she does not stop "mollycoddling" him.

Back in school, Hans and his classmates salute a picture of Hitler while pictures of Göring and Goebbels look on approvingly. The paintings show more texture in their rendering but also caricature their subjects: Göring's medals spill over his frame, and Goebbels peers from the corner of his tilted frame to the sound of rat-like chittering.

The teacher sketches on the chalkboard the outlines of a hare and a fox which come to life, with the fox chasing, cornering, and eating the hare. When Hans expresses sympathy for the hare, the teacher angrily sends him to sit in the dunce's corner and calls him a *dummkopf.* The paintings of Hitler, Göring, and Goebbels (again with chittering accompaniment) glare in disapproval. While Hans sheds a tear, other students give the correct answer that the world belongs to the strong and the brutal, and Hans comes around to that way of thinking. The boys *heil* while the teacher rants about German superiority. Hans then vehemently renounces his sympathy for the hare. The narrator comments on the effectiveness of the teaching, and the portrait of Hitler winks.

The scene changes to a nighttime rally with torches where books by Einstein, Spinoza, Mann, Voltaire, and possibly Marx (only MA is visible on one book cover) are burned, as are paintings and Mendelssohn's *Wedding March.* A Bible transforms into *Mein Kampf*, and a crucifix into a sword with a swastika on the hilt and a swastika shadow on the blade. Marching shadows play across a church wall, and a painted swastika materializes on the wall. A brick crashes through a stained glass window showing Mary and the infant Jesus, recalling the window Democracy fled through earlier.

Hans is then seen marching and *heiling.* He and his companions transform into *Hitlerjugend* and then into soldiers with rifles and bayonets. He is now a good Nazi. In a close-up, blinders appear when the narrator says that he sees only what the Party wants him to see. A muzzle appears, showing that he says nothing but what the Party wants him to say, and chains around his neck and those of the others in his rank indicate that he does nothing but what the Party wants him to do. Hans and his comrades march off into the background and turn into rows and rows of Nazi grave markers. His education for death is now complete.

The film demonstrates how fear and regimentation produce Nazi followers. The rendering tends to be more realistic, except for the cartoon fairy tale, but ironically it also becomes more symbolic in the last sequence as the trappings of Nazi control accrete on the marching Hans.

Education for Death is also perhaps the least Disney-like of the propaganda films. The scenes involving the faceless representative of Hitler's regime with their use of expressionistic light and shadow (also associated with earlier German Expressionist films) and more natural bodily proportions recall what the Fleischers had been doing in their Superman cartoons. And the fairy tale sequence has a decidedly Warner Bros. feel to its character design, level of satire, and mild bawdiness.

***Reason and Emotion* (1943).** Directed by Bill Roberts, *Reason and Emotion* is perhaps the most psychologically oriented of the propaganda films in that it specifically purports to explain common psychological processes, albeit in very simplified terms. The title processes are personified with cartoon characters drawn from contemporary Hollywood stereotypes, with examples of typical sensible and emotional behavior similarly derived from the paradigms of the day.

The outline of a scale appears with neon letters spelling out the title as the narrator explains that "within the mind of each of us these two wage a ceaseless battle for mastery." An infant boy pushes a flower pot off a window sill, pulls a cat's tail and tumbles down a flight of stairs at the behest of Emotion, a little caveboy figure (wearing a leopard skin) in his head who has complete control since Reason has not been born yet. Reason shows up after the toddler's fall, dressed in a baby bonnet and gown and wearing glasses. Emotion kicks him into his suitcase.

When the infant reaches adulthood, Reason is literally in the driver's seat and behind the steering wheel in his head. Reason has a big head in proportion to his body, a receding hairline, and a weak chin, and he wears glasses and a business suit. In short, he looks— and speaks— much like a typical middle manager in a screwball comedy. Emotion is under control in the back seat. He still wears a leopard skin caveman outfit and looks unkempt with a heavy five o'clock shadow.[37] When he spots a young woman at a bus stop, he argues with Reason about talking to her and finally seizes control of the steering wheel, knocking out Reason. "Hi, Babe! Going my way?" gets only a slap in the face, and a caution from the narrator against letting Emotion take control.

The narrator then "borrows" the young woman's "pretty head" for a moment to demonstrate female versions of Reason and Emotion. Reason is thin, has her dull brown hair in a bun, and wears glasses, a conservative outfit, and sensible shoes (a stereotypical movie librarian or school teacher of the 1930s and 1940s). Emotion is plump and sensual, has flaming red hair, wears lipstick and a short, tight, off-the-shoulder dress, and thinks the guy Reason just slapped was cute. She suggests doing something fun — namely, eating. Although Reason favors a light lunch, Emotion goes wild and seizes control. As she lists what she wants to eat, graphs of the woman's chin, profile, and figure expand and set off alarms-evidence that "uncontrolled emotion can cause you trouble."

As alarming war-related headlines pile up in a stack of newspapers, the narrator warns that in these troubled times we especially need to keep emotion in check, A new exemplar, John Doakes, tries to keep up with the news but becomes anxious over what he hears on the radio. Phantom rumormongers spring up around his easy chair with more disinformation and turn symbolic (a ventriloquist puppet, a parrot, a braying jackass); an old woman complaining that all their food is being sent overseas and that they will starve turns into a skeleton.

Reason and Emotion grapple in his head over whether to believe the rumors, and Emotion is about to brain Reason with the steering wheel when the narrator intervenes and says that would be good ... for Hitler! The narrator proceeds to discuss how Reason and Emotion operate in a typical German. A caricatured Hitler exerts control over a particularly dense-looking German soldier by appealing to his Emotion (who wears a spiked helmet) with fear, sympathy, pride, and hate. As Emotion swells throughout Hitler's tirade, Reason shrinks. Emotion bashes him with a spiked club and puts him in a tiny concentration camp. As Emotion marches around Reason saluting, the camera focuses on his legs and dissolves to realistic legs in jackboots (with a swastika on them) marching through a ruined city. After this example of the effects of unrestrained emotion, the narrator tells John Doakes's Reason and Emotion what they need to do and be: Reason needs to think and plan while Emotion must love "his country, his freedom, his life." Reason and Emotion become pilot and co-pilot in a fighter pilot's head in a fleet of U.S. bombers.

The figures of Reason and Emotion do not present the same sort of oppositions represented by Thrifty and Spendthrift or the angel and the devil of *Donald's Decision*. After all, Emotion explicitly has the potential of being "a good Emotion" and helping serve his country. But the drama implicit in the conflict between the two throughout the film certainly engages the viewer's attention. It was effective enough in any case to garner an Oscar nomination for Best Animated Short.

***Chicken Little* (1943).** Directed by Clyde Geronimi, *Chicken Little* looks much like a Silly Symphony in that it tells a familiar fable in cartoon style.[38] The film warns against listening to rumors and giving in to unfounded fears, both very real dangers on the home front. It, too, deals with psychological processes but demonstrates them in action without having the narrator belabor the point with analyses or explanations and without the surreal images of fear used in *Reason and Emotion*. In fact, the narrator seems to be here mainly to tell a story which, it turns out, he has no control over.

Originally this film was to have had more topical references. The book Foxey Loxey refers to for guidance was to have been *Mein Kampf*, and the grave markers at the end were to be swastikas. Disney was already perhaps looking forward to a possible re-release of this film after the war, however, and changed the book to a general psychology text, eliminated the swastikas, and changed a few words of dialogue as well.[39]

The narrator introduces all the characters. The chickens and other farm fowls wear clothing and engage in human activities (gossiping, knitting, drinking and smoking, getting their hair done, dancing). They live complacent, sheltered lives behind a tall fence with a padlocked gate; the farmer's shotgun also stands nearby ready to repel predators. Undaunted, however, Foxey Loxey resorts to psychology to capture his prey. He quotes from a psychology text that "To influence the masses, aim first at the least intelligent." That would be Chicken Little, who can barely cope with his yo-yo.

Foxey Loxey also quotes, "If you tell 'em a lie, don't tell a little one, tell a big one." He takes a star from a wooden astrologer's sign[40] and drops it on Chicken Little's head. Then, speaking through a knothole in the fence as "the voice of doom" he tells Chicken Little that the sky is falling. Chicken Little panics and alarms all the other birds, but Cocky Locky correctly identifies the "star" as a piece of wood and sends everyone back to business as usual.

The narrator mocks Foxey Loxey over his plan not working, but the fox returns to his text to quote "Undermine the faith of the masses in their leaders." Donning various disguises matching each group he addresses through knotholes, he starts a whispering campaign questioning Cocky Locky's ability to lead.

After reading "Through the use of flattery insignificant people can be made to look upon themselves as born leaders," Foxey Loxey convinces Chicken Little he should lead the fowls. When Cocky Locky asks why the supposedly falling sky doesn't it hit him, the fox knocks him flat with another wooden star. All the birds panic, and Foxey Loxey (his fangs particularly evident and menacing) advises Chicken Little to send them to the cave. They burst out of their safe yard and rush to the cave where the fox seals them in. The narrator assures the audience that everything will work out all right, but a dissolve shows a bloated Foxey Loxey sucking clean a wishbone and planting it in a little graveyard laid out with ranks of wishbone markers. The narrator objects that that's not how it ends in his book, and Foxey Loxey responds, "Don't believe everything you read, brother."

Chicken Little and *Education for Death*, both directed by Clyde Geronimi, present the grimmest endings in the Disney cannon—both end with rows of graves. Both present the forces of Nazism (implicit in the case of Foxey Loxey's use of Hitlerian strategy) ascendant with no obvious balancing element of hope (the graves ending *Education for Death* represent the deaths of German soldiers but not explicitly the defeat of Nazi Germany). These dark tales defy the good exemplar/bad exemplar paradigm that Disney was developing and instead present only the negative side but in such a way that the viewer is compelled to see the evil it represents and automatically reject it.

Conclusion

Although Disney continued to make military training films and Good Neighbor health films for the duration, government demand for, and hence the studio's production of, propaganda films for American theatrical release ceased after an impressive climax in 1943.

Parts of *Reason and Emotion* were re-used (minus World War II references) in a segment for *Walt Disney's Wonderful World of Color* on NBC in 1962 entitled *Man Is His Own Worst Enemy*. Some of that footage was then used under that title as a 16mm educational release in 1975.

The Nazi teacher's chalkboard outline drawings which came to life in *Education for Death* served as a model for the illustrative drawings in *How to Catch a Cold* (1951) and the *I'm No Fool* educational series. This series, starring Jiminy Cricket, was made for the *Mickey Mouse Club* TV series in the 1950s and later released on 16mm. After instructing the viewer on the right way to swim, ride a bicycle, deal with electricity, and so on, Jiminy would draw first a "fool" on the chalkboard and then "you." The fool would do everything wrong and wind up a pile of chalk dust while "you" would do everything right. This also continued the tradition of good and bad exemplars as teaching tools, which appeared in *The Spirit of '43*, *Reason and Emotion*, the Canadian bond rally film *Donald's Decision*, and, arguably, *Der Fuehrer's Face.*

The off-screen voice of authority, a feature of all the propaganda films except *Der Fuehrer's Face*, turns up in Disney's later educational films such as *Toot, Whistle, Plunk, and Boom* (1953), *Donald in Mathmagic Land* (1959), and the science films *Man in Space* (1954), *Man and the Moon* (1955), *Mars and Beyond* (1957), *Our Friend the Atom* (1958), and *Eyes in Outer Space* (1959).[41] While this might seem an obvious device to use in such films, it was by no means Disney's only option. He frequently used on-screen narrators, both live (Deems Taylor in *Fantasia*, Major Seversky in *Victory Through Air Power*, Werner von Braun in the Tomorrowland space exploration documentaries, and himself as host for the *Disneyland* TV series) and cartoon (most notably, Jiminy Cricket and Prof. Ludwig von Drake).

The mixing of different types of animation within the same film worked so well in the propaganda films that Disney once again used all three types as well as live-action in the Tomorrowland films about space exploration and atomic power for his TV series.

The strategy of setting out the history of a subject, describing how it works in the present, and making projections for the future, which appeared in *The Grain that Built a Hemisphere, Education for Death,* and *Victory through Air Power*, operates also in the science films of the 1950s. And historical overviews played significant roles in the Oscar-winning *Toot, Whistle, Plunk and Boom* and the Oscar-nominated *Donald in Mathmagic Land.*

The Silly Symphonies of the 1930s allowed Disney to try out technical innovations that would become significant factors in the feature films while nonetheless providing top quality cartoon entertainment in their own right. The propaganda films of the 1940s served very specific functions during the war years but also became in effect a similar testing ground for various sorts of rhetorical and storytelling experimentation that Disney capitalized on in his postwar ventures into edutainment.

Notes

1. Richard Shale, *Donald Duck Joins Up: The Walt Disney Studio during World War II* (Ann Arbor: UMI Research Press, 1982), 24.

2. The propaganda films discussed here and many of the other wartime Disney films can be found on the two–DVD set *Walt Disney on the Front Lines: The War Years* released 2004 in the Walt Disney Treasures series.

3. See Walton Rawls, *Disney Dons Dogtags: The Best of Disney Military Insignia from World War II* (New York: Abbeville Publishing Group, 1992) for further discussion and copious examples. Any variances from Rawls's discussion here are based on items from the author's own collection.

4. Shale, 86. See also Rawls, 12–13, for an example of a Mickey Mouse "Appreciate America" poster.

5. In 1941 alone (and, of course, before the Pearl Harbor attack), Abbot and Costello made three: *Keep 'em Flying, In the Navy*, and *Buck Privates.* That same year Bob Hope weighed in with *Caught in the Draft*, and Laurel and Hardy appeared in *Great Guns*. The Three Stooges wound up in the army the previous year in the short *Boobs in Arms.*

6. *Donald Gets Drafted, Sky Trooper*, and *The Vanishing Private* (both 1942); *Fall Out, Fall In* and *The Old Army Game* (all 1943). Donald also tried to command his nephews in a Civil Defense unit in *Home Defense* (1943). All of these titles were directed by Jack King. Donald even took an active combat role in *Commando Duck* (1944), in which he improbably demolished a Japanese airbase singlehandedly with a hyperinflated rubber life raft. This gave him the distinction of being the only regular Disney character whose engagement with the enemy formed the central plot element in a film

7. *The Army Mascot* (1942), *Private Pluto* (1943), and *Dog Watch* (1944).

8. See Ollie Johnston and Frank Thomas, *Disney Animation: The Illusion of Life* (New York: Abbeville Press, 1981) for discussion of the Disney style as it developed during this period.

9. The early adoption of sound in cartoons rocketed Disney to the top of his industry, but with notable exceptions such as *The Three Little Pigs* (1933), most Disney shorts of the 1930s kept dialogue between characters to a minimum.

10. See in particular Don Peri, ed., *Working with Walt: Interviews with Disney Artists* (Jackson: University of Mississippi Press, 2008).

11. These comedies of instruction were so effective that the series endured for more than twenty years. When the Disney studio recently began experimenting once again with theatrical shorts, they re-teamed Goofy with his more knowledgeable narrator in *How to Set Up Your Video System* (2007).

12. I have not seen these extremely rare films, but they are discussed in Russell Merritt and J. B. Kaufman's *Walt in Wonderland* (Pordenone: Edizioni Biblioteca dell'Immagine, 1992).

13. See Johnston and Thomas for an illustrative inside look at classical Disney animation methods and the demands of character animation.

14. Peri, quotes (p. 64) animator and director Wilfred Jackson, who played a significant role in helping Walt synchronize music with animated images, "Walt wanted people to believe his characters were actual things, not just drawings jumping around on the screen, and that they were real, individual beings with minds of their own and individual personalities of their own."

15. The 1930s gave rise to a whole genre of cartoon shorts in which books, toys, and other objects in shops came to life and held jam sessions—for example, Disney's *The Clock Store* (1931). Conversely, in *The Band Concert* (1935) it comes across as something of an anomaly when the benches of Mickey's audience run away from an approaching tornado.

16. A transitional stage appears in *The Goddess of Spring* (1934) wherein Persephone has a human-looking face and five-fingered hands but arms which seem to have no joints, and Pluto (not the dog this time, but the lord of the Underworld) has a torso

and limbs that are properly proportioned for a human. Compare this noble-looking underworld ruler with the "cartoonish" version in *Hell's Bells* (1929).

17. The anthology features had no problem accommodating different styles in different sections. *Victory Through Air Power* used all three to significant degrees.

18. By contrast, Warner Bros. cartoons frequently employed the negative aspects of rationing and short supply of foodstuffs and vital materials as a source of usually rueful humor.

19. Shale, 32–33.

20. This sequence echoes shots from Pare Lorentz's *The Plow That Broke the Plains* (1936). That live-action documentary, made for the Resettlement Administration, had looked at how uncontrolled farming in the Great Plains led to the Dust Bowl; *Food Will Win the War* represents something of an antithesis to that negative image of the American farmer.

21. The *Toons at War* web site includes a photo from a January 28, 1942 press release of Walt Disney presenting the insignia to Secretary of Agriculture Claude Wickard (posted 7 June 2007, on http://toonsatwar.blogspot.com/2007/06/department-of-agriculture-lend-lease.html.

22. The film carries a 1942 copyright but was released in 1943.

23. In only the second year that the Academy of Motion Picture Arts & Sciences awarded Oscars to documentary films, they took the unique tack of allowing twenty-five nominations, both features and shorts, in a single Documentary category and gave out four awards.

24. The figure here is clearly male although this task would have been performed by the women of the tribe.

25. This includes glue for putting up posters (a circus poster is shown) and starch for clothes (a dickey springs out from a jacket on a mannequin torso). While neither image comes directly from *Dumbo*, both seem to derive from that feature. That the poster shows a clown seems hardly coincidental, and the ringmaster's shirt front curls up when Dumbo's mother goes on her rampage.

26. Shale, 52.

27. It also hints at another positive response to the negative picture of American agriculture presented by *The Plow That Broke the Plains*.

28. Richard Holliss and Brian Sibley, *The Disney Studio Story* (New York: Crown Publishers, 1988), 47–48.

29. The most extensive treatment of this episode appears in Shale, 27–35. See also Neal Gabler, *Walt Disney: The Triumph of the American Imagination* (New York: Alfred A. Knopf, 2006), 384–385.

30. Donald's total income for 1941 was $2501. The average salary in America was $2050 according to the web site *Television History— The First 75 Years* http://www.tvhistory.tv/1941%20QF.htm. Donald owes $13 in taxes and pays with check #13 drawn on the 13th National Bank on 13 February 1942.

31. Donald had earlier had a less positive experience with a radio voice in Jack King's *Self Control* (1938).

32. That footage in any case had already been re-used in *Donald's Decision* (1942) to sell war bonds for the National film Board of Canada.

33. Even in insignia Mickey appeared without actual weapons and usually in those related to home front services.

34. Germans provided bread made with sawdust to prisoners in concentration camps and P.O.W. camps, and the citizens of Leningrad resorted to bread made from sawdust during the German siege.

35. The book also served as the basis for Edward Dmytryk's 1943 live action feature *Hitler's Children*.

36. A scene of school children saluting in front of *Der Bannerträger* appears in *Prelude to War*.

37. He is modeled after animator Ward Kimball. See Shale, 149.

38. The last Silly Symphonies were made in 1939, however.

39. Shale, 65.

40. Other signs on the tree advertise Holoboff Varnish (Mike Holoboff was an uncredited assistant director on *Snow White, Pinocchio, Fantasia*, and *Bambi*) and Ryman Tires (Herb Ryman was art director on *Fantasia* and *Dumbo*).

41. The first four were all made for the Tomorrowland portion of the *Disneyland* television series; *Eyes in Outer Space* was actually a theatrical release.

Bibliography

Gabler, Neal. *Walt Disney: The Triumph of the American Imagination*. New York: Alfred A. Knopf, 2006.

Holliss, Richard, and Brian Sibley, *The Disney Studio Story*. New York: Crown Publishers, 1988).

Johnston, Ollie, and Frank Thomas, *Disney Animation: The Illusion of Life*. New York: Disney Editions, 1995.

Merritt, Russell, and J. B. Kaufman's *Walt in Wonderland*. Pordenone, Italy: Edizioni Biblioteca dell'Immagine, 1992.

Peri, Don, editor. *Working with Walt: Interviews with Disney Artists*. Jackson: University of Mississippi Press, 2008.

Rawls, Walton. *Disney Dons Dogtags: The Best of Disney Military Insignia from World War II*. New York: Abbeville Publishing Group, 1992.

Shale, Richard. *Donald Duck Joins Up: The Walt Disney Studio During World War II*. Ann Arbor, MI: UMI Research Press, 1982.

4

Cartoon Combat

World War II, Alexander de Seversky, and Victory Through Air Power

JOHN D. THOMAS

On 8 December 1941, the United States officially entered the Second World War, a conflict that had drastically altered national boundaries since it began in the latter half of 1939. Since that time, the German army had conquered most of mainland Europe, defeated British forces in several Mediterranean and North African conflicts, and advanced approximately 700 miles into Russia, an eastward offensive that would, by November of the following year, proceed as far as Leningrad, Moscow, and Stalingrad. Meanwhile, in what came to be known as the Pacific Theatre, Japan's military had extended its empire from Manchukuo (a puppet state established in Mongolia and China) to Hong Kong and French Indo-China, from the Dutch East Indies and the Philippines to Guam and other Pacific islands. Its navy had just dealt a crippling blow to U.S. forces stationed at Pearl Harbor, destroying four battleships and 200 aircraft and killing more than 2,300 American servicemen and civilians.

Following the United States' declaration of war, however, a unique counter-offensive began in, of all places, the Walt Disney Studios. For the first eight months of 1942, the U. S. army nearly monopolized Disney's soundstages. Nevertheless, Disney, at the request of several military officials, began producing an assortment of animated cartoons in support of the Allied war effort. By mid-year, almost every studio production was in some way relevant to the war.[1] Often financed by government contracts, Disney's wartime cartoons were, for the most part, educational shorts (*Thrifty Pigs*, *Donald Gets Drafted*, and *Food Will Win the War*, for example) and training films (*Stop That Tank*, *Four Methods of Flush Riveting*, and *Wings/Engines/Fuselage/Tail*, to name a few).[2] However, despite the attention received by many of these animated productions, Disney's *Victory Through Air Power*—a semi-animated, feature-length film shown to American audiences in 1943—would eventually be the most widely seen, and possibly the most influential, wartime production released by the studio. Amalgamating the many artistic techniques that he had employed in his more popular shorts, such as *Der Fuehrer's Face* and *Education for Death*, Disney's film, an adaptation of the 1942 bestseller *Victory Through Air Power*, translated the aeronautical theories of Major Alexander P. de Seversky into a visual medium accessible to citizens of all ages.

After emigrating to the United States in 1918, Seversky, a Russian naval pilot and veteran of World War I, founded two companies in the inter-war period that specialized in advanced flight technology (the Seversky Aero Corporation in 1923 and the Seversky Aircraft Company in 1931) and produced such planes as the SEV-3 (an amphibian monoplane) and the P-35 (one of the Army's first modern fighters).[3] More importantly, he had, since the early 1920s, worked alongside General "Billy" Mitchell, a controversial army officer whose book *Winged Defense* (1925) was one of the first major publications that argued for the creation of an autonomous air force.

Throughout his life, Seversky considered Mitchell an exemplar and praised the latter's apparent foresight regarding the future of military aviation. In 1942, he wrote *Victory Through Air Power*, in which he argued that long-range bombing would, through the destruction of industrial and military sites far within enemy territory, hasten the end of the global conflict and provide the American military with "interhemispheric" attack capabilities. Appearing less than five months after the bombing of Pearl Harbor, it seemed to offer answers for the many Americans who were anxious about future attacks from the sky. Beginning with an apocalyptic vision of "giant bombers" invading the U.S. mainland "[f]rom every point of the compass," the book concludes with a reverse scenario—Alaska and the Aleutian Islands would, according to Seversky, provide perfect locations for long-range bombings of Tokyo and other Japanese-held territories.[4] Unlike Mitchell's earlier work, Seversky's publication was immensely popular and was read by tens of thousands of Americans. And here, in the many varied responses to the book that appeared in national newspapers and magazines, we can begin to understand the origins of what would become one of the most interesting collaborations Disney every undertook.

Disney, Seversky, and Victory

After multiple delays and a third advance printing, Simon & Schuster published Seversky's *Victory Through Air Power* on April 20, 1942. With an initial release of 30,000 copies, the book immediately made *The New York Times* bestseller list and remained there for the next twenty-one weeks.[5] On May 10th, a writer for the *Times* reviewed Seversky's much-acclaimed work and concluded the following:

> In no other war have books played as important a part as they have done and will continue to do in the present conflict.... Books are not only supplying information. [T]hey are furnishing weapons for the successful prosecution of the war.
>
> They will not only play a part in the determination of war policy; they will help to keep vividly alive in us the values for which we are fighting. They will, too, help to lay the foundations for the new world structure which must follow when the war is won....
>
> This is a war which is being fought for and about and with ideas, to an unprecedented degree, and books, which are the repository of ideas, are weapons of might in that war.[6]

Overstated as they may seem to modern ears, such claims epitomize the general response to Seversky's book. Its array of arguments, controversial as they were at times, dazzled its audience even as its conclusions provoked debate amongst all types of readers, from civilians to the most decorated military brass. While Seversky was not the first aviator to propose the creation of a modernized, autonomous air force (such claims had already been circulated by Billy Mitchell, Ira Eaker, and Henry Harley Arnold, to name a few), his book more clearly articulated and popularized the arguments made by previous military strategists.[7] Moreover, the book's seemingly pragmatic approach to strategic, long-range bombing appealed to a readership worried about American involvement in the Pacific, and thereby generated many public discussions of Seversky's aeronautical theories.

For instance, *Victory Through Air Power* was called "the most brilliant book yet to appear on the war," a "bombshell that exploded in the faces of both the military and the lay public," a "very efficient firecracker to drop into the pants' [sic] of the allied high command."[8] The historian Charles Beard wrote, "In my opinion, this book is more important to America than all the other war books put together"; Lewis Gannett of the *New York Herald Tribune* argued that Seversky's work, "if read and heeded, might become a turning point in the war"; and Clifton Fadiman of *The New Yorker* suggested that "it is the duty of every adult citizen who can lay his hand on $2.50 to buy it and ponder its message."[9] In fact, for the first time in its sixteen-year history, the Book-of-the-Month Club distributed the Russian-born major's work, alongside a previously chosen novel, to its nearly 500,000 members, beginning a trend of "dual selection" that would continue "due to the urgent timeliness of the [second] book chosen," usually a nonfiction work related to the war.[10] But not all reviewers echoed these paeans. Orville Prescott, a contributor for *The New York Times*, cautioned readers of Seversky's work: "Either he is right and most of our military concepts and defensive and offensive plans must be changed at once; or else he is wrong and is unnecessarily scaring the daylights out of every reader of his sensational book." After quoting a particularly disturbing section of *Victory Through Air*

Power—one in which Seversky suggested that "advanced peoples must, if possible, be reduced to impotence beyond easy recovery, through the annihilation of the industrial foundations of their life" so that no military "comeback" could possibly be achieved—Prescott warned, "Is this war going to reduce us to the same moral level as the Nazis and are we going to have a literature that can be quoted by our enemies with the same propaganda effectiveness in Germany as 'Mein Kampf' has had here?"[11] Despite a few such objections, within a month after the book's release, Seversky had become a celebrity. He immediately joined the lecture circuit and was thereafter invited to Harvard's "War Institute," a gathering of military minds to discuss a variety of important matters related to the worldwide conflict. As time passed, Seversky's work would even be referred to as "prophetic," and the author called a "hero" and an "apostle" of air power.[12]

During this period, Walt Disney became, as one scholar has suggested, Seversky's "most fervent disciple."[13] As early as 1940, the U.S. military "recognized the potential for 'direct propaganda films couched in the simplicity of the animation medium,' and recruited Walt Disney as goodwill ambassador in South America to counter Nazi propaganda."[14] Upon his return to the United States, Disney contacted Seversky and obtained the rights to produce an animated, feature-film of the best-selling book. Although the government had already financed many short training films for each branch of the military, no financial arrangement was made with Disney for this particular project due to the overwhelming political pressure exerted by Navy officials who were ardently opposed to the creation of an independent air force. This lack of financial support, however, did not alter Disney's resolve, and he decided to produce the film independently with his own company's money, aware that such a decision might prove financially disastrous for his studio. During the previous year, from May until September of 1941, most of Disney's staff had organized a labor strike and delayed the production of numerous films.[15] Moreover, on the day after the bombing of Pearl Harbor, five hundred soldiers requisitioned several of Disney's sound stages, installed antiaircraft repair machinery, and stored millions of rounds of ammunition there before setting up a temporary barracks.[16] Despite these obstacles, Disney began animating *Victory Through Air Power* in mid-1942, and the segments that included Seversky were filmed later that year.[17]

The film opened at New York's Globe Theatre on July 17, 1943, and ran for six consecutive weeks, but its critical reception varied.[18] One reviewer called the movie an "unusual document," a film that was "frankly propaganda" yet, oddly enough, one that was also "prophetic" and a "technical *tour de force*."[19] Another writer claimed that *Victory Through Air Power* was "[m]ost interesting from a cinematic viewpoint ... a landmark in the ideographical usage of the screen. Its digestive method of teaching almost frightens you with its scope."[20] *Time* magazine called it "65 minutes of highly unorthodox film fare, and an exceedingly potent instrument of propaganda.... It may drop with the effect of an incendiary bomb into the long-smoldering argument on whether the U.S. should have a separate Air Force."[21] The Hollywood producer Walter Wagner explained how "every once in a while a motion picture flashes across the horizon to prove our industry an instrumentality of human enlightenment," and a reviewer for *Life* magazine suggested that Disney's movie was "good history and fine entertainment."[22] Finally, according to Thomas Pryor, a writer for the *Times*, "Mr. Disney has adroitly blended the documentary technique of presentation with his own highly skilled cartoon form of infectious humor. The result is a delightful and stimulating combination entertainment-information film.... If 'Victory Through Airpower' [sic] is propaganda, it is at least the most encouraging and inspiring propaganda that the screen has afforded us in a long time."[23]

Despite these approbations, some reviewers disagreed. One writer claimed that the film was "completely devoid of human values" and that it "fail[ed] to give the impression of the loss of human life," and Howard Barnes of the *New York Tribune* suggested that the "ideological content of the offering ... is likely to give one pause."[24] Similarly, in a cautionary review for *The Nation*, James Agee wrote:

> I only hope Major de Seversky and Walt Disney know what they are talking about, for I suspect an awful lot of people who see "Victory Through Air Power" are going to think they do. Certainly I am not equipped to argue with them. I have the feeling I was sold something under pretty high pressure which I don't enjoy, and I am staggered by the ease with which such self-confidence, on matters of such importance, can be blared all over a nation, without cross-questioning....
>
> I noticed, uneasily, that there were no suffering and dying enemy civilians under all those proud promises of bombs; no civilians at all, in fact.

Agee then concluded by criticizing the film's artistic medium. "I realized," he said, "that animated cartoons, so weak — at least as Disney uses them — in the whole human world, would be particularly inadequate to human terror, suffering, and death."[25]

Unfortunately for Agee, Disney's production proved to be more than a mere "weak" cartoon. Before the film's release, Theodore Strauss, in an article for the *Times*, had written of the "sudden new importance of the cartoon medium" and had explained how "Donald [Duck], who used to be just another noisy neighbor, has by some odd token of fate become a sort of ambassador-at-large, a salesman of the American Way.... He has become one of this country's No. 1 propagandists."[26] Likewise, during one of his many interviews, Seversky discussed his initial reaction to Disney's proposed collaboration. He said, "As for becoming an actor — when Walt Disney informed me that I was to appear in the picture as myself — well, anyone in the studio within a hundred yards of my voice at the time can tell you how passionately I tried to persuade him that animations are much more explicit than any human action can be."[27] Accordingly, Disney defended his own aesthetic preferences:

> The war ... has taught us that people who won't read a book will look at a film. It's shown that you can take knowledge out of a dusty tome somewhere, and wrap up the effort of many teachers in one can of film. You can show that film to any audience and twenty minutes later it has learned something — a new idea, or an item of important information — and it at least has stimulated further interest in study.[28]

Responding to his critics, he added, "[T]hese are times for radical departures.... Of course I want to make the kind of pictures that make people laugh — and in *Victory Through Air Power* I've tried to do so in some sequences. But we believe that the basic ideas of this picture must be carried out before people are going to be able to laugh very much again."[29] For Disney, books were not the only "weapons of might" in World War II; cartoons were as well.

Regardless of its critical reception, the movie was a commercial failure. Audiences endeared to the memorable characters that Disney had hitherto created were confused by the didactic nature of the film. Although *Victory Through Air Power* failed at the box office, its propagandistic value, for Disney and others involved in the film's production, far outweighed financial compensation.[30] At the Quebec Conference attended by Franklin D. Roosevelt and Winston Churchill, "many military and naval experts" attended a private showing of the film. According to Roy Disney, Walt's brother, "The film had wide distribution ... because the air force sent it far and wide to other countries and to military establishments. As a motion picture for the theatre it was a big flop. We lost most of our money [$436,000] on that picture, but we did it as a patriotic gesture." It seems that the "gesture" may have been worth the effort. Churchill was given a special screening and thought that it was a "superb film."[31] And according to H.C. Potter, the film's director:

> The British Air Force thought this was the greatest thing that ever came down the pike, and the picture was much better known in England than it was here, in official circles, and early in the game. Walt told me this story, and swore this was what happened. When Churchill came over to the Quebec conference, they were trying to get Roosevelt interested in this long-range bombing idea, and Roosevelt didn't know what the hell they were talking about. Churchill said, "Well, of course, you've seen *Victory through Air Power*..." and Roosevelt said, "No, what's that?" Air Marshal Tedder and Churchill worked on Roosevelt until Roosevelt put out an order to the Air Corps to fly a print of *Victory through Air Power* up to Quebec. Churchill ran it for him, and that was the beginning of the U.S. Air Corps Long Range Bombing.[32]

Although Disney, as well as Potter, inflated the political influence of their film after its release and subsequent financial failure — the "Combined Bomber Offensive" had been organized by American and British generals in January of 1943 and implemented in June of that year; the Quebec Conference was not held until August — they recognized the fact that their film was being circulated among military personnel and was, at the very least, contributing to national debates regarding the strategic use of long-range bombers.

Moreover, Disney and his supporters responded to those who criticized the cartoon medium for its inability to depict death and destruction by arguing that animated films had vast pedagogical potential. Richard Schickel, one of Disney's early biographers, believed that cartoons were the "ideal educational medium" due to the "hard-outline precision possible in animation."[33] Discussing this aspect of his productions, Disney claimed, "Mass education is coming.... It's coming because it's a necessity. Democracy's ability to survive depends on the ability of its individuals to appreciate their duties as citizens and to comprehend the complex problems of the changing world we live in."[34] Disregarding his critics, Disney wholeheartedly believed in the didactic power of the screen (as seen in his many post-war educational films), and so did many others. In "Film Phenomena," a short review of several Disney movies published prior to the release of *Victory Through Air Power*, Wagner insisted that a "new education of the free world" would issue from the Disney studios. In a later article, which appeared in September of 1943, he again suggested that Disney's films had great pedagogic potential: "We know that people want to be informed today, and information means education. Today, through the film, education can be carried to the entire world—to the remotest village—and a medium like Disney's which every day is turning out pictures in three and four languages—and has made them in as many as ten—is a logical means of carrying out such a mission."[35] Calling the "motion picture" a "medium of enlightenment," Wagner believed in the instructional power of the genre.

However, others considered the impartation of knowledge less important than the manner whereby Disney cultivated political support for a particular military credo. J. P. McEvoy, a writer for *This Week Magazine*, called Disney "a propaganda genius for whom the Axis would give a dozen divisions," and two artists who worked for Disney in the 1940s, Joe Grant and Dick Huemer, claimed that "[i]n this war, humor and fantasy have enlisted on the side of the United Nations.... They're fighting, and fighting hard.... No other weapon of propaganda can ridicule the Axis, expose its absurdities, as deftly."[36] Although the propagandistic nature of *Victory Through Air Power* is not quite as shocking as that of *Der Fuehrer's Face* or *Education for Death*, two of Disney's most (in)famous animated shorts, the film both entertained and indoctrinated audiences through the animation of ideology. It contained many scenes designed to convert as many men and women (and even children) of all ages as possible into supporters of an independent air force and a wartime strategy based on long-range bombing.

In light of the discrepancies between this film's critical reception and its cultural influence, one might wonder why *Victory Through Air Power* so bewildered reviewers and general audiences alike. Why was it labeled an "unusual document," "unorthodox fare," a "weak" cartoon, and propaganda while simultaneously praised as a "technical *tour de force*," a "documentary" filled with "good history" that functioned as an instrument of "human enlightenment"? What could engender such ardent vilification and glowing praise? On another note, why did it escape any sort of criticism in Argentina, a country whose government had already censored most of Hollywood's anti–Axis films? And why, if the movie was such blatant propaganda (as so many claimed), did the "Schools Motion Picture Committee of the National Board of Review, a voluntary organization of teachers and parents of pupils in local public and private elementary and high schools," recommend Disney's wartime picture as "suitable for children between the ages of 8 and 14 years"?[37] Such questions, at this time, remain largely unanswered due to several reasons. First, most biographers and scholars have critiqued the historical and social context of *Victory Through Air Power*, but have not examined the film itself nor subjected it to any sort of critical investigation. Second, after 1944, the Disney studios withheld the movie and did not allow anyone to see it (excepting a few rare instances) until 2004, when the company released *Walt Disney: On the Front Lines*, a two-disc DVD compilation of Disney's most famous World War II animated pictures.

Not surprisingly, when examining this film, any attempt at categorization encounters immediate problems. As Bill Nichols suggests, "When stories set out to represent the world around us, they enter into the realm of those blurred genres like historiography and documentary that use imaginative techniques to tell the tale of actual occurrences."[38] In Walt Disney's case, not only is *Victory Through Air Power* "one of the most curious motion pictures in his studio's history,"[39] it also represents a marked departure from more popular film genres. For example, it is a documentary animated by a team of professional artists; it is propaganda in cartoon form; it is political ideology disguised as entertainment. In order to understand the film's heterogeneity, we must avoid general observations and examine each of the aforementioned features in detail. Only then might we understand why the movie elicited such remarkably different reactions from theatergoers in 1943—from enthusiasm to aversion, interest to apathy, edification to perplexity.

Victory *as Propaganda: Selling Air Power*

Throughout the film, from the introductory statements to the concluding commentary, Disney creates, or attempts to create, a "cult of personality" around its inspiration and main character, Major Seversky, an already-accredited aeronautical expert. As the opening credits end, an introduction of sorts appears on screen:

> Our country in the past, has struggled through many storms of anguish, difficulty and doubt. But we have always been saved by men of vision and courage, who opened our minds and showed us the way out of confusion. One of the men who foresaw the present mortal conflict, who tried desperately to awaken and prepare us for the issue, but who was ignored and ridiculed, was General Billy Mitchell.[40]

Before valorizing Seversky's military achievements and promoting his strategy for long-range bombing, Disney and his team of animators situate his argument within a history of overlooked, unnoticed warnings regarding the need for an autonomous air force. In 1919, General Mitchell believed that another world war was inevitable, and he claimed that the American military needed to develop and enhance its aerial capabilities before the recurrence of global hostilities. As I have already suggested, Mitchell worked alongside Seversky and others to promote these hypotheses and test their validity, and in 1925, he published *Winged Defense*, a book that warned of a possible future attack by Japan on U.S. bases located in the Pacific Ocean but was ultimately ignored by military officials.[41] Less than a year later, he was court-martialed for publicly criticizing his superior officers and thereafter resigned from active duty. In 1936, three years prior to the start of World War II, he died of influenza.

Although the film ignores the details of Mitchell's career, the sequences that follow caution viewers not to disregard such dire and, according to Disney, undeniably prophetic warnings. As the introductory text fades, the colorful background darkens, the melodic music becomes ominous, and the year "1919" appears before a looming newspaper that bears the front-page headline "Future War in Air." Although that year followed the cessation of worldwide conflict, it inaugurated a period of hostility toward efforts aimed at bolstering support for an independent U.S. air force. After various newspaper columns devoted to Mitchell's theories appear in a chronological montage that proceeds from 1921 to 1934, the *Los Angeles Examiner*, a newspaper associated with the latter date, expands to fill the screen. Suddenly, a photograph of Mitchell superimposed upon the front page of the *Examiner* becomes cinematic, and a short filmed sequence follows in which Mitchell, recorded in an unidentified archival video, addresses Disney's audience. "Today," states Mitchell, "a war is very different than the last European war was," but the "today" discussed by the general has been removed from its original historical context and transcribed into that of *Victory Through Air Power*. Thus, another type of "animation" takes place than that commonly employed by Disney. Instead of using fictional characters throughout this portion of the film, Disney visually resurrects the deceased Mitchell—or, more properly stated, a cinematic simulacra of him—and not only reanimates the man, but vitalizes his military exhortation as well. Nevertheless, although the film acknowledges its indebtedness to General Mitchell, the introductory material insinuates that Seversky is, like the unheeded general, also a man "of vision and courage," one who will "open" the minds of civilians and officers alike to the necessity of air supremacy.

Thereafter, during a sequence in which an animated copy of the book *Victory Through Air Power* appears on screen, the narrator praises the "vision and persistence of pioneer airmen," especially Seversky, a "friend, advisor, and disciple of General Billy Mitchell." For the next few minutes, the movie proceeds through a biographical sketch of Seversky's career—from his military training and martial accomplishments to his tactical inventions and awards— using both animation and a photographic montage, and the narrator explains that "[w]ith his background as a combat pilot, aeronautical designer, engineer, manufacturer, and military strategist, Major Seversky's advanced viewpoint and opinions are of vital importance to every citizen." Alongside the description of Seversky's many inventions and accomplishments, the cartoon sequence both accompanies and complements the biographical information presented to the audience; however, the paucity of factual details and the accelerated pace of the narrative renders the sequence more didactic than informative. For instance, during a brief description of the fifty-seven aerial battles in which Seversky participated, the film depicts at least sixteen German airplanes concurrently ablaze and plummeting to earth, each presumably destroyed by the accomplished Russian pilot. Next, an animated shadow box appears onscreen containing a variety of medals and other prestigious military decorations, a cinematic assemblage of diverse, generic awards. Finally, as the narrator explains the patents developed by Seversky for the U.S. military, the film depicts an assortment of diagrams, sketches, blueprints, and drafts. These scenes progress rapidly, creating a visual experience more akin to a cinematic mosaic than a realistic biography; thus, the film quickly recapitulates the many reasons why Seversky should be trusted, why his opinions in aeronautical matters cannot be ignored. The hurried pace of these sequences enables the makers of the film to lengthen the didactic segments and overwhelm their audiences with a barrage of diverse images. Through such sequences— which integrate a doctrinaire narrative voice with a frantic montage of animated pictures and photographs— Disney encourages an outright acceptance of both Seversky's authority and his postulations while also discouraging a cautious, critical approach to the film's didacticism.

Between the segments linking Mitchell and Seversky are the moments when *Victory Through Air Power* is more "docutoon" than cartoon, more closely associated with the documentary technique. These sequences boldly assert the film's historicity. In one, an animated book entitled *History of Aviation* opens to a page labeled "1903," and the narrator, the "voice of God" so familiar in documentaries,[42] discusses the airplane's development during the first decade of the twentieth century. For the next few minutes, as the pages turn and the years pass, the Wright brothers perform their first takeoff, various inventors modify the airplane's design, the U.S. Army requests its own aircraft, and aviators create and break aeronautical records. This story proceeds in a seemingly innocuous manner until the page turns to the year 1914. Here, the narrator describes how the airplane, "at the tender age of ten, went off to war." What follows is a series of animated scenes that force upon the reader a skewed historical rendering of the events precipitating the First World War.

"When documentary films are at their best," one scholar claims, "a sense of urgency brushes aside our efforts to contemplate form or analyze rhetoric and encourage a reexamination of the previous material."[43] And here, temporarily anesthetized to the supposedly historical narrative by the nature of Disney's artistic medium, one must pause and reexamine the content of these scenes. In the first place, this animated sequence begins with the opening of a book. This image is, in itself, suggestive of several things. If documentaries move "between the public and private, personal and political spheres by becoming simultaneously an aesthetic and archival object—part fiction, part truth," then "[w]e may think we hear history or reality speaking to us through a film, but what we actually hear is the voice of the text, even when that voice tries to efface itself."[44] The aforementioned book, even though it is animated, suggests a degree of historical authenticity, yet this portion of the film is more story than history. In fact, it is the story of a story, a narrative (Disney's) of a narrative (the fictional book *History of Aviation*)—one that is chronicled by a seemingly knowledgeable narrator, drawn by artists, and captured by the camera—a series of simulacra that suggest the dubious nature of the re-telling. Thus, as Alan Rosenthal suggests, "[I]nstead of having the past clarified and illuminated, we simply have a new mythologizing of history."[45]

For instance, as the story unfolds, the narrator discusses the manner in which airplanes were used during the First World War. According to the aforementioned fictitious, pseudo-historical book, German and French pilots often flew near other, waved, and took pictures of one another in what the narrator describes as "a spirit of sportsmanship." However, one day, after Pierre (the French pilot) develops his photographs, he sees a mocking image of Fritz (the German) and immediately exclaims, "*Sacré bleu*! This is outráge!" The following day, Pierre throws a brick at Fritz, and since the latter is, as the narrator recounts, both a "hothead as well as a square-head," he responds by firing his pistol at Pierre. Thus, according to Disney, mid-flight duels began and eventually intensified due to mounted machine guns, especially after the development of the "synchronizing device," the timing mechanism that allowed bullets to travel between the blades of the propeller. Clearly, during this animated portion of the movie, history and story have become indistinguishable. Historical events have been reconstructed and reinterpreted, and the "real" catastrophes of World War I have been reduced to a series of caricatures created by the Disney studios.

Furthermore, in an artistic aesthetic that Disney scholars have commonly referred to as "imagineering,"[46] Disney animates a peculiar type of aerial historiography, one indebted to pseudo-factual recreations of military and aviation history. For instance, during the sequence involving General Mitchell, and throughout much of the film, Disney supports many of his claims using animated newspapers, virtual replicas of both actual and fictional publications. In fact, he intersperses journalistic reproductions between various chronological sequences at least fifteen times during the remainder of the film. While some of these newspaper segments provide factual information—the U.S Army's purchase of the first warplane, the development of modern aerial technologies, the conclusion of World War I, Hitler's militaristic aggression, and the attack on Pearl Harbor—others appear as support for Seversky's military proposals. To achieve a decisive, succinct victory over the Japanese, Seversky argues, long-range bombers capable of attacking mainland Japan would have to be developed and then deployed from bases situated on the Alaskan Peninsula. In support of such argumentation, Disney juxtaposes Seversky's plan with those proposed by other military strategists—aerial attacks based in China and Siberia, an offensive launched from a Pacific fleet of aircraft carriers, or an aeroamphibious island-to-island campaign. In each of these instances, a newspaper appears with a headline that promotes a plan other than Seversky's, but the latter thereafter explains the shortcomings of each strategy and summarily dismisses them as both illogical and futile. Although these cartoon reproductions resemble actual papers, the images on the front page belie such direct historical correspondence since each animated photograph appears in color (as opposed to the black and white publication) and artistically resembles the film's other cartoon segments. In each of these visual manipulations, Disney subtly revises military history, blurs the distinctions between fact and fiction, and imbues Seversky's theories with ideological authority.

Moreover, Disney consistently relies upon an aesthetics of transmutation. Throughout the film, many diverse animated metamorphoses occur. Objects undergo constant artistic transliterations, and in the process, these images promote a type of illustrative didacticism. For instance, after the narrator explains the importance of C. S. Rolls's solo flight across the English Channel in 1910, the "voice-of-God" ends, and another narrative voice begins. "Departing from England," the voice-of-Rolls explains, "the flight across the channel was quite uneventful. Reaching the other side and being recognized, dropped greetings. And without stopping, returned home safely without mishap." During this scene, a small plane navigates a thunderstorm and drops letters addressed to "The Aero Club de France" near a sleeping French shepherd, disturbing a flock of sheep in the process. Immediately thereafter, the chronological sequence continues with a turning of the page from the aforementioned *History of Aviation*. However, later in the film, during a description of the technological advancements in World War II aerial bombardment, the narrator explains, "Today, the historic flight of C. S. Rolls is repeated daily." As the voice-of-Rolls begins a verbatim repetition of his earlier statements, the images shown are no longer merely that of Rolls's plane, a thunderstorm, and the French countryside. Instead, Allied bombers cross the channel. Upon reaching the "other side," now a designation for German-controlled territory, they are "recognized" by enemy artillery before "dropp[ing] greetings," payload after payload of explosive materials. In both of these instances, Disney not only renders an artistic continuity between various segments of his film; he also suggests that these bombing raids will effectively destroy German forces and allow Allied soldiers to "return home safely without mishap," like Rolls, amidst the billowing smoke of decimated enemy munitions.

This is only one of the many such instances where Disney relies upon this stylistic aesthetic. Elsewhere the transmutations are much more overt. For example, during a description of the recently-developed B-19, the Wright brothers' first flight takes place on the wings of the aircraft[47]; in a later scene, a French flag atop the Eiffel Tower mutates into a German one; and soon thereafter, several German swastikas become the propellers of enemy fighters.[48] Likewise, Allied planes become a protective bridge for boats navigating the English Channel at the Battle of Dunkirk, the U.S. mainland evolves into a large industrial factory, a celebratory bottle of champagne is replaced by a destructive torpedo, the Japanese islands and Manchukuo become the jaws of a deformed monster, and the Alaskan Peninsula transforms into a large finger pointing in the direction of Japan. Finally, in a scene indebted to an original illustration from Seversky's book, an eagle (the United States) attacks an octopus (Japan) and alights upon a miniature globe. Immediately, both eagle and globe become the adornment of a golden flagpole, and an American flag waves in the breeze while "America the Beautiful" crescendoes. These transliterations underscore the propagandistic pedagogy of *Victory Through Air Power*, and their consistent deployment throughout the film intensifies its didacticism. By relying upon images *en mouvement*,[49] that is, pictorial transmutation, Disney augments Seversky's arguments with a dynamic array of visual metamorphoses, artistic manipulations designed to enhance both the viewer's visceral experience of the film as well as its persuasive potential.

Alongside this creative manipulation of images, Disney relies upon elaborate cartographic sequences throughout *Victory Through Air Power* that are underscored by animated maps, globes, diagrams, and directional arrows. These illustrations function both metaphorically and metonymically. They are used to simulate the movements of military forces across continental and transnational boundaries and the expansions and contractions of the German and Japanese empires, but they also simplify the complexity of these changes by reducing the scale of military engagements and expansionist agendas to a few manageable sequences. In each, Disney uses a wide variety of animated illustrations to connect the conceptual to the concrete in order to vitalize what might have otherwise been a bland recitation of geographic facts or a convoluted representation of global conflict.

Seversky's critique of Maginot Line, for example, is illustrated by a large map with a string of French fortifications highlighted in yellow, adjacent to darkened regions under the control of Nazi Germany. The film then depicts the advance of the "Nazi hordes," but what begins as a more realistic portrayal of Hitler's armed forces evolves into a hybrid sequence involving arrows and miniature tanks. In another transmutative sequence, one of Hitler's fighter planes transforms into three large red arrows, and the scene evolves from landscape to topographic map as recurring arrows destroy a series of small turrets representing the Maginot Line. One particularly effective arrow penetrates the French defenses and, like the metaphoric "bridge" over Dunkirk, becomes a "shield of air power" under which Hitler's tanks proceed into French territory.

In a later segment, these somewhat realistic representations of military operations all but disappear, and metonymic images alone illustrate Seversky's arguments. During a scene in which the narrative voice discusses supply lines, a map of Europe appears, but fades shortly thereafter as a swastika positioned over much of the continent grows larger and becomes the center of a massive, horizontal wheel: "the hub—[Hitler's] powerful industrial center," "the spokes—his supply lines," "the fighting fronts—the rim of the wheel." As yellow arrows representing industrial production emerge from the red hub and travel down the spokes, green arrows surround the wheel and attempt to penetrate its outer rim, and a cinematic close shot reveals numerous miniature tanks destroying one another. For nearly two and a half minutes, this sequence continues almost entirely uninterrupted as Seversky explains the advantages of long-range air attacks designed to destroy the hub of the wheel, the center of wartime production, and not the rim and spokes, individual military units or supply lines. These cartographic sequences condense the pictorial apparatuses associated with Seversky's arguments into simple, understandable images and enable Disney to avoid intricate, realistic recreations of military engagements. They are the most didactic elements of *Victory Through Air Power* and render intelligible a large number of simultaneous, diverse military operations that would have otherwise been too artistically complex for a single film.

Furthermore, Disney uses visual transmutations to illustrate pertinent technological advancements in aeronautics, yet he does so without explaining how or when such improvements in long-range bombing might be accomplished. Thus, during these segments of the film, he encourages an uncritical acceptance of the supposedly easy path to aeronautical evolution. For instance, immediately after the transmutation of the Alaskan Peninsula into a large finger, a blueprint entitled "Long Range Combat Fighter" appears onscreen, followed by a montage of other diagrams that, in greater detail, artistically envision the production of such advanced weapons of war. Concurrent with this animated sequence, Seversky explains: "Bombers that can take off from our own shores, fly across the ocean, strike at the enemy, and return non-stop are not only possible, but practical. It is no longer a question of whether it can be done, but of making up our minds to do it. The science of aviation is ready to give us powerful, long-range combat planes far exceeding anything in the air today."[50] As Seversky's narration ends, the final blueprint of one of these "practical" machines transmutates into the plane itself, and the scene scrolls from right to left in order to provide audiences with a more detailed visualization of the plane in mid-air. Simultaneously, the narrator explains, "They'll be heavily armed and bristling with large-caliber cannon" and "maneuverable" guns, military technologies that will provide these bombers with a distinct advantage over "[s]mall single-seater fighters" whose guns "are not maneuverable" and "can only fire forward." Interestingly enough, the airplanes envisioned by Seversky and animated by Disney not only exceed "anything in the air today," but most aircraft in the *today* of postwar military technologies.[51] For instance, the proposed long-range bomber of the film has eleven individual, independent rotating gun turrets and two cannons located in the rear and nose of the plane; however, in this portion of the film, the bomber not only successfully targets military installations on enemy territory, it also effectively destroys small enemy fighters during a massive mid-air conflict. According to Disney, as the smaller enemy planes "jockey" into position, "They're under the constant and deadly fire of the combat plane which is always in firing position." As the scene progresses, the bomber's turrets and cannons independently fire in thirteen separate directions, and within the next few moments, the plane destroys at least twenty enemy aircraft, due to the "scientific accuracy" of its guns, and achieves "complete mastery" of the air.[52]

In order to support Seversky's claims that such machines were technologically feasible if Americans, especially military personnel, "[made] up our minds to do it," Disney consistently, and rather ingeniously, refers to the possibilities inherent in "Science," an inclusive, generic term employed throughout the film. During the aforementioned segments, he and Seversky promote the "science of aviation," the "scientific accuracy" of military technology, and a "science of demolition" that will enable long-range bombers to destroy the enemy's industrial centers. In the earlier transliteration of C.S. Rolls's historic flight, the narrator claims that massive "bombloads of the most devastating explosives" have been "conceived by science." Later, alongside a critique of land and sea warfare, the "new scientific devices" used by the enemy effectively destroy Allied warships and other important wartime vessels. Nevertheless, Disney suggests that "scientific bombing," those air raids conducted by Seversky's theoretical squadrons of long-range bombers, will eventually "conquer Hitler's submarines." And although the German navy protected its U-boats with concrete structures and fortifications, "[S]cience," according to Disney, "is developing an armor-piercing bomb employing the rocket principle. As it nears its target, a rocket in the tail ignites, driving it down with such terrific speed it can knife its way through steel and concrete." Thereafter, Disney implies that "science" will also develop a bomb that can penetrate the earth's crust and initiate a small earthquake, a devastating series of tremors that will destroy every one of the enemy's nearby industrial sites.[53] Like the cartographic effects used throughout the film, the recurrence of this abstract concept allows Disney to avoid any detailed explanations and visualizations of the scientific and industrial processes necessary for the development of such weaponry. For those unacquainted with physics or aeronautical engineering, arguably most individuals involved in the production and reception of *Victory Through Air Power*, this simplistic yet suggestive term implies that — given enough time, financial assistance, and military support — "science" will ensure an Allied victory over both Germany and Japan.

Unlike his wartime shorts, Disney's *Victory Through Air Power* presented a sustained, propagandistic argument regarding the importance of an autonomous air force and the necessity of long-range bombing missions. Although the movie was a commercial failure, Disney warned audiences not to dismiss Seversky like those contemporaries of General Mitchell had done years before, and he believed that his animated productions, especially this feature-film, could motivate American citizens to participate more actively in the war effort and convince military officials that Seversky's theories, if put into practice, would inevitably result in an ultimate Allied victory. After its release, the film provoked a wide variety of critical responses— some denigrated it as a polemic, others worried about its didacticism, many praised it as sound pedagogy. Undoubtedly, it remains to this day one of the oddest movies that the Walt Disney Studios ever produced. Unlike many others that appeared during the Second World War, this one received no government financing. It was a privately-funded attempt to influence public policy, one aimed at both military officials and the general public; it was a semi-animated, propagandistic pseudo-documentary that attempted to entertain as well as instruct; it was a peculiar, but fascinating, vision of aeronautical history and its future potential; and it was a collaboration that advocated specific wartime strategies and lobbied for the formal organization of what would become, less than five years later, the newest branch of the U.S. armed forces. Unavailable for decades, the film's re-release in 2004 enables twenty-first century viewers to reexamine Disney's legacy, to revisit a wartime production that appeared during a particularly bleak period for Allied troops, and to watch and re-watch a film that Disney believed might actually alter the course of American history.

Notes

1. According to Steven Watts, "[B]y mid–1942 over 93 percent of Disney production was connected to government contracts" (229). For more on Disney' wartime films, see Watts, *The Magic Kingdom: Walt Disney and the American Way of Life* (New York: Houghton Mifflin, 1997), 228–242; and Michael S. Shull and David E. Witt, *Doing Their Bit: Wartime American Animated Short Films, 1939–1945* (Jefferson, NC: McFarland, 2004) 74, 129.

2. For Leonard Maltin (*Walt Disney: On the Front Lines*, DVD, Walt Disney Video, 2004), such films made military objectives "more tangible" since they conceptualized three-dimensional reality and taught pilots many "practical, life-saving tips." However, the efficacy of these films eventually came into question as the war progressed, especially the 1942 *Wings/Engines/Fuselage/Tail* (WEFT). After "this system fell into disrepute," Watts explains, "the acronym WEFT was said to stand for 'wrong every fucking time'" (229). Thereafter, the Navy "regularly rejected films in the series because of rampant errors"— Sean Griffin, *Tinker Belles and Evil Queens: The Walt Disney Company from the Inside Out* (New York: New York University Press, 2000), 32–33.

3. For more on Seversky, see Edward Maloney, *Sever the Sky: Evolution of Severksy*

Aircraft (California: Planes of Fame Publishers, 1979) and Judy Rumerman, "Alexander de Seversky and Seversky Aircraft," *U.S. Centennial Flight Commission*, accessed1 March 2010 at <http://www.centennialofflight.gov/essay/Aerospace/Seversky/Aero42.htm>

4. Alexander P. de Seversky, *Victory Through Air Power* (New York: Simon and Schuster, 1942), 7, 337–343.

5. *The New York Times*, April 17, 1942, 15. *The New York Times*, September 13, 1942: BR8.

6. "Speaking of Books—," *The New York Times*, May 10, 1942: BR2.

7. For more on the early debates regarding the efficacy of an autonomous air force, see Michael Sherry, *The Rise of American Air Power* (New Haven: Yale University Press, 1987), 47–69.

8. Fletcher Pratt, "Air Power's Part in the War," *The New York Times*, May 3, 1942: BR1. Prescott, "Books of the Times," *The New York Times*, December 18, 1942: 35. Brooks Atkinson, "Our Huge War Task Traced at Harvard," *The New York Times*, May 31, 1942: 20.

9. *The New York Times*, May 3, 1942: BR13. *The New York Times*, May 18, 1942: 13. For other reviews of Seversky's book, see Donald Mitchell, "The Dominance of Air Power," *The Nation* 154.21 (May 23, 1942), 603–604; and G. W. McGinty, "Victory Through Air Power," *Southwestern Social Science Quarterly*, 23.3 (Dec. 1942), 295–296.

10. "Notes on Books and Authors," *The New York Times*, April 24, 1942: 15. Isaac Anderson, "Books and Authors," *The New York Times*, August 2, 1942: BR10.

11. Orville Prescott, "Books of the Times," *The New York Times*, April 20, 1942: 19.

12. Pratt, BR1. Hanson W. Baldwin, "Air Power's Role in the Atom Age," *The New York Times*, July 3, 1949: BR1. Hanson, "Can Air Power Do the Trick?" *The New York Times*, September 24, 1950: BR4.

13. Leonard Mosley, *Disney's World* (Maryland: Scarborough House Publishers, 1990), 206.

14. Elizabeth Bell, Lynda Haas, and Laura Sells, "Introduction: Walt's in the Movies," *From Mouse to Mermaid: The Politics of Film, Gender, and Culture* (Bloomington: Indiana University Press, 1995), 5.

15. For a detailed description of the strike and an analysis of its aesthetic repercussions, see Michael Denning, *The Cultural Front: The Laboring of American Culture in the Twentieth Century* (New York: Verso, 1997), 403–422.

16. Bob Thomas, *Building a Company: Roy O. Disney and the Creation of an Entertainment Empire* (New York: Hyperion, 1998), 150–151.

17. "Screen New Here and in Hollywood," *The New York Times*, June 22, 1942: 19; and Oct. 14, 1942: 29.

18. According to Walt's nephew Roy Disney, he and the Disney family traveled to New York for the premier. The day before the film opened, as Roy and his mother sat in their hotel room, they grabbed a box of crayons and wrote "Go see *Victory Through Air Power*" on sheet after sheet of paper, which they then folded into paper airplanes and threw out of their hotel window.

19. "Air Power on the Screen," *The New York Times*, July 26, 1943: 18.

20. Bosley Crowther, "Summer Harvest," *The New York Times*, August 5, 1943: X3.

21. *The New York Times*, July 29, 1943: 36.

22. Walter Wagner, "Mickey Icarus, 1943: Fusing Ideas with the Art of the Animated Cartoon," *The Saturday Review*, September 4, 1943: 18–19; in Eric Smoodin, *Disney Discourse: Producing the Magic Kingdom* (New York: Routledge, 1994), 44–47.

23. Thomas M. Pryor, "The Screen," *The New York Times*, July 19, 1943: 13.

24. Watts, 236–237.

25. James Agee, "Films," *The Nation* 157.3 (July 17, 1943), 82. When Agee critiqued the missing civilians in *Victory Through Air Power*, he entered into an ongoing public

debate regarding precision bombing and its alternatives. Adopted in the post–World War I years and celebrated throughout the 1930s and early 1940s, daylight precision bombing missions were believed to be an effective, even humane, way to attack enemy installations. But after the destruction of London and what came to be known as the "Baedeker Blitz" (the bombing of non-military, historic sites culled from German editions of the popular Baedeker tourist guides), as well as the mounting losses due to German anti-aircraft guns, the RAF and the USAAF began to consider alternative bombing strategies proposed by Seversky and other like-minded officials. By 1945, daylight precision raids diminished as officials began to prefer more large-scale bombings campaigns, such as those carried out against Dresden and Tokyo in February of that year. For more on the rise and decline of precision bombing, see Sherry (49–58, 260–267); for the Baedeker Blitz, Martin Gilbert, *The Second World War: A Complete History* (New York: Holt, 1989), 319.

26. Theodore Strauss, "Donald Duck's Disney," *The New York Times*, Feb. 7 1943: X3.

27. Alexander P. de Seversky, "A Joint Statement about the Motion Picture 'Victory Through Air Power' by Walt Disney and Major Alexander P. de Seversky," *The New York Times*, July 29, 1943: 36.

28. Walt Disney, quoted in Strauss, X3.

29. Disney, "A Joint Statement," 36.

30. Although "propaganda" is often associated with the dissemination of information by governmental or quasi-governmental organizations, I recur to the term throughout this essay in order to highlight the fact that many of Disney's productions during these years were not mere lobbying efforts by the head of an American corporation. From his government-sponsored trip to South America to the requisitioning of his studios by the army in late 1942 to the financing of his many wartime educational films, Disney often cooperated and collaborated with military officials to bolster homefront support for American involvement in a two-theatre campaign against the Axis alliance. Although *Victory Through Air Power* received no such financing, Disney quickly established himself as a man with close ties to the U.S. military throughout the remaining years of the war.

31. John H. Criders, "Eden Joins Quebec Parley; Political Phase Is Reached," *The New York Times*, August 19, 1943: 1. Roy Disney, quoted in Thomas, 155. Mosely, 206.

32. Leonard Maltin, *The Disney Films* (New York: Crown, 1973), 64. In his introduction to *On the Front Lines*, Maltin restates this hypothesis: "H.C. Potter was told by Walt that it was only after Roosevelt saw *Victory Through Air Power* that our country made the commitment to long-range bombing. And that, after all, was the reason Walt committed to making this movie in the first place."

33. Richard Schickel, *The Disney Version: The Life, Times, Art and Commerce of Walt Disney* (New York: Simon and Schuster, 1968), 269.

34. Walt Disney, "Donald Duck Disney," X3.

35. Walter Wagner, "Film Phenomena," *Saturday Review of Literature*, Feb. 6, 1943; and "Mickey Icarus," quoted in Smoodin, 42–47.

36. J.P. McEvoy, "Disney Goes to War," *This Week Magazine*, July 5, 1942: 8. McEvoy, Grant, and Huemer are quoted in Watts 233–234.

37. "Matter of Censorship," *The New York Times*, April 23, 1944: X3. "Films Chosen For Young," *The New York Times*, Dec. 23, 1943: 23. "Films for Young," *The New York Times*, Jan. 6, 1944: 18.

38. Bill Nichols, *Blurred Boundaries: Questions of Meaning in Contemporary Culture* (Bloomington: Indiana University Press, 1994), ix.

39. Watts, 234.

40. *Victory Through Air Power*, dir. H. C. Potter, perf. Alexander P. de Seversky, United Artists, 1943. For a detailed analysis of Mitchell's efforts to promote the autonomy and

augmentation of American air power, see Chapter 5 of H. Bruce Franklin's *War Stars: The Superweapon and the American Imagination* (New York: Oxford University Press, 1988), 91–100.

41. William Mitchell, *Winged Defense: The Development and Possibilities of Modern Air Power— Economic and Military* (New York: G. P. Putnam's Sons, 1925).

42. Bill Nichols, *Representing Reality: Issues and Concepts in Documentary* (Bloomington: Indiana University Press, 1991), 34–35.

43. Ibid, x.

44. Paula Rabinowitz, *They Must Be Represented: The Politics of Documentary* (New York: Verso, 1994): 6. Bill Nichols, "The Voice of Documentary," *New Challenges for Documentary*, ed. Alan Rosenthal (Berkeley: University of California Press, 1987), 52.

45. Rosenthal, *New Challenges for Documentary*, 429.

46. See Mark Clague, "Playing in 'Toon: Walt Disney's *Fantasia* (1940) and the Imagineering of Classical Music," *American Music* 22.1 (2004), 91–109; Scott Schaffer, "Disney and the Imagineering of Histories," *Postmodern Culture: An Electronic Journal of Interdisciplinary Criticism*, 6.3 (1996), Last accessed 8 Feb. 2008 at <http://muse.jhu.edu/journals/postmodern_culture/toc/pmc6.3.html>.

47. The Douglas XB-19 was an expensive prototype that never saw formal production; it had a wingspan of more than 200 feet.

48. Schaffer (cit. n. 46)

49. In *Cinema 1* (Minneapolis: University of Minnesota Press, 1986), Gilles Deleuze analyzes the "movement-image," and its relationship to a diverse variety of films. However, he mentions the cartoon medium only once:

> [C]inema is the system which reproduces movement as a function of any-instant-whatever that is, as a function of equidistant instants, selected so as to create an impression of continuity.... Any other system which reproduces movement through an order of exposures [*poses*] projected in such a way that they pass into one another, or are 'transformed,' is foreign to the cinema. This is clear when one attempts to define the cartoon film; if it belongs fully to the cinema, this is because the drawing no longer constitutes a pose or a completed figure, but the description of a figure which is always in the process of being formed or dissolving through the movement. (5)

50. Seversky's theories regarding transcontinental bombing were, in this instance, an accurate assessment of proposed military technologies at the time. In 1941, the first blueprints were developed for what would eventually become the B-36 Peacemaker, though it would take the company later known as Convair nearly five years to develop the first working prototype.

51. One might argue that there a few exceptions: the Phalanx Close-In Weapon System (CWIS) is similar to what Seversky imagined, but it is strictly used on Navy combat ships. And one of the most approximate realizations of Seversky's vision, the B-36 (which had machine-gun turrets and cannons), did not formally emerge from the production line until 1948; however, it did not, like the B-29 Superfortress before it, have independently operated gun turrets and was not designed for mid-air fighting. It was also bulky and costly and required constant maintenance in order to avoid engine fires. Eventually, after the development of the jet engine, the B-36 became obsolete and production ceased in 1958. For more information on these aeronautical developments, see John Taylor's *Combat Aircraft of the World; from 1909 to the Present* (New York: Putnam, 1969), Michael Sherry's *The Rise of American Air Power* (New Haven: Yale University Press, 1987), and Timothy Moy's *War Machines: Transforming Technologies in the U.S. Military, 1920–1940* (College Station: Texas A&M University Press, 2001).

52. In these segments, Disney and Seversky recapitulate the arguments (which were

later disproved) made by various USAAF officials that bomber squadrons could, with the proper weaponry, protect themselves from fighter squadrons.

53. Barnes Wallis designed two bombs for the RAF, the 12,000-pound "Tallboy" and the 22,000-pound "Grand Slam," that were designed to penetrate the ground near large structures and destroy them with shockwaves. Although these bombs were dropped several dozen times during the final few years of World War II (most often on bridges, submarine shelters, and railway tunnels, but also alongside the moored battleship *Tirpitz*), they did not have anywhere near the explosive potential of those envisioned by Disney and Seversky. See Paul Brickhill, *The Dam Busters* (1951; Pan Books, 1999).

Bibliography

Agee, James. "Films." *The Nation* 157.3 (17 July 1943): 82.
"Air Power on the Screen," *The New York Times*, 26 July 1943: 18.
Anderson, Isaac. "Books and Authors," *The New York Times*, 2 August 1942: BR10.
Atkinson, Brooks. "Our Huge War Task Traced at Harvard," *The New York Times*, 31 May 1942: 20.
Baldwin, Hanson W. "Air Power's Role in the Atom Age," *The New York Times*, 3 July 1949: BR1.
_____. "Can Air Power Do the Trick?" *The New York Times*, 24 September 1950: BR4.
Bell, Elizabeth, Lynda Haas, and Laura Sells. *From Mouse to Mermaid: The Politics of Film, Gender, and Culture*. Bloomington: Indiana University Press, 1995.
Brickhill, Paul. *The Dam Busters*. 1951. Pan Books, 1999.
Clague, Mark. "Playing in 'Toon: Walt Disney's *Fantasia* (1940) and the Imagineering of Classical Music," *American Music* 22.1 (2004), 91–109.
Criders, John H. "Eden Joins Quebec Parley; Political Phase Is Reached," *The New York Times*, 19 August 1943: 1.
Crowther, Bosley. "Summer Harvest." *The New York Times*, August 5, 1943: X3.
Deleuze, Gilles. *Cinema 1*. Minneapolis: University of Minnesota Press, 1986.
Denning, Michael. *The Cultural Front: The Laboring of American Culture in the Twentieth Century*. New York: Verso, 1997.
"Films Chosen For Young," *The New York Times*, 23 December 1943: 23.
"Films for Young," *The New York Times*, 6 January 1944: 18.
Franklin, H. Bruce. *War Stars: The Superweapon and the American Imagination*. New York: Oxford University Press, 1988.
Gilbert, Martin. *The Second World War: A Complete History*. New York: Holt, 1989.
Griffin, Sean. *Tinker Belles and Evil Queens: The Walt Disney Company from the Inside Out*. New York: New York University Press, 2000.
Maloney, Edward. *Sever the Sky: Evolution of Severksy Aircraft*. California: Planes of Fame Publishers, 1979. Rumerman, Judy. "Alexander de Seversky and Seversky Aircraft," *U.S. Centennial of Flight Commission*. http://www.centennialofflight.gov/essay/Aerospace/Seversky/Aero42.htm>
Maltin, Leonard. *The Disney Films*. New York: Crown, 1973.
"Matter of Censorship," *The New York Times*, 23 April 1944: X3.
McGinty, G. W. "Victory Through Air Power," *Southwestern Social Science Quarterly*, 23.3 (December 1942), 295–296.
Mitchell, Donald. "The Dominance of Air Power," *The Nation* 154.21 (23 May 1942), 603–604.
Mitchell, William. *Winged Defense: The Development and Possibilities of Modern Air Power — Economic and Military*. New York: G. P. Putnam's Sons, 1925.
Mosley, Leonard. *Disney's World*. Maryland: Scarborough House Publishers, 1990, 206.

Moy, Timothy. *War Machines: Transforming Technologies in the U.S. Military, 1920–1940*. College Station: Texas A&M University Press, 2001.
Nichols, Bill. *Blurred Boundaries: Questions of Meaning in Contemporary Culture*. Bloomington: Indiana University Press, 1994.
_____. *Representing Reality: Issues and Concepts in Documentary*. Bloomington: Indiana University Press, 1991.
_____. "The Voice of Documentary." In *New Challenges for Documentary*, edited by Alan Rosenthal. Berkeley and Los Angeles: University of California Press, 1987.
"Notes on Books and Authors," *The New York Times*, 24 April 1942: 15.
Pratt, Fletcher. "Air Power's Part in the War," *The New York Times*, 3 May 1942: BR1.
Prescott, Orville. "Books of the Times," *The New York Times*, 20 April 1942: 19.
_____. "Books of the Times," *The New York Times*, 18 December 1942: 35.
Pryor, Thomas M. "The Screen," *The New York Times*, 19 July 1943: 13.
Rabinowitz, Paula. *They Must Be Represented: The Politics of Documentary*. New York: Verso, 1994.
Schaffer, Scott. "Disney and the Imagineering of Histories," *Postmodern Culture: An Electronic Journal of Interdisciplinary Criticism*, 6.3 (1996). http://muse.jhu.edu/journals/postmodern_culture/toc/pmc6.3.html
Schickel, Richard. *The Disney Version: The Life, Times, Art and Commerce of Walt Disney*. New York: Simon and Schuster, 1968.
"Screen New Here and in Hollywood," *The New York Times*, 22 June 1942: 19; 14 October 1942: 29.
Seversky, Alexander P. de. "A Joint Statement about the Motion Picture 'Victory Through Air Power' by Walt Disney and Major Alexander P. de Seversky," *The New York Times*, 29 July 1943: 36.
_____. *Victory Through Air Power*. New York: Simon and Schuster, 1942.
Sherry, Michael. *The Rise of American Air Power*. New Haven CT: Yale University Press, 1987.
Shull, Michael S., and David E. Witt. *Doing Their Bit: Wartime American Animated Short Films, 1939–1945*. Jefferson, NC: McFarland, 2004.
"Speaking of Books—," *The New York Times*, 10 May 1942: BR2.
Strauss, Theodore. "Donald Duck's Disney," *The New York Times*, 7 February 1943: X3.
Taylor, John. *Combat Aircraft of the World; from 1909 to the Present*. New York: Putnam, 1969.
The New York Times, 29 July 1943: 36.
The New York Times, 3 May 1942: BR13.
The New York Times, 18 May 1942: 13.
Thomas, Bob. *Building a Company: Roy O. Disney and the Creation of an Entertainment Empire*. New York: Hyperion, 1998.
Wagner, Walter. "Film Phenomena," *Saturday Review of Literature*, 6 February 1943.
_____. "Mickey Icarus, 1943: Fusing Ideas with the Art of the Animated Cartoon," *The Saturday Review*, 4 September 1943: 18–19.
Watts, Steven. *The Magic Kingdom: Walt Disney and the American Way of Life*. New York: Houghton Mifflin, 1997.

Section II: Science, Technology, Mathematics and Medicine

5

The Promise of Things to Come

Disneyland and the Wonders of Technology, 1954–1958

A. Bowdoin Van Riper

Before there was *Nova*, *The Undersea World of Jacques Cousteau*, or the *National Geographic* specials ... there was *Disneyland*. The weekly anthology series that premiered on the ABC network in October 1954, though better known for recycling Disney Studios' theatrical productions and promoting upcoming projects, also offered viewers some of the first science- and technology-themed documentaries aired on American television.[1] Two dozen such programs were planned, and nine were actually produced. Aired between the fall of 1954 and the spring of 1958, they transported viewers to otherwise-inaccessible places: the distant past and the near future, the inside of a nuclear reactor and the bridge of a spacecraft, the Antarctic ice cap and the dusty surface of Mars. Produced by Disney writers, artists, and camera crews in cooperation with outside experts, they chronicled the technological breakthroughs of the postwar era: atomic bombs and atomic power, superhighways and supersonic flight, and the opening of new frontiers on and beyond the Earth. They also captured the brightly burnished optimism of the era, which regarded technology as an unambiguous, unmixed blessing.[2]

Disneyland, created in 1954 as a complement to the soon-to-open Anaheim theme park, originally featured four rotating weekly themes corresponding to the park's four main areas. Fantasyland weeks would feature fairytales and talking animals viewers to the world of fairytales and talking animals, Adventureland segments would explore the wonders of nature, and Frontierland would offer "tall tales and true" of heroes from America's past. *Disneyland*'s trips to Tomorrowland—less frequent, because the lack of existing material that fit the theme—would reveal "the promise of things to come," symbolized by a sleek rocket ship and a stylized atom. The future that unfolded in the six programs produced specifically as Tomorrowland segments was—like the theme park it helped to promote—bright, clean, and efficient. They celebrated—along with three contemporary Disney documentaries on the exploration of Antarctica—the power of technology to reshape the world, transform everyday life, and open new doors to adventure. Conceived and aired in an era (1954–1958) when movies reflected the public's ambivalence about technology, the nine technology-themed films that aired on *Disneyland* were unreservedly and unabashedly cheerful.

Technology on Disneyland*: An Overview*

The *Disneyland* programs dealt with subjects familiar enough to Eisenhower-era audiences to need no introduction, but exotic enough to pique the viewers' interest. Three focused on space travel (*Man in Space, Man and the Moon, Mars and Beyond*), three on Antarctic exploration (*Antarctica: Past and Present, Antarctica: Operation Deep Freeze,* and *Antarctica: To The South Pole for Science*) one each on highways (*Magic Highway USA*), aviation (*Man in Flight*), and atomic energy (*Our Friend the Atom*). Eleven similar programs—conceived but never produced—reflect the same pattern, covering subjects such as *The Wheel, Communications, The Story of Trains,* and *Man and His Earth.*

Had all the planned episodes been produced, there would have been 20 such programs aired—at a rate of roughly five per year—in the first four seasons (1954–1958) of *Disneyland.* In fact, only nine aired, seven of them between September 1956 and May 1958. The high cost of producing such programming from scratch took its toll, however, and production schedules repeatedly slipped. *Atomic Energy,* slated for the first season, appeared in the fourth season as *Our Friend the Atom.* A multi-part episode on the past, present, and future of aviation—scheduled for the second season—became a single third-season episode titled *Man in Flight,* which relied heavily on repurposed footage from *Victory Through Air Power* (1943). The episodes that *did* air were each rebroadcast at least once, and several were re-edited for theatrical release, in order to amortize their production costs. *Man in Space, Man and the Moon,* and *Mars and Beyond* were all released as half-hour featurettes, and the three Antarctica films were condensed into a single film titled *The Seven Cities of Antarctica* and released as part of the People and Places series.

Science and technology documentaries disappeared from *Disneyland,* without fanfare or clear explanation, after the program's fourth (1957–58) season. The name of the series was changed, for the fifth (1958–59) season, to *Walt Disney Presents,* the idea of a rotating weekly theme was dropped. The existence of a designated Tomorrowland segment had, for four seasons, created both a home and a need for programs like *Man in Space* and *Our Friend the Atom.*

When the need for "Tomorrowland" programming disappeared, episodes dealing with science and technology disappeared along with it. Outlines for projects dealing with artificial satellites, weather control, geology, and oceanography (originally scheduled for the fourth season) remained on the table, along with plans for biographies of Leonardo da Vinci and astronomer Edwin Hubble and a set of episodes titled *The Magic of Mathematics* (originally scheduled for the fifth season). Elements of these projects resurfaced as theatrical featurettes—*Eyes in Outer Space* and *Donald in Mathmagic Land*—in 1959, but none was produced for television.

The nine *Disneyland* episodes that dealt with science and technology were neither conceived as a branded series (like the "True Life Adventures" wildlife films or the "People and Places" travelogues) nor made in a distinctive "house style." Eclecticism—in style and content—was their hallmark. All nine episodes were motivated, however, by an effort to educate (and so reassure) audiences about the technologies transforming their lives, while keeping them entertained. The "Tomorowland" segments of *Disneyland* were, in that sense, Disney edutainment in its purest form: "fact-packed," at Walt's insistence, and yet (beneath their genuine seriousness, and considerable intellectual sophistication) as playfully entertaining and inherently optimistic as any Mickey Mouse short.

Content

Disneyland's science and technology programs were designed to make cutting-edge science and technology interesting to a non-specialist, all-ages television audience. They did so by emphasizing, wherever possible, practice over theory, action over speech, and the concrete over the abstract. It was an approach that played not just to the medium of television, but to the strengths of the Disney Studio, which had built its reputation on its exquisite visuals more than (as in the case of the Warner Brothers cartoon unit) on clever writing and deft characterization. The nine programs may have been *about* ideas, but wherever possible they *showed* people and things—preferably in vigorous and varied motion. Even when they used live-action footage the films were always, in the broader sense, animated.

Disney's preference for the concrete over the abstract was apparent in the Antarctica trilogy of films. Shot by Disney cameramen who accompanied a 1955–56 U. S. Navy expedition to Antarctica, the three films chronicle, the establishment of seven research stations—"seven cities for science," as the narration describes them—on the south polar ice. Aside from a historical segment at the beginning of *Antarctica: Past and Present*, the trilogy is really the story of a complex, high-tech military operation. It depicts a peaceful "invasion" in which the weapons are bulldozers and prefabricated buildings, the only defenders are annoyed penguins, and the principal enemies are the sudden storms and ever-present cold. The films of the Antarctica trilogy, like those shot during the Allied invasion of Normandy a dozen years before, depict exotic machinery in constant motion. Icebreakers smash channels through the pack ice with their reinforced bows, bulldozers shear off ridges of snow and ice and plow them into newly opened crevasses, giant transport aircraft parachute supplies to the construction crews waiting below, and snow tractors on broad tank-like treads haul supplies inland in a steady stream. The high-visibility colors of the equipment — red for the bulldozers, bright orange for the outer wing panels of the airplanes— stand out starkly against the all-white background, accentuating the motion.

The human figures in the Antarctica trilogy are like the soldiers in wartime combat documentaries: competent, purposeful, and anonymous. The film does not reveal their backgrounds, their motivations, their job titles, or — except for a handful of men killed in accidents during the operation — even their names. Anonymous and interchangeable in their heavy clothes, they are shown striding through underground ice tunnels, raising prefabricated buildings, and setting off dynamite explosions to expose dangerous crevasses. They are objects, moving in a landscape, and their function in the films is the same as that of icebreakers and the caterpillar tractors: to *act,* not to comment or reflect or their actions. The unsolved scientific questions that motivated the massive operation in the first place are effectively absent from the Antarctica trilogy. Even in the third film, titled *To the South Pole for Science*, the most memorable moments are about logistics: the air-dropping of supplies to build the Amundsen-Scott research station at the bottom of the world. Scientists wait patiently off-screen, waiting for the men of action — the icebreaker crews, the transport pilots, and the construction gangs— to create a sheltered place for them to do their contemplative work.

The Antarctica films, because they chronicled a large construction project in an exotic landscape accessible to camera crews, had visual interest to spare. *Man in Flight* and *Magic Highway USA,* though they depicted the development of particular machines across a variety of times and places rather than a variety of machines at work in a particular time and place, had similar advantages. The space trilogy and *Our Friend the Atom* presented Disney filmmakers with greater challenges. Much of their content was inherently abstract (like the laws of motion), many of their settings were beyond the reach of cameras (the inside of an atomic nucleus, the surface of the Moon), and most of the machines they described had yet to be built. All four succeeded, however, by applying the same basic preference for showing over telling, but at a markedly higher level of sophistication.

Man in Space, the first of the films to air, set the tone for the three to follow. It began by explaining Newton's law of action and reaction — the basis of all rocket propulsion — then turned to the combination of gravity and inertia that causes spacecraft to "fall around" the bodies they orbit. Between the two halves of this primer in rocket physics came an introduction to rocket engineering: explanations of the principal components in a single-stage V-2 rocket and of the performance advantages of that multi-stage rockets offer over single-stage ones. The extended discussion of "space medicine" covered the basics of that subject, such as the human body's response to high g-forces experienced during acceleration (loss of consciousness) and low g-forces experienced in orbit (disorientation and possible nausea). It was, however, much broader than the "space medicine" label suggests. The enumeration of the problems of living in space touched on the deeply counterintuitive physics of low gravity—an environment where an unanchored astronaut pushing on a wrench will turn himself instead of the bolt he is trying to tighten. It also explored astronomy, pointing out that the cosmic radiation and micrometeorites absorbed daily by Earth's atmosphere would be dangerous to astronauts who traveled beyond it, and touched on the psychological effects of being "trapped in a tiny metal box, floating through the incomprehensible nothingness of space." Each of these explanations was deftly illustrated by snippets of animation: sneezing dogs, speeding sports cars, and a hapless space traveler who suffers one low-gravity indignity after another.

The other three episodes followed a similar pattern, and broadened still further the range of scientific subjects covered. *Our Friend the Atom* explained atomic structure, the nature of radiation, how a nuclear chain reaction works, and how the controlled chain reaction in a power plant differs from the uncontrolled one in a bomb. *Man and the Moon* and *Mars and Beyond* inventoried the nine planets and thirty-one moons then known to comprise the solar system, discussed the formation of the solar system as a whole, and evaluated the possibilities of finding life elsewhere within it.[3] They described surface conditions on their titular worlds in as much detail as the available data permitted, noting (for example) the existence of dust storms and polar ice caps on Mars and two distinct geological provinces—light-colored highlands and dark-colored basins—on the Moon.[4] *Mars and Beyond* also delved deeply into biology, summarizing the evolution of life on Earth and speculating on the path that evolution might have taken on Mars had life emerged there.

All four programs took similar approaches toward advanced technology, first introducing and explaining its design features and then showing it in action. *Our Friend the Atom* covered the functioning of nuclear reactors in great detail, and then offered a more general discussion of their applications in electric power generation, transportation, agriculture, and medicine. The three space-themed programs introduced audiences to a trio of increasingly capable space ships, each of which it showed in action on an imaginary mission depicted at the end of the episode. *Man in Space* featured a sleek three-stage chemical-fuel booster capable of lifting a reusable, rocket-powered spacecraft and its ten-member crew into Earth orbit for a day. *Man and the Moon* showed a four-person ship, assembled in Earth orbit, capable of going to the Moon and back (though not landing) in less than a week. *Mars and Beyond* presented a 500-foot-wide disk-shaped, nuclear-powered ship that could reach Mars in a little over a year. Other space technology, featured alongside the ships, received similar treatment: satellites, self-propelled spacesuits for zero-g construction work, and a 100-person space station.

A viewer who paid close attention to all four programs would, in exchange for the four hours they invested, have received a solid (if somewhat idiosyncratic) introduction to planetary astronomy, classical mechanics, nuclear physics and engineering, astronautical engineering, space medicine, historical geology, evolutionary theory, and what would today be called exobiology.[5] The programs' greatest strength, however, was not the broad range of topics they covered but the surprising sophistication with which they approached those topics.

One mark of this sophistication is the extent to which all four programs assumed *some* knowledge on the part of the audience. *Man in Space*, for example, referred to but did not explain the use of a centrifuge to simulate g-forces in astronaut training, assuming that an average television viewer would be able to extrapolate its function from seeing it in operation. *Man and the Moon*, depicting construction of an Earth-orbiting space station, left viewers to make connection that the fleet of winged rockets making daily deliveries to orbit were production versions of the prototype shown in *Man in Space*. Similarly, *Mars and Beyond* implied but never stated that the space station constructed in *Man and the Moon* served as an orbital home base for the six Mars-bound spacecraft seen in the final segment. *Our Friend the Atom* evoked the destructive power of nuclear weapons (a critical contrast for its main storyline about the peaceful uses of nuclear energy) with a handful of mushroom-cloud images and an oblique sentence or two. It presumed the audience capable of filling in the gaps.

A second aspect of the programs' sophistication was their currency. The step-by-step plan for putting humans in space outlined in *Man in Space* and its two sequels fell squarely into that category, though the distance between it and the plan actually used makes it hard to see that today. *Disneyland* viewers already interested in space would have recognized the plan (the four-stage winged rocket, the 100-man space station, the moon ship) as that outlined in an eight-part series that had appeared in *Collier's* magazine in 1952–53. They would also have recognized the program's onscreen experts—Wernher Von Braun, Willy Ley, Heinz Haber, and Ernst Stuhlinger—as the authors of that series, and Ley as the author of a follow-up book: *Across the Space Frontier*.[6] Von Braun's detailed explanation of a flight-test program for the rocket, his specification of hydrazine and nitric acid (then new and experimental) as its fuel, and the minute level of detail in which the construction of the space station is described suggest a real plan, worked out in complete earnest. So, too, do the details of the mission plan that Von Braun describes in *Mars and Beyond*—4 months accelerating in Earth orbit, 45 days in a spiraling deceleration toward

Martian orbit, 13 months total in transit. Indeed von Braun's plan, which Disney gave life on the screen as *Collier's* and Viking Press had given it life on the page, *was* the most detailed, plausible vision of the future available.[7]

The last, and most striking, mark of the Disney programs' sophistication was their willingness to tackle complex issues. *Our Friend the Atom* explained the physics of nuclear chain reactions, *Man in Space* introduced the deeply counterintuitive principles of orbital mechanics, and *Man and the Moon* described what would be (if carried out) the most complex construction project in human history. *Mars and Beyond*, rather than describing its Mars-bound fleet of spaceships as vaguely "atomic powered," had Ernst Stuhlinger carefully explain how a nuclear-electric ion drive would work.[8] Nuclear physics and "rocket science" were standard symbols of scientific complexity in the 1950s, but *Disneyland*— the product of a studio better known for singing dwarfs and talking animals— tackled them with aplomb.

Style

Perhaps *because* of its strong, long-standing association with fantasy, Disney Studios took care to distinguish its "science-factual" Tomorrowland programs from science fiction. Cultural context helped. Each of the *Disneyland* programs on science and technology had close ties to current events: the introduction of the first jet airliners, the launch of the nuclear-powered submarine *Nautilus*, the construction of the interstate highway system, the International Geophysical Year. The technologies they described were, by the mid–1950s, discussed not only in technical journals but hobbyist magazines like *Popular Mechanics*, general-interest magazines like *Collier's* and *The Saturday Evening Post*, and books aimed at squarely at the general public (including children). This, along with the studio's successful forays into documentary filmmaking — the *True-Life Adventures* and *People and Places* series—created a presumption that the programs were serious documentaries.

A variety of visual elements in the programs themselves reinforced the point. The films of the Antarctica trilogy consisted almost entirely of live-action footage, and the rest made extensive use of it: stock footage, costumed dramatizations, and lectures and demonstrations filmed on studio sets. Where the films used animation, it ranged from limited character animation that owed more to Mister Magoo than Mickey Mouse to the stylized realism used a decade earlier in *Fantasia* (1940), *Bambi* (1942), and *Victory Through Air Power* (1943). The colorful, rounded, fully animated characters and richly detailed backgrounds that had made Disney Studios famous was conspicuously absent.[9] The decision behind this may have been practical — traditional Disney animation was expensive — or it may have been a conscious attempt to distance the programs from the fantasy-themed shorts and features for which the studio was known.

Onscreen lectures by established authority figures—used everywhere *but* the Antarctica films—reinforced the air of factuality. Each of the three space-themed episodes opened with brief introductions in which Walt Disney and writer-director Ward Kimball assured audiences that the program to follow was based on scientific fact. Each of the three then turned, after an animated historical segment narrated by Kimball, to formal presentations by scientists and engineers such as Willy Ley, Wernher von Braun, and Heinz Haber. *Our Friend the Atom* used a more streamlined version of the same formula, making Haber the sole onscreen expert and giving him Kimball's old role as narrator-host. *Magic Highway USA*, meanwhile, contented itself with a nameless, suited and bespectacled "traffic engineer."

The filmed lectures instantly established an air of seriousness by recreating the atmosphere of a classroom. The physical positioning of the onscreen expert, sitting at a desk or standing beside a chalkboard on a studio set, established him as the teacher and the viewing audience as the class. *Man in Space* even provided an *actual* audience: a group of Disney artists seated in straight-backed wooden chairs with notepads and drawing boards in their hands. Linking studio and living room to form a virtual classroom signaled the viewing audience that the upcoming segment would be dense and information-rich, requiring their full attention. It was ideal, therefore, for subjects that were conceptually difficult, such as orbital mechanics in *Man in Space* and nuclear chain reactions in *Our Friend the Atom*. The format was also well suited to subjects far beyond the audience's everyday experience, such as space station construction in *Man and the Moon*, ion-drive spaceships in *Mars and Beyond*. The lecture format lent an air of instant seriousness to such seemingly outlandish subjects. The possibility that a soberly dressed expert seated behind a desk would deliver anything *other* than a serious lecture simply did not exist in the world of 1950s television.[10]

Disney's use of émigré German scientists as onscreen experts reinforced the seriousness of the lecture segments.[11] Their gray suits, formal style of speaking, and thick European accents linked them to scientific authority figures both real (Freud, Einstein) and imaginary (*Flash Gordon*'s Dr. Zarkov). The German experts were notably stiff in front of the camera, however, and their deliberate, uninflected speech slowed down already slow-paced segments. Wherever possible, Disney tried to soften the German experts' stiff formality by providing visual distractions for the viewer. Willy Ley's lecture on rocket physics in *Man in Space* was illustrated by chalkboard diagrams that briefly come to animated life. Heinz Haber's descriptions of the physical challenges confronting astronauts—multi-g acceleration, weightlessness, disorientation—were accompanied by a cartoon of a space-faring "everyman," who experiences them in comically exaggerated ways. Von Braun's detailed explanations of future spacecraft in all three space-themed program were delivered next to large, meticulously crafted models of spaceships and space stations. His narrative of a space station being built in *Man and the Moon* were accompanied, storyboard-style, by close-up shots of detailed artists' renderings. Haber's lecture on nuclear chain reactions in *Our Friend the Atom* had the best visual aid of all: A tabletop demonstration in which cocked mousetraps represented unstable atomic nuclei (of uranium 235, for example) and ping pong balls, balanced atop them, represented the neutrons set free when they split. A single ping pong ball, dropped onto the table from above, triggered a spectacular flurry of activity and enders the concept of chain reactions instantly memorable.

Disney's stylized, animated realism conferred a different kind of gravity on the segments in which it was used. Disney studios had used it before: not only in its most serious-minded feature-length films, but also in the most self-consciously serious segments *of* those films. It lent a sense of majesty to the forests in *Bambi*, as well as to the early scenes of Bambi's father and the concluding scenes of the adult Bambi. The animators of *Fantasia* used it to recreate the world of the doomed dinosaurs in the "Rite of Spring" segment. Three years later, it was used for the apocalyptic climax of *Victory Through Air Power:* scenes of American heavy bombers crossing the Pacific and blasting the cities of Japan into oblivion. The use of stylized realism signaled, in all four cases, a break from lighthearted moments elsewhere in the same film and an understanding that the events depicted should be understood as "real" even though their details had been imagined by Disney animators.

The *Disneyland* programs used stylized realism to depict events for which there had not been (or could not be) human observers: events for which the details were, by definition, invented. The stylization — deep shadows, clean outlines, and minimal surface detail — signaled that the events on-screen had been freely imagined, rather than "drawn from life." The realism — normally proportioned human figures, slightly muted "natural" colors, and practical-looking machines— simultaneously signals that they are tied as closely as possible to reality, and not "just made up." Stylized realism was the preferred motif for depictions of the distant past and the future. In *Man and the Moon*, for example, it was used for a sequence showing the well-understood but never-observed early history of the solar system, and in still images showing construction of the orbital space station. The first manned orbital flight in *Man in Space* and the first manned mission to Mars in *Mars and Beyond* were rendered in it, as were sequences depicting the future uses of nuclear energy in *Our Friend the Atom*, next-generation air travel in *Man in Flight* and the "highways of tomorrow" in *Magic Highway USA*.[12]

Stylized realism also served to illustrate subjects that were inaccessible for reasons other than chronology: the behavior of subatomic particles in *Our Friend the Atom*, for example. *Mars and Beyond* exemplified both approaches. Stylized realism was used not only in the mission-to-Mars segment, but also to depict conditions on the surfaces of other worlds, the formation of the primordial Earth, and the surface of a hypothetical Mars (discussed in the next section) inhabited by complex life. The images of this "living Mars" recall the images of prehistoric Earth in the "Rite of Spring" segment of *Fantasia*, but (unlike the dinosaurs in *Fantasia*) are based not on fossil evidence but on informed speculation about how life *might* have adapted to a dry, dusty world. The use of stylized realism to depict the Martian creatures signaled viewers to treat them, like dinosaurs in *Fantasia* the rockets in *Man in Space*, as products of serious scientific thought.

Segments that dealt with the past gave Disney filmmakers more stylistic freedom. They *could* be depicted in conventional documentary style — using live-action footage of real events as in *Antarctica: Past and Present* or *Man in Space*, or stylized animation as in *Our Friend the Atom*— but they did not have to be. The history of the automobile, the airplane, and the rocket were familiar, at least in their broadest outlines, to most members of the audience. A straightforward recounting of any of them would, therefore, come across as truthful even if illustrated with less-than-serious images. *Man in Flight*, for example, uses comic-book-style visuals in World War I sequences to illustrate a wholly serious point: the escalating levels of aerial violence over the Western Front in the early months of the war, as shouted insults gave way to pistols, rifles, and machine guns. *Magic Highway USA* featured costumed members of a California antique-car club simulating the travails of early motorists: choking dust, frequent blowouts, and narrow, rutted roads. Shot in black-and-white,[13] the segment was deliberately sped up and accompanied by frenetic piano music, imitating the frenzied action of a silent film comedy. Later in the program, modern road-building equipment is shown at work: first at normal speed and then, their reality having been established, over-cranked into a blur of motion supposedly representing "the highway engineer's dream" of rapid road construction. The normal-speed original serves as an anchor in reality, allowing the high-speed version to be used for comic effect without sacrificing the seriousness of the program as a whole.[14]

The three space-themed films indulged in similar visual excess when depicting the past, but they used limited animation — a style pioneered by the United Productions of America (UPA) animation studio in the late 1940s— to add levity. UPA had already won two Academy Awards for its work by the time *Disneyland* premiered in the fall of 1954.[15] UPA's style was the antithesis of that traditionally used by Disney and Warner Brothers. It featured human characters rather than talking animals, featured consciously two-dimensional drawings, and set its simplified figures against even more simplified backgrounds. More than Warner Brothers and far more than Disney, UPA used its animation to suggest, rather than recreate, the real world.

Limited animation was well suited to the historical segments of space programs because the audience knew many of the individual facts and the basic outlines of the historical background. Unfamiliar names (John Herschel) and concepts (steam rockets) slipped easily into a litany of familiar individuals (Galileo, Newton, Cyrano, Jules Verne), facts (the Chinese invented rockets), and periods (the "Dark Ages," the Renaissance, the French Revolution).[16] The animators for the historical segments were thus free to use limited animation—particularly its exaggerated human figures—for comic relief. The use of rockets for warfare in medieval China was illustrated in *Man in Space* by two figures in conical hats firing ever-larger weapons across a gorge at each other, until both are singed and covered in soot.[17] Scenes of a dog sneezing and blowing himself backward illustrate Newton's law of action and reaction. The "Dark Ages" are symbolized in *Man and the Moon* by a procession of robed, hooded figures across a darkened landscape. A few scenes later, Cyrano de Bergerac is pulled through the sky by his fictional rocket, spouting random French phrases (*Cherchez la Femme ... Liberté, Egalité, Fraternité!*) in cartoon-style speech balloons as he goes.

The historical segment of *Mars and Beyond* is played even more conspicuously for laughs, and climaxes in a parody of science fiction stories about invaders from Mars, featuring a pipe-smoking scientist, his beautiful secretary, and a gigantic robot who kidnaps her and hauls her away to Mars. Having set up a classic pulp-science-fiction plot—heroic scientist rescues passive woman from (implied) rape by aliens—the parody gleefully turned it inside out. The scientist is a clueless dolt who fails to notice the hulking robot, the secretary turns out to be a capable action hero, and by the time the scientist belatedly arrives on Mars she has done "his" job by rescuing herself and vanquishing the Martians. The "Martian invasion" segment of *Mars and Beyond* was, by design, further from reality than any other part of the program. It was also the only segment in any of the nine programs that was—in the sense of Disney's traditional shorts and features—entirely "made up." The segment also featured Disney's most assured, innovative use of limited animation. The conjunction is not surprising. Throughout the nine programs, style routinely reflected content.

Message

Disneyland's nine programs on science and technology presented audiences with a wealth of specific information: observed facts, well-tested theories, and informed speculation. They did so straightforwardly and explicitly, in a series of brief "lessons" designed to entertain as well as instruct. The nine programs also, however, conveyed messages about science, technology, and those responsible for their advancement. These messages—unlike those in Disney's wartime propaganda films and educational shorts—were presented subtly and obliquely. They were delivered by implication, rather than proclamation. The extent to which viewing audiences absorbed them is unknown and unknowable, but it seems clear that Disney intended them. The two central ones—that scientific and technological progress is beneficial, and that scientists and engineers embody American values—are fully consistent with Walt Disney's (and thus Disney Studios') essentially conservative worldview.[18]

The advancement of science was a relatively minor theme in the *Disneyland* programs, but it was always presented earnestly. The heroically animated scientists in *Our Friend the Atom* and the double-time parade of broadly drawn sight gags and caricatured history in the space trilogy present a uniform message: that exploring the universe is an essential part of the human experience. All four programs treated science as a routine activity that takes place wherever and whenever humans are free to exercise their minds, and see it as always productive, never destructive. The only dark moments in their historical segments are those in which free inquiry is squelched by ignorant authorities. *Mars and Beyond*, for example, portrayed the millennium between 500 and 1500 AD as "a black period of stupidity, superstition, and sorcery," and illustrated it with a collage of devils, demons, and skulls. Society, Disney implied, had nothing to fear from science—only from those who would stifle it.

The advancement of technology was a far more prominent theme, and Disney's trademark optimism was more prominently on display. The history of technology was, in all nine programs, an opportunity for celebration the ways in which humankind's expanding control of nature improved its quality of life. *Man in Flight* and *Magic Highway USA*, for example, were primarily historical and explicitly celebratory. Contrasting past and present, they invited the audience to marvel at how far "we" (nominally the human race, but practically the industrialized world and specifically the United States) had come in less than a century. The Antarctica trilogy briefly acknowledged the first explorers' brief, tenuous forays onto the continent before celebrating, in detail, the U. S. Navy's massive efforts to reshape pieces of it in permanent homes for scientists. Both the Antarctica trilogy, *Mars and Beyond*, and *Our Friend the Atom* all linked, to varying degrees, the advancement of technology to the more efficient control of nature and the access to untapped pools of natural resources—both seen as clearly and unambiguously good.

The possibility that the advance of technology might *not* be wonderful was alien to Disney's outlook. The nine episodes sidestepped, glossed over, or altogether ignored the consequences that often make new technologies a mixed blessing. *Man in Flight* borrowed footage freely from *Victory Through Air Power*, but dropped the earlier film's bellicose narration and used virtually none of its animated depictions of bombers blasting apart enemy cities. *Magic Highway USA* did not dwell on accidents, road rage, or the seas of asphalt that engulfed the countryside as car travel pushed the suburban frontier outward.[19] Indeed, *Magic Highway USA* goes on at length about the process of clearing rights-of-way for new highways, celebrating the clear-cutting of trees as evidence of man's power over nature, and treating the demolition of existing neighborhoods as a triumph of democracy. Man *in Space* failed to note that a rocket capable of putting a spacecraft into orbit could also lob a nuclear warhead hundreds of miles into enemy territory, despite the fact that von Braun was then employed designing such weapons for the United States Army.[20]

Our Friend the Atom was the only one of the nine episodes that even acknowledged a possible downside to technological progress. It was also, not coincidentally, the episode that offered the most explicit statement of Disney's optimism about technological change. *Atom* began by retelling a folktale from the *Arabian Nights*. A fisherman find a bottle caught in his net, opens it, and in so doing releases a powerful genie that threatens to kill him. The fisherman first cowers in fear and then, desperate, tricks the genie back into the bottle and seals it up again. The genie, trapped but still powerful, promises the fisherman three wishes *if* he is released from the bottle. The story itself takes only a few minutes to tell, but its plot served as the organizing metaphor of *Our Friend the Atom*. The genie of atomic energy is released from his bottle when the first nuclear chain reaction is carried out in 1938. The genie first manifests itself in the form of atomic weapons—a "devastating force" that "posed a fearful threat"—but is soon imprisoned in nuclear reactors. Thus "tamed," he becomes a powerful but obedient servant eager to grant his new masters' wishes for unlimited energy, more productive agriculture, and new cures for diseases.

Our Friend sidestepped the traditional, cautionary ending of the genie-and-fisherman story, in which the hero chooses his second or third wish unwisely and winds up no better off (or, in some versions, far worse off) than he was before.[21] It twice acknowledged that nuclear weapons can be deadly, but each time does so briefly and obliquely, with bomb-test footage that shows mushroom clouds but *not* disintegrating buildings or scorched target ships. Even these mild images of destruction are quickly followed, however, by reassurance from the narrator. "An atomic blast is more than a threat," the narrator intones in the first instance. "It is also a regretful waste of heat and radiation" that could be harnessed to generate electricity or benefit agriculture and medicine. "Our third wish," he proclaims the second time around, "should be for the atomic genie to remain our friend ... since he holds the power of both creation and destruction." *Our Friend the Atom* thus acknowledged that new technologies may bring new risks, but insisted that eliminating those risks requires only that we make wise choices. True to Disney's optimism, the episode never even suggests that we might not.

The second major theme in the *Disneyland* programs—that science and technology reflect mainstream American values—was presented implicitly rather than explicitly and by example rather than proclamation. The value of teamwork, for example, was promoted and celebrated throughout. The historical segments of *Man and the Moon*, *Mars and Beyond*, and *Our Friend the Atom* reflected (even though they did not quote) Isaac Newton's famous acknowledgement of the intellectual debt he owed his predecessors: "If I have seen further, it is because I have stood on the shoulders of giants." There was no room for revolutionaries or iconoclasts in Disney's history of science, in which knowledge is built up by team players who expand and refine the work of those who went before. *Man in Flight* and *Magic Highway USA* presented the history of technology in similar terms, though the individual engineers and inventors were less often named. The films of the Antarctica trilogy depicted teams of scientists cooperating with one another and with the U. S. Navy. The International Geophysical Year, the ever-present background of the Antarctica films, was itself designed to foster international cooperation in science.

The dramatized space missions in each of the three programs depicted the same model of close collaboration between specialists. The four-stage rocket that makes the first flight to Earth orbit in *Man in Space* carries a crew of ten that includes a pilot, a navigator, a communication specialist, and various scientists. Its launch site—a large complex on a remote atoll in the Pacific—implies the existence of a massive support staff: engineers, technicians, construction crews, and sailors to run the ships that ferry in supplies and rocket components. The construction of the Earth-orbiting space station in *Man and the Moon* requires the launch of one such rocket a day, and weeks of work by specialized construction gangs used to living and working in zero gravity. The 50-man crew of the finished station includes entire departments of astronomers, biologists, meteorologists, doctors, and military observers as well as (presumably) engineers, technicians, and a command staff. Aboard the ship that departs the station for the first flight to the Moon, the crewmembers address one another almost exclusively by job title. The man responsible for maintaining contact with Earth is never "Johnson" or "Bob" or even "Sparks," but "Radio Operator." Space will, in Disney's version of the future, be conquered by the Organization Man.

The scientists and engineers who appeared live in *Man in Space*, *Man and the Moon*, *Mars and Beyond*, and *Our Friend the Atom* were models of 1950s middle-class propriety. They dressed in conservative suits, had neatly combed hair, spoke in measured tones, and illustrated their talks with slick, professional-looking charts and models. Wernher von Braun, explaining his design for a four-stage rocket in *Man in Space*, could just as easily have been a senior executive at General Motors unveiling a new model of luxury sedan. The animated scientists depicted in the historical section of *Our Friend the Atom* had the same square-jawed, well-groomed look. The traffic engineers in *Magic Highway USA* could have walked out of a Rotary Club meeting in any medium-sized American city. The scientists and engineers who ride the spaceships in *Man in Space* and its sequels could all have stepped out of the same air force recruiting poster as the pilots. Even in broadly comic animated sequences, scientists were never the butt of the jokes. The lone exception—the clueless scientist whose secretary is kidnapped by aliens in *Mars and Beyond*—appeared in a sequence explicitly designed to satirize pop culture clichés.

The Disney programs' messages about science and technology were not new. The idea that scientists and engineers were solid citizens whose work improved everyone's quality of life had been a staple of corporate and government public relations for decades, and inspired a brief cycle of Hollywood films about scientists and inventors in the 1930s and early 1940s.[22] The dominant image of science and technology in popular culture was, in the 1950s, far less flattering. Malevolent scientists—heirs of the half-mad Dr. Frankenstein—joined with their hapless or dangerously naïve colleagues to cause mayhem in films like *The Thing from Another World* (1951), *Monkey Business* (1952), *Tarantula* (1955), *Forbidden Planet* (1956) and *X: The Man with X-Ray Eyes* (1957). Even positive portrayals of cinematic scientists and engineers—Sam Jaffee's advocate of interspecies friendship in *The Day the Earth Stood Still* (1951), James Stewart's principled metallurgist in *No Highway in the Sky* (1954), and Spencer Tracy's amiable computer engineer in *The Desk Set* (1957)—emphasized their eccentricity.

The Disney programs presented scientists and engineers as sober, steady team players rather than eccentric visionaries. They presented scientific and technological progress as forces that helped to *sustain* the routines of everyday life, rather than subverting or disrupting them. Doing so, Disney helped to rescued scientists from their exile to the fringes of American culture, and made a bid to reintegrate them into polite society. The *Disneyland* programs, in short, created an image of science and technology that their middle-American audience could comfortably embrace.

Decline, Fall, and Afterlife

Magic Highway USA, the last of the Tomorrowland segments, aired in May 1958, but the nine science-and-technology-themed segments made for *Disneyland* never entirely faded away.

Beginning with the 1961–62 season, Disney Studios moved the series from ABC to NBC, in order to take advantage of the latter network's color-broadcasting capability.[23] Re-titled *Disney's Wonderful World of Color*, it featured a number of episodes that recycled cartoon segments (all color and nearly all comic) from the Tomorrowland programs. Professor Ludwig von Drake, a new animated character created specifically for television, served as the addle-brained "expert" narrator of the programs (an unacknowledged parody of Ley, Von Braun, and Haber) and newly animated segments featuring him linked the older pieces. Elements of *Man in Flight* became *Fly with Von Drake* and the least-serious bits of the three space episodes were collected into *Inside Outer Space*.[24] The Von Drake episodes were rebroadcast several times during the early years of the Disney Channel (1985–1990). Several of the original *Disneyland* episodes were also rebroadcast, late at night, as part of the network's "Vault Disney" programming track aimed at animation enthusiasts and nostalgic Baby-Boomers. The three space episodes, along with *Our Friend the Atom*, were released on a limited edition *Tomorrowland* DVD in 2006, as part of the Disney Treasures series.

Disney's decision to exploit the (considerable) comic and nostalgic value of the programs is understandable. It has tended, however, to obscure the purpose for which they were originally produced and the context in which they were originally viewed. The programs were meant to entertain, but also to educate and reassure Disney's middle–American target audience about the science- and technology-laden future that was taking shape around them. Over the course of four television seasons, they did so: always ambitious, and occasionally brilliant.

Notes

1. Bill Cotter, *The Wonderful World of Disney Television: A Complete History* (New York: Disney Editions, 1997), chapter 2; and J. P. Telotte, *Disney TV* (Detroit: Wayne State University Press, 2004), chapter 1 offer historical overviews of the Disney anthology series.

2. William L. O'Neill, *American High: The Years of Confidence, 1945–1960* (New York: Free Press, 1986) and David Halberstam, *The Fifties* (New York: Villard, 1993) are useful overviews of the decade and its *zeitgeist* by a social historian and a journalist, respectively. Useful treatments of the popular image of science and technology in the 1950s include: Marcel C. LaFollette, *Making Science Our Own: Public Images of Science, 1910–1955* (Chicago: University of Chicago Press, 1990); Peter Biskind, *Seeing Is Believing: How Hollywood Taught Us to Stop Worrying and Learn to Love the Fifties* (New York: Pantheon, 1983), chapter 3; Patrick Lucanio and Gary Colville, *Smokin' Rockets: The Romance of Technology in American Film, Radio, and Television, 1945–1962* (Jefferson, NC: McFarland, 2002); Michael Scheibach, *Atomic Narratives and American Youth: Coming of Age with the Atom, 1945–1955* (Jefferson, NC: McFarland, 2003); and Paul Boyer, *By the Bomb's Early Light: American Thought and Culture at the Dawn of the Atomic Age* (Chapel Hill: University of North Carolina Press, 1985).

3. Pluto, discovered in 1920, was classified as a planet until 2007. Astronomers using Earth-based telescopes had, by the mid–1950s, identified both of Mars's moons, twelve of Jupiter's, nine of Saturn's, five of Uranus's, and two of Neptune's in addition to Earth's own large satellite. Those numbers remained essentially stable until the *Pioneer* and *Voyager* probes reached the outer planets beginning in the mid–1970s.

4. A more detailed understanding of the two worlds did not begin to emerge until flybys and landings by robot probes began in the 1960s.

5. The *word* exobiology was coined (by Joshua Lederberg) in 1960, but the idea of a science of extraterrestrial life existed at least as early as 1953, when the term "astrobiology" was coined to describe it. On the origins and early history of the field, see Richard Sullivan, "Exobiology," *Perspectives in Biology and Medicine 43* (Winter 2000), 277–285.

6. Leibermann, "The *Collier's* and Disney Series." Cornelius Ryan, ed., *Across the Space Frontier* (New York: Viking, 1953).

7. On the shift from Von Braun's gradualist approach to the headlong rush of Mercury, Gemini, and Apollo, see McCurdy, *Space and the American Imagination* and Walter A. McDougall, *The Heavens and the Earth: A Political History of the Space Age* (1985. Baltimore: Johns Hopkins University Press, 1997).

8. Stuhlinger's design used the heat from a nuclear reactor to heat silicone oil, which would then be passed over a turbine before being cooled and re-circulated. The drive itself, using electricity from a generator coupled to the turbine, would force a high-

velocity stream of electrically charged atoms (ions) out the back of the spacecraft by passing them between a pair of electrically charged metal plates or grids. The result, for the spacecraft, would be a slow-and-steady acceleration that could be effortlessly maintained for months at a time.

NASA built its first ion engine in 1960, and flew its first ion-drive spacecraft (the robot probe *Deep Space 1*) in 1998. For details, see the Jet Propulsion Laboratory web page *Deep Space 1: Solar Electric Propulsion FAQ*, accessed 25 September 2007 at http://nmp.nasa.gov/ds1/tech/ionpropfaq.html

9. On the history of Disney animation generally, see: Frank Thomas and Ollie Johnston, *Disney Animation: The Illusion of Life* (New York: Abbeville Press, 1984); John Canemaker, *Walt Disney's Nine Old Men and the Art of Animation* (New York: Hyperion Books, 1984); Bob Thomas, *Walt Disney and the Art of Animation* (New York: Simon and Schuster, 1958) and Leonard Maltin, *The Disney Films*, 4th ed. (New York: Disney Editions, 2000).

10. They have since, of course, become an established feature of American television, with a lineage that reaches from *That Was the Week That Was* in the 1960s to *The Daily Show* and *The Colbert Report* in the early twenty-first century.

11. The best treatment of Von Braun's work on the Disney programs is Mike Wright, "The Disney-Von Braun Collaboration and its Influence on Space Exploration," Marshall Space Flight Center History Office, http://history.msfc.nasa.gov/vonbraun/disney_article.html (accessed 27 September 2007). See also Bob Ward, *Dr. Space: The Life of Wernher von Braun* (Annapolis: Naval Institute Press, 2005), 87–93; and Dennis Piszkiewicz, *Wernher von Braun: The Man Who Sold the Moon* (Westport, CT: Praeger, 2005), 83–91.

12. These later films, though clearly part of the same tradition, exhibit a slightly greater degree of stylization. Their bolder use of color and self-consciously "heroic" figures are somewhat reminiscent of WPA murals from the 1930s.

13. *Disneyland* was originally aired in black-and-white, but except for a few segments the science and technology programs were shot in color.

14. For an alternate reading of the over-cranked segments, see J. P. Telotte, "Disney in Science Fiction Land," *Journal of Popular Film and Television 33* (Spring 2005), pp. 12–21, on pp. 16–17 and 4–5.

15. *Gerald McBoing-Boing* (1951) and the Mister Magoo short *When Magoo Flew* (1953)

16. On the history of secondary-school history teaching and the role of a theoretically undisputed "master narrative," see: Frances FitzGerald, *America Revised* (New York, Vintage, 1980); James Loewen, *Lies My Teacher Told Me: Everything Your American History Textbook Got Wrong* (New York: Simon and Schuster, 1995); and Gary B. Nash, Charlotte Crabtree, and Ross E. Dunn, *History on Trial: Culture Wars and the Teaching of the Past* (New York: Knopf, 1997).

17. It is almost irresistible, in hindsight, to read the sequence as a sly commentary on the doctrine of "mutual assured destruction" promulgated by the Eisenhower administration and its Secretary of State, John Foster Dulles. The studio's history of cultural conservatism suggests, however, makes easy laughs elicited at the expense of the Chinese a more plausible motivation.

18. On this worldview, see Leonard Moseley, *The Disney Version*, 3rd edition (Chicago: Ivan R. Dee, 2007), Neal Gabler, *Walt Disney: The Triumph of the American Imagination* (New York: Knopf, 2006), and especially Watts, *Magic Kingdom*.

19. Disney *did* take up these issues, lightheartedly, in short films like "Motormania," considered elsewhere in this book.

20. Both the United States and the Soviet Union routinely used medium- and long-range ballistic missiles as launch vehicles for satellites and spacecraft. See T. A. Heppenheimer, *Countdown: A History of Spaceflight* (New York: Wiley, 1999), chapters 4 and 5.

21. One of the best-known examples is W. W. Jacobs' 1902 short story "The Monkey's Paw," widely anthologized and available at: http://gaslight.mtroyal.ab.ca/mnkyspaw.htm (accessed 26 September 2007). Spider Robinson's science fiction novel *The Callahan Touch* (New York: Ace Books, 1993) includes a chapter in which the patrons of a bar, collectively granted three wishes, analyze how best to use them *without* falling into such a trap.

22. Christopher Frayling, *Mad, Bad, and Dangerous? The Scientist and the Cinema* (London: Reaktion Books, 2005), 133–166. The subjects of these films included Louis Pasteur, Paul Ehrlich, Marie Curie, Thomas Edison, and Alexander Graham Bell.

23. Gabler, *Walt Disney*, 570–571.

24. Von Drake, voiced by Paul Frees, made a total of eighteen appearances over three seasons. See Don Markstein, "Ludwig Von Drake," *Don Markstein's Toonopedia* (accessed 22 September 2007), http://www.toonopedia.com/vondrake.htm; and Jeremy Sovereign, *The Ludwig Von Drake Authority* (accessed 22 September 2007), http://www.geocities.com/TelevisionCity/Set/4591

Bibliography

Biskind, Peter. *Seeing Is Believing: How Hollywood Taught Us to Stop Worrying and Learn to Love the Fifties*. New York: Pantheon, 1983.

Boyer, Paul. *By the Bomb's Early Light: American Thought and Culture at the Dawn of the Atomic Age*. Chapel Hill: University of North Carolina Press, 1985.

Canemaker, John. *Walt Disney's Nine Old Men and the Art of Animation*. New York: Hyperion Books, 1984.

Cornelius Ryan, editor. *Across the Space Frontier*. New York: Viking, 1953.

Cotter, Bill. *The Wonderful World of Disney Television: A Complete History*. New York: Disney Editions, 1997.

FitzGerald, Frances. *America Revised*. New York, Vintage, 1980.

Frayling, Christopher. *Mad, Bad, and Dangerous? The Scientist and the Cinema*. London: Reaktion Books, 2005.

Gabler, Neal. *Walt Disney: The Triumph of the American Imagination*. New York: Knopf, 2006).

Halberstam, David. *The Fifties*. New York: Villard, 1993.

Heppenheimer, T. A. *Countdown: A History of Spaceflight*. New York: Wiley, 1999.

Jacobs, W. W. "The Monkey's Paw." 1902. http://gaslight.mtroyal.ab.ca/mnkyspaw.htm

LaFollette, Marcel C. *Making Science Our Own: Public Images of Science, 1910–1955/* Chicago: University of Chicago Press, 1990.

Leibermann, Randy. "The *Collier's* and Disney Series." In *Blueprint for Space: Science Fiction to Science Fact*, edited by Frederick I. Ordway, 135–146. Wshington, DC: Smithsonian Institution Press, 1992.

Loewen, James. *Lies My Teacher Told Me: Everything Your American History Textbook Got Wrong*. New York: Simon and Schuster, 1995.

Lucanio, Patrick, and Gary Colville. *Smokin' Rockets: The Romance of Technology in American Film, Radio, and Television, 1945–1962*. Jefferson, NC: McFarland, 2002.

Maltin, Leonard. *The Disney Films*, 4th edition. New York: Disney Editions, 2000.

Markstein, Don. "Ludwig Von Drake," *Don Markstein's Toonopedia*. http://www.toonopedia.com/vondrake.htm

McCurdy, Howard E. *Space and the American Imagination*. Washington, DC: Smithsonian Institution Press, 1997.

McDougall, Walter A. *The Heavens and the Earth: A Political History of the Space Age*. 1985. Baltimore: Johns Hopkins University Press, 1997.

Moseley, Leonard. *The Disney Version*, 3rd edition. Chicago: Ivan R. Dee, 2007.

Nash, Gary B., Charlotte Crabtree, and Ross E. Dunn. *History on Trial: Culture Wars and the Teaching of the Past*. New York: Knopf, 1997.
National Aeronautics and Space Administration. "Deep Space 1: Solar Electric Propulsion FAQ," http://nmp.nasa.gov/ds1/tech/ionpropfaq.html
O'Neill, William L. *American High: The Years of Confidence, 1945–1960*. New York: Free Press, 1986.
Piszkiewicz, Dennis. *Wernher von Braun: The Man Who Sold the Moon*. Westport, CT: Praeger, 2005.
Robinson, Spider. *The Callahan Touch*. New York: Ace Books, 1993.
Scheibach, Michael. *Atomic Narratives and American Youth: Coming of Age with the Atom, 1945–1955*. Jefferson, NC: McFarland, 2003.
Sovereign, Jeremy. *The Ludwig Von Drake Authority* http://www.geocities.com/TelevisionCity/Set/4591
Sullivan, Richard. "Exobiology," *Perspectives in Biology and Medicine 43* (Winter 2000): 277–285.
Telotte, J. P. "Disney in Science Fiction Land," *Journal of Popular Film and Television* 33 (Spring 2005):12–21.
Telotte, J. P. *Disney TV*. Detroit: Wayne State University Press, 2004.
Thomas, Bob. *Walt Disney and the Art of Animation*. New York: Simon and Schuster, 1958.
Thomas, Frank, and Ollie Johnston, *Disney Animation: The Illusion of Life*. New York: Abbeville Press, 1984.
Ward, Bob. *Dr. Space: The Life of Wernher von Braun*. Annapolis, MD: Naval Institute Press, 2005.
Wright, Mike. "The Disney-Von Braun Collaboration and its Influence on Space Exploration," Marshall Space Flight Center History Office. http://history.msfc.nasa.gov/vonbraun/disney_article.html

6

A Nation on Wheels

Films About Cars and Driving, 1948–1970

A. Bowdoin Van Riper

"Keeping on the move," Walt Disney told television audiences in May 1958, "is an old custom ... and a good one." Introducing *Magic Highway USA*, an hour-long episode of the TV anthology series *Disneyland*, he described America as "a nation on wheels," its citizens as people who "like to go places," and the highway its "the most important symbol of progress." That progress, however, was a double-edged sword. The automobile and the expanding national highway system nourished Disney's version of the American dream (and brought millions of visitors to his theme park) but in doing so they corroded the small towns that he idealized.

Disney's vision of the ideal American community—given physical form in the Main Street U.S.A. section of Disneyland (and later Walt Disney World), and recreated on screen in films such as *Pollyanna* (1960) and *Summer Magic* (1963)—was modeled on the small Midwestern towns of his childhood.[1] It featured a slow pace of life and a strong sense of community. Citizens moved by foot, by horse, by bicycle, or perhaps occasionally by open-topped car, and had ample opportunity to interact in the town's parks, cafés, stores, and other public spaces. The modern automobile that emerged in the 1930s—fully enclosed, sound-proofed, and climate-controlled—isolated those inside from pedestrians and fellow motorists alike. Widening roads and rising speeds also played a role, reducing interactions between motorists to a small set of messages communicated by flashing lights or simple gestures.[2] The new cars—more capable, more reliable, and more widely available—encouraged longer journeys, and gradually redrew the built environment of small towns.[3] The filling station on the highway replaced the railway station, the quick-service hamburger joint competed with the local café, and the roadside motel challenged the inn on Main Street.[4] Social atomization replaced the social cohesion that Walt Disney cherished.

Disney Studios produced five films expressly *about* the relationship of automobiles and society between the end of World War II and it its founder's death in 1966: the animated shorts *Motor Mania* (1948), *The Story of Anyburg USA* (1957), *Freewayphobia* (1965) and *Goofy's Freeway Troubles* (1965), and the hour-long live-action documentary *Magic Highway USA* (1958). Ward Kimball, producer-director of *Magic Highway* and one of Disney Studios' fabled "Nine Old Men," added a sixth — the hybrid featurette *Dad, Can I Borrow the Car?*— in 1970.

The films' underlying assumption was that automobiles magnified the effects— good and bad — of their users' behavior. Cars allowed Americans' wanderlust to manifest itself as cross-country family vacations and visits to distant relatives, but they also allowed seemingly minor vices such as impatience and inattention to trigger catastrophic accidents. The films, therefore, explained to viewers how to enjoy the benefits of the automobile while minimizing its costs to society. Their prescription echoed messages in Disney's wartime propaganda films and tales from American history: trust the system, respect authority figures, and (when necessary) subordinate your needs to those of the group. Good driving was, in the Disney universe, an extension of good citizenship.

Trust the System

The decades immediately following the end of World War II marked the peak of Americans' love affair with experts: with people who knew how things worked and presumably, therefore, how to improve them. Heroic doctors (Richard Widmark in *Panic in the Streets*), wise judges (Spencer Tracy in *Judgment at Nuremberg*), brilliant scientists (Sam Jaffe in *The Day the Earth Stood Still*), ingenious engineers (John Archer in *Destination Moon*), and even principled politicians (Henry Fonda in *Fail-Safe*) appeared on screens large and small.[5] The idea that putting "the best and the brightest" in charge would make things better, not worse, still seemed reasonable. That love affair with experts, and consequent faith in the System they controlled, was fully on display in Disney's automobile-themed films. They presented American cars and the American highway system as the products of a long process of progressive improvement, guided by the steady hands of experts. Historical accident, enlightened self-interest, political opportunism, and other random elements barely register in the Disney's streamlined history of the automobile in America. Cars and roads are the way they are because experts made them that way.

Magic Highway USA, a history of American roads, used the construction of the then-new Interstate Highway System as its centerpiece.[6] In one segment, an unnamed traffic engineer — marked as an expert by his glasses, serious manner, and command of factual detail — explains the system's virtues. It will cover all 48 states, he notes, stretching from "coast to coast and border to border without a stoplight" and paying for itself with new revenue generated and lives saved. It represents the triumph of the planned over the accidental, the organized over the *ad hoc*, and "we know" or "we think." The onscreen expert's lack of either a name or an affiliation implies that he is no lone genius, but one small part of a much larger organization of experts

The next long segment of the film shows other experts at work on a new road. Serious-looking urban planners bends over maps and complex charts, identifying traffic problems that make citizens' daily lives more complicated. Equally serious-looking engineers follow, plotting possible routes for a new highway in order to choose the one that represents the greatest good for the greatest number. Detailed plans for the new highway arise, by their hands, from a sea of data: charts, aerial photographs, measurements by surveying crews, and "an avalanche of mathematics." Other representatives of the Authorities describe the new road at public meetings and negotiate with those whose homes will be bought up and demolished to make way for it. Both scenes end with individual citizens signaling their approval with purposeful nods and (in the case of the displaced homeowners) firm handshakes. The climax of the segment shows giant machines rolling along the route of the new highway, shouldering aside Nature and leaving a perfectly designed strip of concrete and asphalt in their wake. The construction scenes suggest godlike powers at work, but the Authorities who wield them are neither cruel nor capricious. They have, *Magic Highway* implies, only the best interests of society in mind.

The Story of Anyburg USA—a seven-minute parable about a town that literally puts the automobile on trial—introduces a small crowd of experts. Called as witnesses, a series of engineers and inventors recite, in rhyming couplets, their contributions to auto safety. "We invented the a safety tire," declare identical twins in lab coats, standing over a comically extreme testing device. "And windshield wipers the law requires," continues a different, baritone voice. I developed safety glass, confides a gray-haired man, swinging a golf club against a car windshield and watching it crack into pieces. There are, the film implies, countless more engineers and inventors just like them.

The most prominent of the film's other experts is introduced as "Cyrus P. Sliderule, of the Department of Highways." He is balding and bespectacled, with the dome-like head (and implied large brain) that connoted "genius" in the visual language of 1950s cartoons. Everyone in *Anyburg* speaks in rhyming couplets, but Sliderule (voice of Thurl Ravenscroft) sings his testimony in an operatic tenor. He explains how his department "labored late from early dawn, leveling hills and straightening byways, building concrete superhighways." The resulting roads, he testifies, were "perfect" in their execution: subdivided by lines, edged with curbs, and posted with "helpful signs" to guide motorists. They were everything, in short, that a motorist could want or need.

Or perhaps not *everything*. The last segment of *Magic Highway USA* is speculative, and contemplates the future of cars and highways. Citing "serious experts," again unnamed, it imagines nuclear-powered tunneling machines, tubular highways through hostile terrain, self-steering cars, and cars with turbine, jet, nuclear, and magnetic-levitation propulsion systems. The experts, will give us a future brighter than we can imagine ... if we will only trust them.

Lawful Authorities

The signs that Cyrus Sliderule describes so proudly in *Anyburg USA* are tangible expressions of the law. They permit certain behaviors on the road, and prohibit others. A different set of laws, meanwhile, limits access to the roads by setting licensing requirements, typically excluding the very old and (especially) the very young. Both types of limits are imposed by on the individual driver by (and for the good of society). Not surprisingly, the Disney films counseled the individual to accept those limits gracefully. The nameless, faceless Authorities who impose traffic laws, and enforce licensing restrictions are treated with the same respect as more traditional authority figures like Yensid the Sorcerer in *Fantasia* (1940), the King of the Forest in *Bambi* (1944), and Pa in *Old Yeller* (1957). They are owed respect and deference, even if their decisions seem arbitrary, and their motives unclear.[7]

No such authority figures appear onscreen in *Anyburg USA*, but — perhaps not surprisingly for a movie set in a *courtroom* — it takes the law very seriously. The defense attorney sets out to exonerate the automobile by demonstrating that bad drivers are the *real* cause of highway mayhem. With the aid of a "magic screen" (like a portable movie screen) he shows three such drivers "as they really are": dangerous criminals whose seemingly "minor" and "harmless" transgressions are akin to armed robbery and murder.

Standing side-by-side against a backdrop that suggests a police line-up, they appear to be ordinary law-abiding citizens. Each is transformed into a violent criminal, however, as the defense attorney describes their violation of the traffic laws. A stooped, slightly built man carrying an umbrella (guilty of "reckless driving, two counts") morphs into a satanic figure with reddish skin, wild eyes, and a crazed expression. His umbrella becomes a submachine gun, and he fires it indiscriminately into the audience. A primly dressed housewife in a pillbox hat (charged with "hit-and-run") undergoes a similar transformation, blazing away with an automatic pistol pulled from her handbag. A short, glowering older man, in a dark suit becomes (for his crime of "speeding") a snarling, black-cloaked anarchist wielding a round black bomb with a lit fuse. "This is not an exaggeration," the lawyer insists, preemptively defending his implied equation of speeding and mass murder. Exaggerated or not, however, the message is clear: The traffic laws demand the same respect that a good citizen pays to The Law in general.

Dad, Can I Borrow The Car? preaches a similar message to its nominally teenaged audience. Its visual style—rapid-fire editing, visual non sequiters, and self-conscious surrealism—owes more to *Laugh-In, The Monkees*, and *Monty Python's Flying Circus* than to *The Wonderful World of Disney*, but its deference to authority reflects the Disney worldview.[8] The original, 20-minute version of *Dad* released to theaters in 1970 follows its unnamed hero on his quest to become a licensed driver, a car owner, and thus—though the film never makes the connection explicit—an adult. Along the way, he encounters a succession of adult authority figures, who offer him guidance and present him with challenges he must overcome. The disembodied voice of a driving simulator keeps up a running stream of advice on safety and proper technique. His father lectures him on the costs he'll be liable for if he borrows the family car. The examiner (and the signs he drives by) keep up a steady stream of instructions during the road test he must pass for his license. A used-car dealer sings the (dubious) praises of the vehicles on his lot, challenging him to find the truth beneath the layers of exaggeration.

The film treats all these encounters as comic, and wraps them in surrealist touches, but treats the adult authority figures with respect. Even as the driving simulator runs out of control, or his on-the-road driving test becomes a blur of quickly passing signs, the intrepid teen hero does his best to keep up and follow the instructions. He sighs to himself—but *only* to himself—about his father's lecture on responsibility. He watches the clownish used-car dealer on television, but contents himself with an expressive "Wow" as he turns off the set. He does not even voice—much less act on—his sense that the Authorities who regulate his access to driving are capricious. *Dad*, for all its superficial surrealism, remains a Disney film at its core, and in its world—far from that of *If* ... (1968), *Easy Rider* (1969), or *M*A*S*H* (1970)—there are no disaffected youth.

Individual and Group

The unseen narrators in *Motor Mania, Freewayphobia*, and *Goofy's Freeway Troubles* are both experts and authority figures. Using Goofy as an onscreen model of bad driving habits, they explain (as experts) why his behavior is dangerous and (as authority figures) admonish the audience to avoid it. Made nearly twenty years apart (the former in 1948 and the latter two in 1965), they belong to different parts of the Disney Studios' output. *Motor Mania*, eight minutes long, stands on its own and has the string-of-gags structure of a typical Disney cartoon short, while *Freewayphobia* and *Goofy's Freeway Troubles*, each fifteen minutes long, are clearly companion pieces, and (when viewed together), have the structure of an illustrated lecture punctuated with visual gags.[9] The three films present a single message, however: The individual driver must be willing to put others before himself, and to rein in his own needs and desires for the good of the group.

All three films are broadly similar, in structure, to the Goofy "How To..." shorts, which began with *The Art of Skiing* in 1941 eventually included nine installments, of which the last was *How to Relax* in 1957. Though not uniformly titled, the "How To" shorts shared a common format: the off-screen voice of a stern, authoritative narrator described the proper technique for doing the activity of the title, while the visuals showed Goofy doing it comically — often spectacularly — wrong.[10]

Motor Mania is primarily concerned with the power of the automobile to encourage — and then to amplify — bad behavior. The reason, it implies, is that cars isolate us from our surroundings. The film opens with a scene of Goofy, dressed in a suit and pince-nez glasses, stepping out the front door of his suburban home and striding purposefully toward the garage. The narrator identifies him as "Mr. Walker," an average citizen of average intelligence steps out of the front door of his suburban home and strides purposefully toward his garage. His actions (tweeting at a small bird, not stepping on an ant, cordially greeting the narrator) mark him as a kindly man, and the narrator speaks of him glowingly. All that changes, however, when Mr. Walker slides behind the wheel of his car. His face darkens, his placid expression turns crazed, and eyes grow wild. "Mr. Walker," the narrator intones, "is charged with an overwhelming sense of power, and his whole personality changes. Abruptly he becomes an uncontrollable monster, a demon driver: Mr. Walker is now Mr. Wheeler, *a motorist.*" The last word is the same grim emphasis that, in a different context, might be reserved for "axe murderer" or "terrorist."[11]

Mr. Wheeler lives up to the narrator's billing. One transgression follows another on his trip into town, which becomes a catalog of bad driving habits. Mr. Wheeler is inattentive when he hits a car, and nearly hits a pedestrian, while backing out of his driveway ... then maliciously precise when he swerves through a puddle in order to splash a passerby. He is a dawdling "road hog" one moment, straddling the centerline and moving well under the speed limit the next ... then fuming at the delay caused by a red light, and lamenting "thirty seconds of my life gone." He swerves and flits between lanes on the freeway ... then single-mindedly smashes his way into a tight parking space at the expense of the cars ahead of and behind him. Of all the bad drivers portrayed in the six Disney automobile films, he is the only one who is not simply self-absorbed or impatient, but deliberately violent and hateful — a poster boy for road rage.

The rampage ends, and the film delivers its message, when Mr. Wheeler climbs out of his car and once again becomes the placid Mr. Walker. Going about his pedestrian business, he finds himself at the mercy of a town full of cars — all of them seemingly driven by clones of his alter ego. He sets a foot in the crosswalk and it is promptly run over. He tries to cross the street again, thinking a waiting driver has waved him on, but is knocked back to the curb again. He steps into the street a third time and, "hunted" by a driver whose hood ornament looks like a gun sight, is knocked back a third time. Several indignities later, he winds up clinging to the upper portion of a lamppost while two anthropomorphized cars snarl and snap at its base like wild dogs. He finds safety, at last, in his own car, having gained (the narrator observes) "a knowledge of how the other fellow feels." To the narrator at least, the lesson is obvious: "Drive safely. Play fair. Give the *other* fellow a break."

Motor Mania thus envisions driving as a series of discrete interactions between individuals. It defines cooperation (and thus good driving) as "giving the other fellow a break" and trusting that you will be given a break in turn. *Freewayphobia* and *Goofy's Freeway Troubles*, on the other hand, envision driving as the banding together of many individuals in pursuit of a common goal. They define cooperation (and thus good driving) as acknowledging and conforming to what the narrator of *Freewayphobia* describes as "certain practical rules and courtesies necessary for mutual protection." Conformity, the narrator insists, is the key to highway safety "Any individual who does not, or will not, recognize this is a menace to everyone."

The balance of *Freewayphobia*, and all of *Goofy's Freeway Troubles* present a taxonomy of such menaces—each given a mock-Latin name, and each personified by Goofy.[12] *Driverius timidicus*, the timid driver, "refuses to adjust to freeway speeds." He drives well below the speed limit, dawdles in the slow lane, and attempts to merge by accelerating from a dead stop at the top of the entrance ramp. *Motoramus fidgetus*, the impatient driver, ceaselessly searches for a chance to get ahead: weaving through traffic, abruptly changing lanes, and riding the bumper of slower drivers ahead of him. *Neglectorus maximus*, the inattentive driver, keeps his attention on everything but the road ahead. He eats, drinks, shaves, reads the newspaper, and holds face-to-face conversations with his passengers—even when they're in the back seat. *Stupidicus ultimus* commits a variety of sins. He fails to maintain his car properly; ignores strange noises, loose parts, and other signs of trouble; and fills his back seat with unsecured objects that become projectiles in the event of a collision or sudden stop.

Each of these drivers personally pays the comically animated price for his transgressions. Goofy is, over the course of the two cartoons, subjected to crashes, explosions, disintegrating cars, and burial in flying cargo from his own back seat and garbage from a truck he has rear-ended. They also cause chain-reaction collisions, each involving a dozen other drivers and implicitly inconveniencing hundreds or thousands more blocking the free flow of traffic. The films refer to such an accident as a "boxcar effect," invoking the image of a string of railroad cars derailing. Goofy's various avatars cause a half-dozen of these catastrophes in the course of the two films, and the narration implies that they—*because* they injure or inconvenience so many others—are far greater transgressions than any single-car accident. Goofy sins, in *Freewayphobia* and *Goofy's Freeway Troubles*, not against fellow motorists as individuals but against the community. The freeway system is efficient, but its efficiency is fragile: The selfish behavior of even a single driver is enough to temporarily bring the flow of traffic to a halt, making life worse for everyone.

Conclusion

Disney's automobile-themed films presented a consistent message that equated good driving—putting the needs of the community ahead of one's own desires—with good citizenship. It was a vision that, despite overtones of socialism, is consistent with Walt Disney's vision of an ideal America, echoing the calls to individual sacrifice made in Disney's wartime propaganda cartoons and paralleling the message of Disney's tales from American history: that national unity must, for the good of all, trump even the most deeply held political commitments.

Unlike the studio's propaganda shorts and the heroic tales from the past, however, Disney's films about driving are imbued with a deep pessimism about the possibility of *achieving* the ideals they promote. Humans are, they seem to imply, naturally selfish and thus naturally bad drivers, determined to pursue their own needs and desires at the expense of other motorists' well-being. All the films except *Dad, Can I Borrow the Car* lecture simultaneously to the characters onscreen and to the audience, but all seem to assume that their messages will have, at best, a temporary effect. *Motor Mania* ends not with the narrator's encouragement to "give the other fellow a break" but with Mr. Wheeler's snarled response: "Ahhh—shut up!" *The Story of Anyburg USA* reports that, after a brief period of politeness following the trial, local drivers reverted to their homicidal ways. *Freewayphobia* and *Goofy's Freeway Troubles* simply assume that terrible drivers—the four species of "menace" that Goofy portrays—will always exist. The apparent goal of the films is not to reform them, but to persuade new drivers—whose habits are not yet formed—not to emulate them. *Dad, Can I Borrow the Car?* meanwhile seems to abandon even *that* small hope, with its teenager's-eye-view of driver education and licensing as surreal and incomprehensible.

Only *Magic Highway USA* offers an unmistakably optimistic view of a better, safer highway system and an end to accidents. Its final segment, describing the highways of the future, shows a family riding from suburb to city in their bubble-canopied, computer-guided car. The father—directing their interactions with the wider world in good 1950s fashion—programs their destination into the dashboard, and the car (in conjunction with computerized highways) does the rest: accelerating, decelerating, and steering while the family chats and plays games.[13] The segment thus reinforces a theme that ran through all Disney's automobile-themed films: better technology makes for a better life. The family of the future is, when they set out on a journey, allowed to express one wish: Where they want to go. All decisions, large and small, about how to get there are made by the computer. In that respect, it takes Disney's view of highway citizenship to its logical extreme: the individual surrendering a (large) measure of their autonomy to the computer system that looks out for the good of the community

Notes

1. See, for example, Neal Gabler, *Walt Disney and the Triumph of the American Imagination* (New York: Random House, 2007), p. 18.
2. Tom Vanderbilt, *Traffic: Why We Drive the Way We Do (And What It Says About Us)* (New York: Knopf, 2008), 19–39.
3. On the intersection of technological change and social change in the case of the automobile, see: James J. Flink, *The Automobile Age* (Cambridge, MA: MIT Press, 1988) and Rudi Volti, *Cars and Culture: The Life Story of a Technology* (Baltimore: Johns Hopkins University Press, 2006). On the culture of cars and driving in America, see: David L. Lewis and Laurence Goldstein, editors, *The Automobile in American Culture* (Ann Arbor: University of Michigan Press, 1983); Cotton Seiler, *A Republic of Drivers: A Cultural History of Automobility in America* (Chicago: University of Chicago Press, 2008); and John Heitmann, *The Automobile in American Life* (Jefferson, NC: McFarland, 2009);
4. On the history of roadside conveniences in the automobile age, see Chester H. Liebs, *Main Street to Miracle Mile: American Roadside Architecture* (Boston: Little, Brown, 1985); John A. Jakle and Keith A. Sculle, *The Gas Station in America* (Baltimore: Johns Hopkins University Press, 1994); John A. Jakle, Keith A. Sculle, and Jefferson S. Rogers, *The Motel in America* (Baltimore: Johns Hopkins University Press, 1996); and John A. Jakle and Keith R. Sculle, *Fast Food: Roadside Restaurants in the Automobile Age* (Baltimore: Johns Hopkins University Press, 2002).
5. Peter Biskind, *Seeing Is Believing: How Hollywood Taught Us to Stop Worrying and Love the Fifties* (1983. New York: Holt, 2000).
6. Dan McNicholl, *The Roads that Built America: The Incredible Story of the U. S. Interstate System* (New York: Sterling, 2006) echoes Disney's pro-highway view and lavish visuals. For a more detailed, balanced treatment see Tom Lewis, *Divided Highways: Building the Interstate Highways, Transforming American Life* (New York: Viking, 1997).
7. Lee Artz, "Animating Hierarchy: Disney and the Globalization of Capitalism," *Global Media Journal* vol. 1, issue 1, article 9 (Spring 2002). Accessed 24 June 2010 at: http://lass.calumet.purdue.edu/cca/gmj/fa02/gmj-fa02-artz.htm
8. Christopher P. Lehman, *American Animated Cartoons of the Vietnam War Era: A Study in Social Commentary in Films and Television Programs, 1961–1973* (Jefferson, NC: McFarland, 2006), 147.
9. Cf. Lehman, who sees (p. 53) the 1965 Goofy cartoons as evidence that Disney was abandoning slapstick humor in its cartoon shorts.
10. The arc of Goofy's career as a character is traced in Flora O'Brien, *Walt Disney's Goofy: The Good Sport* (New York: Macmillan, 1985).
11. On the psychology of driving, see Vanderbilt (cit. n. 2).
12. From 1949 to 1962 Chuck Jones' "Roadrunner" cartoons for Warner Brothers included freeze-frames in which the two principal characters were identified with similar mock-Latin names.
13. On similar visions of future transportation systems, see Joseph J. Corn and Brian Horrigan, eds. *Yesterday's Tomorrows: Past Visions of the American Future* (Baltimore: Johns Hopkins University Press, 1996), 87–108; and Eric Dregni and John Dregni, *Follies of Science: 20th Century Visions of Our Fantastic Future* (Golden, CO: Speck Press, 2006), 13–32.

Bibliography

Artz, Lee. "Animating Hierarchy: Disney and the Globalization of Capitalism," *Global Media Journal* vol. 1, issue 1, article 9 (Spring 2002). http://lass.calumet.purdue.edu/cca/gmj/fa02/gmj-fa02-artz.htm

Biskind, Peter. *Seeing Is Believing: How Hollywood Taught Us to Stop Worrying and Love the Fifties.* 1983. New York: Holt, 2000.

Corn, Joseph J., and Brian Horrigan, eds. *Yesterday's Tomorrows: Past Visions of the American Future.* Baltimore: Johns Hopkins University Press, 1996.

Dregni, Eric, and John Dregni. *Follies of Science: 20th Century Visions of Our Fantastic Future.* Golden, CO: Speck Press, 2006.

Flink, James J. *The Automobile Age.* Cambridge, MA: MIT Press, 1988.

Gabler, Neal. *Walt Disney and the Triumph of the American Imagination.* New York: Random House, 2007.

Heitmann, John. *The Automobile in American Life.* Jefferson, NC: McFarland, 2009.

Jakle, John A., and Keith A. Sculle, *Fast Food: Roadside Restaurants in the Automobile Age.* Baltimore: Johns Hopkins University Press, 2002.

_____ and _____. *The Gas Station in America.* Baltimore: Johns Hopkins University Press, 1994.

_____, _____, and Jefferson S. Rogers, *The Motel in America.* Baltimore: Johns Hopkins University Press, 1996.

Lehman, Christopher P. *American Animated Cartoons of the Vietnam War Era: A Study in Social Commentary in Films and Television Programs, 1961–1973.* Jefferson, NC: McFarland, 2006.

Lewis, David L., and Laurence Goldstein, editors, *The Automobile in American Culture* (Ann Arbor: University of Michigan Press, 1983.

Lewis, Tom. *Divided Highways: Building the Interstate Highways, Transforming American Life.* New York: Viking, 1997.

Liebs, Chester H. *Main Street to Miracle Mile: American Roadside Architecture.* Boston: Little, Brown, 1985.

McNicholl, Dan. *The Roads That Built America: The Incredible Story of the U. S. Interstate System.* New York: Sterling, 2006.

O'Brien, Flora. *Walt Disney's Goofy: The Good Sport.* New York: Macmillan, 1985.

Seiler, Cotton. *A Republic of Drivers: A Cultural History of Automobility in America.* Chicago: University of Chicago Press, 2008.

Vanderbilt, Tom. *Traffic: Why We Drive the Way We Do (And What It Says About Us).* New York: Knopf, 2008.

Volti, Rudi, *Cars and Culture: The Life Story of a Technology.* Baltimore: Johns Hopkins University Press, 2006.

7

"A Journey Through the Wonderland of Mathematics"

Donald in Mathmagic Land

MARTIN F. NORDEN

A door opens, and a mysterious streak of light pierces a huge darkened environment. An animated white pintail duck wearing a beige short-sleeved shirt and matching pith helmet enters the undefined space, casting an enormous shadow as he does so. Carrying a rifle, he looks about warily. "Mighty strange," he says in an immediately recognizable quackish voice.

Strange, indeed. So begins *Donald in Mathmagic Land,* a 27-minute featurette produced by the Disney studio and released in late June 1959. Starring the eponymous Donald Duck, this episodic, Oscar-nominated film combines animated and live-action sequences to introduce its viewers to basic math concepts, a history of mathematical thinking, and the relevance of math to music, art, architecture, nature, sports, board games, and other aspects of everyday life. Supplemented by a similarly titled Dell comic book published a few months later,[1] *Donald in Mathmagic Land* remains one of the Disney studio's best-known educational films.

In a number of respects, *Donald in Mathmagic Land* is a transitional film in the Disney canon. Following in the tradition of the many didactic animated shorts produced by the studio during World War II and the years thereafter, *Donald in Mathmagic Land* was designed as a theatrical film. Initially paired with the feature movie *Darby O'Gill and the Little People* in 1959, it was an instant hit. Nevertheless, it played on the big screen at a time when theatrical short films were in serious decline as a result of the rise of television, and the film itself—running more than three times longer than the traditional Disney short—received only limited exhibition in movie theaters.[2] Fittingly, perhaps, it became the first Disney animated film to be broadcast in color when the company included it in its premiere episode of *Walt Disney's Wonderful World of Color* on NBC-TV in 1961.

Its greatest impact, however, was still to come. Abundant anecdotal evidence suggests that *Donald in Mathmagic Land* enjoyed, and continues to enjoy, considerable success well after its days as a theatrical-featurette-turned-TV-episode. A key achievement in the company's quest to become a major provider of K-12 educational materials during the 1950s and 60s,[3] *Donald in Mathmagic Land* has been a staple of math classrooms from the elementary through collegiate levels for decades. Even today, it is regarded as a mathematics teaching tool virtually without peer.[4]

Since *Donald in Mathmagic Land* depends heavily, but by no means exclusively, on factors that had guided previous Disney productions, and this article examines much-beloved film in light of those precedents. The Disney studio had absorbed many lessons as a result of its experiences creating wartime propaganda and instructional films, and it codified what it learned into a workable set of principles that included: (1) an instantly familiar and popular character to which the studio already owned the rights and who could serve as a stand-in for the audience, (2) a male narrator whose "voice of authority" would make unequivocal statements, (3) a visual style that could facilitate relatively quick and inexpensive production, and (4) the Alice-in-Wonderland idea of placing the lead character in an unfamiliar environment in the hope that the audience will share that character's sense of wonder and discovery. These factors, based on prior Disney successes and failures and abetted by the growing prominence of Disneyland and its emphasis on fabricated lands, strongly guided the making of *Donald in Mathmagic Land* and its comic-book tie-in.[5]

* * *

"The cartoon," said Walt Disney in late 1959, "is a good medium to stimulate interest. It is an ideal medium for teaching and it has always been my hope that we could do something that way. But it would have to be of general interest, yet helpful in teaching. It should be used for opening people's minds and meeting their needs. We have recently explained mathematics in a film and in that way excited public interest in this very important subject. *Donald in Mathmagic Land* stimulated interest in mathematics and turned out very well."[6]

At the time Disney uttered these comments, *Donald in Mathmagic Land* was a recent and highly conspicuous addition to the long line of educational animated films produced by his studio.[7] In retrospect, it is hardly surprising that his company should develop a general-interest mathematics film at that particular historical juncture. In October 1957, the Soviets kicked off the Space Race when they launched the first Sputnik satellite into a low elliptical orbit around the earth. The surprise announcement humiliated the United States, touched off waves of near-panic in some sectors of American society, and considerably increased Cold War tensions. Fearing further setbacks, the federal government mounted an aggressive campaign to promote educational projects that enhanced scientific, technological, and mathematical learning among all levels of American society.[8] The Disney studio, which had already positioned itself as a significant educational force in the fields of science, nature, and technology years before the Sputnik launch, was primed for such an eventuality (indeed, it had anticipated the launch more than a year earlier)[9] and needed no further bidding.

Even if the Sputnik crisis had not occurred, the idea of a mathematics teaching film fit squarely within the studio's educational agenda. Disney himself had long identified arithmetic as a "basic" and argued that its "advancement by means of the motion picture screen will give more people in this world an opportunity to learn" it, in his words.[10] Importantly, his studio already had some experience creating math-themed films. During World War II, it produced two animated shorts—*The New Spirit* (1942) and *The Spirit of '43* (1943)—that deployed its emergent star, Donald Duck, on two of his most difficult missions: to convince wartime audiences of the need for income taxes and, furthermore, to show those audiences how to calculate them. Though the "Spirit" films differed notably from *Donald in Mathmagic Land* in their patriotic and financially pragmatic dimensions, the studio was keenly aware of their major impact on the millions who saw them. The films' success left a deep impression on the studio and helped shape its postwar educational philosophy.[11]

An additional consideration that had bearing on the studio's decision to produce a general-interest mathematics film was the decades-long success of *Mathemagic: Magic, Puzzles and Games with Numbers,* a book written by Royal Vale Heath and originally published by Simon & Schuster in 1933 during the depths of the Great Depression. Heath, a long-time member of the New York Stock Exchange, was an accomplished amateur magician who had accumulated an extensive collection of mathematical games, tricks, and puzzles as a part of his avocation. Impressed by Heath's vast knowledge of recreational mathematics, the president of the Society of American Magicians, Bernard Ernst, persuaded Heath to take all the math tricks he knew and publish them as a book. The result was a limited-edition volume that gained a cult following of sorts during the 1930s. By decade's end, *Mathemagic* was fetching high enough prices at used-book stores to prompt Simon & Schuster to reissue it in 1940 and to lead a rival publisher, Doubleday, to produce a competing book two years later.[12] Sensing correctly that the market for Heath's work remained strong, Dover Publications acquired the rights to *Mathemagic* in 1953 and kept the book in print well into the 2000s. Though the Disney studio did not formally acknowledge Heath or his (by then) widely available book in the credits for *Donald in Mathmagic Land* (and was careful to exclude the "e" in "mathemagic" in the film's title),[13] the enduring popularity of *Mathemagic* assured the studio that there would be high interest in a mathematics film, particularly one that made learning fun.[14]

With general subject matter in hand, the team assembled to create the film — supervising director Hamilton Luske; sequence directors Wolfgang Reitherman, Les Clark, and Joshua Meador; story contributors Milt Banda, Bill Berg, and Heinz Haber; and myriad artists and technicians— began working with narrative and visual strategies that the company's founder had put into play as early as the 1920s. The team members agreed that the central ingredient in those strategies should be an instantly familiar leading character, and for that figure they needed to look no further than the sailor-suited waterfowl that the studio had been cultivating for a quarter-century and that had eclipsed Mickey Mouse in popularity: Donald Fauntleroy Duck,[15] voiced since his initial 1934 appearance by the redoubtable Clarence Nash. The studio had "test-driven" Donald in numerous propaganda and training films during World War II (such as *The New Spirit* and *The Spirit of '43,* noted above) to much acclaim, and, even before the war had ended, it was making plans to use him for general teaching purposes. As a *Look* writer breathlessly observed in April 1945, "Symbolically speaking, a celluloid duck is emerging from World War II as the greatest potential educational force this world has ever known. His name is Donald Duck, and he stands for the international picture language developed and perfected over 25 years by his 43-year-old creator, Walt Disney."[16]

Though Donald had provided the Disney studio with a solid track record of didactic accomplishment from the early 1940s onward, the *Donald in Mathmagic Land* team decided a change was in order and modified this most serviceable character for its new film. Luske and his animators transformed him into a kinder, gentler (if still trouble-prone) soul far removed from the apoplectic, much put-upon Donald that had appeared in countless other Disney shorts. By accident or design, this "new" Donald bore more than a passing resemblance to the much more cooperative "Everyduck" version of Donald that for years had populated the Dell comic books penned by Carl Barks.[17] To enhance their Donald's toned-down qualities— or, at least, not detract from them — Luske and his colleagues jettisoned the bouncy, ironic theme song that had begun many a Donald Duck short ("Who's got the greatest disposition? One guess, that's who!")[18] in favor of an orchestral score as bland as the name of its composer: Norman "Buddy" Baker.

The *Donald in Mathmagic Land* team also needed a character that could serve as a foil to Donald but not remind audiences of Donald's earlier, explosive self. In particular, the team wanted an authority figure whose information-laden utterances would be taken by Donald and audiences alike as the Truth with a capital T. Beginning with its first World War II training film —*Four Methods of Flush Riveting* (1941), a nine-and-a-half-minute animated short produced on behalf of its Burbank neighbor, Lockheed Aircraft — the Disney studio frequently employed voice-over narrators who commented authoritatively on the proceedings depicted in the films. Though the narrator of *Four Methods* was a nonprofessional speaker who offered his comments in a monotone, the studio quickly learned the value of having an unseen speaker, almost always male, in the seat of authority. As Nicholas Sammond has suggested, the studio's experience creating government training films allowed it to develop "a voice of scientific authority" that eventually extended into its postwar educational productions.[19] It might be added that the studio had a very practical reason for keeping the narrator off-screen in at least some of its films; he was one less character that needed to be animated, a consideration that helped the studio contain costs while speeding up the production process.[20] Freed from the laborious, multi-step process of visualizing and animating a major character, the studio could focus instead on turning the narrator into a major vocal presence. Taking its cue from such radio-trained pontificators as Orson Welles and Westbrook van Voorhis (the latter of whom served for years as the *March of Time* newsreel's "Voice of Doom" narrator), the Disney studio turned its voice-over speakers into all-knowing, sagacious, God-like figures. In keeping with the studio's newfound "edutainment" philosophy, the studio often leavened the narrators' pronouncements with doses of ironic humor.

In what may have been a nod to the "spirit" suggested by the titles of *The New Spirit* and *The Spirit of '43,* Luske and his team dubbed the voice of authority in *Donald in Mathmagic Land* "the True Spirit of Adventure," or, as Donald calls him, "Mr. Spirit." Unlike earlier Disney voices of authority, such as those provided by Fred Shields and John McLeish in such quasi-instructional shorts as *How to Play Golf* (1944), *How to Be a Sailor* (1944), and *How to Ride a Horse* (1950), the Spirit frequently engages Donald in conversation and gives him much individualized attention while serving as his guide. For this new type of teacherly narrator, the studio turned to journeyman voice actor Paul Frees, who had worked opposite Clarence Nash in at least one other film (the 1947 animated Disney short *Crazy with the Heat*) and also provided voice-over work for the *Disneyland* television program in 1954. Famed for his versatility and in particular for his imitations of Orson Welles, Frees was a natural for the voice of the Spirit of Adventure. Though Frees and Nash did not receive on-screen credit for their contributions to the film,[21] Frees's biographer, Ben Ohmart, was hardly alone in his opinion that Frees's work as *Donald in Mathmagic Land*'s subdued, patient narrator was among the actor's best vocalizations and helped make the film a classic.[22]

The film's general visual style was another element that the Disney team needed to modify. During the war years, the studio out of economic necessity began pursuing a variety of strategies for producing animated films more simply and efficiently.[23] These strategies, which went well beyond keeping the narrator an off-screen presence in many of its productions, were to have a major impact on the studio's aesthetic values as expressed in its films. The visual style that characterized Disney animation during the 1930s and early 1940s—a lush, heavily detailed realism that featured rounded shapes and subtle gradations of color and lighting—had given way by the 1950s to modernist visualizations that emphasized flatness, angularity, rather blotchy uses of color and lighting, and reduced background detail. Rooted solidly in concerns both economic and pragmatic, this new visual sensibility characterized many animated productions of the time and defined the general "look" of *Donald in Mathmagic Land*.[24]

The film's simplified visual style was complemented by the effects of another cost-cutting measure, one that harkened back to Disney's "Alice" films of the 1920s: a reliance on rather prosaic live-action imagery. To help illustrate the relationship of mathematics to such topics as music, architecture, nature, and sports, Luske and his team included photographic images of such subjects as a jazz band, a concert pianist and orchestra, the Manhattan skyline, a spider web, a honeycomb, various flora and sea fauna, and, most famously, a billiards player who uses the small diamond shapes on the sides of the table to calculate his shots. Some of the film's shots consist of simple zoom-ins and/or include low-level animation (such as the superimposed outlines of a pentagram or the so-termed "golden rectangle," for example), while others— the ones featuring humans— are exceptionally dark and shadowy, perhaps to make them comparable to the animated shots in their relative lack of background detail. Collectively, the live-action images take up a generous amount of screen time; indeed, the billiards sequence, directed by Les Clark, represents about a fifth of the film's overall running time and is its longest narrative unit. Despite their prominence, the images are, virtually without exception, bland and unremarkable.

Before Luske and his associates could gather and edit these images, however, they needed to develop a narrative spine for their film. They quickly settled on the story strategy of injecting a lone protagonist into an unfamiliar world with its own laws and landscapes: in brief, the "Alice-in-Wonderland" narrative as distilled from Lewis Carroll's 1865 novel *Alice's Adventures in Wonderland* and its 1871 sequel, *Through the Looking-Glass, and What Alice Found There*. This fundamental strategy, which allowed Luske and his team to steer *Donald in Mathmagic Land* into decidedly surrealistic terrain, was nothing new at the Disney studio; it had fascinated its founder for decades. In fact, Disney had begun his animation career in 1923 by producing *Alice's Wonderland*, a short film that featured a very young girl named Alice (played by four-year-old Virginia Davis), who after visiting an animation studio goes home, falls asleep, and dreams she has traveled to "Cartoonland." By the time Disney concluded his "Alice" series in 1927 with *Alice in the Big League*, he had produced more than fifty such films, each featuring a live-action young actress interacting with cartoon characters in animated fantasy settings.[25] Though the studio began moving away from the idea of mingling live-action and animation by the start of the sound-film era (only to return to it with its postwar educational films), it did not forget its founder's love of the Carroll material. Among the studio's many animated sound-era shorts, for example, was *Thru the Mirror* (1936), in which Mickey Mouse, voiced by Disney himself, falls asleep while reading a book titled *Alice Through the Looking Glass* and passes through his own looking glass into a Wonderland dominated by troublesome household furnishings and hyperactive playing cards.

The studio had already featured Donald Duck in a short loosely modeled on the Alice-in-Wonderland framework: the Oscar-winning *Der Fuehrer's Face* (1943), one of the studio's most famous pieces of wartime propaganda. In this eight-minute film, Donald inexplicably finds himself in a bizarre environment — a swastika-festooned land populated by strangely proportioned, goose-stepping (and duck-kicking) soldiers— only to discover by film's end that he had been dreaming. The film's original title —*Donald Duck in Nutziland*— left little doubt about the film's thematic kinship to other Disney films inspired by the Carroll works.[26]

The principal film among those productions was of course *Alice in Wonderland,* the studio's 1951 feature-length animated film that borrowed heavily from both Carroll novels.[27] The whimsical, tune-laden production had been a critical and box-office flop, but its failure did not deter the studio from revisiting the narrative premise in the late 1950s. In a move that practically guaranteed a visual and thematic bond between the two films, the studio assigned the *Mathmagic Land* project to a number of senior animators who had brought *Alice in Wonderland* to the screen eight years before. The three men listed as *Donald in Mathmagic Land*'s sequence directors— Wolfgang Reitherman, Les Clark, and Joshua Meador — had all worked on *Alice in Wonderland* as animators, and supervising director Hamilton Luske, a longtime Disney director/animator renowned for his mentoring abilities, was one of *Alice*'s three credited directors.[28] In addition, one of *Mathmagic Land*'s three story contributors, Milt Banta, had helped develop the *Alice* script.

The Alice-in-Wonderland qualities of *Donald in Mathmagic Land* are evident from the very start. Within moments after Donald's unexplained arrival in the number-bedecked *terra incognita*, he follows footprint like numerals on the ground, which the film quickly reveals to be the work of an entity that would be quite at home in Alice's imaginary world: a bird-like, backward-walking, pencil-headed creature. The creature wordlessly challenges Donald to a game of tic-tac-toe. The creature uses its pencil head to make its marks on a crosshatch it etched on the ground, while Donald uses the barrel of his rifle to make his. The creature defeats Donald in mere seconds, prompting the exasperated duck to complain, "What kind of a crazy place is this?" He hops over a waterfall-fed stream that features cascading numbers that divide into smaller numbers when they strike rocks in the stream, and he ends up in an odd forest filled with trees bearing (and baring) roots bent at ninety-degree angles. "Well, whaddaya know! Square roots!" he exclaims. He then encounters a collective creature that exhibits some thematic resemblance to *Alice in Wonderland*'s Cheshire Cat: a circle, a triangle, and a rectangle perched on a tree branch. The geometric figures, each with their own set of legs, coalesce to form a single creature that, like the Cheshire Cat, imparts information from on high to the story's lost and confused protagonist. Unlike the cat, whose grin is the first and last thing the audience sees, the composite creature's mouth appears only after the three animated geometric shapes come together. After the creature recites the value of pi — erroneously, as it turns out — its mouth disappears and it splits back into separate geometric shapes.[29] It's an Alice-in-Wonderland moment, to be sure.

Lest any viewer miss the connection, Donald's "Hello?" that echoes through the bizarre countryside immediately thereafter sets the stage for another reference. The disembodied voice of the True Spirit of Adventure answers the wayward waterfowl and tells him where he is. Donald exclaims, "What's next?" to which the Spirit replies: "A journey through the Wonderland of mathematics."

Donald in Mathmagic Land contains numerous other connections to the studio's *Alice in Wonderland,* the most conspicuous of which occurs when the Spirit, moving to a discussion of mathematics and games, invokes the centuries-old mathematical game of chess. While the Spirit observes that Lewis Carroll, a noted mathematician, used a chessboard for a setting in *Through the Looking-Glass,* Donald finds himself on a large chessboard confronted by various chess pieces taller than he. The Spirit then engages in a bit of gender-bending by transforming Donald into an Alice-like figure. Now wearing a light-blue dress, a white apron, and a headband — the same outfit worn by *Alice in Wonderland*'s title character — a bewigged Donald immediately finds himself in trouble; he's harassed by the red king and the red queen who think he's a lost pawn, and he tries to escape, only to be slowed down and then pursued by a red knight. Still in drag, he is buffeted about the chessboard like a pinball until he does an ungraceful swan dive off the board. He slides along the floor and crashes into the front of a large box, its hinged lid open to reveal what appear to be bakery items and a sign that reads "HURRY EAT ONE." He grabs one, downs it, and, in a very Alice-like development, grows incredibly large incredibly fast. He looks down on the board, and his high-angle perspective allows the filmmakers the opportunity to use simple animated movements to show how chess is played. Though the *Donald in Mathmagic Land* team had cut a number of visual-design corners in the process of producing this film, it did so only minimally here; the similarity of this brief episode's iconography to that of *Alice in Wonderland* is unmistakable.[30]

The Alice-in-Wonderland quality is even more pronounced in *Donald in Mathmagic Land*'s comic-book counterpart, an important tie-in product.[31] Adapted from the film by a Dell team consisting of writer Don R. ("Don Arr") Christensen, penciler Tony Strobl, and inker Steve Steere,[32] the comic book omits the Donald-on-safari and the Donald-in-drag material but includes a framing story that explains Donald's arrival in and eventual departure from Mathmagic Land. At the start of this framing narrative, Donald finds himself at the mercy of his uncle, Scrooge McDuck. We learn that Donald had borrowed a mere 89 cents from Scrooge, but the crafty financier had engineered a loan for his unsuspecting nephew at the eye-popping interest rate of 30 percent. Donald's own nephews Huey, Dewey, and Louie lend him a book titled *Complete Mathematics,* and he works late into the night hoping to come up with a solution. The more he reads, the more frustrated he becomes. "Numbers ... Figures ... Nothing but trouble! I wish mathematics had never been invented!" he exclaims to no one in particular before falling asleep at his desk. His lamentations are answered by a visualized entity calling itself the "Spirit of Mathematics," who leads Donald through a numerical universe far more detailed than, but otherwise similar to, the one depicted in the film. Donald's adventures in Mathmagic Land conclude when a character named Nimble Numbo (imagine Elmer Fudd clad in Mickey Mouse's bright red robe and pointy blue sorcerer's hat from *Fantasia*) reveals a secret to Donald that could help him escape the clutches of his usurious uncle. Armed with this new information, Donald awakens from his dream and tricks Scrooge into agreeing to a variation on the "wheat-and-chessboard" mathematics problem as a means of settling his debt.[33] Prefiguring *Scrooge McDuck and Money,* an educational animated short directed by Hamilton Luske in 1967, this framing story reveals a pragmatic, dollars-and-cents side to math that is completely lacking in the film and, more importantly, provides an Alice-like context for Donald's improbable sojourn.[34]

Given the Disney company's lengthy and ongoing history of cross-promotional activities, it is probably no accident that the Alice-in-Wonderland dimension of *Donald in Mathmagic Land*, in both its film and comic-book incarnations, coincided remarkably well with the philosophy behind a relatively new extrafilmic development in the Disney universe: Disneyland. The Magic Kingdom had opened in Anaheim only four years before the film's debut, and Disney himself saw a distinct parallel between the theme park and the narrative formula that he and his studio had worked with for so many years. "Disneyland is like Alice stepping through the Looking Glass," he said simply, adding that "to step through the portals of Disneyland will be like entering another world."[35] From Disney's perspective, it made sense to encourage audiences to think of the learning process as an adventure that would take them through an unfamiliar land full of marvels. Just as Donald, who initially looks as if he is in the midst of an Adventureland safari, is whisked away to ancient Greece to learn about Pythagoras, pentagrams, and the relationship of mathematics to music, so too would Magic Kingdom visitors be transported to the theme park's various lands and learn from their exhibits and installations. At least, that was the way Disney claimed to have originally envisioned Disneyland: as an educational venue. It is a place, he said, "for people to find happiness and knowledge" and "for teachers and pupils to discover greater ways of understanding and education." Noting further that Disneyland will offer "the wonders of Nature and Man for all to see and understand," Disney observed that his theme park "will remind us and show us how to make these wonders part of our own lives."[36] The perspectives that governed *Donald in Mathmagic Land* hardly differed.

* * *

The factors sketched here — the instantly recognizable lead character, the off-screen voice of authority, the modernist look that combined simplified graphics with fundamental live-action imagery, the general Alice-in-Wonderland narrative — do not tell the full story of *Donald in Mathmagic Land*'s enormous popularity in the classroom.[37] Nevertheless, I do think the studio was well aware of these factors and, with an eye toward the postwar educational-materials market, carefully modified and packaged them into a production that contained far more information than the typical Disney short but at 27 minutes could easily fit within a typical classroom period. Though *Donald in Mathmagic Land* shows its age in a number of areas (particularly in its representations of then-current technologies) and contains some problematic assertions, such as the incorrect pi value, it amply demonstrates the point that the studio had drawn upon past successes and failures in its approach to it. As Disney observed several months after the release of *Donald in Mathmagic Land,* "We learned a great deal during the war years when we were making instruction and technological films in which abstract and obscure things had to be made plain and quickly and exactly applicable to the men in the military services. These explorations and efficiencies of our cartoon medium must [be used] and extended in the entertainment field."[38] *Donald in Mathmagic Land*— a theatrical film that lent itself exceptionally well to the classroom — was very much the product of that way of thinking.

The author presented a slightly different version of this essay at Hampshire College's "Art on the Brain: Exploring the Intersections of the Arts, Neuroscience, and Society" conference, held on June 3–4, 2010, in South Hadley, MA.

Notes

1. The full bibliographic citation for the comic book is *Walt Disney's Donald in Mathmagic Land,* No. 1051, Dell Publishing Co., August 1959.
2. For a sample review, see "Esquire Short with 'Darby' Puts Donald in Math Land," *Dallas Morning News,* 1 August 1959, p. 4. It is possible that the studio envisioned the film all along as something other than a theatrical film and released it to theaters mainly to get Academy-Award recognition.
3. As Richard Schickel has noted, the company was renting 16mm copies of its films to schools as early as 1952 and had become heavily invested in the production of classroom materials such as 35mm filmstrips. See Richard Schickel, *The Disney Version: The Life, Times, Art and Commerce of Walt Disney* (New York: Avon, 1968), 12.

4. For example, see the numerous viewer comments online at Amazon.com's listing of the film.

5. While I have learned to be wary of secondary sources, especially those found online, this chapter has benefited from the collective efforts of the webmasters at DisneyBox.com, an unofficial communication center and forum designed primarily for Chinese fans of Walt Disney and his work. The site contains a stunning number of Walt Disney quotations culled from multiple primary sources. Unfortunately the bibliographic citations are often rather murky, but the quotes strike my historian's eye as authentic. Whenever I cited quotations from this website, I would first state the source as indicated at the site and then follow up with a "reprinted in" reference to the Disney quotes section of DisneyBox.com.

6. Walt Disney, "From the Wisdom of Walt Disney," *Wisdom: The Magazine of Knowledge for Lifetime Learning and Education*, December 1959, 79. Part of this quotation is reprinted in Dave Smith, *Disney A to Z: The Official Encyclopedia*, 3rd ed. (New York: Disney Editions, 2006), p. 198.

7. By the mid–1950s, the Disney studio was turning out educationally oriented animated films in earnest. A rash of films, typically bearing titles beginning with "I'm No Fool" or "You and Your," appeared during this time. They included *I'm No Fool with Fire* (1955), *You and Your Senses of Smell and Taste* (1955), *You and Your Food* (1955), *I'm No Fool with a Bicycle* (1955), *You and Your Five Senses* (1955), *You and Your Sense of Touch* (1955), *I'm No Fool with Fire* (1955), *You the Human Animal* (1955), *You and Your Ears* (1956), *I'm No Fool Having Fun* (1956), *I'm No Fool in Water* (1956), *How to Have an Accident in the Home* (1956), and *I'm No Fool as a Pedestrian* (1956). These films, along with the *People and Places* and *True-Life Adventure* series of films, set the stage for *Donald in Mathmagic Land.*

8. Robert A. Divine, *The Sputnik Challenge: Eisenhower's Response to the Soviet Satellite.* (New York: Oxford University Press, 1993).

9. On Oct. 5, 1957—the day after the first Sputnik's launch—Disney was asked if he was startled by the Soviets' accomplishment. "Not too much," he replied and went on to explain that space expert Wernher von Braun had predicted the event on "Man in Space," a 1955 episode of Disney's *Disneyland* TV show. Disney cited in Larry Wolters, "Wonderful World Was Born in the Chicago Winter of 1901," *Chicago Tribune,* 11 September 1968, B6.

10. Disney cited in *Walt's Files—Byline Stories by Walt Disney,* folder 1; reprinted in <www.disneybox.com/wiki/index.php?title=Disney_Quotes>.

11. "Walt Disney: Great Teacher," *Fortune,* August 1942, 94

12. The book in question is *Mathematics Made Easy* by Henry Thomas. It promised "magic with figures" along with time-saving short cuts and mathematic trickery. Typical newspaper ads for *Mathematics Made Easy* suggested that the book would reveal all sorts of "Startling Feats of 'Mathemagic' YOU Can Do!" See *New York Times,* 1 February 1942, book review section, 32; and *New York Times,* 9 August 1942, book review sect., 24.

13. However, when Donald asks the True Spirit of Adventure where he is, the Spirit, voiced by Paul Frees, adds an extra syllable in his reply: "Math*e*magic Land."

14. Heath became something of a celebrity during the 1940s; he deftly entertained troops with his mathemagical acumen while on the USO circuit during World War II, and in 1947 he dazzled more than a thousand fellow prestidigitators as a featured performer at the Society of American Magicians' convention in Chicago. Heath would seem the perfect "expert" to have consulted on *Donald in Mathmagic Land,* but the studio elected to go instead with Heinz Haber, a UCLA–based physicist who had served as scientific advisor on the "Man in Space" (1955) and "Our Friend the Atom" (1957) episodes of the *Disneyland* television program. Background information on Heath may be found in Philip Brooks, "Notes on Rare Books," *New York Times,* 17 Mar. 1940, 102; "Magical

Days Are Here Again, and No Fooling," *Chicago Tribune,* 30 May 1947, 8; "Royal Vale Heath," *New York Times,* 27 July 1960, 29; and Gloria W. Heath, "Numbers up his Sleeve," *Christian Science Monitor,* 15 Jan. 1981, 22. For reviews of *Mathemagic,* see "New Publication," *Wall Street Journal,* 27 June 1933, 5; Theodore Hall, "No End of Books," *Washington Post,* 3 May 1934, 9; and Lorine Letcher Butler, "Mathematics as a Pastime," *New York Times,* 2 May 1937, sect. 10, 8.

15. Donald's rarely mentioned middle name is visible on his draft notice in the Disney animated short *Donald Gets Drafted* (1942).

16. "Walt Disney—Teacher of Tomorrow," *Look,* 17 April 1945, 23.

17. The studio never quite abandoned the "old" Donald, however. Even the Donald Duck films that immediately preceded and followed *Mathmagic Land*—the instructional shorts *How to Have an Accident in the Home* (1956) and *How to Have an Accident at Work* (1959), developed by other Disney animation teams—featured the highly temperamental Donald that audiences had come to love. For more information about Carl Barks and his important contributions to popular culture, see Thomas Andrae, *Carl Barks and the Disney Comic Book: Unmasking the Myth of Modernity* (Jackson: University Press of Mississippi, 2006).

18. The complete lyrics are as follows: "Who's got the greatest disposition? One guess, that's who! Who never, never starts an argument? Who never shows a bit of temperament? Who's never wrong, but always right? Who'd never dream of starting a fight? Who gets stuck with all the bad luck? No one, but Donald Duck."

19. Nicholas Sammond, *Babes in Tomorrowland: Walt Disney and the Making of the American Child, 1930–1960* (Durham: Duke University Press, 2005), 248.

20. Of course, the Disney studio did not put all of its narrators off-screen. For example, *How to Have an Accident in the Home* and *How to Have an Accident at Work* both feature an animated bird named J. J. Fate, who shares considerable screen time with Donald (though the two never converse). The studio's most famous on-screen narrator was Ludwig von Drake, who first appeared in the television series *Walt Disney's Wonderful World of Color* in September 1961.

21. In a 1977 interview, Nash remembered Walt Disney's reaction upon learning that Nash's carefully hidden identity had been revealed to the public. Said he: "They had a policy in those days that we voices [sic] were not supposed to get any publicity, and somehow or other, my name leaked out. I had nothing to do with it, but he was giving me—he could chew you out. He could do that real well. He can make you feel mighty darn small." Nash cited in Don Peri, *Working with Walt: Interviews with Disney Artists* (Jackson: University Press of Mississippi, 2008), 54.

22. Ben Ohmart, *Welcome, Foolish Mortals: The Life and Voices of Paul Frees* (Albany, GA: BearManor Media, 2004), 93–94. Frees would go on to provide the voice of authority in other Disney productions, most notably as Ludwig von Drake of *Disney's Wonderful World of Color* and the "Ghost Host" of the Haunted Mansion rides at Disneyland and Walt Disney World.

23. The studio itself acknowledged this point in a marvelously transparent statement at the beginning of *Four Methods of Flush Riveting.* A title card reads: "The following film uses a simplified technique developed by the Walt Disney Studio to demonstrate the *quickest & cheapest* method whereby the animation medium can be applied to national defense training" [italics in original text].

24. Disney's "It's a Small World" attraction, featured at the 1964 New York World's Fair before moving to Disneyland in 1966, reflects a similar modernist visual style. The most prominent non–Disney animation examples of this trend are the television productions of William Hanna and Joseph Barbera, including *The Huckleberry Hound Show* (1958–62), *The Flintstones* (1960–66), and *The Yogi Bear Show* (1961–62).

25. For information on the individual "Alice" films, see Graham Webb, *The Animated*

Film Encyclopedia: A Complete Guide to American Shorts, Features, and Sequences, 1900–1979 (Jefferson, NC: McFarland, 2000), 12–17.

26. According to Disney archivist Dave Smith, the studio changed the film's title only because of the popularity of the "Der Fuehrer's Face" song, written by Oliver Wallace. See Smith, 166.

27. This production is not to be confused with the similarly titled live-action sequel directed by Tim Burton and co-produced by the Disney studio in 2010.

28. For information on Luske, see <legends.disney.go.com/legends/detail?key=Ham+Luske>. The individual contributions of these four directors to the film are largely undocumented. Clark, who along with Reitherman was one of Disney's "Nine Old Men of Animation" and had worked on such earlier productions as *Snow White and the Seven Dwarfs* (1937) and *Pinocchio* (1940), stated in a 1978 interview with Don Peri that he directed only the billiard-table sequence; see Peri, 132. Reitherman had a special knack for handling major action scenes, such as key moments from *Fantasia* (1940), *Sleeping Beauty* (1959), and *Pinocchio,* and may well have directed *Mathmagic*'s chess-board sequence, but the specifics of his participation are unknown. For more information on Reitherman, see <legends.disney.go.com/legends/detail?key=Wolfgang+Reitherman>.

29. Voiced by Paul Frees, the collective geometric character states, "Pi is equal to 3.141592653589747, et cetera, et cetera, et cetera." Mathematicians, tending to be a precise lot, have observed that pi's correct value to the same number of decimal places is actually 3.141592653589793.

30. Paul Frees provided the voice for the red king, while Jane Fowler Boyd (who, intriguingly, served as the live-action model for Maleficent in Disney's *Sleeping Beauty* that same year) did the honors for the red queen. See Webb, 125.

31. According to one estimate, Dell's Donald Duck comics sold around three million copies per issue at the height of their popularity in the 1950s; see Larry Kart, "Happy Birthday, Uncle Donald," *Chicago Tribune,* 3 June 1984, M26. It is difficult to say how frequently or in what capacity the *Donald in Mathmagic Land* comic book was used as a supplement for the film — indeed, it is difficult to imagine teachers countenancing comic books of any sort in the classroom, even ones as informative as this one — but Dell did make it available shortly before the start of the 1959–60 school year.

32. Though Carl Barks was the principal artist associated with the comic-book version of Donald Duck, the definitive source on Disney comics—coa.inducks.org — explicitly credits the *Donald in Mathmagic Land* comic book to Christensen, Strobl, and Steere. See <coa.inducks.org/s.php/x/W+OS+1051-01>. For more information on Christensen's involvement in the *Mathmagic Land* comic book, see Mark Evanier, "Notes From Me," POVonline, 16 June 2002 <www.povonline.com/notes/Notes061602.htm>.

33. For a brief discussion of this age-old mathematical problem, see Theoni Pappas, *The Joy of Mathematics: Discovering Mathematics All Around You,* 2nd ed. (San Carlos, CA: Wide World Publishing/Tetra, 1993), 17.

34. Though Scrooge had been a prominent figure in the Dell comic books for years, the Disney studio did not produce any animated films with him in them until 1967 with the aforementioned *Scrooge McDuck and Money.* However, a Scrooge prototype replete with tam, kilts, and thick Scottish burr appears in *The Spirit of '43* as the "Voice of Savings."

35. Disney cited in *Walt's Files — Disneyland Folder*; reprinted in <www.disneybox.com/wiki/index.php?title=Disney_Quotes>.

36. Disney cited in Marty Sklar, *Walt Disney World — Background and Philosophy,* 1967; reprinted in <www.disneybox.com/wiki/index.php?title=Disney_Quotes>.

37. They also do not directly address the issue of commercial encroachment into the classroom. This worthy topic I leave to other researchers.

38. Disney, "From the Wisdom," 77.

Bibliography

Andrae, Thomas. *Carl Barks and the Disney Comic Book: Unmasking the Myth of Modernity.* Jackson: University Press of Mississippi, 2006.

Brooks, Philip. "Notes on Rare Books," *New York Times,* 17 March 1940, 102.

Butler, Lorine Letcher. "Mathematics as a Pastime," *New York Times,* 2 May 1937, sect. 10, 8.

Disney, Walt. "From the Wisdom of Walt Disney." *Wisdom: The Magazine of Knowledge for Lifetime Learning and Education.* December 1959, 79.

_____. "Walt's Files—Disneyland Folder" www.disneybox.com/wiki/index.php?title=Disney_Quotes

Divine, Robert A. *The Sputnik Challenge: Eisenhower's Response to the Soviet Satellite.* New York: Oxford University Press, 1993.

"Esquire Short with 'Darby' Puts Donald in Math Land," *Dallas Morning News,* 1 August 1959, 4.

Evanier, Mark. "Notes From Me," POVonline, 16 June 2002 <www.povonline.com/notes/Notes061602.htm>.

Hall, Theodore. "No End of Books," *Washington Post,* 3 May 1934, 9.

Heath, Gloria W. "Numbers up his Sleeve," *Christian Science Monitor,* 15 January 1981, 22.

"Magical Days Are Here Again, and No Fooling," *Chicago Tribune,* 30 May 1947, 8.

"New Publication," *Wall Street Journal,* 27 June 1933, 5.

Ohmart, Ben. *Welcome, Foolish Mortals: The Life and Voices of Paul Frees.* Albany, GA: BearManor Media, 2004.

Pappas, Theoni. *The Joy of Mathematics: Discovering Mathematics All Around You,* 2nd edition. San Carlos, CA: Wide World Publishing/Tetra, 1993.

Peri, Don. *Working with Walt: Interviews with Disney Artists.* Jackson: University Press of Mississippi, 2008.

"Royal Vale Heath," *New York Times,* 27 July 1960, 29.

Sammond, Nicholas. *Babes in Tomorrowland: Walt Disney and the Making of the American Child, 1930–1960.* Durham: Duke University Press, 2005.

Schickel, Richard. *The Disney Version: The Life, Times, Art and Commerce of Walt Disney.* New York: Avon, 1968.

Sklar, Marty. *Walt Disney World—Background and Philosophy.* 1967.

Smith, Dave. *Disney A to Z: The Official Encyclopedia,* 3rd edition. New York: Disney Editions, 2006.

"Walt Disney—Teacher of Tomorrow," *Look,* 17 April 1945, 23.

"Walt Disney: Great Teacher," *Fortune,* August 1942, 94.

Walt Disney's Donald in Mathmagic Land, No. 1051, Dell Publishing Co., August 1959.

Webb, Graham. *The Animated Film Encyclopedia: A Complete Guide to American Shorts, Features, and Sequences, 1900–1979.* Jefferson, NC: McFarland, 2000.

Wolters, Larry. "Wonderful World Was Born in the Chicago Winter of 1901," *Chicago Tribune,* 11 September 1968, B6.

8

Paging Dr. Disney

Health Education Films, 1922–1973

Bob Cruz, Jr.

Films promoting health education were first produced during World War I with the object of raising soldiers' awareness of malaria and venereal disease. They were intended as adjuncts to, or replacements for, lectures by medical officers, and the stern, voice-of-authority tone associated with health education films ever since reflects those origins. The use of film as a health-education tool expanded after the war. In 1922, a U.S. study on the effectiveness of film in public venereal disease campaigns identified two goals: to "increase popular knowledge," and to "arouse an emotional attitude in the public which will ... lead to significant changes in behavior."[1] These can be presumed to be the goal of *any* health education film, the emphasis on changing viewer behavior making such films unique among educational films. The Disney studio's contributions to the genre, though not it's best known work or even its best known educational films, covered a wide range of topics. It touched on familiar public health subjects with films such as *Winged Scourge* (1943, about malaria) and *VD Attack Plan* (1973, about venereal disease), and ventured into unexplored territory, with *The Story of Menstruation* (1946) and *Defense Against Invasion* (1943).

The public-health that Disney and his studio produced between 1922 and 1973, though varied in topic, share three key elements that set them apart from the better-known parts of the Disney canon. First, unlike the bulk of Disney's other peacetime ventures into "edutainment," most were never intended for theatrical release or television broadcast. They were, rather, designed for institutional use: meant to be screened in classrooms and meeting halls for audiences whose attendance was, if not compulsory, then at least not wholly voluntary. Second, they were usually produced in partnership with the government or a business entity, as a means of generating income during periods of limited cash flow at the Studio. They thus document the rare instances where the Studio had to yield ultimate control to a higher authority (which is why so many have fallen into public domain). Finally, these films were always conceived with specific demographics in mind: members of the Latin American working class, American school-age children, and so forth. Despite these intentions and limitations, however, these films invariably reflect the perspective — white, American, and middle-class — that Walt Disney and his creative team brought to virtually every film the studio produced.

Disney and the "Decay" of the American Midwest

The earliest Disney films associated with health focus on dental hygiene, *Tommy Tucker's Tooth* (1922) and *Clara Cleans Her Teeth* (1926). *Tommy* was produced in Kansas City, Missouri, where Walt Disney had started out as an animator. His studio, Laugh-O-Grams, Inc., started out making modern versions of *Little Red Riding Hood* and *Cinderella*, but the bankruptcy of the buyer for these films meant the fledgling company had no income. By late 1922, Disney had become so destitute that a local dentist, Dr. Thomas B. McCrum, after compassionately paying Disney's shoe repair bill, offered him $500 to produce a live-action film about dental health,[2] which resulted in *Tommy Tucker's Tooth.* Disney moved to Los Angeles in 1923 and found success there with his "Alice" comedies (featuring a live-action child, Alice, in a world of animated animals), but by 1926, while the name "Disney" had become fairly recognizable, a new contract with his distributor resulted in delayed payments and limited cash flow. Disney then produced a second film for Dr. McCrum, *Clara Cleans Her Teeth*, for an undisclosed amount (Disney saving money by casting his niece, Marjorie Sewell Davis, as Clara[3]). *Tommy* was distributed to the Missouri school system,[4] and while no such information is known for *Clara,* it presumably shared the same fate since available records indicate it lacks a copyright.[5] The films' title cards are telling. *Tommy*'s lists McCrum's name below the title simply as "Thos. B. McCrum DDS," while Disney's is absent. The title card for *Clara* lists credit to the "Walt Disney Studio" *below* the title; meanwhile, *above* the title, McCrum is credited as the presenter, his name in upper-case letters. The target audience for these films is white American middle-class schoolchildren, and both are live-action narratives (cheaper than animation), set in the sunny environs of a typical American suburb of the 1920s. However, in this halcyon landscape, as depicted in both films, deviations from the social norm — such as poor-looking teeth — invite disdain. *Tommy* opens up with small school-age children sitting around a female teacher who tells them the "true story" of two pre-teen boys: Tommy Tucker and Jimmie Jones. Tommy takes care of himself and brushes his teeth; Jimmie doesn't brush because he believes it's "only for girls." The teacher then cites three reasons for brushing: to avoid toothaches, to maintain better health overall, and because "You will be better looking." When both boys apply for the same job in an office (what the job is or what the company does is never explained), Tommy is hired while Jimmie is told by the employer that "Tommy's neat appearance and good teeth show that he takes pride in himself." Jimmie promptly visits a dentist (the actual visit is not shown), then revisits the potential employer, who, impressed by Jimmie's makeover, rewards him with a job alongside Tommy. Subsequently, there is a demonstration of the proper method of brushing teeth, using a large toothbrush and an enlarged set of teeth and gums. The film ends with Jimmie brushing, followed by the words "KEEP YOUR TEETH CLEAN."

Clara, meanwhile, opens with the title character—a grade-school-age girl—making friends with a male playmate on her first day of school, as the entire class enjoys a snack of crackers and milk. Clara, however, because her teeth are presumably rotten and painful, downs her food without chewing it. Later, while the rest of the class brushes their teeth, Clara admits to her male playmate that she never bothers to brush. The other schoolchildren soon notice how her front teeth appear to be broken, prompting them to ridicule her as "Snaggle Tooth Susan" while openly declaring they will not play with her. That night, while Clara is asleep, she is visited by an animated trio—a toothbrush, a rinsing mug and a set of pliers—the last of whom delivers a stern ultimatum: that Clara's teeth must either be filled or else extracted. The dream scares Clara into going to the dentist (her presumably extensive dental work is only alluded to by a title card which reads "After several visits to the dentist—"—after which she is seen exiting the dentist's office, smiling). Subsequently, she wins back all of her friends.

Animation in both films is sparse. In addition to the aforementioned trio in *Clara*, in *Tommy* depicts the cause of a toothache as spoiling leftover food which invokes mallet-wielding, antennae-bearing "acid demons" who repeatedly assail the tooth until the nerve is painfully exposed. And when Jimmie himself develops a toothache, animated lightning bolts radiate from his jaw. There is also animation recycled from the Laugh-O-Gram *Puss in Boots*: winged alarm clocks flutter across the screen, in *Tommy*'s case, to bridge the passage of time during Jimmie's makeover. *Tommy*, having preceded *Clara*, is more explanatory about basic dental hygiene: the correct method to brush one's teeth is shown, while a cavity is likened to a hole in a sock that only gets bigger if not darned. *Tommy*, however, also implies that poor dental hygiene leads to poor bodily health, by having a gym instructor remark to Jimmie that he seems underweight compared to Tommy (who is noticeably portly). And the condition of Jimmie's teeth is confusing: he sports a buck tooth that disappears after his makeover, but how it got fixed is never explained.

The actual message of both films, however, emanates straight from the George Babbitt school of health education: it is important to be well-thought-of, and that such respect is not possible without conforming to social norms. In *Tommy*, to visually emphasize Jimmie's ignorance of dental hygiene, in addition to his buck tooth, his hair is noticeably disheveled and his clothes baggy compared to Tommy, whose combed hair and necktie are in place from the start. In *Clara*, the film's closing sequence illustrates the rewards of middle-class conformity: Clara smiles as she and her schoolmates all brush together. Of significance is the fact that the outcomes differ according to gender. For Jimmie, the payoff is economic: he is rewarded with a job. Meanwhile, Clara benefits socially: she is content to win the respect of her male classmate. The "good vs. bad behavior" premise of *Tommy Tucker*, already a common theme in anti-venereal disease and anti-liquor films of the time, would resurface in later Disney health films. McCrum certainly was the expert on dental health, but the fact that both films use "bandwagon" advertising (e.g., presenting social acceptance as the real impetus for proper dental hygiene) suggests that Disney, a former employee of the Kansas City Ad Company, carefully shaped and refined the narratives.

Blobs and Parasites Fight the Nazis

The success of Mickey Mouse resulted in Disney and his studio releasing the first animated feature, *Snow White and the Seven Dwarfs* (1938), a nearly one-and-half million dollar investment which grossed $8.5 million in its initial release.[6] But soon the loss of the European market due to war, an employee strike and the commercial failures of *Pinocchio* and *Fantasia* placed the studio in dubious financial straits. Consequently, in 1941, Disney went back to making educational films, the first of which were war bond commercials for the National Film Board of Canada, using the Three Little Pigs and the Seven Dwarfs. Later, the Army and the Navy turned to Disney for training and instructional films (among them *A Few Quick Words #7*, a film on venereal disease now presumed lost). Eventually, through the efforts of Studio Vice-President and legal advisor Gunther Lessing, Disney entered into a partnership with the Coordinator of Inter-American Affairs (CIAA), a U.S. agency set up under Nelson Rockefeller to monitor Axis presence in South America.[7] After making a goodwill tour of South America for the CIAA (which resulted in the features *Saludos Amigos*, 1942, and *The Three Caballeros*, 1943), Disney offered to increase his involvement (and revenue) by making films to support the agency's health- and educational-related activities in Latin America.

To demonstrate his studio's capabilities, Disney produced three films, the first of which was *The Winged Scourge* (1943), a ten-minute short focusing on the anopheles mosquito and malaria (a common subject during the war[8]). The film is an odd mix of drama and whimsy. Dark-hued graphics dramatize the facts of malaria infection: a color-coded world map identifies regions where the disease is problematic; transmission is graphically illustrated as a mosquito goes from host to host, spreading the individual malaria parasites via the infected human blood in its proboscis; and, finally, the debilitating effect to humans are shown which inevitably includes death. In one particularly dramatic graphic, a gigantic mosquito stands over a farmer's homestead, its proboscis plunging through the roof. When the film presents various methods of prevention and eradication, however, it switches moods. The Seven Dwarfs from *Snow White* take center stage to demonstrate the various corrective measures, accompanied by a brighter color scheme, upbeat music (from *Snow White*'s score) and a change in the presentational scale of the mosquito (it is the size of a housefly compared to the onscreen Dwarfs, thus making it seem less menacing).

Winged Scourge, however, despite oversight by the CIAA,[9] appears to have been made with no thought to its intended foreign audience, instead featuring imagery that was more familiar to white middle-class Americans of the time. The farmer who eventually succumbs to malaria, for example, is portrayed as a white middle-aged male who, in healthier times, oversees his rolling productive acres, tobacco pipe in hand, from the comfort of a rocking chair on the steps of his clapboard home. Although Disney cautioned the story crew to avoid indulging in gags that would dilute the seriousness of the film's message.[10] other aspects of the film thwart information delivery. For instance, the film starts off with mosquito pictured on a "Wanted" poster — a device familiar to American movie audiences but problematic in this context (even if translated into Spanish or Portuguese) because illiteracy rates at the time in many Latin American countries exceeded fifty percent.[11] Later in *Winged Scourge,* visuals are presented — enlargements of mosquito larva as well as of the malaria parasite itself — which would confuse those unfamiliar with microscopes. The film was received favorably overseas in English-speaking countries like Australia, with the CIAA reporting that by mid–1945 the film had been shown to 1,109,186 people in Central and South America via "outdoor showings where two, three and four thousand people are present."[12] Later, however, Latin American educators found fault with it, criticizing how the farmer in the film represented more a malaria-savvy, wealthy landowner than the "underprivileged masses who, through their ignorance and utter destitution, fell prey to the scourge."[13]

Disney's second film for the CIAA, *Water — Friend or Enemy* (1943) features "Water" speaking on its own behalf, explaining how it is used by humans, whether as a drinking source or a means of waste disposal. The humans this time are brown-complexioned individuals (although their faces remain obscured); after drinking contaminated water (colored red, with skulls appearing to indicate its toxic nature), however, they succumb to the diseases it carries (later identified as typhoid, cholera and dysentery). The emphasis of the film is on how to protect a water source from contamination (such as lining a well with cement), with specific mention of how outhouses must be well-distanced from water sources. The film ends with the assurance that, if such procedures are followed, "Water" will remain a friend. Unfortunately, for all its attempts to portray indigenous Latin Americans, *Water*'s depictions of rural life emanate from the American Midwest experience: a family eats at a table which has place settings, tumblers and a centerpiece; the water wells shown all appear to serve a single household rather than an entire village. Also, the water collection devices shown seem extravagant for rural Latin America, requiring substantial amounts of building materials (namely cement and piping), as well as a rudimentary knowledge of engineering skills. Some of the visual information is confusing: water gets contaminated when used to flush human refuse, but not when used to bathe children or wash clothes. Completely out-of-place is the film's closing recommendation that the viewer have water tested at "your local Health Department."

Eventually, such culturally-skewed representation reached its breaking point in the third and last film of Disney's "demo" films, *Defense Against Invasion* (1943), deemed by the CIAA something that "would go way over the heads of the Latin American people," and subsequently never approved.[14] The reasons are obvious: *Defense Against Invasion* uses visual metaphors that presume a high degree of familiarity with human biology, focusing as it does on the immune system and the importance of vaccination. The film starts off with a live-action segment wherein four boys—in the style of "Our Gang" (replete with one portly member, one African-American member, and a scraggly mutt)—visit the doctor to get vaccinated. There is no dialogue; instead a narrator speaks for all the characters, even when the film switches to animation. Once the doctor presents a conventional medical "cutaway" diagram of a male torso, the interior of the human body is visually likened to a "modern city" along the lines of Lang's *Metropolis*, rife with factories and roadways, and populated by millions of identically-rendered anthropomorphized red-blood cells. Pathogens—drawn as black, four-tentacled blobs—subsequently threaten this happy state. A war ensues, the blood cells fire artillery at the invaders, but, ultimately, the black pathogens overwhelm the city, everything gets covered in black ooze, and (in the film's only somber moment) the infected human succumbs. The film then goes on to explain how vaccination benefits the immune system: harmlessly mimicking lethal pathogens and fooling the blood cells into stocking up on defenses so that, when genuinely potent pathogens finally do invade, the blood cells have enough resistance to vanquish them.

Obviously, American middle-class audiences of the time would have had no problem understanding this metaphoric premise, as evidenced by the fact that the young boys in the film know enough medical science to understand how the doctor's story relates to their bodies (although the information is wrong: antibodies are produced by white blood cells, not the red ones.) But for rural illiterate adult Latin Americans, such medical knowledge would have been lacking, thus preventing the images from being understood as a metaphor. The depiction of the body's "city" as a gleaming technocracy would have been somewhat confounding. Ironically, at the end of the "city" sequence the dead victim is represented by a coffin with two candles burning atop it, and a crucifix on the wall behind—a very specific, presumably conscious, nod to the film's intended, overwhelmingly Catholic audience.)

Fortunately, in 1943, two Disney employees assigned to the CIAA project, Bill Cottrell and Jack Cutting, decided to gain a better understanding of their target audience. First, they traveled to Central America and met with local doctors, concluding that educational aids "on personal hygiene and nutrition would be among the most valuable items of education for large masses of people."[15] Later that same year, Cottrell and Cutting held the "Seminar on Visual Education," which invited Latin American educators to the Disney Studio to meet and confer with the staffs of the Disney Studio and the CIAA.[16] Feedback from the other side of the cultural divide noted many disconnects. In addition to the previously-cited criticism of *The Winged Scourge*, *Water—Friend or Enemy* was faulted for emphasizing where to locate outhouses when, in fact, 80 percent of rural Latin Americans had no such facilities.[17] *Water*'s use of red to indicate contaminated water was also a major cultural misfire: red, the Disney staff was told, connotes "life and joy" to Latin Americans, while contaminated water is usually thought of as being black ("*aguas negras*").[18]

Out of such discussion came "Health for Americas," a series of films that were substantially more culturally aware. These films entertained less but educated at a more appropriate level for its Third World audience. In *Tuberculosis* (1945) and *Cleanliness Brings Health* (1945), for instance, emphasis is on the human behaviors that affect disease transmission (preparation of food, washing of hands, etc), rather than on how bacteria work. *Cleanliness* also re-deploys the "good vs. bad hygiene" premise of *Tommy Tucker's Tooth*, by comparing the lifestyle habits of two Latin American families. *Infant Care*, on the other hand, simply focuses on the "proper" way to feed an infant. *Hookworm* explains the workings of yet another parasite, its central human figure "Careless Charlie" ("Ramon" in the Spanish-language version) drawn to appear more like a conventional Disney "character." (Names were changed in the Spanish and Portuguese versions, but the rest of the foreign language tracks were simply translations of the original English script.) Additionally, these films display a comic strip garishness ordered by Walt Disney himself, who felt that the boldness of the imagery would counter the fact these films would be shown in 16mm, poorly projected,[19] usually from flatbed truck onto a hanging bedsheet.[20]

Both Disney and the CIAA carefully monitored production. In one instance, after the CIAA nixed the showing of a high chair in *Infant Care* (1945), Walt Disney discovered an "albino baby" that had somehow made its way into the closing scenes and ordered it repainted.[21] Instances of White American middle-class superiority still persisted, however. In *Planning for Good Eating*, the narrator disdains a family's habit of subsisting on a diet of corn and beans (which *are* nutritious, and the traditional mainstay of many diets in Mexico and Central America), and they are shown as being miserable due to their limited fare. Later, portly Charlie tries to measure himself up to a portrait of a tall, athletic, angularly-profiled European male, but is told his poor condition is due to his limited diet. At times, the advice seems out-of-touch. *Cleanliness Brings Health*, for instance, recommends using lots of soap when washing everything from bodies to clothes, as if soap and detergent are as readily available in rural Latin America as they are in an American supermarket. And there is the continuing implication of the benefits of a Protestant work ethic. In *The Human Body*, for instance, the narrator tells the film's strapping Latino farm worker (whose shirt gets ripped off by the hand of his animator for exhibition purposes) "An industrious man like you deserves a nice house to live in." *Body* also presents the issue of good health in materialistic terms, citing it as the "the most valuable possession you have" when compared to a house and livestock, while emphasizing how other things are easily replaceable (through hard work of course), a perspective not necessarily familiar to the impoverished. The net effect of all this ultimately yields what others have since described as a "repetitive and paternalistic discourse."[22]

Eventually, the CIAA partnership fell apart. The production of a companion series, "Reading for the Americas," intended to promote literacy while still discussing health, led to heated clashes between educators. The criticism of one educator made its way to the Mexican press: "...the truth is many illiterates do not eat well, not because they may not know how ... but because they can't, they are poor."[23] In late 1945, the CIAA terminated its partnership with Disney.

Murder of an Anatomy

Beginning in 1945, Disney expanded his client base for educational films to include corporations such as the Johnson and Johnson, General Motors, and International Cellucotton Company—whose film *The Story of Menstruation* (1946) has since become infamous for its depiction (or, rather, lack of depiction) of female sexual anatomy. As with any educational piece on the topic, the film first explains the biological facts of the process, then advises the viewer on how to personally address it. *Menstruation* opens with pastel-colored flowers (reused from *Fantasia*'s "Nutcracker Suite" segment) drifting into a room, accompanied by a lullaby-like blend of strings that segues into an oboe solo. The camera pans over to a plush, pink and white-colored bassinette, where a baby lies sleeping. The female narrator's calm, reassuring tones proceed to explain how "Mother Nature" works when it comes to growing up. When the baby awakens, it smiles into the camera, whereupon it freezes into position and its body is shown in silhouette; subsequently, the pituitary gland is identified and its role explained, with diagrams then presented to illustrate how the burgeoning female uterine tract and its ovaries function. The rest of the film advises the viewer on the care and monitoring of oneself during the menstrual cycle, eventually referring them to the sponsor's accompanying booklet "Very Personally Yours" for more information. The film's closing iterates the notion of growing up, although implicit this time around is an increased awareness of what it means to be female (e.g., the female infant who is shown maturing into a woman subsequently becomes a mother and smiles at her own female infant). The film depersonalizes, however, what it presents as a very personal process. Females of various ages and body types are shown throughout the film, yet none have names. Even the female narrator remains anonymous. None of the figures speak. With the exception of the mother and child at film's end, they do not even acknowledge each other, even when sharing the same frame.

The film gives the distinct impression of female disempowerment. Phrases such as "as a girl grows up ... her body is obeying the orders issued by the pituitary gland" and "the ovary ... tells the cells in the uterus to multiply and fill with blood" convey a sense that the female body is at the mercy of biological processes. In many instances, the featured females remain motionless while the things around or within them move. When it comes to visualizing the cyclic nature of menstruation, a girl with braids appears center screen, wearing a pinafore-like dress; subsequently, under her, a clockface appears marked off with names of the months, its shadowy hand ticking away successive menstrual periods by the month—yet the girl herself remains still. In another instance, hormonal flow is shown as a series of arrows descending in military-like fashion from pituitary down to the ovaries, while the female figure that contains them stays rigid. And while certainly "cutaway" representations of sexual anatomy at the time were deliberately abstract, Disney's visual approach to the female uterine tract seems more akin to what the Studio employed when identifying hardware in *Four Methods of Flush Riveting* for the U.S. military, complete with labels in the same sans-serif font. Even more abstract is the side-view diagram which illustrates how the uterus lies between the bladder and the rectum: respectively, they have been stylized to resemble a segment of garden hose and two upended golf clubs. Thus, in what is perhaps one of the greatest ironies in the history of the animated film, the very studio which prided itself on lifelike-animation (i.e., the bare-breasted centaurettes in *Fantasia*, as well as the hyperrealism of *Bambi*) avoided it when it came to ovaries and fallopian tubes.

Ultimately, *Menstruation*'s view of femininity is clinical and distanced, thus reflecting the all-male perspective of its production team. The cold expertise of the film's consulting gynecologist Dr. Mason Hohn fails to mask the obvious discomfort of Disney's all-male animation staff with the subject. Whenever the unclothed female body is called upon to frame inner anatomy, only its silhouette is presented—indicating, perhaps, a feeling on the part of the male heterosexual animators that *any* detail on the female body would somehow sexualize it (previously, however, they had had no such qualms when it came to the unclothed male figures in the "Health for the Americas" films, in particular the aforementioned shirtless male in *The Human Body*, who is actually complimented by the narrator on his muscles). And, in what amounts to a startling complement to the misrepresented immunity-fighting cells in *Defense Against Invasion*, the blood in *Menstruation* is white! Such a deliberate choice invites all sorts of speculation. Did the animators feel the color red would give the impression of injury? Were they afraid that flowing red liquid would raise questions about leakage and the staining of clothes? (Perhaps this explains the lack of inclusion of the sponsor's product — sanitary napkins— along with instructions on their use.) Despite the use of a female narrator, the abstract representation of the subject yields the distinct impression of information emanating from someone with no personal stake in the matter. The relationship between menstruation and babies is never made clear, leaving the potential for some young girls to presume that eggs could develop on their own). Musical chords bookend the film, but in-between, there is no music, indeed no sound other than the narrator's voice, thus creating a somber mood, devoid of all emotion.

Credits are unavailable for this film; to date, no Disney employee has admitted to working on it. Whether American Cotton approached Disney first — or vice-versa — is also unknown. It is noteworthy, however, that, at the time of *Menstruation*'s production, Walt Disney's daughters, Diane and Sharon, were, respectively, twelve and ten years old. This may be the true genesis of the film, as well as better explain its sterile, abstracted view of female sexuality. The film had a long, extended shelf life. As late as 1969, it was still being shown to pre-pubescent female audiences (with the stipulation that the subject not be "discussed with the boys"[24]).

In 1951, as if to send the pendulum of gender swinging the other way, Disney and Cellucotton produced another film, *How to Catch a Cold*, a promotional for Kleenex tissues. The storyline features the character of the "Common Man" learning about the care and prevention of the common cold from his anthropomorphized conscience — an bespectacled male imp named "Common Sense." The Common Man lives in tract housing in the suburbs (with a wife who has breakfast waiting for him), sports a business suit, commutes by subway to his office, and works at a desk in an office filled with other white males just like him. He also square-dances and golfs (despite rain) for recreation. Eventually, he comes down with a cold and ends up in bed. Meanwhile, Common Sense lectures him about cold germs, using a blackboard and animated chalk drawings to show how germs spread, then, later, using the analogy of a football game which pits the Common Man's health against the common cold. The film ends with the man understanding the need to remain in bed, and a shot of his hand grabbing many tissues from a Kleenex box. Presumably because of its innocuous nature, *Cold* was released theatrically; consequently, it has a rich palette, a musical score throughout, and full animation (including cold germs made of red

"Disney Dust"). Both characters are voiced by Bill Thompson, a well-known industry talent, who also voiced the White Rabbit in *Alice in Wonderland* that same year. In contrast to *The Story of Menstruation*, *Cold* reeks of white male empowerment: the Common Man's wife and son (both drawn less-detailed than him) yield to his authority (his wife has breakfast waiting on the table, his son loses his toy gun when the "pop" of its cork wakes his napping father, who then breaks it in two). A driving Protestant work ethic even compels him to go to work despite his being sick. Of course, this was the audience that Disney and his staff knew best, right down to the Common Man's blue silk pajamas. Unlike the Latin American men in the CIAA films who were constantly being nudged to become more active for health's sake, the Common Man *gets ill* because of *over*activity. And unlike the young girls in *Menstruation* who were advised to limit exertion, the Common Man pushes on in the face of physical and environmental adversity. A comic snapshot of the post-war White American middle class male, *Cold* was the last of Walt Disney's corporate co-productions.

Safety First, VD Last

In the mid–1950s, Disney produced two series on health and safety education for television broadcast on the *Mickey Mouse Club* show: *You the Human Animal* and *I'm No Fool*, both hosted by Jiminy Cricket (sporting less detail than in *Pinocchio*, and drawn with thick black lines), each with its own theme song sung by Jiminy. Episodes were fully-animated and ran 8–10 minutes long. *You* was a pleasantly informative, science-based series, presenting information on the anatomy and physiology of human organs connected to the five senses (i.e., the eye, the ear, etc). *I'm No Fool* re-used the blackboard-and-chalk-drawings technique of *How to Catch a Cold* to teach lessons on safety, with Jiminy cast in for the role played by Common Sense (an appropriate choice given Jiminy's original role as Pinocchio's conscience). *Fool* also re-deployed the "good vs. bad behavior" premise of *Tommy Tucker's Tooth.* Jiminy would first present a humorous historical review of an activity such as bicycling. Then the unsafe and safe ways of how to do the same activity were presented, pitting the goofily-drawn "Fool" (who appeared to be a teenage boy) against the character which represented the viewer (almost always a small boy). The humor seems deliberately low-key (e.g., bad things would happen to the Fool, but not to point of being ridiculously violent), presumably so that it would not distract from the main message of safety. The pedagogic tone of *Fool* was further enhanced by always featuring Jiminy among stacks of books or in a schoolroom.

Fool's safety messages come through loud and clear because its advice is simple, and because its target audience was very familiar to Disney and his staff. More than likely, *Fool* was concocted as an edutainment alternative to the finger-wagging child safety films of the 1950s, the grimmest of which were those of Sid Davis, producer of films like *Live and Learn* (1950), about children suffering the consequences of careless behavior ("Supposing this were you?" the narrator asks while presenting a boy with a bandaged eye, the result of a gun accident), and *Why Take Chances?* (1952), which combines drawings and live-action footage that show children getting hurt. Prior to *I'm No Fool*, Disney had touched on the subject of safety in the Goofy cartoons of the 1940s that cast the character as an inept beginner trying to learn a sport or other recreational activity (*The Art of Skiing*, 1941, *How to Play Golf*, 1944). Goofy was also cast as a smoker trying to quit in *No Smoking* (1951). Later in the 1950s, Donald Duck starred in two *How to Have an Accident* shorts. But these endeavors were played strictly for laughs (in *No Smoking*, for instance, Goofy *doesn't* quit at film's end). The *I'm No Fool* series, on the other hand, stresses *viewer* safety, pleasantly but repeatedly. Jiminy even addresses the viewer directly, much as the narrator in a Sid Davis film does. Eventually, both the *I'm No Fool* and *You the Human Animal* series were eventually distributed to schools as 16-millimeter prints, proving so popular that as late as 1973, new episodes were being produced.

In the late 1960s, *Fantasia* and *Alice in Wonderland* found new popularity with members of the counterculture, many of whom had been among the youngest viewers of the original Mickey Mouse Club. Indeed, *Alice*, with its hookah-smoking caterpillar and size-altering mushrooms, proved *too* popular: the film was withdrawn from 16mm rental.[25] With Walt Disney gone, perhaps the studio felt it was time to acknowledge the new social climate by producing the *Triangle of Health* series (the title refers to a triangle whose sides represent Physical, Emotional and Social health), a joint venture with Upjohn Pharmaceuticals. Four one-reel films were released: *Steps Toward Maturity and Health* (1968), *Understanding Stresses and Strains* (1968), *Physical Fitness and Good Health* (1969) and *The Social Side of Health* (1969), this last-named probably the closest the Disney studio ever came to making something "hip." The film focuses on the human need to socialize, its male narrator explaining how "How we get along with others may greatly improve the social side of our health" to its target audience of young adults. The animation is not standard Disney but resembles more the far-less-detailed work of rival studio Hanna-Barbera. A jazzy score bookends the film, while ragtime predominates in the middle. Live-footage from Disney's nature films is used at one point to illustrate the gregariousness of animals and insects. Like Disney's dental films, *Social* also explores the notion of conformity, but in updated an: the diversity of groups is acknowledged, along with the possibility that one may prefer the companionship of only a few friends rather than a group. Unfortunately, at times, the narration comes off more like a Sid Davis film: the social group, whose members sport long hair and beards, is described as "dedicated to smoking it up, drinking it down, and experimenting with sex and dangerous drugs, frequently with tragic consequences." And the film's depiction of a drug trip turns out to be more visually engaging than foreboding: after a young man and woman swallow small white pills, psychedelic patterns float behind them; then their bodies swirl away in the same manner as the wraiths in the "Night on Bald Mountain" sequence of *Fantasia*. The film closes with an acknowledgement that *Social* is part of Upjohn's continuing program toward a "better understanding of health."

A similar effort aimed at children was the *What Should I Do?* series: *The Flight* (1969), *The Game* (1969), *Lunch Money* (1970), *The New Girl* (1970), and *The Project* (1970). These were released by the Walt Disney Educational Media Company, an independent subsidiary created in 1968 from the 16mm rental division.[26] The animation style here is also Hanna-Barbera-like, with characters that are racially diverse. The name of the series is the question each child asks when faced with a troubling decision (i.e., whether to tell the truth). The repetitive strategy, however, grows tiresome after awhile.

By the early 1970s, however, the Sexual Revolution was in overdrive. But with the free love made possible by the Pill there came consequences. From 1965 to 1975, gonorrhea infections tripled, to over 1 million cases per year.[27] A 1970 *Time* article stated that the new sexual climate was clearly suspect.[28] The year 1972 turned out to be a banner one for venereal disease awareness: there was *Newsweek* cover story; a documentary by acclaimed filmmaker Richard Leacock, *VD*; a film by Sid Davis, *Summer of '63*; and PBS Emmy award-winning special, *VD Blues*, a one-hour television show featuring music and skits which *Time* described as "unprecedentedly frank."[29] Perhaps so inspired, in 1973, the education director of the Walt Disney Media Educational Media Company, Donna George, decided to make *VD Attack Plan*, which was ultimately released despite resistance from studio executives such as Disney son-in-law, Ron Miller.[30]

The title of the film is a double entendre: implying preventative strategy, it actually refers to a planned assault. Like *Defense Against Invasion*, it employs an aggressively comic metaphorical approach to the subject of disease. The seriousness of the issue, however, is made evident from the film's start: after a series of explosions, a narrator announces "This is a war story.... It could only take place within the human body." The main character is the infectious agent itself: a sergeant in the Contagion Corps, drawn as a purplish blob with a face but no limbs. Voiced by Keenan Wynn (known both for tough-guy roles in mainstream movies, and for playing comic heavies in Disney comedies like *The Absent-Minded Professor*, 1961 and *Herbie Rides Again*, 1974), he expounds on the vulnerability of humans to an audience of similarly-drawn but differently-colored blobs, the green ones representing gonorrhea, the red ones syphilis. The human traits which promote the spread of venereal disease are identified and personified as amorphous shapes as well ("Shame," "Fear" and "Ignorance"). The war theme continues throughout: the pathogens are humorously outfitted to appear as a battalion (the Sergeant wears a German World War I spiked helmet while his troops sport guerrilla berets), and the Sergeant extols the consequences of chronic infection ("Maim 'em for life!") along with the possibility of death. Actual human forms, on the other hand, are much more abstract, depicted only by angular outlines, with gender differentiated via the broad shoulders of the male vs. the hourglass shape of the female, perhaps to de-sexualize them and thus avoid any sort of arousal (as might have happened in Davis' film). Sexual intercourse is mentioned specifically, visualized as an abstraction by overlaying the male and female human figures. When genitals are discussed, they are identified only by region, via the highlighting of a circle that covers the hip region in both sexes. The film is surprisingly contemporary. Same-sex transmission is acknowledged, and the diseases are referred to their slang names—"clap" and "syph"—as is a condom (i.e. a "rubber"). There is even an allusion to racial diversity when the human figure designated as a doctor has an obvious tan complexion. Myths about how one can catch venereal disease (e. g., from toilet seats) are cited, with the pathogens derisively laughing at such human ignorance. Rather than imply that such disease is associated with certain types of individuals (the prostitutes in Davis' *Summer of '63*, for example), the point is made that infection is random, with the frequency of sexual encounters and the probability of infection likened to gambling. Condoms are also mentioned by name, though, because of their effectiveness as a barrier, are discussed as being something of a problem for the pathogens (the reference, however, was cut in the version released to public high schools). The majority of the visuals illustrate modes of transmission, the randomness of infection and, like the early World War I films on the subject, the consequences of infection eventually documented by photographs of chancre sores and inflamed skin. Shortcomings do occur, however: the score is by George Bruns, who worked on many Disney films during the 1960s; consequently, the musical accents in *VD* seem lifted from the battle of the toy soldiers in Disney's *Babes in Toyland.* Ultimately, the film's effectiveness depends on how much one recoils at the sight of glistening red lesions on human bodies (such horrific visuals would more than likely remain in the viewer's consciousness than the narrator's stern warnings in Davis' *Summer of '63*).

VD Attack Plan did not endure to the same extent as *The Story of Menstruation,* probably because herpes and AIDS overtook gonorrhea and syphilis as major STDs, and because the incurable—even fatal—nature of these new diseases made the humorous tone of *VD* inappropriate.

Conclusion

How exactly does one assess Disney's health films as edutainment? To begin with, the concept of "edutainment" didn't originate until sometime in the late 1940s. Prior to that time, Disney's health films were considered as legitimate *approved* learning aids. His experience when making the Latin American films affirms this commitment: he tolerated numerous revisions to his staff's creative concepts by the CIAA, as well as lengthy periods of review for each film. But after his falling-out with the CIAA and the mundane nature of his corporate projects proved, his frustrated need to entertain won out and he allegedly told Ben Sharpsteen "Let's stick to entertainment. We'll make educational films, but they'll be sugar-coated."[31] This is where "edutainment" really begins: when Disney abandoned the need for anyone's approval of his films. He went from being an earnest communicator of knowledge to crowning him and his studio as the inarguable source of it, in charge of all sugar-coated representation. But health and medical advice cannot be sugar-coated as easily as live-action seals and beavers. Therefore, in Disney's new edutainment-oriented kingdom, there was little room for health films, except for those that focused on simple matters like the common cold and safety. That, of course, would later change with the death of Disney and the creation of the Walt Disney Educational Media Company, the so-named entity presumably committed to fortifying the "edu" in edutainment. Films such as *Lunch Money* and *VD*, then, while they may have the aura of edutainment, were produced by academically accredited people like Donna George (who earned a PhD while working at the studio). As such, these later films are distinct from those made by a staff whose academic credentials were lacking.

But whether officially edutainment or not, *all* Disney health films are a mix of fancy and fact to some degree. Yet because of this, the only valid assessment of their texts rests with their ability to make an impact on their target audiences. Did this *ever* happen? In spite of all the cultural disconnects, unfamiliar modes of representation, entertainment and sugar-coating, to what degree — if any — did the messages in these films about changing human behavior reach the viewer? Unfortunately, other than ubiquitous fond memories and personal anecdotes about films such as *The Story of Menstruation*, the *I'm No Fool* series, or even *VD Attack Plan*, there appears to a dearth of such documentation.

There is, fortunately, one notable exception: In 1951 and 1953, in Uganda and in the Gold Coast (now Ghana) respectively, the Social Welfare and Community Development Department analyzed the reactions of illiterate audiences to the films *Hookworm*, *The Winged Scourge* and *The Way Disease Spreads*.[32] The results were reported in 1955, in the *Health Education Journal*, in an article by Ken Pickering, an officer with the Development Department. There were, of course, the expected disconnects: replacement of the soundtracks with "vernacular commentary"[33] to improve clarity of action, while animated gags—such as the one in *Hookworm* where a latrine ends up automatically built despite the bumbling antics of its builder, Charlie — were attributed to "white man's magic." In the end, however, because audiences understood the need for the building of something like a latrine, the animated gags were not seen as an impairment to learning. However, unlike the Ugandan audiences, the Gold Coast audiences, prior to viewing the films, had not been exposed to relevant medical information. This had been deliberate: an experiment to determine audience reaction "if it had never heard of the disease, although suffering from it."[34] What Pickering found upon following up with the Gold Coast audiences a few weeks later was that, although they retained visual images, the images were out of sequence, and attempts to reconstruct the action "produced grossly distorted ideas,"[35] thus documenting the power of Disney's vibrant imagery to make an impact without necessarily educating. But Pickering's report also discusses how such films *affect* members of an illiterate society, where superstition can block the reception of new knowledge about disease. Under these circumstances, Disney's animated imagery acts as more of an opportunistic distraction than a pedagogic device. The real value of the Disney health films, Pickering wrote "is less in teaching the new than in breaking down the traditional belief where it is too erroneous to be used as a starting point for teaching the truth ... by presenting a graphic and credible picture to the mind so realistically that temporarily the mind's resistance to it is overcome."[36] He concluded that the Disney health films, when carefully monitored and combined with other forms of teaching, would be valuable in the fight against disease in Africa.

At the same time, however, the potential for the images in a Disney health film to impact without necessarily teaching raises questions, namely "Did films made for American middle class audiences ever induce similar consequences as those in the Gold Coast audiences?" Is it possible that, despite the obvious high level of literacy of American audiences, Disney's imagery can overwhelm even the educated mind and simply implant itself with muddled connotations? While the answer might seem a resounding "no," consider *The Story of Menstruation*— and how its reductive images of female sexuality were implanted in developing female minds over the course of two decades. Was the film's oblique treatment of the subject a reflection of cultural attitudes— or were such cultural attitudes only furthered over the years because this film, along with its surreptitious, ritualized viewings, indoctrinated adolescent girls into believing this was how they should regard their own bodies? Or consider the term "female biological clock," which goes at least as far back as 1987 (when it was uttered by Sally Field in the movie *Surrender*). Is its ultimate source *Menstruation*'s image of a rigid young girl on a sundial, which was regularly imprinted into the collective American female consciousness over the course of two decades? In the world of Disney health films, such a connection seems as possible as one between Jiminy Cricket and Sid Davis.

Notes

1. Karl S. Lashley and John B. Watson, *A Psychological Study of Motion Pictures in Relation to Venereal Disease Campaigns* (Washington: United States Interdepartmental Social Hygiene Board, 1922), pg 3–4.

2. Bob Thomas, *Walt Disney: An American Original* (New York: Simon and Schuster, 1976), 64.
3. Russell Merritt and J. B. Kaufman, *Walt in Wonderland: The Silent Films of Walt Disney* (Pordenone, Italy: Le Giornate del Cinema Muto; Baltimore: Dist. by Johns Hopkins University Press, 1993), 79.
4. Merritt and Kaufman, 111.
5. Merritt and Kaufman, 146.
6. Richard Holliss and Brian Sibley, *The Disney Studio Story* (London: Octopus Books, 1988), 34
7. Holliss and Sibley, 44.
8. Marianne Fedunkiw, "Malaria Films: Motion Pictures as a Public Health Tool," *American Journal of Public Health* 93, no. 7 (July 2003): 1050.
9. J.B. Kaufman, *South of the Border with Disney: Walt Disney and the Good Neighbor Program, 1941–1948* (New York: Disney Editions, 2009), 131.
10. Kaufman, 132.
11. Pablo Astorga, Ame R. Burgés and Valpy Fitzgerald, *The Standard of Living in Latin America during the Twentieth Century*, Discussion Papers in Economic and Social History, no. 54 (Oxford: University of Oxford, 2004), 32.
12. Kaufman, 134.
13. Kaufman, 141.
14. Kaufman, 145.
15. Kaufman, 138.
16. Kaufman, 141.
17. Kaufman, 148.
18. Kaufman, 141.
19. Kaufman, 146.
20. Sean Griffin, *Tinker Belles and Evil Queens: The Walt Disney Company from the Inside Out* (New York: New York University Press, 2000), 35.
21. Kaufman, 150.
22. Lisa Cartwright and Brian Goldfarb,"Cultural Contagion: On Disney's Health Education Films for Latin America," in Eric Smoodin, ed., *Disney Discourse: Producing the Magic Kingdom* (New York: Routledge, 1994), 170.
23. Kaufman, 172.
24. Personal correspondence with Montana State University female employees Jeanette Goodwin, Vicki Miller and Diane Steffan (Bozeman, Montana, February 2010).
25. Leonard Maltin, *The Disney Films* (New York: Crown, 1973), 104.
26. Wade Sampson, "Disney Attacks VD: The Rest of the Story," *Mouseplanet. Accessed* 10 June 2009 at http://www.mouseplanet.com/8854/Disney_Attacks_VD_The_Rest_of_the_Story.
27. Alan B. Brandt, *No Magic Bullet: A Social History of Venereal Disease in the United States Since 1880* (New York: Oxford University Press, 1985), 175
28. Medicine: "VD: A National Emergency," *Time*, July 27, 1970.
29. Show Business: "The VD Blues," *Time*, October 9, 1972.
30. Sampson, *Mouseplanet*.
31. Thomas, *Disney*, 206.
32. James Gibbs, "Ken Pickering: Who Is Kofi Basake?" in *Nkyin-Kyin: Essays on the Ghanaian Theatre* (New York: Rodopi, 2009), 18.
33. Ken Pickering, "Another Walt Disney Experiment," *Health Education Journal* 13, no. 78 (1955): 78.
34. Pickering, 78.
35. Pickering, 80.
36. Pickering, 80.

Bibliography

Astorga, Pablo, Ame R. Burgés and Valpy Fitzgerald. *The Standard of Living in Latin America during the Twentieth Century.* Discussion Papers in Economic and Social History, no. 54. Oxford, UK: University of Oxford, 2004.

Brandt, Alan B. *No Magic Bullet: A Social History of Venereal Disease in the United States Since 1880.* New York: Oxford University Press, 1985.

Cartwright, Lisa, and Brian Goldfarb. "Cultural Contagion: On Disney's Health Education Films for Latin America." In *Disney Discourse: Producing the Magic Kingdom,* edited by Eric Smoodin, 169–180. New York: Routledge, 1994.

Fedunkiw, Marianne. "Malaria Films: Motion Pictures as a Public Health Tool" *American Journal of Public Health* 93, no. 7 (July 2003): 1050.

Griffin, Sean. *Tinker Belles and Evil Queens: The Walt Disney Company from the Inside Out.* New York: New York University Press, 2000.

Holliss, Richard, and Brian Sibley. *The Disney Studio Story.* London: Octopus Books, 1988.

Kaufman, J. B. *South of the Border with Disney: Walt Disney and the Good Neighbor Program, 1941–1948.* New York: Disney Editions, 2009.

Lashley, Karl S., and John B. Watson. *A Psychological Study of Motion Pictures in Relation to Venereal Disease Campaigns.* Washington: United States Interdepartmental Social Hygiene Board, 1922.

Maltin, Leonard. *The Disney Films.* New York: Crown Publishers Inc, 1973.

Medicine: "VD: A National Emergency," *Time*, 27 July 1970.

Merritt, Russell, and J. B. Kaufman. *Walt in Wonderland: The Silent Films of Walt Disney.* Pordenone, Italy: Le Giornate del Cinema Muto; Baltimore: Dist. by Johns Hopkins University Press, 1993.

Pickering, Ken. "Another Walt Disney Experiment," *Health Education Journal* 13, no. 78 (1955): 78.

Pickering, Ken. "Who is Kofi Basake?" in *Nkyin-Kyin: Essays on the Ghanaian Theatre,* edited by James Gibbs. 17–24. New York: Rodopi, 2009.

Sampson, Wade. "Disney Attacks VD: The Rest of the Story," *Mouseplanet.* http://www.mouseplanet.com/8854/Disney_Attacks_VD_The_Rest_of_the_Story.

Show Business: "The VD Blues," *Time*, 9 October 1972.

Thomas, Bob. *Walt Disney: An American Original.* New York: Simon and Schuster, 1976.

9

"Nature Is the Dramatist"

Documentary, Entertainment and the World According to the True-Life Adventures

EDDY VON MUELLER

Seal Island may have won Walt Disney his most unexpected Oscar. RKO Pictures, Disney's standing distributor, had balked at handling the two-reeler, apparently assuming there wasn't much market for a nominally non-fiction short chronicling the family life of the fur seal. It must have seemed especially out of step with the kinds of movies that had made the Disney studio famous, animation. With a stable full of talking, singing and dancing animals to choose from, Walt Disney was promoting, of all things, a *documentary* in which the seals were stuck being nothing more than, well, seals.

The cartoon mogul had been struck by a popular children's story, *Matka and Kotik: A Tale of the Mist-Islands*, written by eminent ichthyologist (and, unfortunately, ardent eugenicist) David Starr Jordan. Jordan, who had helped negotiate a moratorium on sealing in the remote Pribilof Islands in the Pacific, where the seal populations had plummeted and where rapacious hunting threatened the animals with imminent extinction, wrote the story from the seals' point-of-view.[1] Disney commissioned the picture after seeing the work of pioneering nature cinematographers, Alfred and Elma Milotte, who were shooting research footage near the famed fur seal breeding grounds that had been saved, in no small measure, by the conservation treaty Jordan helped to draft, and presumably, the sentiments his story helped to stir.[2] Wildlife documentary production was an undiscovered country for the Disney studio, but Disney put some of the studio's oldest and steadiest hands to work culling and cutting the footage, and writing and recording a suitable narration. He also ordered one of his cartoon units to make an animated introduction, to give it his signature touch. Bypassing RKO, Walt's dedicated brother Roy, his perennial Right Hand

and the man in charge of much of the studio's day-to-day operation, set up an in-house distribution arm to push the picture. Christened Buena-Vista, the subsidiary undertook the first steps by Disney as a distributor in the fateful year 1948,[3] promoting the first of what would become a profitable, critically acclaimed and immensely influential series of nature documentaries, the *True-Life Adventures.*

While there had been many films made featuring actuality footage of animals in the wild and captivity—in fact, animal subjects had made for popular cinema since the very birth of the medium (such as Edison's grisly 1903 spectacle of industrialized cruelty, *The Electrocution of an Elephant*, or Jean Painlevé's groundbreaking 1927 underwater views in *L'oeff D'epinoche* [*The Stickleback Eggs*], to name but a few), Disney's *True Life Adventures* would become as paradigmatic to the nature documentary as the studio's fairy-tale inflected musicals are to the animated feature. The longevity of the franchise certainly helped. New and re-released films in the series, which included both shorts and anthological features, played theatrically into the early '70s, and enjoyed an extensive afterlife on the small screen, appearing on Walt's long-running ABC showcase, which premiered as *Disneyland* in 1954 and finally gave up the broadcast network ghost as *The Wonderful World of Disney* in 2008. The nature films also played to captive audiences in countless classrooms as part of the studio's "educational" film service that opened new revenue streams and cultivated life-long consumers after the war. The Baby Boomers would see *True-Life Adventures* in school as 16mm dubs of dubs; as would their kids, born into the brand, on VHS. In other words, the style, the technique, and, as we will see, the rhetorical peculiarities of the series born on *Seal Island* became familiar, at an early age, to generations of viewers. Which no doubt explains why so much of what we see today on series like *Nature* or on niche cable networks like Animal Planet are so powerfully reminiscent of works orchestrated by the Disney studio decades ago.

Seal Island was, relatively speaking, a substantial hit even in its initial run, returning $434,000 on the studio's $84,000 investment.[4] Legend has it that when the film won an Academy Award, Walt advised his brother to go hit someone at RKO over the head with it.[5] Interestingly, the award was not in a documentary category. The overwhelming majority of winners for that year, both feature and short documentaries had been war pictures or propaganda films of one kind or another, made by various government-sponsored film units. In fact, the documentary category had emerged precisely to acknowledge those kinds of films, the first "special" award being given to a non-fiction film in 1942, honoring four military films—including *Prelude to War*, the first of the *Why We Fight* series of propaganda films, for which the Disney Company had made animations.[6] *Seal Island* was acknowledged instead in the now-defunct "Best Short-Subject, Two-Reel" category, a grab-bag race that included comedies, musical reviews, social problem pictures, and news and non-fiction films

(*Seal Island*'s competition in '48 included *Samba-Mania*, a dance-craze themed melodrama, and *Snow Capers*, a round-up of winter sports footage).

It is perhaps fitting that the inaugural True-Life Adventure wasn't honored in the documentary category. The series raises vexing questions about the purpose and practice of commercial non-fiction filmmaking. Since the late 1960s, filmmakers and critics alike have energetically challenged the claims to authenticity made by documentary films, and questioned as well the tactics and techniques use to substantiate those claims. Like many documentaries, Disney's nature films position themselves in a kind of hazy no-man's-land between education or information and entertainment, banking — literally, in the case of the commercial exploitation of such content, on television or in classrooms — on the notion that these two terms are not, as is sometimes suggested, antithetical. Documentary content frequently employs a variety of technical, narrative, or aesthetic devices (such as, in the contemporary context, unsteady hand-held video footage, or "talking-head" interviews with persons strategically framed against appropriately authoritative back-drops, say, maps or walls of leather-bound tomes) to reinforce the films status as a "document," as having some greater fidelity to some truth or reality beyond its own discourse. Documentaries also borrow extensively from the vast tool-kit of commercial and fiction media, to keep viewers attentive and emotionally engaged (using "reaction shots," for instance, or ironic music, or cross-cutting between multiple temporalities to generate commentary or suspense). Indeed, the fact that the documentary is so frequently and fluently imitated in so many fiction films and television shows, from big-screen "mockumentaries" like *This Is Spinal Tap* and *The Blair Witch Project* to faux reality and news programs like *Flight of the Conchords* and *The Daily Show* bears witness to the degree to which "documentary" is as much a calculated construction or a set of formal and narrative devices as it is a cinema with any uncontested or *de facto* claim to factuality or (capitalized) Truth.[7]

Regardless, then, of who photographed the material we see in the *True-Life Adventures*, the creatures and environments the films reveal to us are shown only through the often distorting lens of men Walt Disney trusted to execute his own very particular vision of entertainment, of his audience, and of the world. Disney, as much discussed and as extensively biographied as any American filmmaker, or indeed, as any American, emerges even in profiles created by his own studio, as a man passionately if not obsessively preoccupied with the making and maintaining of meticulously controlled imaginary worlds — from his toy trains and soda fountains and miniatures at home, to the Main Streets and frontiers and jungles in his theme parks, to the Cartoon-lands and Neverlands and Wonderlands of his animations. All of these environments, executed at different times in different forms for different constituencies or modes of consumption, share a fundamental order, or at least, an orderliness, they are benign microcosms, miniature histories and miniature worlds from which ugliness and complexity and chaos all are banished. Coming from a company and a creator so singularly preoccupied with control, it is perhaps to be expected that the live-action nature films made under the *True-Life Adventure* banner have much more in common with the company's cartoons that our conventional understanding of the nature of non-fiction film would seem to allow.

"The World as Only Walt Disney Could Show It to You"

As with so many of the texts constituting the Disney canon, Walt cannot be in any linear way said to be the author of any of the *True-Life Adventures*. Made, like most documentaries, by means of monkish patience during principal photography and strategic editing in post-production, the studio's nature films were outsourced — not to an army of artisans working in a quasi-factory setting, as was the case with the animations, but to a small highly specialized group of researchers and technicians, many of whom might spend months on end in the field in distant locales, far from the watchful eyes of the boss. The people responsible for the images captured for the series were, moreover, strangers to the Disney way of doing things, and to the studio's peculiarly focused view of filmed entertainment. Draftsmen, illustrators, performers, painters, sculptors, and salesmen were all longstanding features of the organization's creative community, but the *True-Life Adventures* front line was held by a very different breed, filmmakers more used to tents and torrents than studio politics and the assembly-line system of industrialized production.

The Milottes were prototypical: amateur naturalists, avid conservationists, and professional photographers, the couple worked on numerous projects for the series. The couple contributed to *Seal Island, Beaver Valley* (1950), *Nature's Half-Acre* (1951), *Bear Country* (1953), and *The African Lion* (1955), among others, and captured stunning images of places and behaviors never before recorded on film. Their work represents the merging of aesthetic, scientific, and to some extent polemic concerns that would become prominent in literary and documentary discourses as the modern environmental movement began to coalesce.[8] Wildlife and nature photographers and cinematographers were part of what has been described as a "fraternity" of scientists, writers and image-makers whose work took them to ever more distant frontiers,[9] in quest of the new, the exotic, and the as-yet-unseen. Recording that quest challenged the limits of cinematic ingenuity and technology. The Milottes and fellow cinematographers Murl Deusing, Robert Crandall, Paul Kenworthy, Dick Borden and Jack Couffer all found ways to adapt the apparatus to conditions and applications previously undreamt of in commercial production. Many of them won the acclaim of their more conventional colleagues, and nature documentaries continue to demand constant innovation. New wonders gave rise to means of filming them, and the naturalist-filmmakers of the *True-Life Adventures* found themselves adding simultaneously to the scientific record and to the art of cinematography[10].

And yet, there is a powerful sense when watches the *True-Life* features and shorts, that you are seeing a *Disney* movie. Walt, well on his way to becoming more brand-master than movie-maker already, had virtually no exposure to the people gathering the eye-popping, award-winning footage for his nature films, and no experience at all of the places they were working. Still the finished films, whether shot in a swamp or a desert or under the sea, are absolutely consistent with the tone and worldview of the studio's other content. Though the ramblers off shooting the films were outsiders, the construction of the films was completed in California, and overseen by old-school Company Men. The nominal producer of the series (he wrote and directed several as well), Ben Sharpsteen, had directed dozens of animated sequences and been a principal producer on both *Pinocchio* and *Fantasia*. James Algar, who is credited as the director of *Seal Island*, the Oscar-winning *The Living Desert*, and dozens of other non-fiction films, also made his reputation in the animation arm, helming the enormously popular "Sorcerer's Apprentice" segment in *Fantasia*. Even Winston "Hib" Hibler, the mild and tireless voice of the series, and one of the main writers for the *True-Life Adventures* aided in the adaptation of story material for the animations, helping to pen the scripts for *Cinderella*, *Alice in Wonderland*, and *Peter Pan*.

It is perhaps in part due to this shared cartoon lineage among the top brass at the live-action documentary unit that the *True-Life Adventures* bear so striking a resemblance to the company's renowned animated films. Walt Disney did not (and in fact, as we shall see, he *could* not) exert the kind of direct personal pressure to mold the new documentary into a form he favored. But looking at the way the documentary series paints in eerily identical hues such dizzyingly diverse environments, and how perfectly those portrayals compliment the fictive universes of *Bambi* and "The Nutcracker Suite" in *Fantasia*, it seems clear that the architect had so effectively shaped the sensibilities of his disciples and lieutenants, so persuasively promulgated a vision for the works of his company, that even the unruly raw materials of actuality could be crafted to fit it.

The bringing of the natural world, or at least the parts of the natural world that fortune and skill contrive to capture on film, into line with the Disney aesthetic and ethos begins with a brush. Each of the *True-Life Adventures* kicks off with an animated sequence in which a painted paintbrush enters the frame and deftly renders the scene or setting we are about to explore. Most often, the painted scene becomes a literal framing device, bordering a space or window in which the live-action image appears. The paintbrush, or more broadly, the hand of the Creator *of* the text appearing *in* the text, is an old animation conceit. Indeed, the trope appears in the very first animated film, J. Stewart Blackton's 1900 film, *The Enchanted Drawing*. But instead of a live-action conjurer stirring to life a fictional reality formally defined by the medium is shown using—in short, a "real" cartoonist is filmed drawing a cartoon character who then proceeds to frolic about in a two-dimensional, artificial environment—here the animated paintbrush is seen to be painting the "real" world. These new animals and landscapes are not so much discovered and described (the goal and procedure employed by scientists) by the Disney operation as they are *rendered* by it, the natural world being processed and delivered for a consumption as an entertainment. As if by the some kind of inverse rotoscope, the marvelous machine that allows animators to make a cartoon atop the actions of a living being, the *True-Life Adventures* make family-friendly fantasies out of recorded realities.[11]

The use of sound, too, in these films, hearkens back to the studios root's as a cartoon-mill. Very little audio material recorded in the field makes it into the mix in the *True-Life Adventures*, sync sound recording frequently being the last thing on the minds of one and two-man camera units filming in less than optimal environments. Some post-synchronous "authentic" animal calls are used, but the majority of what we hear in these films, aside from Hibler's hyperbolical commentary, is music. Music is absolutely fundamental to Disney cinema. Mickey Mouse was, after all, not the first cartoon superstar (that was Felix the Cat); he was the first *sound* cartoon superstar. Disney's early *Silly Symphonies* were organized around music, and set the stage for a host of music-minded imitators, including the *Looney Tunes* and *Merrie Melody* series. All of the Disney animated features were musicals, until the disastrous *Black Cauldron* in 1985 (now, obviously, the musical model is back). As in 1940's *Fantasia*, a series of animations made to illustrate classical compositions, music in Disney's cartoons is often an elemental force, an irresistible rhythm compelling all things to keep time with it. The practice of putting every motion to music is so closely associated with the studio that the technique is still called "Mickey Mousing."[12]

Like the primeval Mickey and his pals bobbing constantly to the beat, and like the marvelously choreographed chases and slapstick brawls animators had skillfully set to music in the features, the editing and scoring of the *True-Life Adventures* keeps actuality carefully in tune. In *The Living Desert*, for instance, which won the company their first documentary award, viscous fumaroles splatter in syncopation to become a "symphony of the mud-pots," and in *Secrets of Life*, windborne seeds rise with the violins, spin with the harp, and float down with the flutes. Elsewhere on the soundtracks, still other echoes of the cartoons can be heard, in the various zings, boings, raspberries, toots, whistles, plunks and booms foleyed in to punctuate any misstep or accidental collision. These sound effects, routinely laid down during post-production as acoustic punctuation in cartoons comedies and even some knockabout live-action comedies (they're ubiquitous in Paramount's Three Stooges shorts, for instance, and for that matter, on FOX's popular *America's Funniest Home Videos*), seem outlandish contrapuntal when synchronized with ostensibly spontaneous events taking place in wilderness locales.

Beyond the animated prologues and distinctly silly symphonic approach to sound, we can see this processing of recorded reality into Disney-style fiction entertainment in almost every aspect of the discourse of the *True-Life Adventures*. Rather than emphasizing the naturalness of the natural world, the settings for the film's are portrayed with an eye towards the otherworldy: the desert is "fantastically ugly, yet strangely beautiful" and "seemingly without meaning"; the Arctic is "unknown," the Everglades a "chapter out of prehistory," the Amazon "untouched by man and all his works"; Australia a "real-life Wonderland." Even quotidian Nature gets a coat of fairy-dust glamour, the lives of familiar insects, ducks and even squirrels becoming "secret," "mysterious," and "fantastic" in *Nature's Half-Acre, Water Birds*, and *Perri*.[13] And like the imaginary realms of fiction and folklore, these are discursive spaces, their boundaries and features fixed not by cartography but by language, representation and narrative. We cannot visit the Brazil of *Jungle Cats* or the savannah of *African Lion* or *The Living Desert*, because they do not fit on a map, only in the movies— they are, like most cinematic environments, constructions, composites made from images recorded in disparate places and times.

The "characters" in the films (the players in what we are told again and again is pageant, story, drama, or saga spontaneously authored for us; "Nature," we are told, "is the dramatist") are also composite creations, as artificial as the Frankensteinian entities made in fiction films by the carefully stitching together movie stars, stunt-doubles, and the backs of stand-in's heads. Filmmakers had known since the late teens how fluidly cinematic space and time could synthesized through editing (for instance, using shots taken from roughly complimentary angles to create the illusion of spatial proximity between the two images), and the same "continuity" approach to editing is used in *Seal Island* to make several seal pups into one, an adorably Chaplinesque waif waddling around the crowded rookeries in search of "his" mother. Other conventions of continuity obscure elaborate production practices necessary to make possible the filming of otherwise invisible animal behavior. In *The Vanishing Prairie*, prairie dogs in a custom-made cutaway burrow match on the actions of others filmed months before in situ. Animal "eye-lines" are created, making the camera's object the cinematic subject, an apparently agitated jaguar made through montage angry *at* the mischievous monkey whose hooting image preceded the cat's. In terms of technique, then, the *True-Life Adventures* are very much conventional Hollywood fiction films, albeit fictions built in large part from materials gathered by documentary camera crews working thousands of miles away.

Such film narratives, of course, obey their own "natural" laws, and here the technically groundbreaking films in the *True-Life* series play very safely by the rules. Each film, for instance, reveals a powerful protagonal impulse, pulling a handful of creature's from the abundant wilderness "cast" (to retain for a moment the series' own theatrical conceits), and foregrounding their stories. The selection of headliners conforms nicely to the kinds of critters favored by animators and tellers of children's tales. Cuteness is definitely preferred, something small, furry and fleet. Cuddly little animals are, after all, the staples of the Disney brand. Rodents, unsurprisingly for the Mouse House, come off particularly well (except for, as we shall see, from the lemmings): prairie dogs are central to *The Vanishing Prairie*, the focus of *Beaver Valley* is self evident, a ground squirrel dubbed "Skinny" steals the show in *The Living Desert*, and a gray one is the title "character" in *Perri* (which was adapted by Hibler from a story penned by the author of the source material for *Bambi*, Felix Salten). Otters, also, get plenty of play, appearing in five of the films as comic relief, fun-loving "clowns," "gypsies," and "carefree vagabonds of the swamp." How Walt refrained from having them fitted with tiny hobo costumes is a mystery.

When predators appears, they are either cast as heavies—various carnivores are introduced as "killers," "assassins," and "executioners"—or softened up by focusing on their families. Big Bad Wolves are evidently acceptable, when playing parent, and their offspring are an irresistible attraction. Juvenile jaguars, lions, grizzlies, polar bears, foxes, wolves, and even alligators appear in the *True-Life Adventures*, which frequently use coming-of-age arcs as part of their narrative formulae. Presumably such stories resonate well for children and their parents, increasingly, after World War II, the Disney studios core consumers. It is worth noting that *Earth*, a theatrical documentary feature inspired by the mammoth *Planet Earth* miniseries (itself a production very much in the mode of the *True-Life* films) and financed and distributed through a new Disney subsidiary, frequently focuses on newborn animals and their "families." In addition to storylines related to rearing the young (*Jungle Cat*, *White Wilderness*, *The African Lion*, *Prowlers of the Everglades*, *The World's Strangest Animals*) and/or growing up to win a mate (*Seal Island*, *The Olympic Elk*, *Perri*, *Birds of the World*), the building and maintenance of dwelling places is also a prominent theme in both *The Vanishing Prairie* and *Beaver Valley* (home-making, literally and figuratively, is a frequent motif in Disney product, from the Granny's Cabin attraction to *The Three Little Pigs*) The wild, in the *True-Life Adventures*, turns out to be rather domestic.

"Authentic, Unstaged and Unrehearsed"

The adoption of continuity editing and animation aesthetics, the contrapuntal construction of animal lives as domestic and animal habitats as fabulous, the insistent manipulation of music and sound, all seem to speak to Disney's preoccupation with control. Animation is, of course an ideal medium for a control freak, since, as a means of making motion pictures, animation, for all its labor-intensiveness, affords the filmmaker a formal freedom utterly impossible in live-action production. Since the entirety of the animated image, at least the kind of animated image that was the specialty of the Disney animation works, is entirely synthetic, every aspect of motion and *mise-en-scene* can be directly guided. Hypothetically, there can be in animation no happy accidents (or accidental gaffes), no spontaneities or improvisations (or flubbed takes to reshoot, or petulant stars to humor). The real world, its drearily confining physics, its inconstant weather and its sloppy unpredictable people, cannot scupper the vision and intentions of the animator. Walt Disney, when he was most energetically engaged in directed the cartoon operation, made the most of what Sergei Eisenstein called the "imagined omnipotence" of animation.[14] He brought that enthusiasm to other projects, especially his personal tourist Utopia, Disneyland. The park recreated in miniature, an idealized composite landscape, encompassing in a single destination the frontier, the jungle, the American small town, the landscape of the European fairy tale. As long as it was *not* authentic, as long as it was caricature and not replication, Walt Disney discovered he could make of his Magic Kingdom anything he wanted.[15]

Needless to say, this concept of control through artifice creates a bit of a dilemma for the documentarian, and even more so for the nature photographer, whose work is understood in the context of a long and even noble tradition of natural history that stretches back for hundreds of years. It is well beyond the scope of this humble work to encompass the vigor and vitriol of the running debate over authenticity, actuality and truth in documentary cinema, which indeed constitutes a significant part of the critical and theoretical literature on the subject. Suffice it here to say that opinions are strongly held, rigorously defended and varied, and that in non-fiction filmmaking, authenticity and truthfulness are always an issue. It is seldom a subject of concern in fiction filmmaking, and in animation, never. Whether the Disney brothers, Sharpsteen, Hibler or Algar ever troubled over the veracity of their rendering of animals and of the wilderness, they certainly traded on truth as watermark and a fetish. Even the name of the series, *True-Life Adventures*, seeks to wed the excitement and entertainment to truth, the conceptual cornerstone of non-fiction media.

Truth, as it turns out, does not stand easily beside Disney's conceptual cornerstone, control. Logistics, and the practical facts of wildlife prevented Walt Disney from tweaking with the footage being shot for the True-Life films. Post-production manipulations aside, Disney could not insist, as he often did with other projects, that the players or animators pump up the gag or that a sequence redone. Filmmakers shooting animal behavior had to negotiate not the tastes and tirades of a micromanaging mogul, but wind and water and the moods of spiders and the benevolence of bears. In fact, nature photographers and cinematographers often resorted to artifice themselves, albeit for different reasons than Walt Disney. Reality, ever an elusive quarry for the cinematographer, was often far more easy to contrive than to capture. Staging certain events is by no means unheard of in nature cinematography, or rather, creating stages on which certain events can take place; animals and plants are invariably unpredictable. Vivariums, aquariums, camera traps and other devices had long been used to make photographic records of hard-to-film behaviors.[16] Many such tricks of the trade were used in the making of the *True Life Adventures*, and some new ones invented.[17] Which brings us to *White Wilderness* and the case of the lemmings.

This *True-Life* feature, exploring the Arctic north, includes a variety of striking animal sequences, as well as the series' stunning trademark landscapes. One core sequence, though, would eventually create a scandal and threaten the studio's vigorously protected and squeaky-clean image. The controversy erupted in 1983 when *Cruel Camera*, an award-winning exposé produced by the Canadian Broadcasting Corporation, revealed that images included in the film of the tiny arctic rodents rushing en masse over a precipice and into the sea, images that hundreds of thousands if not millions of viewers, many of them credulous children, had seen, had been faked. The lemmings, loathe to stay on-script and take the plunge, had to be systematically herded sea-ward, and then shoved over the brink with the aid of an ingenious, improvised sweeping devices rigged by one of the camera operators. The scandal, in retrospect, seems perhaps a trifle overblown. They were lemmings, doing what we all expected them to do; accounts of vast populations of lemmings suddenly appearing and racing into the sea had circulated for centuries (prior to the late 1600s and the work of naturalist John Ray, prevailing opinion held that the varmints periodically fell from the sky, or sprung spontaneously from decaying vegetation).[18] As late as the 1920s, stories of mass "suicide" among lemmings were repeated by naturalists ("it is the most puzzling phenomena I know of in animal life," wrote one respected essayist and observer),[19] and the seemingly suicidal behavior was well enough known to be the basis for a story in one of print cartoonist Carl Barks' Scrooge McDuck comics, published by Disney in 1954.[20] Its currency was such that it provoked a somewhat arch admonition against fostering misinformation in a 1968 issue of *The American Biology Teacher*,[21] and it remains a common-knowledge cliché today, whether we believe it or not. If there is one thing, then, lemmings are known for, it is for seething up out of the tundra tussocks and heading for the nearest cliff.

Biologists knew long before the film was made that lemmings were no more prone to suicide than they were products of spontaneous generation. Some lemming species are irruptive, reproductive cycles producing periodic springtime swarms, but these were rodent baby booms don't lead to suicide — though a given migratory path might terminate in the ocean. As the author of the 1968 critique noted, "movement to the sea is merely the result of the passive action of topography." What's more, the lemmings appearing in the Disney film, the collared lemming, isn't known to be irruptive in the first place. But a lemming is a lemming, apparently, and we all know what lemmings do. Of course, hand-wringing from do-gooders in the ASPCA aside, why should anyone be shocked to discover that the event had been synthesized in the first place? There is so much artifice in the *True-Life Adventures*: the music, the multiple cameras recording the event, the staged encounters and seamless match-cuts, all in the service of creating for the viewers an engaging and dramatic glimpse at the animal world, what matters one more act of manipulation? The hue and cry over the film's treatment of the lemmings (which excited far more outrage than did the film's treatment of scientific accuracy) suggests that there are limits to how far a documentary is allowed to go in manufacturing entertainment out of actuality, especially a documentary by bearing the Disney name, a name that by the time *White Wilderness* was released was already iconic?[22]

With the discovery of the deception, a trust is broken. It is not a reasonable trust, or a well-founded one, being based in part of the self-styled virtuousness of a commercial entertainment company and in part on our own volitional faith in the "self-evident" authenticity of the documentary image. Disney's name, and the products associated with it, had become by the mid–1950s virtually synonymous with wholesome, middle-class, family entertainment. The whiff of dishonesty, let alone of callousness or cruelty, that came with the revelation of the tactics used in *White Wilderness* sours the atmosphere of safety and purity the company and its founder strove to create. What's more, the atmosphere of authenticity so central to documentary cinema. Brand, content, rhetoric and technique merge in the *True-Life* films to generate a kind of credibility we are loath to contradict, further seduced as we are by music and the mythopoeic utterances of the unseen and apparently omniscient narrator. It may be naïve for anyone to take at face value the promise in the title sequence, that the film we are about to see reveals reality "authentic, unstaged, and unrehearsed." Yet that naiveté is essential to our enjoyment of almost any of Disney's entertainments, or indeed, any entertainment.

One might argue that Disney's foray into cutaway prairie dog dens, lemming herding and all the other means by which the *True-Life* crews got their shots are ultimately no different from the re-enactments and dramatizations routinely used in all manner of "non-fiction" media, from small-screen true-crime shows to lavishly produced Hollywood historical epics and "docudramas" like *Tora! Tora! Tora!* or *Gettysburg*. There, too, events to which cameras were not originally privy are staged to create a record of what we are encouraged to assume had actually happened. Such techniques create, as motion pictures always do, a novel temporality or synthetic present, an *is* which becomes post-factum proof of a *was* (in some cases, the recreation is so effective that viewers have mistaken filmed recreations for documentary footage of actual events!) By making us all eye-witnesses to the film's version of an events, we become a crucial part of a mechanism by which that version is sustained, and by which alternate interpretations are sidelined. And yet in the popular imagination, natural *history* had become natural *science*. The former is open to bias and revision, it is a product of human culture and prone to all the ills and excesses that attend it. Science, on the other hand, is objective, empirical, absolute. In the popular imagination, scientific truth is discovered and proven, and it then becomes permanent. History is written by the winners. Science is written by no one (or God). Once established, a fact does not change with a new administration, a new millennium. Science *is.*[23]

But given the awesome indelibility of "fact," the machinations of the makers of the *True-Life Adventures* make a certain sense. Unlike historical dramas and many other documentaries, the priority in many wildlife films is not fidelity to the actuality of an event, but rather fidelity to "Nature." That is to say, rather than limiting themselves to recording only what occurred spontaneously before the camera, the makers of films like *The Living Desert* and *White Wilderness* undertake rigorously to generate events and behaviors *known* to occur ("known" here in the sense of having been established in the scientific literature or documented through observation by professionals). If lemmings don't happen to decide to hurl themselves into the sea when the film crew is on hand to capture the magic moment, that happenstance in no way negates the fact that lemmings *do* hurl themselves into the sea from time to time. To provoke such a stampede for the purposes of making a film, then, merely provides a more complete picture of lemming nature then the little creatures were able to deliver on their own. Like a taxonomist, extrapolating a type specimen for a species from the statistics or from fragmentary remains of dozens of individuals, a kind of scientific montage is at work, to create as whole a picture as can be made.

The Endless Pageant

Yet we have seen that these films are more than Technicolor natural histories or scientific illustrations on celluloid. As narratives and as commercial entertainments, the *True-Life Adventures* also fulfill a variety of economic and social functions, and do other kinds of cultural work. As products of a particular historical moment and of a particularly influential media source (one which is if anything even more powerful today), these films also validate a set of conceptual and ideological positions vis-à-vis the natural world and about us. Ironically, while the *True-Life Adventures* show so many vivid and memorable images of the lives of animals, they say a great deal more about our own.

In these films, the animal kingdom presents as both the antithesis and the avatar of human society. Animals are anthropomorphized in the *True-Life Adventures* in a way not inconsistent with the talking-animal fantasies the studio produced, from the anarchic anthropomorphized menagerie from which Mickey sprang to Goofy's apotheosis as a hapless Eisenhower-era everyman, to retoolings of classic tales with animal casts as in *Robin Hood* or *The Great Mouse Detective,* to folkloric sagas set in worlds without people like *The Lion King.* As in those animated films, animals in the *True-Life* documentaries are presented in roles we readily recognize and are assigned human motivations and traits. They don't speak, sing, or wear hats, but their behaviors in the series are interpreted through a distinctly human lens. A juvenile beaver takes a puritanical turn when he is soberly "apprenticed" in his "father's trade" in *Beaver Valley*, and a young bull fur seal "throws his weight around" to impress "the ladies" in *Seal Island*. In *The Living Desert* a female tarantula appears as a "lethal lady" who devours unwary visitors to her "parlor," until her criminal career is cut short by a female Pepsis wasp, a femme even more fatale — the Pepsis female paralyzes tarantulas and inters them alive in a burrow to act as a living food supply for her larval offspring.[24]

There is a conspicuous tension in these films, then, between an impulse to humanize the animals, to make them into furry, feathered or fanged people, and a contrary desire to imagine and image the natural world as it would be were there no people in it at all. There are virtually no humans to be seen in any of *True-Life Adventures*.[25] In fact, a great deal of emphasis is placed on the remoteness of the locales where they are filmed, on the defining absence of human interference in the events of which we are to be given a privileged glimpse. Like their predecessors in the 18th and 19th century — Georg Stellar, Alexander von Humboldt, Charles Darwin and the other great amateur explorers— the wildlife documentary cinematographers in the '50s and today seem rapturously fascinated with filming that a somehow unsullied Nature that is unaltered by the actions of "civilization," even as the narrative whittles wonder down to a suburban scale. Indeed, there are present in the *True-Life Adventures* (and in many of the films that follow, including *Earth*) two distinct kinds of time. One temporality belongs to individuals, and is measured by the milestones of their singular life. It is story-time (or if you prefer, run-time), made dramatic by the finite and finally terminal experience each living thing has of the world. For a specific fledgling, as for a certain person, there will be a first flight, and there will be a last breath. But there is also a deep time in the films, a temporality in which individuals are expendable and interchangeable precisely because, telescoped over millions of years, nothing is traumatic, nothing is a shock. For an animal character, life can be a "desperate struggle," or a "gripping drama," or "one long romp." For the desert or the Amazon, or more abstractly still, for Nature, Life, Earth, on the other hand, it is an "eternal pageant," a "continuous cycle," an "eternity."

Thus, the *True-Life Adventures* are hybrids in yet another sense, combining elements of the funny-animal animation tradition (and of its long line of progenitors in print, fable, and folk culture), in which animals serve as stand-ins or camouflage for recognized human types, and the conventions of classical Natural History and the literary "Wild Animal Story," which seeks to passionately and precisely engage a world in which creation operated under an unalterable order that was unstirred by the domineering interference of man. The Wild Animal story attempts to portray animals "living on their own terms," rather than defined by their relationships, hostile or congenial, with human beings.[26] Jordan's *Matka and Kotik*, which had been so instrumental in drawing Disney's attention to the remote Pribilofs, was one such story. Several others, such as Felix Salten's *Bambi: a Forest Life*, Ernest Thompson Seton's 1898 *Lobo* and a number of tales collected in Jack London's 1903 smash, *Call of the Wild*, were inspirational to Disney and other filmmakers. The form, which enjoyed a revival with Rachel Carson's clarion 1941 best-seller, *Under the Sea Wind* (her first book), and since has seen a number of major works, some of which, including *Watership Down*, inspired animated adaptations. In most cases, Wild Animal Stories are based on direct and intimate knowledge of animal habitats and behavior.[27] When people appear in Wild Animal Stories, they appear most often as inscrutable interlopers or unfeeling alien threats, in other words, in roles frequently played by animals in other wilderness narratives. In the landscape of the Wild Animal Story, it is man who is the Other.

This is certainly the case in the *True-Life Adventures*, though even when humanity is edited out, the fact that human beings are doing the editing in the first place is one that must be weighed in the balance. Many of the great labors of Natural History, and the works of the Wild Animal story writers, take place in the shadow of the Industrial Revolution and the rise of the secular state, a time during which nature was far more dramatically driven back (some would say decimated) by the engines of civilization and culture. Naturalists traveled to the remotest corners of the globe, in part to fulfill the encyclopedic project of post-renaissance scientific inquiry, which envisions modes of knowing in which all things can be contained and cataloged, and in part to find an authentic nature free from the taints of human action. Mapping, trapping, dissecting, describing the flora and fauna of the Antipodes, the islands of the Pacific, the interiors of Amazonia and Africa and the Americas, these gentlemen adventurers (most of them, Darwin, Clark, Humboldt and the lot, *were* men and moreover men of some position and privilege) were seeking Edens—all of which one by one vanished as their own efforts put such places in the path of their homelands' insatiable appetite for material, markets, and manpower. This quest remains central to conservationist discourses and to constructions of the natural world in contemporary media. "This nature is cast as that which existed prior to the impact of human action," notes Elizabeth Garland, "it is nature in a *state of nature*, not yet subsumed by the modern, social domain."[28]

Ironically, the wonder, beauty, and abundance natural historians sought and found in the world's wildernesses gave abundant incentive to the industries and institutions that were eager to tame and exploit them. The representations they made, the lavish, and in many cases, very popular, accounts they wrote, and the collections they assembled paid tribute to the wonders of the wildernesses that remained, and perversely accelerated their erosion.[29] Voyages of discovery inevitably blaze trail for voyages of exploitation. If we imagine these Brave New Worlds as having no people in them (well, no people that matter anyway) it is all the easier to take what we want from them —whether that be raw materials for industry or a restorative experience as an antidote to modernity.

The same desire to find and to fix by representation an emphatically inhuman state of nature, one uncorrupted by our avarice, is evident throughout the series. With a sweep of the magic wand, or in this case, brush, the *True-Life Adventures* take us from Eden to Eden, from all of which we are banned as by an angel with a fiery sword — or at least a park ranger with a sour glance. Nearly all of the films in the series were made in uncritical cahoots with the National Park Service, the Department of the Interior, tourism boards, chambers of commerce and other bureaucracies of with a stake in regulating and usually monetizing nature. None of which is to say the love of Nature with which these films are romantically redolent is in any way disingenuous. Far from it; there is a keen sense in many of the films that they are revealing the "last resorts" of the Wild — the prairie, you will recall, is vanishing. And yet for all the elegiac intonations, the musicality and the anthropomorphizing narration are constantly there to stifle interpretation, to forestall reflection. And even if humanity is invisible in the film, its presence is pervasive, like that of whatever unseen entity, presumably an employee in the Cosmic Ink and Paint Department, makes those opening brush strokes at the beginning of each film that paint a window in the wall through which we are able to see, possibly distorted and somehow shrunken, but still lovely, some of what we have lost.

Notes

1. Beyond a romantically anthropomorphic tendency in the characterization of the seals, little trace of Jordan's story can be detected in *Seal Island*. It is difficult to imagine Disney green-lighting even the most oblique adaptation of some of the episodes from grim lives and deaths of Matka's kin, which include scenes of horrific violence and wholesale slaughter (Jordan, *The Story of Matka: A Tale of the Mists,*1921, 66). Indeed, the commercial exploitation of the species, Jordan's raison d'être, is excluded entirely from the pristine wilderness the Disney documentary depicts.

2. It is no coincidence that the Pribilof Islands were at the time commercially, politically and to some extent, ideologically significant. A treaty negotiated in 1905 between Russia, Japan and the United States to regulate the hunting of fur seals was a landmark piece of conservation legislation — a five-year moratorium was declared when the treaty was ratified six years later — and remains an almost unequalled example of international cooperation. It was also a landmark acknowledgment of how close an expanding America had become to once remote "foreign powers." In 1950s, the islands in the frigid seas between Alaska and Russia were a point where the Cold War superpowers very nearly intersected. See Kurkpatrick Dorsey, "Putting a Ceiling on Sealing: Conservation and Cooperation in the International Arena, 1909–1911," *Environmental History Review*, vol. 15, no. 3 (August 1991), p. 44.

3. In 1948, an cluster of anti-trust actions against the vertically integrated studio system, *United States vs. Paramount et al.*, long delayed by Depression, the excellent attorneys hired by the Hollywood elite, and the Second World War, finally culminated in the consent decrees that effectively ended the stranglehold on first-run exhibition the so-called Big Five had enjoyed. It is ironic, and a testament to Disney's occasionally eerily

good timing, that the studio was integrating distribution at the very moment the bigger fish in the film industry pond were beginning to disintegrate. RKO, his reluctant distributor, would in fact be the first of the major studios to collapse.

4. The series continued to be profitable; *Beaver Valley*, the follow-up to *Seal Island*, made $664,000 and cost only $102,000. *The Living Desert* did still more robust business, returning over $4 million on an investment of around $300,000 (Lutts, p. 14). Like the reality television producers of today, Disney discovered that profit margins were broad when real life provided the stuff of cinema. See Barrier, *The Animated Man: A Life of Walt Disney* (Berkeley and Los Angeles: University of California Press, 2008), 208; and Ralph H. Lutts, *The Nature Fakers: Wildlife, Science and Sentiment* (Golden, CO: Fulcrum, 1990), 14.

5. Gabler, Neal. *Walt Disney: The Triumph of the American Imagination* (New York: Knopf, 2006), 446.

6. It is tempting to see in *Why We Fight* the forebear of Disney's documentary methodology, combining actuality footage, images excised from other sources, including newsreels and even fiction films, and animation, all orchestrated to the exhortations of an openly jingoistic and shamelessly manipulative voice-over. Many similar tactics appear in all of the *True Life Adventures.*

7. Much of documentary criticism and theory wrestles with just such questions, emphasizing the role played by biases and agendas of the filmmakers, exhibitors, and audiences in shaping what "truths" there are in non-fiction cinema (see Winston, 2005, and Nichols, 1981, for excellent and still wholly current overviews of the complexity and variety of documentary thought and practice). Walt Disney and the *True-Life Adventures*, having touched so many viewers and shaped so much content, have an important part to play in these ongoing inquiries

8. In the late 19th century, movements within Western culture and in particular American culture valorized encounters with what was perceived to be a retreating "natural" world as a scientific, medical, aesthetic and even moral remedy for various maladies afflicting the modern, industrial age. Photography, itself very much a product of that age, was somewhat ironically, the dominant representational instrument in making an unspoiled and restorative natural world available, at the same time accelerating the its commodification. Middle-class practitioners who abandoned urban environments to photograph animals and the wilderness in the field were both embodying the back-to-nature ethos that attended these movements, and providing a practical substitute for them; by providing images of the natural world to those unable or unwilling to escape to it. See Kevin C. Armitage, *The Nature Study Movement: The Forgotten Popularizer of America's Conservation Ethic* (Lawrence: University of Kansas Press, 2009).

9. Tucker, Jennifer. *Nature Exposed: Photography As Eyewitness in Victorian Science*, p. 64.

10. Walt Disney recognized the dual role played by these globetrotting photographer-scientists, referring to them as "naturalists who shoot birds." (Barrier, 209)

11. The rotoscope, patented in 1917 by Max Fleischer, one of Disney's most potent competitors in the silent and early sound eras, is a machine that allows animators to trace frames from live-action films. The conceptual forerunner of contemporary motion capture and digital tracing technologies, the device was used extensively at the Disney studio to create "realistic" movement, particularly in the animation of human figures.

12. Chuck Jones, "Music and the Animated Cartoon," *Hollywood Quarterly*, Vol. 1, No. 4 (July, 1946), 365

13. The language of the voice-overs, many of which were written as well as delivered by Hibler, echo precisely the studio's buzz-speak: the same lexicon from which the descriptions of the natural world are drawn in the *True-Life* films supplies the language used to push the other elements of Disney's now-sprawling brand.

14. O'Pray, Michael. "Eisenstein and Stokes on Disney: Film Animation and Omnipotence," in *A Reader in Animation Studies*, ed. Jane Pilling (London: John Libbey, 1997).

15. The park's "real-life dreamworld," the positioning of Main Street U.S.A. cheek by jowl with Sleeping Beauty's Castle creates a collision of fantasy and actuality that strongly recalls the blending of documentary cinematography and cartoon aesthetics in the *True-Life Adventures*. Steven Watts, *The Magic Kingdom: Walt Disney and the American Way of Life*. (Boston & New York: Houghton Mifflin, 1997), 289.

16. There is a distinction to made here, perhaps a fine one, but a significant one nonetheless, between *landscape* photography and *wildlife* photography, both of which are important in the production of documentaries like the ones under discussion. Landscape photography presupposes, and indeed rests wholly upon, the placement of the apparatus in the place being photographed. Wildlife photography affords far greater latitude in terms of methodology. Staged scenes of real animals in artificial environments, meant to be seen as views of Africa or Asia, were commonplace by the middle of the 19th century, and filmmakers, like their peers in the biological sciences, are frequently compelled to create controlled environments in which the phenomena they wish to record or study can be incited and observed.

17. Filming in remote locales and in often extreme conditions, not to mention trying to photograph creatures often swift, cryptic or dangerous, demanded innovation on the part of the *True-Life* cinematographers.

18. Robert Huxley, ed. *The Great Naturalists* (London: Thames & Hudson, 2007), 96.

19. John Burroughs, "A Sheaf of Nature Notes," *The North American Review*, vol. 212, no. 778 (September 1920), 329.

20. Barks, 1954.

21. Henry E. Childs, Jr. "Biological Myths: The Lemming Legend," *The American Biology Teacher*, vol. 30, no. 8 (October 1968), 660

22. Watts, 405

23. The ontological absoluteness of fact, so essential to empirical science, is shared to some extent by photography itself, which has long intertwined the two. See John Tagg, *The Burden of Representation: Essays on Photographies and Histories*. Minneapolis: University of Minnesota Press, 1988), 66.

24. The duel of the spider and the wasp, incidentally, is one of the film's triumphs of documentary stagecraft. UCLA entomology grad student N. Paul Kenworthy, devised a means of filming the conflict as part of his work towards his PhD.

25. In fact, Disney insisted that footage of both white and indigenous people were very deliberately excised from the inaugural *Seal Island* (Gabler, 444); Walt wanted his "True-Life" to be a life without of human beings. A somewhat farcical instance of the erasure of humanity from the natural world as seen in *True-Life Adventures* comes in *White Wilderness* in which the human "presence" is established only by the cave paintings, as if man, too, is as absent from the current scene as are the Wooly Rhinos and mammoths.

26. Ralph H. Lutts, ed. *The Wild Animal Story* (Philadelphia: Temple University Press, 1998), 7

27. Some of the authors associated with *The Wild Animal Story*, most notably Seton and Carson, were amateur or professional naturalists, and produced scientific as well as popular descriptions of animal behavior. Thus, some of the patina of "scientific" authority with which the documentary is often imbued is shared by some Wild Animal Stories, a fact which made these tales occasionally quite controversial. Seton and Charles G. D. Roberts were taken on in print by a number of prominent hunters, not least future president Theodore Roosevelt, who felt the form's insistence on interpreting animal conduct as the product of consciousness and for stirring up anti-hunting sentiment

(Roosevelt, Theodore. "Nature Fakers," *Everybody's Magazine* no. 17 [September 1907]: 427–430.) Similar controversy attended Walt Disney's 1942 animated adaptation of *Bambi*, which so alarmed hunters that the mini-mogul moved the film's American premiere from rustic Maine to the Roxy in New York.

28. The author further notes that for the *people* already resident in these Edens, this First-World Idyll of a depopulated, primal wilderness effectively negate them as cultural and political actors, which opens new questions regarding the unpeopled planet seen in the *True-Life* films. Elizabeth Garland, "The Elephant in the Room: The Colonial Character of Wildlife Conservation in Africa," *African Studies Review* vol. 51, no. 3 (Dec. 2008), 63–65.

29. Of countless instances, the case of Steller's sea cow will serve to illustrate this tragic irony. First described and drawn by Georg Steller on his voyages in the Bering sea (later the site of the Milotte's work for *Seal Island*), and made known in posthumous 1751 publication of his *Des Bestiis Marinis* or *Beasts of the Sea*. A relative of the manatee nearly 30 feet long, and the largest animal of its kind in the world, Steller's sea cow was hunted into extinction in a mere 27 years, surviving not even long enough to be photographed. Leonhard Stejneger, "How the Great Northern Sea-Cow (Rytina) Became Exterminated," *The American Naturalist*, vol. 21, no. 12 (Dec. 1887), 1068.

Bibliography

Armitage, Kevin C. *The Nature Study Movement: The Forgotten Popularizer of America's Conservation Ethic.* Lawrence: University of Kansas Press, 2009.

Barks, Carl. "The Seven Cities of Cibola," *Uncle Scrooge #7*. New York: Dell Publishing, September, 1954

Barrier, Michael. *The Animated Man: A Life of Walt Disney*. Berkeley and Los Angeles: University of California Press, 2008.

Burroughs, John. "A Sheaf of Nature Notes," *The North American Review* 212, no. 778 (September 1920): 329.

Childs, Henry E., Jr. "Biological Myths: The Lemming Legend," *The American Biology Teacher* 30, no. 8 (October 1968): 660–661.

Dorsey, Kurkpatrick. "Putting a Ceiling on Sealing: Conservation and Cooperation in the International Arena, 1909–1911," *Environmental History Review* 15, no. 3 (August 1991): 27–45.

Gabler, Neal. *Walt Disney: The Triumph of the American Imagination*. New York: Knopf, 2006.

Garland, Elizabeth. "The Elephant in the Room: The Colonial Character of Wildlife Conservation in Africa," *African Studies Review* 51, no. 3 (Dec. 2008): 63–65.

Huxley, Robert, ed. *The Great Naturalists*. London: Thames & Hudson, 2007.

Jones, Chuck. "Music and the Animated Cartoon," *Hollywood Quarterly* 1, no. 4 (July, 1946): 364–370.

Jordan, David Starr. *The Story of Matka: A Tale of the Mists*. Yonkers-on-Hudson, New York: World Book Company, 1921.

Lutts, Ralph H. *The Nature Fakers: Wildlife, Science and Sentiment*. Golden, CO: Fulcrum, 1990.

Lutts, Ralph H. ed. *The Wild Animal Story*. Philadelphia: Temple University Press, 1998.

Nichols, Bill. *Ideology and the Image: Social Representation in the Cinema and Other Media*. Bloomington: Indiana University Press, 1981.

O'Pray, Michael. "Eisenstein and Stokes on Disney: Film Animation and Omnipotence," in *A Reader in Animation Studies*, edited by Jane Pilling, 195–202. London: John Libbey, 1997.

Roosevelt, Theodore. "Nature Fakers," *Everybody's Magazine*, September 1907, 427f–430.

Stejneger, Leonhard. "How the Great Northern Sea-Cow (Rytina) Became Exterminated," *The American Naturalist* 21, no. 12 (Dec. 1887): 1068.

Tagg, John. *The Burden of Representation: Essays on Photographies and Histories.* Minneapolis: University of Minnesota Press, 1988.

Tucker, Jennifer. *Nature Exposed: Photography As Eyewitness in Victorian Science.* Baltimore: Johns Hopkins University Press, 2006.

Watts, Steven. *The Magic Kingdom: Walt Disney and the American Way of Life.* Boston & New York: Houghton Mifflin, 1997.

Winston, Brian. "The Tradition of the Victim in Griersonian Documentary." In *New Challenges for Documentary*, second edition, edited by Alan Rosenthal, 269–287. Manchester, United Kingdom: Manchester University Press. 2005.

10

Sex, Love, and Death
Disney's True-Life Fantasies

RONALD TOBIAS

The Circle of Life

During the production of the *True-Life Adventures* (1948–1960), Disney found himself hampered by the constraints of his own demand that the *Adventures* be "completely authentic, unstaged, and unrehearsed." While his quest for authenticity didn't exactly preclude the types of narrative that had made his studio famous, it did inhibit them. Consequently, he conceived the idea of the *True-Life Fantasy* as a way to bridge documentary realism with the types of narrative fantasy that characterized such successful animated features as *Snow White* and *Bambi.* Disney's intentions were simple: he wanted, in his own words, to "use the documentary material straight from nature, *but give it a plot* [emphasis added]."[1] He abandoned his claim to remain faithful to nature as it "really was" but to create a hybrid of fiction and non-fiction that emphasized the sorts of familial and social values that he personally valued as an American. Whereas "nature" had previously provided the plots in the *True-Life Adventures*; Disney would now provide them, unabashedly.

Perri (1957) was the first — and technically the only — example of a category Disney labeled a *True-Life Fantasy.* The story of a young female pine squirrel who negotiates her life in a complex and violent world of the forest, *Perri* falls more under the category of an animal fable than of a biological treatise about the life of *Tamiasciurus.* Disney later dropped the oxymoronic *True-Life Fantasy*, but the film served an important function for many years as a transitional template for a new species of nature fantasy film that started coming out of its studios during the 1960s, such as *Flash, the Teenage Otter* (1961), *The Legend of Lobo (1962)*, and *Yellowstone Cubs* (1963).

In many respects, *Bambi* served as the narrative model for *Perri.* Both stories share the same cast of characters and virtually the same plot; in fact, both stories were adapted from works by the Austrian writer Felix Salten. Both Bambi and Perri suffer similar familial tragedies: Bambi's mother dies and Perri's father dies. Both are threatened by and survive a raging fire. Both stories start in spring at birth and complete one full reproductive cycle. Both of the main characters explore their worlds with innocence, both find themselves at some point in danger of losing their lives, and both fall in love and procreate. And, curiously, both films rely on concepts of realism.

When *Bambi* premiered in 1942, critics in certain circles decried Disney's use of realism in animation. Eastern establishment elites who were out of touch with (or didn't care about) the popular taste made the argument that the inherent promise of animation lie in its ability to free the world from the laws of physics. The joy of animation was its ability to defy natural law. If you ran over a man with a steamroller, then he could either re-inflate or turn into a dozen tiny men who scattered in every direction. Logic did not restrain the imagination. These critics felt that Disney's realism was mundane because it drudgingly obeyed physical law by mimicking nature.

Mainstream animated America, on the other hand, adored Disney's realism. People had grown weary of hallucinogenic fantasies that had no bearing on their interests and lives. The powerful familial themes in *Bambi* resonated with them. Rather than resist the laws of nature, Disney reaffirmed them. More importantly, perhaps, Disney engaged his audience through sentiment. For example, he willingly suspended his demand for absolute realism in depiction in *Bambi* when it came to facial expression. Animals in the wild could not convey the depth of emotional affect the storyline demanded of them; as a result, Disney ordered his animators to exaggerate the physiognomy of characters so as to communicate the full range of sadness, joy, curiosity, puzzlement, and anger. Bambi's round, over-expressive eyes are emblematic of his cuteness and innocence. But when it came to Disney's renditions of the physical world (which he had already prefigured in the 1937 *Silly Symphony* cartoon, *The Old Mill*), he demanded precision and accuracy.

Disney turned to realism again when he started shooting wildlife on camera. The eleven episodes of *True-Life Adventures* produced before 1957 had served as both a starting and a departure point for his *True-Life Fantasy*. First, the dramatic appeal of nature on film had proved irresistibly cost-effective in comparison to labor- and cash-intensive animation. Secondly, Disney's claim that he was recording nature—not inventing it—served as proof to a willing public that nature indeed reaffirmed middle class American social values such as family, monogamy, and citizenship. And lastly, Disney's nature films reinforced the popular and deeply rooted conception of nature as a self-regulating, or homeostatic system.

The ideas of natural stability and resiliency appealed to the public for a variety of powerful psychological reasons. Stability spoke of permanence, constancy, and, however much as Disney characterized nature as unruly and volatile, the audience knew that it nonetheless conformed to a given set of rational and therefore calculable laws. The seasons come and go, animals are born and die, and the sun rises and sets. Even though natural catastrophes might seem capricious, we could nonetheless explicate their etiology.

Disney's nature is an example of classical static stability, a concept derived from the tendency of a mechanical system to return to a steady state after a disruption. According to its principles, even though a dynamic play of forces (either natural or human-made) may deflect nature from its steady state, nature will endure these insults and eventually recover its balance. A powerful and reassuring concept, it treats nature as a perpetual motion machine.

Disney's nature, like the Garden of Eden, exists in a state of static equilibrium. It is a vision of natural perfection in which everyone and everything lives in unwavering abundance and harmony and the cumulative effect of the forces acting upon it as a system equal zero. Change is impossible. For Disney, the essence of nature was its immutability. Its biological processes remained stable, constant, and harmonious. When disruptions occurred, whether by geophysical convulsion or the errancy of human beings, Nature invariably restored itself to its original condition, the same way Disney's elastic cartoon characters snap back into shape no matter how egregious the physical insult to them.

The animals in *Bambi* are sentient, articulate creatures such as deer, squirrels, owls, foxes, and rabbits that live a leisurely life, free of violence save for the calamitous intrusions of Man.[2] They consist of a cadre of small, warm-blooded animals such as rabbits, birds, skunks, squirrels, and a doughty old owl, who are well-behaved, polite, thoughtful citizens. Species that normally prey upon one another, such as the owl and the hare, for example, have reached a peaceful comity. A royal stag that the community collectively reveres as the Prince of the Forest assumes the highest position of power and authority as the forest's distant but ever-present patriarch, a role that Bambi is destined to achieve by virtue of his species, his sex, and his privilege as the stag's son.

Perri's world is equally static — each generation replaces the last — but the tenor of the social community is decidedly different. The animals that got along in *Bambi* are no longer so congenial in *Perri*. In *Bambi* death was an exception, caused by outside forces (the hunters); in *Perri*, however, death is a normalized process that occurs regularly among its citizens. A "mother marten" in search of food for her brood of newborns tries to raid the pine squirrel nest in which Perri lives with his brothers and sisters. "How will nature tip the scale?" the narrator queries in doggerel. "Will life or death prevail?" Perri's father, who like Bambi's father lives outside the home, is motivated "by some ancient instinct" to sacrifice his life in order to lure the marten away from his family. In turn, a raccoon threatens the marten's nest (albeit unconvincingly). In this world, death is an inevitable aspect of life. A mother fox kills a rabbit (which, in turn, a mother bobcat steals to feed her kits) and a goshawk kills a sapsucker. Death, however, is not existentially indiscriminate, as it is in the case of Bambi's mother's. The narrator in *Perri* makes the point, again in ragged verse, that "this is the perfect plan that nature has contrived / Some must die that others may survive / ...[But] many live to run away / And death can wait for another day." For most of the film Perri must duck a series of animals intent on killing her, including her obstinate nemesis the marten as well as a "swift and cunning" weasel and a goshawk that also try to kill her. Curiously, mothers do the bulk of killing in *Perri*. Disney couches the idea of death as a necessary consequence of mothers trying to feed their young.

He also created an annular sense of time so that events that happen are part of a perpetual cycle of re-happening. The film opens with the old saw from Ecclesiastes about there being a time for every purpose under heaven. This idea of time structures the film. "Come with us now," the narrator invites us into the film, "to watch with awe as the seasons change and marvel at the wondrous way in which [nature] has arranged a time for everything." But time in this world is not linear; it is circular because static equilibrium does not allow for change. In *The Lion King*, for example, the baboon prophet Rafiki tells the fledgling lion Simba that we are all part of the eternal cycle that is the "Circle of Life."[3] For the baboon prophet, nature is a closed loop of determined events (a definition of classical static stability) that reinforces a historically evolved teleology that every creature, great and small, has a designated place and a purpose. The same patterns repeat themselves season after season. And so in *Perri* winter is a time of waiting, spring a time of hunting, summer a time of learning, and fall a time of "preparing" followed by the climactic time "of together." Time is, in effect, timeless.

Sex in Disney has always been saccharine. The biological yearning for Perri to follow "nature's basic law" to find a mate during "a time of together." She finds herself irresistibly attracted to a bachelor in the neighborhood (with the echoic name of Porro) who the narrative describes in rhymed couplets as "noisy, brave, and brash / and quite often very rash." Disney erases the aggressive instinct males in the fantasy films; instead, the female indicates her willingness to be courted as she realizes "in some vague way" that her "destiny is entwined with her neighbor in the nearby tree...." In Disney's nature fantasies, the male is as coy and virginal as the female. Porro is polite, deferring, and even a bit ditzy as he "labors hopefully with his vast unruly mess of moss and grass he calls a nest" in preparation of Perri's "moment of fulfillment." The couple comes together as the chorus croons "This is Together Time."

Like Bambi and virtually all the featured animals in the *True-Life Adventures*, Perri lives in a garden that is essentially devoid of human beings.[4] But in *Flash, the Teenage Otter* (1961), the biggest threat of all emerges from the shadows where he had been skulking all along: Man. Born amongst the ruins of an old gristmill, Flash lives on a nature reserve "surrounded but not surrendered" to Man. All around him, the "frontier wilderness (has been) turned under by the pioneer's plow." As long as the animals stay on the reservation, human beings remain benign, but Flash learns the hard way that if an animal trespasses into the world of humans, dire consequences follow.

On the reserve, Flash's world is much like Perri's. He lives with his mother, and for some inexplicable reason his father has been "banished" although he lingers nearby (like the fathers in *Bambi* and *Perri*). The mother, Lutra, is "on a constant shuttle answering the demands of motherhood, [and] responding to the pleas of her mate." The otter pups' greatest virtue is their innocence as they play "tag, follow the leader, and seek-and-find" among the rusting ruins of human technology. There is danger here as well, when a vixen with five kits to feed tries to raid the otters' nest. Later, a bobcat ambles into the scene looking for an easy meal. Flash and his family manage catastrophe adeptly, but when a misstep sweeps Flash downstream from his family, he suddenly finds himself in *terra incognita*, helplessly separated from his mother and the rest of his family.[5]

In the world off the reservation, families of raccoons and skunks turn into families of goats and cattle. Mothers remain the same as they watch over their broods, but Flash must fend for himself in an alien world, and the farther he goes into it, the more precarious his life becomes. In succession he must endure a trapper who wants to kill Flash for the $40 he can get for his pelt, a gamekeeper who wants to kill him because he would compete for fish with fishermen, and finally a pack of dogs that want to kill him out of blood lust.[6] By turns, Flash is trapped, caged, shot at, physically mauled, and then trapped again.

His "odyssey" couched within the film is the trek all otters must take every year as they move between their seasonal hunting, mating, and wintering grounds. This biological trivia is quickly lost to the more powerful emotional odyssey that Flash must make from innocence to experience. The world is a complex—and dangerous—place. And most of that threat comes from Man.

But not all Disney's humans are out of synchronization with nature. A faceless bureaucrat of the "State Conversation Department," who Flash recognizes as a person who "meant him no harm," ultimately returns Flash to the reserve, where he is reunited with his family and his mate-to-be. The cycle of life is restored.

In 1962, one year after *Flash, the Teenage Otter*, Disney released *The Legend of Lobo*, the story of a young wolf who has to adapt to encroaching cattlemen. Lobo undergoes many of the same trials and tribulations as Bambi, Perri, and Flash. As a pup, Lobo nibbles on the ear of an armadillo, gets cornered by an irritable rattlesnake, and makes friends with a tortoise and an antelope. The true conflict of the story, however, is about dispossession as the cattlemen systematically kill Lobo's family and his pack as they move into the wolf's homelands. With their natural prey, the buffalo, nearly extinct, the wolves have been forced to hunt cattle, which brings them into conflict with the cattlemen.

As Lobo matures, he becomes leader of his own pack and so the cattlemen focus their sights on him. He becomes a renegade hero—wanted dead or alive—fighting against insurmountable odds for the rights of his kind. When a trapper captures Lobo's mate, he must come to her rescue, and as he does, Lobo realizes—as his father had—that wolves can't live near people. Forced to leave, Lobo takes his pack and goes off in search of a new home.

The fourth film in what might be called the *True-Life Fantasy* series of films in the late 1950s and early 1960s is *Yellowstone Cubs* (1963). The plot has become formulaic: animals are safe in the wilderness and do not belong in the world of Man. In *Yellowstone Cubs,* twins Tuffy and Tubby get separated from their mother early in the film and get into constant mischief as they come into contact with a series of intolerant tourists in Yellowstone Park. Meanwhile the mother, "old Nokomis," doggedly tracks down her cubs, an act which the rangers of the Park misinterpret as hostile. Branded with yellow paint as a "problem bear," Nokomis refuses to abandon her quest for her cubs, which eventually earns her a death sentence from the rangers. She is reprieved at the last moment when they realize the nature of Nokomis's true quest. Reinvested with the title of a "good bear," she retreats into the forest with her cubs. At the same time Disney produced these nature fantasy-films, he also produced three box office hits about dogs that lived within the human nuclear family: *Old Yeller* (1957), *Nikki, the Dog of the North* (1961), and *Big Red* (1962). *Flash* and *Yellowstone Cubs* did not perform nearly as well at the box office. Even though the public liked the nature-fantasies, it liked sentimentalized stories about canine fidelity and sacrifice even more.

From time to time Disney experimented with stories about wild cats, such as *A Tiger Walks* (1964), *Charlie, the Lonesome Cougar* (1967), and *Napoleon and Samantha* (1972), but the economic successes of domestic dog and cat stories quickly overshadowed the wild animal fantasies. Although the studios kept fabled beasts alive in animated films—most notably *The Lion King* (1994)—the documentary based *True-Life Fantasy* was, for all intents and purposes, dead.

Reality: Nature's Illusion

While critics of high-brow publications panned the nature-fantasies for their extreme anthropomorphism, the popular press embraced Disney as a master of using commercial mass media "in a manner which would make those media educationally beneficial to persons who attend to their messages"—namely children and their parents.[7] Many saw Disney as a moral educator because he presented nature as the ultimate arbiter of what constituted natural *human* social behavior. The domestic melodramas of the nature fantasies presume a certain biological reality because they are presented naturalistically. Audiences understood the fantasies to be realistic portrayals of animal nature when in fact they were idealized portrayals of human nature. "The absorption of ourselves into Nature is simply the absorption of ourselves into ourselves," writes Neil Evernden, "or rather into our conception of how it 'ought' to be."[8] Nature offers compelling models of good and evil, right and wrong, courage and cowardice, and any other behavior for which society at large seeks guidance.

What audiences did not perceive is the function of animal performance in the fantasies. In an essay on *Perri* in 1958, the French film theorist André Bazin wrote in the journal *Cahiers du Cinéma* "It is not the cinema that attributes the human behavior to animals, but the animals themselves acting before the camera according to the predetermination that could preside over a dramatic sequence."[9] Bazin captures the relation of the subject to the camera in Disney's documentary nature fantasies. In the *True-Life Adventures*, the plot came *after* the filming. Filmmakers edited footage shot in the wild to conform to a notion of story (putatively *found* in nature), whereas in the nature-fantasies, the plot came *before* the filming. Animals and their performances were scripted for the camera. Plot, a prototypically human construction, came before any meaningful biological realism.

The traces of reality encoded within the cinematographic image provided a level of access to nature no one had imagined possible as technical advancements in macro- and telephotography gave the camera the power to penetrate the intimate details of nature. "The need to bring things spatially and humanly 'nearer,'" wrote Walter Benjamin, "is almost an obsession today, as is the tendency to negate the unique or ephemeral quality of a given event by reproducing it photographically. There is an ever-growing compulsion to reproduce the object photographically, in close-up...."[10] The viewer quickly came to believe there was no place a camera couldn't go and nothing it couldn't see. The camera went everywhere from the tops of trees to the bottom of ponds. The producers even built sets that prompted viewers to believe they were peeking into the intimate lives of animals in their nests and dens. In the final analysis, the world of reality is as constructed as the artificial world of animation. (Perri, for example, was not a single female pine squirrel; rather, she was one of dozens of squirrels— male and female alike — who died of exhaustion during the rigors of production.) The illusion of nature is compelling because of its constructed visual reality, but in the end the classroom isn't about nature so much as it is about human society.

By the 1960s, film penetrated virtually every city and town in America, and with the advent of television, into virtually every household. As urbanization and industrialization pushed nature farther away from rapidly expanding urban centers, people increasingly accepted Disney as a readily accessible surrogate. [A surrogate, moreover, that validates the separation of Man and wild was necessary for their peaceful coexistence: Man is the disruptive element in *Bambi*.... Flash, Lobo, and Nokomis are endangered by contact with humans ... and humans are endangered in turn when wild animals get too close to their orderly world in *Big Red*, *Old Yeller*, and *A Tiger Walks*.]

Walt Disney is, arguably, our culture's pre-eminent commercial manufacturer of images and stories about nature. Since Walt Disney the man produced his first cartoon short in 1922, his subsequent corporate empire created an enduring archive of popular works that have gained powerful attraction in the minds of hundreds of millions of people over many decades. As one bumper sticker once summarized the Disney effect, "The world is watching the United States, and the United States is watching Walt Disney."[11]

The power of a culture lies in its ability to create myths. Disney's works are woven through the warp and woof of the American cultural tapestry. They have done much to shape our popular myths, beliefs, and fundamental paradigms about nature than any other single cultural force of the last century. The rhetoric of Disney's images employs schemes of knowledge, power and practice that relate to a variety of social and cultural relationships that are grounded in the social interactions between people and between people and nature. By analyzing Disney's narratives about nature (and the way they manipulate the myths within them), we can appreciate their power to shape our sense of what we *expect* of nature, and from it we may begin to limn the moral authority manufactured by Disney Industries over the past century, a moral authority that has become, either by design or default, an American moral compass.

Notes

1. Eric Smoodin, ed. *Disney Discourse: Producing the Magic Kingdom* (New York: Routledge, 1994), 59.
2. I use "Man" in the same way Disney uses it in *Bambi:* the ethos of a society that believes civilization is a place created and protected by males
3. "Circle of Life," Music by Elton John, lyrics by Tim Rice
4. The forest fire in *Bambi* is caused by careless hunters whom the viewer do not see, although their presence is made known by their hunting dogs.
5. Disney relied heavily on the theme of separation anxiety: Bambi, Perri, Flash, and the grizzly twins get separated from their mothers, thus establishing the plotline of reunion.
6. The hunting dogs in *Flash* are the same as the savage hunting dogs in *Bambi*; they are Man's minions.
7. Ralph Izard, Walt Disney: Master of Laughter and Learning," *Peabody Journal of Education*, vol. 45, no. 1 (July 1967), 36.
8. Neil Evernden, *The Social Creation of Nature,* (Baltimore: Johns Hopkins University Press, 1992), 99.
9. André Bazin, "Les Perils de Perri," *Cahiers du Cinéma*, Vol. 83 (May 1958), pp. 50–53.
10. Susan Sontag, *On Photography* (New York: Picador U.S.A., 1977), 191.
11. Quoted in Ralph H. Lutts, "The Trouble with Bambi: Walt Disney's *Bambi* and the American Vision of Nature," *Forest & Conservation History*, vol. 36 (October 1992), 160.

Bibliography

Bazin, André. "Les Perils de Perri," *Cahiers du Cinéma* 83 (May 1958): 50–53.
Evernden, Neal. *The Social Creation of Nature*. Baltimore: Johns Hopkins University Press, 1992.

Izard, Ralph. "Walt Disney: Master of Laughter and Learning" *Peabody Journal of Education* 45, no. 1 (July 1967): 36.
John, Elton, and Tim Rice. "Circle of Life." Burbank, CA: Wonderland Music Company, 1994.
Lutts, Ralph H. "The Trouble with Bambi: Walt Disney's *Bambi* and the American Vision of Nature" *Forest & Conservation History* 36 (October 1992): 160.
Smoodin, Eric, ed. *Disney Discourse: Producing the Magic Kingdom*. New York: Routledge, 1994.
Sontag, Susan. *On Photography*. New York: Picador U.S.A., 1977.

11

It *Is* a Small World, After All

Earth *and the Disneyfication of* Planet Earth

EDDY VON MUELLER

It is always momentous when a noun becomes a verb. The process is organic and informal, so the moment of metamorphosis is often difficult to pinpoint. Consider "disneyfy." While Walt Disney, who had, to say the least, a robust sense of his own significance to modern American culture and indeed to modern world culture, would by no means displeased to find his name thus transformed, there is no evidence that the verb officially originated in the studio. It is in fact unclear when precisely the term appeared. "Disneyfied" was in used in the late 1970s to describe what the work of *enfant terrible* Ralph Bakshi wasn't, and in the mid–1980s to describe what the work of Disney defector Don Bluth was. The word may be much older, however, since that which it aptly describes has been an energetic force in commercial entertainment since the Ub Iwerks' "Springtime" short appeared as part of *Silly Symphonies* series in 1929.[1]

Even if its origins are obscure, the meaning of "disneyfication" is straightforward enough. It refers to a set of practices, neither exclusively confined to animation nor unique to the Disney company, designed to convert existing cultural materials into uncomplicated, unthreatening forms attractive to a specific demographic, the families with small children[2] that have long been the cornerstone of the Disney empire.[3]

Disneyfication is visible in all manner of Disney media, but 2009 provided a superb opportunity to see the process at work. On Earth Day, April 22nd, amid much ballyhoo, the media giant launched a new subsidiary, Disneynature, and premiered the feature-length documentary *Earth*. A live-action, ostensibly non-fiction film, and therefore very different from the kind of content with which Disney has been most closely associated, since the *True-Life Adventure* series of nature films was pulled from production. Bringing *Earth* in line with

Disney's brand and audience make the hallmarks of disneyfication stand out in particularly sharp relief.

That is because *Earth* is not, technically or wholly a Disney production. Rather, it is compilation of sorts, a selection of material shot for the documentary mini-series *Planet Earth*. Aired on the BBC and the Discovery Channel in late 2006, the globetrotting series had been over five years in the making, and had already broken records, won critical plaudits and scooped up multiple media awards before the feature deal with Disney had been inked.[4] But what made for wildly successful television documentary was not evidently suited to Disney's signature mode of theatrical family entertainment. Radically abbreviated to fit into feature length, completely rescored, boasting a different narrative voice and reflecting strikingly different structural strategies and thematic concerns, Disney's *Earth* emerges from its makeover a leaner, friendlier film that ultimately has far more in common with *The Jungle Book* and *The Lion King* than with the eleven-hour epic of 21st century Natural History from which it had been carved.

The "Epic Documentary" Tradition

The disneyfication of *Planet Earth* involves more than shift from one medium to another (from television to theatrical cinema, the small screen to the silver, so to speak), it is also a rebranding, and the transformation of a text made in one documentary filmmaking tradition into and example of another, very different tradition.

In the early 1950s, when airtime was abundant and competition relatively scarce, television producers experimented in long-format documentary content. Created by Henry Salomon, *Victory at Sea* spanned 26 half-hour episodes and aired on NBC in 1952 and 1953. Cobbled together primarily from newsreel and government footage, the series was counted a success, but as the medium matured and situation comedies, Westerns and quiz shows crowded into prime-time, it failed to provide a viable commercial paradigm. In Britain, though, where a national television service was less at the mercy at the marketplace and from whence came so many trailblazing television productions, a number of non-fiction programs were made which took advantage of televisions affinity for serialization and undertook the detailed exploration of topics and issues too vast to be treated by traditional documentary cinema. The first of these, a 13-episode history of Western culture and art called, boldly, *Civilisation*, aired in 1969. It was the brainchild of art historian and museum curator Sir Kenneth Clark and filmmaker David Attenborough, who was then in charge of the BBC2 network and who would go on to make the British nature documentary almost his own for the rest of the 20th century.

The same year, production began on *The World at War*, a British answer to *Victory at Sea*, which ran to 26 half-hour episodes and began airing in 1973. Produced by Jeremy Isaacs for Lew Grade's innovative ITV — Britain's first commercial television network — it covered a smaller time period than *Civilisation*, but had a broader geographical scope, combining interviews and archival footage to create a "video history" of the Second World War. It also featured voice-over narration by Sir Laurence Olivier, Britain's most revered stage and screen actor, which lent dramatic gravitas and a measure of star-power to the production, establishing a device that remains important today.

Other British documentary "epics" followed. Most, including *Civilisation*, ultimately found a place in the American market on public television, which had ample available airtime; a smaller, more exclusive share of the audience; and a longstanding association with "educational" content. The documentaries hewed to a relatively consistent pattern: like *World at War* and *Civilisation*, they are sweeping in scope, feature material shot in a large number of far-flung locales, and deal with the broadest of topics. The titles, often, say it all: *The Ascent of Man*, *The Trials of Life*, *Life on Earth*, *The Power of Art*. The foothold established by British imports ultimately led a number of epic documentarians from the UK to ply their trade stateside, notably Adrian Malone, executive producer of *The Ascent of Man* and one of the series' directors, David Kennard. In 1980, the pair would collaborate on the production of *Cosmos*, a thirteen episode PBS series that sought to encompass not only the history of science and the human species, but universe itself.

Cosmos was the most widely-viewed program in the history of non-commercial broadcasting in the United States and began (or, giving *Victory at Sea* its pride of place, restored) an American tradition of epic documentaries. These projects, like *Vietnam: A Television History* (1983), *Eyes on the Prize* (1987) and Ken Burns' *Civil War* (which broke *Cosmos*' PBS ratings record in 1990), *Baseball*, *Jazz* (2001) and *The War* (2007), as well as such cable epics as *The Presidents* (2005) and *The States* (2007), share with the BBC content the signature scope. Unrestrained by audience attention spans or the exhibitor's insatiable need to turn screens, the documentary epic is free to delve.

On either side of the Atlantic, epic documentaries all feature as well the guidance of a seemingly omniscient narrator, often either an expert in the matter at hand or a celebrity of the more sober and reliable sort. In some cases, the series made the experts into celebrities. *Cosmos* made a star of astronomer Carl Sagan, for instance, and storyteller Shelby Foote gained considerable cache-lending the *Civil War* his Southern drawl. The grandiose reach and the all-knowing voice-over, which link the epic documentary to what Bill Nichols calls the "expository" mode of documentary filmmaking,[5] renders such films, however stirringly scored, dramatically cut, or impressively photographed they might be, essentially didactic.[6] They are encyclopedias in moving pictures, far-reaching and authoritative enough in handling what they do address to create the illusion that they have addressed all.

Planet Earth: *The BBC's High Definition Natural History Epic*

Planet Earth is a quintessential example of epic documentary encyclopedism. Produced by Alistair Fothergill, a filmmaker trained as a zoologist and a pivotal member of the BBC's Natural History Unit, the series includes footage shot by 40 teams working in more than 200 locations, from the Himalayas to the ocean floor. Fothergill has an impressive pedigree in the form, having previously led the production of the epic documentary *The Blue Planet* in 2001 and worked under the supervision of David Attenborough on several of his multi-part nature programs. Attenborough—whose venerable, tweedy voice as been synonymous with wildlife documentaries in the United Kingdom since the 1970s—narrates *Planet Earth*, which certainly adds to the series' air of world-encompassing completeness.[7]

In terms of its audience and its mode of address, *Planet Earth* is not as archly pedantic as many of the BBC epics (including most of Attenborough's films), or as high-minded and elegiac as Ken Burns' work for American public television, *Planet Earth* is nevertheless emphatically not kid stuff—except possibly for kids who happen to enjoy encyclopedias. Like the majority of non-fiction content which fills much of the cable line-up much of the time, *Planet Earth* is geared principally for teens and adults. It contains fairly graphic violence, for example, though sex and violence among the non-hominid fauna is generally deemed relatively innocuous in "educational" programming. The tone and the language of the piece tend toward detail and environmentally ominous conclusions: We are frequently reminded both of the life-and-death struggles faced the creatures we meet, as well as of our own complicity in the destruction of animal habitats.

Though the premier episode promises to show us "places untouched by man," the Hand of Man is constantly felt throughout the series. In addition to the environmentally-conscious alarms sounded in nearly every episode (deserts are growing, the snow leopard population has collapsed, disappearing sea ice is damning the polar bears), humanity is a structuring absence in the program. Few people appear in the main body of *Planet Earth*, but the voice-over makes the viewer acutely conscious of that fact, insisting that we are witnessing events that "rarely seen by human eyes" or "never filmed before," as if we are discovering a New World by our watching.

This privileged glimpse at a world without people is, of course, an illusory, secondhand one. Every episode of *Planet Earth* ends with one or more segments in which the illusion of a pristine "untouched" wilderness is self-reflexively swept away, and the people and the machines that made the elephantine epic possible take center stage. These segments, called "Planet Earth Diaries" reveal an almost fetishistic fascination with the cutting-edge equipment employed, and with trials faced by the "bold," "dauntless," and "determined" people using them. This trope makes them into almost heroic figures. The camera crews become, implicitly, not just recorders of he natural world, but scientist-explorers in their own right—the Darwins and Humbolts of the digital age. Ironically, technology itself is one of the stars of *Planet Earth*. Even had traditional cinematography been able to record the distant, deep, dark and frequently dangerous scenes the more compact, more forgiving high-definition digital cameras capture for the series, the sheer cost of such an undertaking on film would have beggared the BBC and its partners.

Unlike fiction films, which generally go to great lengths to keep the operations of the filmmakers decently hidden lest they puncture the imaginary "reality" of the story-world, *Planet Earth* is at great pains to frame its depictions of the natural world with scenes from *our* world, the real "real world." It is as if the segments featuring the filmmakers are there to assure viewers that yes, someone actually did follow that impala in a helicopter, or loiter in a war-zone waiting for goats, or slither up that mountain of guano, swarming with roaches. In an age when synthetic spectacles made by computers have become routine (consider the computer-generated jungles in Peter Jackson's revision of *King Kong*, or the towering forests and floating mountains in James Cameron's *Avatar*), reality needs all the corroborating evidence it can get. Thus we are finally pulled, every hour, out of the surge of unprecedented, eye-popping images and *Planet Earth* forcefully reasserts the status of the film as a film, or more specifically, a documentary.

Unquestionably, there is beauty here, terrible and splendid, and there is awe, but there is little wonder in *Planet Earth*: we believe what we see to be genuine, and we are made to understand how it all came to be. Indeed, we are almost as awed that the fillmmakers got the shot as we are by what it depicts. In a sense, *Planet Earth* is a series from which mystery and wonder have been banished, since it seems as if there is no place on the planet, from the most ice-bound glacier to the most hidden cave, that cannot be explored, recorded and ultimately understood, no wilderness so remote or creature so cryptic that it can hide from the filmmakers (and by extension, our) all-seeing HD gaze. Considered in the context of epic documentary, nature filmmaking and wildlife photography, *Planet Earth* is certainly a masterpiece, but it is never allowed to be magical.

Magic, however, is what Disney is all about. Much had to change, therefore, before this extraordinary, encyclopedic work could appear in theaters, bearing the Disney brand and standard.

Planet Disney: *Docudrama and the Diminution of an Epic*

The Walt Disney Company is by no means new to documentary. The company has been involved in the making of hundreds of educational and—during the Second World War — training and propaganda films, The *True-Life Adventures* series of short and feature-length wilderness and wildlife films, treated elsewhere in this volume, were seen theatrically around the world, and played in classrooms and on television well into the 1980s. The True-Life format was, like most Disney content, tailored for the family audience, and though the last film in the series was released in 1960, it is in the likeness of these movies that *Planet Earth* was re-made in 2009. The eco-conscious natural history epic was, in the hands of Walt Disney Studios, expertly whittled into an edifying (if occasionally and accidentally educational), emotionally rich family drama.

Earth running time is exactly 90 minutes: traditionally the ideal length for movie-goers with kids in tow, and just about exactly one-seventh the running time of the mini-series. Obviously, a lot of material shot by those "bold, dauntless and determined" HD teams had to hit the virtual cutting-room floor in the process. The priorities and practices of disneyfication can be seen in what is taken out, what is retained, and how it is organized. *Earth* is not a condensed version of *Planet Earth*— a distillation or reduction concentrating into a denser film the essence of the original — but rather a diminution, or juvenilization, in which the concerns and themes of *Planet Earth* (the very world *it* discovers and creates)— are made manageable, miniature, and comfortably familiar.

The kinder, gentler, shorter *Earth* adopts a number of techniques used extensively in other Disney content, including the *True-Life Adventures* and in the sound cartoons on which the studios fortunes were built. The use of music, in particular, is a conspicuous difference between the small-screen epic and the big-screen bauble The sequence in which the mating displays of an eye-catching assortment of Birds of Paradise are syncopated to a thumping base groove, for example, is straight out of the *True-Life Adventures* or the first Silly Symphonies cartoon, *Skeleton Dance*. The same technique, known in the filmmaking world as Mickey-Mousing, is used in a scene in which a troop of baboons wades awkwardly through a flooded inland delta, the mincing rhythm creating a sort of slapstick tone. Both scenes occur in *Planet Earth*, but in the mini-series there is no mood-setting music; the behaviors are acoustically accompanied only by what seem to be natural sounds recorded on location.

Planet Earth has a musical score, and like all film music, it influences the audience's emotional response to the image track. But the music in *Earth* is far more evocative of the kinds of music typical of fiction filmmaking, and it is more pervasive. More pervasive, too, is the use of time-lapse photography. Time-lapse photography is a favorite technique of nature documentarians. After all, many processes, from the melting of snows to the springing of buds, take place to slowly for impatient human observers to mark. The technique appears frequently in *Planet Earth*, usually to illustrate a specific phase or process significant to the animals under discussion: a forest blushing russet with the coming of autumn, or clouds rushing into towering formation to pour rains on the thirsty plains. Time-lapse (and slow-motion cinematography) here may be thought of as a temporal analog to the encyclopedic documentary's apparently all-encompassing breadth of vision, which can take in everything from the highest peaks to the bottommost undersea abyss. Neither events blindingly fast nor glacially slow can elude the cameras.

Fast-motion interludes also offer a formal punctuation mark, facilitating a change in location or focus. Time lapse photography is used in *Planet Earth* because we have so much ground to cover; in *Earth*, because we have so little time. The time-lapse sequences in *Planet Earth* enhance the kaleidoscopic, trans-temporal God's-eye perspective of the encyclopedic documentary. *Earth*, with its smaller scope and briefer span, *Earth* employs time-lapse in ways that often seem disconnected from the natural world. The sequences function as a purely formal gesture—a kind of magical seeing that has less to do with the rhythms of the real world than with the emotions of the audience. Crammed into so (relatively) short a film and frequently set to music, the time-lapse sequences in *Earth* seem like something out of *Fantasia*.

Most of the heavy lifting of disneyfication in *Earth*, though, is done on the level of narrative. Like most works of natural history, *Planet Earth* favors systematics to thematics, and structures each episode around a specific environment—fresh water, desert, forests, and so forth. This allows the film to remain global in its perspective, episodes hop nimbly from the Eastern Europe to the Western United States to Central Asia—and keep it at a certain distance from the actions of individual animals, which admittedly give the film much of its emotional impact. If we were given a nutshell to shove its half-a-day's worth of documentary into, we might say that *Planet Earth* is "about" our planet's many habitats, and the living things those habitats support.

Earth, on the other hand, is about babies.

The film opens with twin polar bear cubs (not just cute, but brand-building, plush-toy peddling cute—Coca Cola has been using CGI polar bear cubs as a seasonal sales tool for over a decade) and proceeds to parade baby animals on the screen throughout—all warm-blooded, by the way (invertebrates and reptiles are most frequently found playing support in Disney cartoons—Evinrude the dragonfly in *The Rescuers*, Sebastian the crab in *Little Mermaid* (the titular amphibians in *The Frog Princess* are the first cold-blooded critters cast in "leading roles"—presuming that the stars of *Dinosaur* were endotherms). The perspective is technically still global, but what links these creatures together is not adaptation and environment, as in *Planet Earth*, but developmental and individualized their shared infancy. Species—elephant, duck, baboon, whale, bear—doesn't make a difference, the film suggests. Babies are babies, . *Earth* plays, as a result, like the zoological equivalent to the famous animatronic "It's a Small World" attraction at Disneyland, in which children of every race and nation hold hands and sing to the audience across a harmonious, bijou Earth.

To drive this focus on the family home, the adult animals in *Earth* are consistently and casually referred as "mom" or "dad." In the end, all of the juveniles on which we have focused (save one) are alive and well, and the parents have proven themselves good and responsible guardians. This is not to say, however, that *Earth* is devoid of drama. Far from it. The film's most gripping (and manipulative) sequences involve baby animals in peril, a favorite theme of the studio throughout its history. A young deer is taken by a wolf in the first act (the wolf, we are informed, has cubs to feed), and later a pride of lions menace try to separate an elephant calf from the protective circle of his herd during a night attack. When they find the vulnerable youngster shielded by trumpeting grown-ups, the disappointed lions shift their hungry attentions to a "solitary male," who they harry off-screen. Their messy meal, like all blood-smeared scenes of animal feasting featured in *Planet Earth*, is not shown in the Disney version.

Finally, bookending the film, a male polar bear, identified as the father of the introductory twins, goes after a newborn walrus. This attempt, like the wolf's, is chalked up to the demands of feeding the family, but the polar bear fails, and is injured—mortally we are told—by one of his would-be victims.

If this seems a lot of violence for a family film, reflect for a moment on the corpse-strewn canon of Disney's animated features, scarcely a single nuclear family survives with both parents intact, and the films are full of orphans. Human children tend to be bereft before the movie begins, as in *Lilo and Stitch* and *Tarzan*, but animals face grimmer prospects. *Bambi*, *Finding Nemo*, *The Fox and the Hound*, and *The Lion King* all include the death of a parent, albeit obliquely. Moreover, most of the cartoon features thrust their young protagonists in deadly harm's way at some point. These events are, of course, handled with care. We do not dwell on explicit scenes of predation or dismemberment, a nicety of feeling shared by the editors of *Earth* which, like the more lethal animations, leave to the real moms and dads watching with their offspring the unpleasant task of explaining what just happened to Bambi's mom or Simba's dad.

How violence is represented and contextualized in *Earth* is a fascinating example of how the same representations of the same events can be spun to different effects for different crowds. "This is the circle of life, that most of us in our urban lives have lost touch with" intones the narration by James Earl Jones (repeating a refrain from *The Lion King*, whose patriarch, Mufasa, spoke in his voice), as a cheetah runs down a gazelle. The pursuit is presented as a bloodless, balletic slow-mo sequence, with the coup-de-grace neatly cut out, accompanied by a lovely, melancholic music. A similar sequence, appearing in both films, shows a great white shark devouring a flailing sea-lion. The slow-motion sequence is cut differently in *Earth*, with the one shot in which the predator's jaws close in unambiguous slow motion on the body of the hapless pinniped is excised. Only shots in which just the sea lion's tail can be seen in the shark's mouth are used. Nature may still be red in tooth and claw in a Disney film, but it is a very *pretty* red, and death, when it comes, is always narratively reconciled.

The film and the voice-over of *Earth* create an unambiguous interpretive framework for understanding the events shown. The shot of the wounded polar bear "dad" breaking off his attack on the escaping walruses, during which we are informed that he will not survive, is followed by a bright, high-angle long shot of the twins jogging along the snowscape. "Their father's brave spirit will always live on in their young hearts," says Jones (the voice not only of Mufasa, but of Darth Vader and CNN), "like all of our children, they are the hope of the future and proof of the resilience of life in this place we all share." Unlike the omniscient narrator in the mini-series, the function of the voice-over in *Earth* is not simply to explain, but also to reassure, to tell us not just what the events pictured literally *are* but what they, in this case metaphysically or spiritually, mean. Here, death becomes paternal sacrifice, and the Jones' sonorous benediction closes the circle of life: an animal's life ends, but animal life endures. This sort of mythic perpetuity, in which drama can punctuate but never ultimately arrest the closed-circuit spin of a stable and impervious cosmos is wholly compatible with the magical thinking that underlies much Disney content. *Every* night in the park is special, and marked by a parade; every ending is finally a happy one.

The most profound mark of *Earth's* disneyfication is, ultimately, that optimistic outlook. Its source-epic, *Planet Earth*, depicts life as perpetually standing on the brink, and puts responsibility for the fragile and threatened natural world squarely on our shoulders. On *Planet Earth*, we appear as newcomers: aliens and usurpers, or, more benignly, chroniclers and collectors. Human ingenuity and perseverance are celebrated in every episode of *Planet Earth*, but so too are human rapacity and neglect decried Whether it is the animals that are under threat or the small, small world itself, as in the case of the vast Lechuguilla cave system, which has to be sealed off lest spelunking nature-lovers inadvertently destroy its wonders, *Planet Earth* is an encyclopedia of the endangered. Even when humanity is not directly implicated in its peril, the natural world is depicted in the epic as painfully prone to cataclysm, as seen in the fantastical (but not, in the literal sense, fabulous!) deepwater environments that cluster round volcanic vents and then are left lifeless when the pattern of eruption changes. *Earth*, in good Disney fashion, plays a dramatically different refrain, reassuring viewers that, though *a* life may be fleeting, Life itself goes on and on.

Notes

1. As Donald Crafton, Karl Malden and others have ably chronicled elsewhere, theatrical animation in the United States was varied and competitive, with many players, series, characters and techniques jostling for screens and market share. Disney's small studio was initially part of this hungry throng. An important harbinger of things to come, "Springtime" sets itself apart from many early sound cartoons, including others made by Disney, by adopting a bluntly but still distinctly Romantic view of nature, setting the processes of seasons and animal life jauntily to music.

2. There is of course an immense market for media targeting exclusively children—content designed in other words to be consumed principally by juveniles absent older co-viewers. Disney, in fact, creates or distributes many such titles (their Baby Einstein products and various Mickey Mouse Club franchises spring to mind). Contrasted with, for instance, Disney's animated and live action features which presuppose that there are adults present in the theater (that most such films are in fact now routinely rated "PG," formally acknowledging this assumption), children's media presents far more simple and streamlined narratives and structures. Disneyfied content, on the other hand, tends to have a kind of doubled discourse, simultaneously presented to two distinct, if not sometimes downright oppositional audiences: kids and their caretakers and/or instructors.

3. Some finessing of terms is called for here: "Disney" as a conglomerate has vast and varied interests in media, many of them, such as ESPN, more or less completely disconnected from the family entertainment operation. However, both historically and colloquially, "Disney" as a *brand* remains more intimately associated with its parks, features, and small-screen content.

4. Anthony Crupi, "Survival Of the Fittest." *Adweek* vol. 48, no. 19 (2007), SR4-SR6, SR8; Hibberd, James. "Discovery, BBC Plot More 'Planet,'" *Television Week*, vol. 26, no. 17 (2007), 3–34.

5. Nichols, Bill. *Introduction to Documentary* (Bloomington: University of Indiana Press) 2001, 105–108.

6. To this, as to all rules of genre and cinematic taxonomy, there are some exceptions. Claude Lanzmann's singular *Shoah* (1985) for instance, was an immense undertaking, and runs some nine hours, but never pretends to offer any kind of totalizing perspective of the Holocaust. While it takes viewers to many of the myriad places where events tragic and brutal and even courageous occurred, it remains fiercely and intimately engaged, with history and with the human subjects interviewed for the project, rejecting the lofty "objectivity" frequently cultivated in films like *Planet Earth*.

7. Documentaries made in the UK are routinely re-recorded with American voice talent. In the case of *Planet Earth*, the American broadcasts on the Discover Channel featured a voice-over by Sigourney Weaver, an actress, now 60, then best-known to most audiences for playing Ripley, the long-suffering protagonist of the *Alien* films. Presumably, her unflappable, coolly feminine stoicism was deemed an appropriate substitute for Attenborough's wry omniscience.

Bibliography

Crafton, Donald. *Before Mickey*. Chicago: University of Chicago Press, 1993.
Crupi, Anthony. "Survival of the Fittest." *Adweek* 48, no. 19 (2007): SR4-SR6, SR8.
Hibberd, James. "Discovery, BBC Plot More 'Planet,'" *Television Week* 26, no. 17 (2007): 3–34.
Nichols, Bill. *Introduction to Documentary*. Bloomington: University of Indiana Press, 2001.

Section IV: Times, Places and People

12

A Past to Make Us Proud

U.S. History According to Disney

MARIANNE HOLDZKOM

In 1630, while traveling to North America from England, John Winthrop, the new Governor of Massachusetts Bay articulated the aspirations he had for the new settlement. In his speech, "A Model of Christian Charity" Winthrop uttered a phrased that spelled out the importance of the colonists' behavior and success in the Western Hemisphere. He told his fellow Puritans that they would be like "a city upon a hill: The eyes of all people are upon us...." Massachusetts Bay would be an example to the world and therefore all colonists must behave accordingly. From this moment on, the idea of America as example has been a constant in our history. The Revolutionary generation insisted that they could break the cycle of history and become the safe-haven of liberty for the entire world. The very existence of America could be "philosophy teaching by example." Abraham Lincoln reminded Americans of their special place in the world in the Gettysburg Address. Even into the 20th and 21st centuries, the United States has taken on the role of guardian of liberty and has dedicated itself, in a number of ways to teach the world how to form democracies and thrive in them. How successful the U.S. has been at this is questionable, but one point is clear: Educating the world—or attempting to—is as American as apple pie.[1]

In this spirit, Walt Disney played the role of educator as well: teaching his middle-class American audience not only about science, nature, health, safety, and geography, but about their own history. "I've always wanted to do American History," Disney told *Newsweek* magazine in 1955. "It's due. We have taken too many things for granted."[2] Disney set out, at the height of the Cold War, to teach his audiences that their past was noble and that they themselves could rise to the greatness of their ancestors. He focused, therefore, on stories of people who—working together—created, preserved and expanded the United States. Disney wanted to present the story of Amerca's history in unapologetically patriotic terms: "history told with head high, chest up, heart bursting with pride...."[3]

Disney films that depict events from U. S. History are too numerous to analyze them all here, but examining selected periods—The American Revolution, The Civil War, the Westward expansion and (in Disney films of the 1990s) the early colonial period—provides a clear picture of Disney's attitude toward American history. Some of these films and television series deal with real historical characters; others recreate the spirit of a time or movement. All show how Disney rewrote the past in order to reshape audiences' view of the present.

According to Scott Alan Metzger, historical films can allow audiences to "think about a better world by imagining a better past."[4] Disney's historical films provided audiences with l entertainment in his historical films while at the same time giving them a past in which they could be proud of and draw inspiration from. The themes of unity (or community) and reconciliation—apparent in all of the films covered in this chapter—were central to this goal. Disney films about the American past never shied away from depicting tension and conflict, but they nearly always told stories of people standing together, working as a team or reconciling their differences in order to move on together and achieve a common goal. These themes are sometimes subtle and other times like hammer blows to the head, but they are always present.

The intense focus on unity and reconciliation in Disney historical films reflects the worldview of Walt Disney himself. It stemmed, in part from his longing for a utopia. In his nostalgia for Marceline, Missouri, the town in which he grew up, Walt remembered that people in that community cared for one another and that there was a tolerance in the town as well. "Everything was done in a community help," said Disney. The town worked as one unit. Disney longed to recapture the sense of "well-being, freedom and community" he felt as a child in that town,[5] The small-town, collaborative values that Disney cherished were—he believed—also those of his Studio. The cartoonists' strike that shook the Studio in 1941 "shattered its' owner's utopianism" and left him shocked and dismayed by this strike, taking it as a personal affront.[6] Disney felt that the strike had "destroyed the spirit of the studio" and he blamed the turmoil on Communist interference (bent on destroying him personally) rather than on his own labor policies.[7] Lingering bitterness over the strike and concern over the worldwide spread of Communism may have led Disney—more than a decade later—to embrace stories of cooperation and ultimate understanding between Americans, and to ignore the historical realities that contradicted his vision. His films provided as much of an escape for him as they did for his audience.The Cold War, was may have sharpened their appeal, to Walt if not to theater audienced: The same ideas that had created the United States and made it a "City Upon a Hill" could now save the world by encouraging Americans to set aside their differences and make common cause against the enemy.

Disney's American history films were designed to teach those broader lessons: to persuade Americans to embrace the values of their past in order to protect their present and insure their future.

The American Revolution

Historians of the American Revolution have interpreted that event in various ways: some as an ideological struggle between power and liberty and others as a conflict over not only home rule but over "who should rule at home" as Carl Becker once put it. In other words, historians have always recognized the complexity of the Revolution and have argued that the participants were motivated by many different factors.[8] Disney's version of the American Revolution was far simpler: The colonists were fighting for the right to freedom, not just for themselves but also for the entire world, and when internal strife arose among them those who remembered that they *were* fighting for liberty won out. The Studio's two principal Revolutionary War productions—*Johnny Tremain* and the slightly darker, more adult *The Swamp Fox*— depict the American Revolution as a clear-cut fight for freedom in the face of tyranny..

The Swamp Fox, a loosely structured six-part serial that ran as part of the *Disneyland* television series from October 1959 through January 1961, told the story of Colonel Francis Marion, nicknamed "The Swamp Fox" by the British. Marion's greatest fame came as a militia leader whose guerilla tactics made life miserable for the British in South Carolina: disrupting supply lines, burning ships and capturing horses and equipment for the Continental Army.[9] To his credit, Walt Disney effectively used his on-screen introductions to each installment of the series to sketch the history—little known to most Americans—of the Revolutionary War in the South. The episodes themselves, however, followed in a long tradition of doing to Marion what Parson Weems (creator of the cherry tree legend) did for George Washington. They made him more a symbol than a human being: always heroic, never dishonest. The series itself however reduced Marion to a crusading outlaw-figure, and in fact referred to Marion as "The Robin Hood of the American Revolution."[10] Disney completed the illusion by casting the tall, handsome Leslie Nielsen as Marion. Nielsen was known for playing heroic leads at this point in his career (the starship captain in *Forbidden Planet*, for example), but given contemporary physical descriptions of Marion, Wally Cox or Don Knotts would have been a better choice. Marion was described as "nearly forty-eight years old, short and a bit on the frail side, with his ankles and knees obviously malformed."[11]

One of the most interesting aspects of the series is its accurate depiction of the war in the Southern colonies as a civil war between "Tories" who were loyal to the crown and "Patriots" who were in favor of independence. The American Revolution in the South offered neighbors an opportunity to settle old scores and both Tories and Patriots were guilty of doing so.[12] *The Swamp Fox* demonstrates the lengths to which such efforts were carried, depicting the Tories as men bent on revenge who resort to burning barns and shooting Patriots even as the British condemn such practices.[13] The Patriots crimes against their Tory neighbors are (in the series) far less serious, and the men of Marion's gang laugh off their antics. For example, in the first episode of the series, one of Marion's men arrives at camp with a pig in his arms. The pig escapes, however, and the man tells Marion that it was a Tory pig anyway—but that he didn't steal it; the pig followed him to camp. The historical reality was far darker, with colonists on both sides resorting to arson and murder.

The second episode, "Brother Against Brother," shows a Tory attempting to burn down his brother's barn and his brother along with it. Marion and his men show up in the nick of time to save him. In this episode as well, Marion's men are ready to take their revenge on the Tories. His sister-in-law tells him that they do not fear the British so much as the "Tory devils" who have just burned down their barn. His brother Gabe says, "A barn for a barn, a house for a house, a life for a life if necessary." Gabe's anger is shared by the rest of the men, but Marion counsels restraint and reminds them that—despite their differences—they are all neighbors. The battles will be forgotten, he warns, but if a neighbor burns down another neighbor's barn or house, those things will *never* be forgotten. Revenge, he argues, is unacceptable because "That's what the enemy does!"[14]

Disney thus maintains a classic good-guys-versus-bad-guys scenario, and glosses over the historical reality that there were atrocities on both sides of this fight. Placing blame on both sides would have complicated the plot and, more importantly, blurred the story's message about the importance of working together and the consequences of disunity. The Patriots in *The Swamp Fox* are strong, Marion tells his men in the first episode, because they are fighting for a cause: for their "land ... their country.... And that's why we'll win."[15] The Tories in this series are clearly the misguided men, having foolishly thrown in their lot with the British enemy rather than making common cause with their Patriot neighbors against them. It was—as the Cold War approached its peak—a particularly powerful message for a staunch anti-communist like Walt Disney

Cold War themes are even more prominent in *Johnny Tremain*—the story of the early days of the Revolution as experienced by Paul Revere's (fictional) teenaged apprentice—takes a still-more-expansive view. It opens with an accurate map of Boston, Massachusetts in 1773, and features such real historical figures as Paul Revere, Samuel Adams, James Warren and James Otis as supporting characters—even touching on Otis's descent into madness—but it is very much a product of 1957. The film is dedicated to "the youth of the world ... in whose spirit and courage rests the hope of eventual freedom for all Mankind."[16] For Walt Disney, the ultimate goal of the American Revolution was freedom for the *world*, and he was explicit about the Cold War significance of that idea. "*Johnny Tremain*, he noted, "is a very pertinent story. What we were fighting for then, we are fight for now."[17]

The film is very clear about *what* the colonists are fighting for. After the disaster of Lexington and Concord, General Thomas Gage, Royal Governor of Massachusetts and commander of British troops there, tells one of his subordinates: "We've experienced more than a defeat, more than a military misfortune. We've been vanquished by an idea, a belief in human rights." It would have been news to the British of the 18th century that they did *not* believe in human rights. According to Robert Middlekauff, the English were even looked down upon by other Europeans because they were considered "an unstable lot, obsessed with parliamentary government, with bills of rights and liberty that cut monarchs down to the size of mayors."[18] The landed aristocracy continued to exercise great influence in England, and would until parliamentary reform began in the 1830s, but the citizens of the country were proud of their mixed monarchy and their established rights. King George III himself admired the system, writing of the "beauty, excellence, and perfection of the British Constitution as by Law established."[19] The British may not have expounded on human rights the way 20th century Americans did, but they certainly saw themselves as head and shoulders above the rest of Europe when it came to protecting the liberty of their people as even the American colonists acknowledged. By putting the imagined words of a Stalin or a Khrushchev into the mouth of a British general, Disney reminded Americans of the 1950s of their new struggle for freedom.

The Cold War themes in *Johnny Tremain* do not stop with human rights. The themes of unity and community are, once again, very prominent. When Johnny is accused of a crime he did not commit, the sons of Liberty provide a lawyer for him. When Johnny he that he cannot afford such an attorney because he is "just a nobody." Paul Revere — a fellow Son of Liberty as well as his master and mentor — responds, "We're all nobodies when we stand alone." The message resonates with 1950s attitudes, but distorts history, glossing over conflicts within the colonial community regarding the nature of the revolutionary movement, perpetuating the notion that the colonists in the northern colonies were homogeneously united against the British and that all Americans would reap the benefits of liberty.[20] The only prominent Tory in the film is Johnny's wealthy uncle, and Johnny's rejection of him — returning the christening cup given to him by his dead mother and stating that "this means more to you than it ever will to me"— is as much about rejecting unearned wealth and power as it is about Tory politics.

Both *Johnny Tremain* and *The Swamp Fox* demonstrate Disney's dedication to historical adventure. Disney himself was concerned with historical accuracy to a point, wishing to get the details of soldiers' uniforms and troop movements correct, but not with the political complexities of the Revolution,[21] The overriding theme in both productions is the righteousness of the American cause and the importance of standing together. Those who reject either are villains, and Disney admits no shades of gray on that point.

Westward Expansion: Part I

One major theme in United States history is that of western expansion. From the time of the Louisiana Purchase in 1803 to the annexation of Texas and the Southwest territories after the defeat of Mexico in the Mexican-American War, the United Sates was looking to add more and more land to its boundaries. The concept of Manifest Destiny led Americans to believe that they had a right to all of the land from the Atlantic to the Pacific. In truth, this desire for Western lands discounted the prior claims of native peoples and earlier settlers from Mexico, who were systematically displaced and dispossessed. None of this is evident in Disney's tales of western expansion and exploration. These focused on trail-blazing heroes and brave pioneers; emphasized their courage, commitment, and hard work needed; and reiterated the themes of unity, reconciliation and community.

Walt Disney had been considering Davy Crockett for an anthology on American heroes long, but hesitated. even as the studio was planning the show because he was afraid that it would feature "too much fighting Indians."[22] Practicality won out. Having structured his new ABC-TV anthology series, *Disneyland*, around four rotating themes tied to the theme park's four "lands," Disney decided that Davy Crockett was a perfect fit for the Frontierland theme. The first of three planned, hour-long programs featuring Crockett debuted on December 5, 1954, and the frontiersman — plain-spoken, fearless and compassionate; able to "lick any problem with his wits and his own two hands," as *Time* magazine wrote — became an overnight sensation.[23] Historian Steven Watts wrote that "Walt Disney, with his instinctive feel for cultural pressure points, half-consciously shaped an ideal, reassuring representation of the American way as it faced a daunting challenge from without."[24] "The Ballad of Davy Crockett" became a standard on the American Pop Charts and ten million coonskins caps were sold in 1955.[25]

Davy Crockett: Indian Fighter, the first of the three original stories, introduces the hero as he is attempting to "grin down a bear" and is therefore unavailable to report to General Andrew Jackson as requested. Instantly the audience is aware that this man does things his own way in his own time, and who serves or defies authority when he feels he needs to. Davy helps the U. S. Army find and fight the Indian warrior Red Stick — defeating him in hand-to-hand combat — but in the end he counsels Red Stick to make paeace, telling him that "White Man's laws" could work for the "Red Man" too, if given half a chance. When Red Stick asks Davy why he did not kill him when he had the opportunity,

Davy answers: "Because of another law that's good for all men, red and white alike: Thou Shalt Not Kill." In the end, Davy and Red Stick shake hands, offering the hope of peace and reconciliation between the Natives and the Whites, and establishing an approach to Indian-White relations that Disney would run through Disney films for decades.

The second in the series, *Davy Crockett Goes to Congress* (aired January 26–31, 1955) follows Davy Crockett through his brief career in politics. Along the way, Crockett again promotes peace with Native Americans–evidence, perhaps of Walt Disney's concerns about "too much fighting Indians." "Injuns got rights." Davy declares on the floor of Congress. "They're folks same as anybody else." He makes a speech against Andrew Jackson's "Injun Bill"—the Indian Removal Act of 1830 which called for the relocation of the Cherokee Nation and other tribes from eastern states to an area west of the Mississippi River—but makes it plain that Jackson has only the best of intentions, an assertion that some historians would find difficult to believe.[26] Disney did not want his hero to go too far, even speaking in opposition to a bill that contemporaries—including Chief Justice John Marshall—found distasteful. The Disney version of Davy Crockett is willing to disagree with the leader of the United States, but only up to a point. He stops short of criticizing the president personally, and instead blames greedy land speculators for wanting to remove the Indians from the East. Crockett holds out great hope that the Natives and the Whites can live together in peace—even though Disney knows how the tension between whites and Indians played out: There was finally peace, but the Indians lost.

The second Crockett tale ends after his speech, leaving Congress and his political career behind. It glosses over Crockett's defeat in the 1834 election (a result of his opposition to Jackson's policies) and his legendary comment that the voters that turned him out "can all go to hell, and I will go to Texas." The last of the original series, *Davy Crockett At the Alamo* (air date February 23rd-28th, 1955) begins with Davy and his pal George on their way to Texas where, he says, Americans are in trouble and need his help. The "trouble" is American immigrants' efforts to wrest Texas from Mexican control or, more accurately, Mexican opposition to those efforts. Davy and George arrive in San Antonio during the siege of the Alamo by Santa Anna's army. Here, as in the previous episode and in *Johnny Tremain*, Disney reduces complex politics to a simple opposition. The last time the audience sees Davy, he is swinging his rifle at the attacking Mexican Army in the walls of the Alamo and the final verse of the ballad ends the film with, "Davy, Davy Crockett! Fightin' for liberty!"

This final scene in the film presented Disney with an unpalatable complication that could not be readily glossed over. The public knew full well that Crockett died at the Alamo, but they did not want to see it in Disney's version. One letter to the studio read: "If you don't get Davy Crockett out of the Alamo unharmed, the Bonniwell family will go back to Arthur Godfrey next week."[27] Disney was torn, but in the end decided that "Everybody knows Davy Crockett died at the Alamo! I wasn't going to tamper with history."[28] Disney stuck to history as it was then known.[29] The ending of the film is quite inconclusive yet gives the audience the *sense* that Crockett's ending was heroic, as his life had been. Disney even managed to resurrect him for another two episodes originally designed to focus on Mike Fink. The shows were revamped to include Davy and George and were re-named *Davy Crockett and the Keel Boat Race* and *Davey Crockett and the River Pirates* in which Davy teams up with Mike Fink to defeat some thieves—apparently Indians, but (in typical Disney fashion) actually white men disguised as Indians—along the Mississippi River.[30]

Though unable to resurrect Davy Crockett himself, Disney brought back Fess Parker in *Westward Ho, the Wagons!* (1956)—another tale of brave pioneers, Manifest Destiny, and reconciliation with between Native Americans and white settlers. The film, set in 1846, centers on a wagon train bound for the Oregon Territory, acquired from Great Britain the previous year. The film opens by reminding the audience that "The ruts of the Oregon Trail were not cut by armies or adventurers but by wagons carrying American families and all their possessions—westward bound with faith in God and the hope of a Promised Land." As the film begins, the settlers are anxious to get to "friendly Sioux territory" and away from the hostile Pawnees. Yet once they reach Fort Laramie in Sioux territory, a French trader informs the group that the Sioux are upset because some of their braves were killed by the last wagon train to pass through the territory. Asked if he thought the Sioux would close the trail, he responds: "How can you guess with an Indian?"

The climax of the film comes when the Sioux chief's son falls off his horse and is seriously injured. While Many Stars, the tribe's healer attempts to save him, the boy is dying. At this point, "Doc" Grayson—who is not a trained physician—approaches the camp in an attempt to help the boy. The Sioux are reluctant, but after the boy's mother begs her husband to let Grayson try, the "Doc" is given access to the child. He is able to save the boy and this brings peace to the two peoples. The Sioux grant the wagon train safe passage through their territory and the settlers continue on their way to Oregon.

Here again we see the importance of reconciliation and unity to Disney. A common humanity between the whites and the Sioux seems to make a resolution between them possible. Yet the reconciliation only takes place when the *white* doctor saves the *native* child. There is a clear implication of white superiority in this scenario. Somehow, the Sioux had survived for centuries without the medical help of the whites, but only "Doc" Grayson—a man who admits to being a better mule driver than a doctor—has the capability to save the boy. The message of unity here does not stem from an acknowledgement of equality. There is a superior race in this film and once everyone understands that, they can be united in a common humanity.[31]

Harmony between the Sioux and the settlers thus restored, the Sioux grant the wagon train safe passage and escort the settlers through their territory. Riding in parallel lines on either side of the wagons, the Sioux serve as protection from the hostile Pawnee who are portrayed as less-than-human, as "wild savages." They show no human emotions, they steal from the settlers and they have a wild party in which they dance and shoot off guns. On the other hand, the Sioux — the "friendly Indians" — are seen in family units with human concerns and desires. These are the people to which the whites are reconciled by "Doc" Grayson's diplomacy and medical knowledge. Clearly, the Disney Studio of the 1950s believed in "good Indians vs. bad Indians." It would appear that even at Disney there were some people with whom one could not reconcile.

The Civil War

The Civil War —for Disney as for other filmmakers— has held greater appeal than the Revolution, but also posed greater challenges: There is no unambiguously heroic Us to take the place of the Patriots, no readily demonized Them to substitute for King George's redcoats, and no single issue to match the Revolution's iconic struggle between freedom and tyranny. Each of Disney Studios' four Civil War films—*The Great Locomotive Chase* (1956), *Johnny Shiloh* (1963), *Mosby's Marauders* (1967), and *Menace on the Mountain* (1970)— solved this problem in essentially the same way. They took a microcosmic view of the war, focusing not on the larger issues that pitted brother against brother, but on the bonds of brotherhood that formed *between* individual soldiers. The two films based on real events—*Johnny Shiloh* and *The Great Locomotive Chase*— illustrate both Disney's embrace of the theme and Disney filmmakers' willingness to distort the established facts in order to serve it.

In *Johnny Shiloh* (1963) Disney retells the story of a real historical figure: Johnny Clem, the Drummer Boy of Chickamauga. In the story, 10-year-old John Lincoln Clem runs away from home to join the Union army, he trains as a drummer, and wins the respect of the rest of the platoon. Clem gets his first taste of fighting at the Battle of Shiloh where he distinguishes himself by boosting the morale of his regiment and picks up his nickname, Johnny Shiloh. Captured by the Confederate army surrounding Chattanooga, e is placed in the care of another young soldier, Private Jones, with whom he strikes up a friendship.

These two boys serve as the film's versions of the archetypal Civil War soldiers, "Johnny Reb" and "Billy Yank," their dialogue providing the audience with a glimpse of the soldier's life. In crucial way, however, the two boys are not typical of either army. They are under eighteen, when the average age of Civil War soliders was twenty-four,[32] and either says much about *why* he is fighting, although there is evidence to suggest that soldiers on both sides had very clear ideas about this issue.[33] Jones simply says that his army will lick "the Yanks." He also tells Johnny that he hates "The Yanks" because they captured his best friend and sent him to a prison camp. Over their time together, Johnny and Private Jones also argue about who can save the country — Abraham Lincoln or Jefferson Davis — but the film largely avoids politics. For Jones, his fight is now very personal. In this way, Disney brings the huge Civil War down to a very simple and human scale.

The two boys become friends despite the power relationship between them. Eventually the trust between them is so complete that Jones — who, again atypically for a Civil War soldier, is illiterate — asks Johnny to read a letter he receives from home.[34] It thus falls to Johnny to tell Jones the letter's terrible news: that Jones' best friend has died in the Union prison camp. Later, when Johnny escapes to avoid being sent to a prison camp himself, Jones discovers the escape attempt, but lets him go, saving his new friend from the fate of his hometown buddy. Johnny returns to his unit, is given a shiny new Union uniform, but also decides to keep the clothes he was given in the Confederate camp because "a friend of mine" gave them to him. Johnny's friendship with Jones surfaces again when he is reunited with his guardian Gabe after his escape. Gabe asks Johnny what the Rebs are like in their camp and Johnny responds that they are "no different from us," and says that he'll be glad when the war is over so that they can stop shooting at one another. *Johnny Shiloh* thus reiterates, subtly, Disney's vision of American history: Consensus is the ultimate good, and disunity leads to tragedies like the Civil War. Glossing over the political tensions that tore the country apart in 1861, the film proposes that, like Johnny and Private Jones, Northerners and Southerners had more in common than they knew and that the issues that brought them together — their common belief in freedom for example — were more powerful than their differences.

The Great Locomotive Chase — the story of an 1862 Union attempt to isolate Chattanooga by cutting the rail line to Atlanta — also features two characters from opposite sides of the war. Adversaries rather than friends, they find (in true Disney fashion) much to admire in one another. The mission, carried out by a party of soldiers led by Union spy James Andrews, involved stealing a train from Big Shanty (now Marietta) Georgia, and driving it north, tearing up track, disabling switches, and cutting telegraph lines as they went. They succeeded in stealing a train, headed by the now famous locomotive The *General*, but its conductor, William Fuller, pursued them — first on a handcar and then (after reaching the next station) in a second locomotive: the *Texas*.[35]

Themes of reconciliation figure prominently in the film. In order for the raid to succeed, the Union soldiers must literally walk in Southerners' shoes: posing as loyal Southerners and even uncomfortably singing "Dixie." This is easier for some of the raiders than for others. Andrews and William Pittinger — the most intelligent and sensitive of the raiders — see Southerners as wayward brothers. Pittinger even remarks that he cannot hate the men he is fighting. Another of the raiders — the rough, belligerent William Campbell — takes exactly the opposite position.[36] His intense, personal hatred of Southerners repeatedly endangers the mission by threatening to blow the raiders' cover or causing him to act rashly when threatened. He must learn to control his loathing in order for the raid to succeed. The film underscores the value of unity in a later scene, where Pittinger and Andrews agree that they are fighting *for* the Union, not *against* Southerners, and Pittinger regrets the "brother-against-brother" nature of the war.

While this story is told strictly from the Union perspective, the Southerners— notably conductor William Fuller, whose quick action foils the raid—are all sympathetic characters. To drive the point of reconciliation home, Disney also includes a scene that is remarkable in its revisionism. Before Andrews is hanged for his role in the raid, he requests to see Fuller, the man most responsible for its failure. Fuller is reluctant to visit the man who lied to him in order to steal his train, but does so anyway, clearly uncomfortable as he approaches the jail cell. The theme of reconciliation continues in the remarkable dialog:

> ANDREWS: I wanted you to know I'm sorry I had to deceive you.... You whipped me fair and square. Now that it's over, I hoped you wouldn't hold a grudge.
>
> FULLER: I haven't much use for a man who poses as a loyal Southerner and isn't.
>
> ANDREWS: I was fighting for my convictions.... My only weapons were the lies a spy must tell. Some day the fightin' will be over and both sides will have to shake hands. I won't be alive to see that day. Could we do it now?

Reluctantly, Fuller shakes Andrews's outstretched hand in the ultimate act of reunion: a lovely scene that elicits strong emotions from those who view it, but one that never took place. It is wholly the creation of the Disney screenwriters— inspired, perhaps, by symbolic handshakes of reconciliation that *did* take place: Grant and Lee at Appomattox in 1865, or Union and Confederate veterans at the 50th-anniversary commemoration of the Battle of Gettysburg in 1913.[37] Here the Disney studio attempted to emphasize a united country by creating a moment of reconciliation in the past, a moment that never occurred, but stood for the real unity that Disney wished to emphasize.

That Disney chose to depict the most divisive period of U.S. history with stories that emphasized the need for unity was, perhaps, a reflection of the times they were made. *The Great Locomotive Chase* premiered in June 1956, in the wake of Brown v. Board of Education (1954) and the murder of Emmett Till (1955), and the midst of the Montgomery Bus Boycott. *Johnny Shiloh* had its first broadcast on telecast in early 1963: the year of "Letter from the Birmingham Jail," the assassination of Medgar Evers, and the March on Washington. The country was, once again, split by regional tensions, and through his Civil War films, Walt Disney called for the American public to reject strife in favor of reconciliation.

Westward Expansion: Part II

In her book *The Legacy of Conquest: The Unbroken Past of the American West*, historian Patricia Limerick laments that the conquest of the West by settlers to that region "dissolved into stereotypes of noble savages and noble pioneers struggling quaintly in the wilderness." The subject of conquest became "the domain of mass entertainment and the occasion for lighthearted national escapism." There would certainly be some regret about the Native Americans, but for the most part, Americans chose to see the struggle for Western settlement as a great adventure.[38] Disney's numerous productions set in the post–Civil-War West—among them *Tonka, The Wild Country, Texas John Slaughter, The Nine Lives of Elfego Baca*—reflect that tendency, glossing over political, racial, and ethnic tensions in favor of adventure and escape. The two films discussed here share these themes (and Disney's trademark focus on unity) but they cover two distinct aspects of western settlement. *Ten Who Dared* follows the first expedition down the Colorado River and is the more adventurous of the two. *The One and Only, Genuine, Original Family Band* deals with issues of Western settlement not often considered: the development of Western territories and their struggle to join the Union.

John Wesley Powell, a Union Army veteran turned geologist, led two expeditions down the Colorado River through the Grand Canyon in 1869 and 1871. Powell and his men mapped the course of the river, proved it was navigable, and made scientific observations. The American public quickly embraced the journey as a great adventure. The feat of running the wild river in open, oar-driven wooden boats was made still more extraordinary by the fact that Powell had lost his right arm during the Civil War, as he acknowledged in a moving portion of his journal's introduction.[39] Powell, however, saw the expedition as a scientific endeavor, nothing more. Asked why no history of his 1869 trip had been published, Powell replied that "I had no interest in that work as an adventure, but was interested only in the scientific results, and that those had been published."[40] Powell was well aware that the adventure story was writing itself. In fact, reports had circulated that all but one member of the expedition had died on the trip, Powell being among the dead. Upon reading his own obituary, Powell wrote "...it was interesting and rather flattering ... to discover the high esteem in which I had been held by the people of the United States" and that "In my supposed death I had attained to a glory which I fear my continued life has not fully vindicated."[41]

The first expedition, carried out by Powell and nine other men, was the basis of the 1960 Disney production *Ten Who Dared*. The film presents the expedition's members as flawed heroes, but heroes nonetheless. One member is an alcoholic whose demon costs the expedition one of its boats. Another, called simply "Missouri," is hiding a prison record. A third, George Bradley, is a veteran of the Civil War who fought for the Confederacy, which greatly disturbs Powell's brother, Walter—a former inmate at Andersonville, the infamous Southern prison camp. Powell says, in the film, that his brother's experiences at the camp made him "savage," and hopes that the expedition will help him to come back to his senses. William Dunn is an astrologer, who reads the stars, and has little use for Powell's science. Two brothers, a newspaper reporter, and an Englishman who leaves the expedition partway through round out the crew.

Powell himself is—like Davy Crockett, Francis Marion, James Andrews, and other Disney recreations—the wise, paternal leader who stands slightly apart from his men and always knows best. Like them, he is driven by devotion to a cause larger than himself—in Powell's case, science. His men do not appreciate this quality, nor do they understand his dedication to science. At one point in the film Dunn, ever-eager to find gold, suspects that Powell has found some but will not share. When Powell reveals that his "treasures" are fossils, the men lose interest in his finds, but the episode demonstrates the differences between Powell and his men. In time, the men begin to see Powell as a liability, but they remain loyal to him as a leader. When he slips off a cliff and is holding on by his one arm, they come together to save him.

As the expedition continues, the men run out of food and some of them begin to doubt Powell's leadership. Three leave the expedition and climb out of the canyon to make their own way to civilization. The six who remain with Powell reach their destination just as he said they would; those who left, the narrator explains at the end of the film, died at the hands of hostile Indians. The closing narration forgives them for their foolishness, stating that they too are heroes who partook in a journey into the unknown, but the message is clear: Those who trust their leaders survive. There is safety in unity.

The film also makes a parallel case for unity in a subplot about the tension between Walter Powell and George Bradley. When Walter attempts to provoke Bradley by asking him to sing "John Brown's Body," Bradley simply replies, "The war is over, Walter." For Walter, however, it clearly is not; he cannot forget the war or his experiences in it. When George goes out hunting one day, Walter follows him with a gun, clearly intending to kill him, but instead it is George who corners Walter at gunpoint. He points his rifle at Walter then lowers it, saying: "As I said, the war is over." He helps Walter to his feet and the two men return to camp after nightfall. They then sing together, evidently having worked out their problems and Walter is a new man. What is interesting about this tension is that it is a complete fabrication. Both Walter and Bradley were described as "moody" by a Powell biographer, but the post–Civil War antagonism did not exist nor could it have because both of the historical characters were Union veterans! As in *The Great Locomotive Chase,* Disney created a scene to emphasize the importance of reconciliation and unity.[42] In 1960, the United States was approaching the one hundredth anniversary of that conflict and the wounds had been reopened by the turmoil of the Civil Rights movement in the South. The Disney writers carefully remind Americans that, in Bradley's words, "the war is over." Once the memories and hatred of that war are put aside, the haunted Union veteran, Walter, can move on. Once again, Disney managed to resolve conflict through reconciliation.

Released nine years after *Ten Who Dared* and set two decades later, *The*

One and Only, Genuine, Original Family Band focuses on a different kind of post–Civil-War reconciliation. Set in 1888, the film tells the story of the Bowers, a large family full of musically talented people. It is clear early on that Grandpa Bowers is a die-hard Democrat, for he is concerned this his oldest granddaughter, Alice, has taken up with a "Ree-publican," Joe Carder. Carder writes a newspaper in which he promotes Republican ideas and the need for statehood for Dakota Territory. Grandpa sees the statehood appeal as a political maneuver, believing that the "Ree-publicans" want to split the territory in two, North and South Dakota, so that the party will get not just two new senators but four. Unaware of Grandpa's political affiliation, Carder tells the family that he is recruiting people — the right kind of people, Republican people — to move to Dakota Territory. He makes his case with an inspiring song about Dakota — similar to the title song of Rogers and Hammerstein's *Oklahoma!* — that promises a "great tomorrow dawning" amid a lush landscape of "virgin fields" with "land for all." The Bowers and other families are convinced (what family interested in westward expansion would not be?) and they pack up and move west. Forty years after the time of *Westward Ho, the Wagons!*, the Bowers' trip seems quite easy and comfortable.

Upon their arrival in Rapid City, the family finds a divided community. There are in fact some Democrats in Dakota Territory and Grandpa sees his chance to influence the debate over statehood. Political passions run high, as they did in the 1880s, and neither side is above a fistfight over the issue.[43] The main issue for Dakota-territory settlers— as the movie makes clear — is admission to the union as a state (or two). The film ends on election night, with Democratic incumbent Grover Cleveland winning the popular vote, but Republican challenger Benjamin Harrison winning the electoral vote and thus the presidency. With this announcement and the rowdy reaction that goes with it, Papa Bowers makes an interesting speech in which he calls for healing. He quotes his father when he tells the people, "There is a time to stand up and fight for what you believe in and a time to join hands and work together or all the fighting doesn't mean a thing." The people soon learn that both North and South Dakota will be admitted to the union, but also that Montana and Washington will become states, evening out out the number of Republican and Democratic senators heading to Washington D.C. With unity restored, everyone is ready to make up — and sing!

Family Band is a wonderful piece of entertainment and even manages to get some of the history correct. Walt Disney died early in its production, but he would have been pleased to know that yet another message of unity was released to a nation in turmoil over war, politics and values. The contrast between the community, reconciled at the end of this film by a powerful speech and music and the battles raging in late 1960s America is striking. The film provided its audiences with a fantasyland in which deep political rifts can be healed with a heartfelt speech and a song — exactly the kind of thing that

Walt Disney liked to do. Like the historical adventures that preceded it at Walt Disney Studios, it gave the American people a past of which they could be proud.

History according to the Disney Studio is entertaining. It is filled with adventure and conflict. It is dramatic and touching. In many cases it is also accurate. Yet Disney's version of American history should be viewed with care. Walt Disney, and his studio after him, represented the values that Disney himself believed in: loyalty, honor, the nobility of the American past. The mistakes made by the people of the past are, in the films, consistently overlooked in favor of the messages of unity, community and reconciliation. Disney's history is an oversimplification of the past, created to remind Americans of their role in the world. He took his role as educator seriously, and even after his death, the education of the American public continued. The message changed somewhat, but the theme was still the same. Disney himself, had he lived to see *Pocahontas*, *Squanto: A Warrior's Tale*, or the cluster of based-on-a-true-story sports dramas the studio released in the 1990s, would likely have been pleased that his dream of national unity was still alive and well, and being taught to a new generation of Americans.

The author wishes to thank her husband, Al Churella, for his loving support.

Notes

1. For the quote from Winthrop's "Model of Christian Charity" see Elliott J. Gorn, et al., *Constructing The American Past: A Source Book of a People's History*, vol. 1 (New York: Pearson/Longman, 2005), 48. For the American Revolution as an example to the world, see Bernard Bailyn, *The Ideological Origins of the American Revolution* (Cambridge: Belknap Press of Harvard University Press), 160.
2. Paul Anderson, *The Davy Crockett Craze: A Look at the 1950s Phenomenon and Davy Crockett Collectibles* (Hillside, IL: R&G Productions, 1996), 14.
3. Steven Watts, *The Magic Kingdom: Walt Disney and the American Way of Life* (Columbia: University of Missouri Press, 1997), 291.
4. Scott Alan Metzger, "Evaluating the Educational Potential of Hollywood History Movies" in *Celluloid Blackboard: Teaching History with Film*, ed. Alan Marcus (Charlotte, NC: Information Age Publishing, 2007), 90.
5. Disney, quoted in Neal Gabler, *Walt Disney: The Triumph of The American Imagination* (New York: Knopf, 2006), 13 & 18.
6. Gabler, xviii.
7. Gabler, 371, 366.
8. For a small sampling of the various interpretations of the American Revolution see Bernard Bailyn, *The Ideological Origins of the American Revolution* (Cambridge, Massachusetts: Belknap Press of Harvard University Press, 1967); Carl Becker, *The History of Political Parties in the Province of New York, 1760–1776* (Madison: University of Wisconsin Press, 1960), 22 (quote); Gary Nash, *The Urban Crucible: Social Change, Political Consciousness, and the Origins of the American Revolution* (Cambridge, MA: Harvard University Press, 1979); Gordon S. Wood, *The Creation of the American Republic* (Chapel Hill: University of North Carolina Press, 1969).

9. For the British perspective on the War for Independence, see Christopher Hibbert, *Redcoats and Rebels* (Chelmsford, UK: Grafton Books, 1990).

10. Bass, Robert D. *Swamp Fox: The Life and Campaigns of Francis Marion* (Lexington, SC: Sandlapper Store, 1959), 3. According to Bass South Carolinians saw Marion as a latter-day Robin Hood. Disney created another, wholly fictional, Robin Hood figure several years later, in the three-part drama "The Scarecrow of Romney Marsh," starring Patrick McGoohan as a country priest who (disguised as "The Scarecrow,") defended his parishioners against the excesses of royal tyranny in 1736 England.

11. Rankin, Hugh F. *Francis Marion: The Swamp Fox* (New York: Thomas Y. Crowell, 1973), 60.

12. John S. Pancake, *This Destructive War: The British Campaign in the Carolinas, 1780–1782* (Tuscaloosa: University of Alabama, 1985), 172.

13. Compare this to the depiction of the British in the Mel Gibson film *The Patriot* (2000) in which the evil British trap Patriots in a church and burn them alive.

14. *The Swamp Fox* , episode 2, "Brother Against Brother" original air date 30 October 1959. Walt Disney Treasures DVD, 2005.

15. *The Swamp Fox*, episode one, "Birth of the Swamp Fox" original air date: 23 October 1959. Walt Disney Treasures DVD, 2005.

16. *Johnny Tremain* (1957).

17. Walt Disney quoted in Watts, 291.

18. Middlekauff, 10.

19. Middlekauff, 18.

20. See for example, Gary Nash, *The Urban Crucible* and Rhys Isaac, *The Transformation of Virginia, 1740–1790*, (Chapel Hill: University of North Carolina Press, 1982).

21. Leonard Maltin introduces "The Swamp Fox" on Disney Treasures DVD released in 2005 and discusses Disney's love for history. He says that Disney spent more on the show than he saw in returns because he wanted it to look good. He also filmed the shows in color even though they would be broadcast in black and white.

22. Gabler, 513–514.

23. Quoted in Gabler, 516.

24. Steven Watts quoted in Gabler, 516.

25. Gabler, 514–515.

26. See, for example Edward Pessen, *Jacksonian America: Society, Personality and Politics* (Homewood, IL: Dorsey Press, 1978). Pessen argues that Jackson was bent on removing the Indians at any cost.

27. Anderson, 75.

28. Anderson, 75.

29. Many historians now suspect that Crockett survived the Battle of the Alamo and was later executed by Santa Anna. This version of events elicits strong feelings from some who cannot bear the thought that Crockett would not have gone down fighting. In fact, one historian received death threats when he suggested that Crockett surrendered. See Albert Churella, "'Remember the Alamo!': The Struggle for Texas Independence" in *Retrieving The American Past* (Boston: Pearson Custom Publishing, 2003). See also Dan Kilgore, *How Did Davy Die?* (College Station: Texas A&M University Press, 1978).

30. Anderson, 77.

31. For an alternate reading of the healing scene, see Douglas Brode, *Multiculturalism and the Mouse: Race and Sex in Disney Entertainment* (College Station: Texas A & M University Press, 2005), 34–37.

32. James McPherson, *What They Fought For, 1861–1865* (Baton Rouge: Louisiana State University Press, 1994), 4.

33. See for example McPherson as well as Chandra Manning, *What This Cruel War Was Over*, (New York: Knopf, 2007). Manning argues that "Whatever else occupied their minds, ordinary Union and Confederate soldiers recognized slavery as the reason for the war..." 4.

34. Eighty percent of Confederate soldiers and ninety percent of Union soldiers were literate. (McPherson, 4.) While Disney was probably unaware of these statistics, given the numbers, it makes sense that Johnny is the one with these skills rather than Private Jones.

35. *The General* is on display at the Southern Museum of Civil War History in Kennesaw, Georgia where it serves as the centerpiece of the museum and the curators use Disney's film as an introduction to it. The *Texas* is on display at the Cyclorama Museum in Atlanta. Buster Keaton's 1926 film *The General* tells the Confederate side of the story, with Keaton's character "Johnnie Gray" taking Fuller's role.

36. Campbell was played by Jeff York, who created several such rough-edged characters for Disney, including brawling keelboat captain Mike Fink in two Davy Crocket adventures and the mercurial Patriot orator James Otis in *Johnny Tremain*.

37. On the Gettysburg celebration, see: John Heiser, "The Great Reunion of 1913." *Voices of Battle: Gettysburg National Military Park Virtual Tour*. National Park Service. Last updated: September 1998. http://www.nps.gov/archive/gett/getttour/sidebar/reunion13.htm

38. Patricia Nelson Limerick, *Legacy of Conquest: The Unbroken Past of the American West* (New York: Norton, 1987), 19.

39. Powell wrote, "I was a maimed man. My right arm gone; and these brave men, these good men, never forgot it ... my safety was their first care..." *Canyons of The Colorado* (New York: Penguin Books, 1987), xvii.

40. Powell, xvi.

41. Powell, xv.

42. For an example of both men's temperament see Wallace Stegner, *Beyond the Hundredth Meridian: John Wesley Powell and the Second Opening of the West* (New York: Penguin Books, 1954), 68.

43. Voter participation in the late nineteenth century was quite high, with one textbook putting the figure at 80 percent of qualified voters participating. See Chapter 20 of John Mack Faragher, et al., *Out of Many: A History of the American People* (Upper Saddle River, NJ: Prentice-Hall, 2006) for a description of Gilded Age politics.

Bibliography

Anderson, Paul. *The Davy Crockett Craze: A Look at the 1950s Phenomenon and Davy Crockett Collectibles*. Hillside, IL: R&G Productions, 1996.

Bailyn, Bernard. *The Ideological Origins of the American Revolution*. Cambridge, Massachusetts: Belknap Press of Harvard University Press, 1967.

Bass, Robert D. *Swamp Fox: The Life and Campaigns of Francis Marion*. Lexington, SC: Sandlapper Store, 1959.

Becker, Carl. *The History of Political Parties in the Province of New York, 1760–1776*. Madison: University of Wisconsin Press, 1960.

Brode, Douglas. *Multiculturalism and the Mouse: Race and Sex in Disney Entertainment*. College Station: Texas A & M University Press, 2005.

Churella, Albert. "'Remember the Alamo!': The Struggle for Texas Independence" in *Retrieving the American Past*. Boston: Pearson Custom Publishing, 2003.

Faragher, John Mack, et al. *Out of Many: A History of the American People*. Upper Saddle River, NJ: Prentice-Hall, 2006.

Gabler, Neal. *Walt Disney: The Triumph of the American Imagination*. New York: Knopf, 2006.
Gorn, Elliott J., et al., *Constructing The American Past: A Source Book of a People's History*. vol. 1. New York: Pearson/Longman, 2005.
Heiser, John. "The Great Reunion of 1913." *Voices of Battle: Gettysburg National Military Park Virtual Tour*. National Park Service. Last updated: September 1998. http://www.nps.gov/archive/gett/getttour/sidebar/reunion13.htm
Hibbert, Christopher. *Redcoats and Rebels*. Chelmsford, UK: Grafton Books, 1990.
Isaac, Rhys. *The Transformation of Virginia, 1740–1790*. Chapel Hill: University of North Carolina Press, 1982.
Kilgore, Dan. *How Did Davy Die?* College Station: Texas A&M University Press, 1978.
Limerick, Patricia Nelson. *Legacy of Conquest: The Unbroken Past of the American West*. New York: Norton, 1987.
Manning, Chandra. *What This Cruel War Was Over*. New York: Knopf, 2007.
McPherson, James. *What They Fought For, 1861–1865*. Baton Rouge: Louisiana State University Press, 1994.
Metzger, Scott Alan. "Evaluating the Educational Potential of Hollywood History Movies" in *Celluloid Blackboard: Teaching History with Film*, edited by Alan Marcus. Charlotte, NC: Information Age Publishing, 2007.
Middlekauff, Robert. *The Glorious Cause: The American Revolution, 1763–1789*, 2nd Revised Edition. New York: Oxford University Press, 2005.
Nash, Gary. *The Urban Crucible: The Northern Seaports and the Origins of the American Revolution*. Cambridge, MA: Harvard University Press, 1979.
Pancake, John S. *This Destructive War: The British Campaign in the Carolinas, 1780–1782*. Tuscaloosa: University of Alabama, 1985.
Pessen, Edward. *Jacksonian America: Society, Personality and Politics*. Homewood, IL: Dorsey Press, 1978.
Powell, John Wesley. *Canyons of The Colorado*. New York: Penguin Books, 1987.
Rankin, Hugh F. *Francis Marion: The Swamp Fox*. New York: Thomas Y. Crowell, 1973.
Stegner, Wallace. *Beyond the Hundredth Meridian: John Wesley Powell and the Second Opening of the West*. New York: Penguin Books, 1954.
Watts, Steven. *The Magic Kingdom: Walt Disney and the American Way of Life*. Columbia: University of Missouri Press, 1997.
Wood, Gordon S. *The Creation of the American Republic*. Chapel Hill: University of North Carolina Press, 1969.

13

Reviving the American Dream

The World of Sports

KATHARINA BONZEL

> "*Invincible* is not just my story but it can be anyone's story as well. It's about having a dream and overcoming the odds, adversity, and obstacles that go with making that dream come true."
>
> —Vince Papale about the Disney film that tells his life story[1]

Time and again Hollywood revisits the magical world of sports. In sports anything can happen, and films make dreams come true—together they become an inspirational mix of fact and fiction that encourages audiences to believe in the American Dream. The 2000s brought a veritable wave of films from the Walt Disney Company—including *Remember the Titans* (2000), *The Rookie* (2002), *Miracle* (2004), *Invincible* (2005) and *Glory Road* (2006)—that dramatize true stories from the recent history of American sports Released in a time of uncertainty and a strained political climate, a time that could be said to have suffered a crisis of confidence in the American Dream, these films invoked its strength and vitality.Underlining this revitalization strategy are the films' claims of authenticity and authority because they are based on true stories and thus the protagonists' dreams and achievements are represented as 'real'—demonstrating that the American Dream is not only still alive in this new millennium, but achievable and worth believing in.

Introduction: The Noughties

Arriving after an era of relative prosperity and growth, in particular in the information technology industries, the new millennium began with the bursting of the dot-com bubble; one of the closest presidential elections in U.S.

history, which gave the presidency to George W. Bush; and the terrorist attacks of September 11, 2001, all in close succession. These crises were followed immediately by the "war on terror," in particular in Afghanistan, and, by extension, the war in Iraq in search of alleged weapons of mass destruction. The new millennium thus shaped up to be one of various crises of confidence: confidence in the electoral process due to the mismatch of the popular and electoral vote majorities in the 2000 election; confidence in the economy with various high-profile economic scandals and crises, such as the Enron scandal, the collapse of the dot-com bubble and more recently the subprime mortgage crisis and ensuing recession; confidence in legitimate sporting successes due to doping scandals such as the BALCO steroid scandal; and, of course, confidence in national security in light of the September 11 attacks. Together these crises of confidence produced an atmosphere of insecurity, instability and fear that shook American society and its self-conception. What does it mean to be American in this new millennium? "America," as Bill Clinton famously intoned, "is far more than a place. It is an idea."[2] In this it is different from many countries, most notably those of the "Old World," from which the early settlers escaped in search for a new home where they could live their lives according to their own ideals and without persecution. Out of this hope and the way immigrants went after this better life grew the American Dream.

It is not surprising that in these trying times reality TV shows that invoke the American Dream and champion stories of success such as *American Idol*, *So you Think You Can Dance* and *The Apprentice*, have proliferated. At the box office, films indebted to fantasy (e.g. the *Lord of the Rings* trilogy) and comic books (e.g. *Spider-Man* trilogy and *The Dark Knight*) dominated, providing welcome relief from reality and featuring clear-cut visions of good and evil.[3] While sports films do not tend to rule the box office, they had a healthy run in the first decade of the new millennium. As Kyle Kusz asserts, "By the mid–1990s an interest materialized among Hollywood executives and American audiences for producing and consuming films centered on sport."[4] Of the top-grossing sports dramas of the new millennium, three were produced by the Walt Disney Company (*Remember the Titans*, *The Rookie*, *Miracle*), with *Invincible* (at number 11 on the list) just outside the top ten. Importantly, eight of these films— including the four by Disney-were based on a true story or famous athlete.[5] These numbers give an indication of the rising interest in "authentic" sports dramas and I will argue that they, in particular those produced by the Walt Disney Company, have revived and valorized the idea of the American Dream for a new millennium audience.

"Based on a True Story"

The Disney sports films based on true stories seem to sit awkwardly in the company of the classic animated Disney fairy tale fare such as *Snow White* and

Aladdin or even the live-action films of the *Pirates of the Caribbean* franchise. The sports films stories, however, are often also a form of legend, differing from fairy tales only in that they are based on "real" people in "real" places in our "real" history. These legendary stories frequently feature unlikely—yet real-life—heroes, such as the Cinderella-like Vince Papale in *Invincible*, who goes, via an open try-out for the Philadelphia Eagles, from being an NFL fan to being an NFL regular. The sports stories are also all set in the past, ranging from the 1960s to the 1990s, a necessary distancing in the process of becoming a sports "legend." *Miracle*, for example, is a film about the surprise win of the United States ice hockey team over the heavily favored Soviet Union team at the 1980 Olympic Winter Games—a win that has often been described as one of the biggest upsets in sports history. *Glory Road* and *Remember the Titans* feature lesser-known stories of racial segregation and subsequent integration in college and high school sports. The former tells the story of the 1966 Texas Western College basketball team that won the national championship with the first all-black starting lineup in NCAA history. The latter follows the exploits of the first integrated football team at a newly desegregated Virginia high school in 1971. Though less well-known than the events in *Miracle*, these stories are elevated to epic journeys, through the narrative dramatization in the films.

Regardless of the legendary status of the actual event/story, the films' claims for authenticity go beyond the "based on/inspired by a true story" tag on the DVD cover. The films' promotional material and the making of featurettes often directly address themes of authenticity, and set out to claim verisimilitude for even the smallest details. Most obvious are the period features of the film, such as appropriate clothing, hair styles, decor and music, as well as correctly depicting physical traits or tics of the real people (coaches, athletes, parents, etc.) involved. All of these aspects and claims to historical authenticity are not specific to sports films and indeed apply to any period film. However, in the depiction of the actual sports content, the filmmakers face various unique problems: Firstly, the style of play must be historically accurate, whether this concerns famous play-by-play reenactments, or general playing style.[6] Secondly, this sporting action must be filmed, anachronistically, in a style that is interesting and engaging to a modern audience, which is accustomed to multiple camera perspectives and endless replays from contemporary sports television coverage. Thirdly, and crucially, the sports action has to be *convincing* in the sense of looking and feeling like real sports action, for, as David Thompson assures us, sports fans "can smell the fake."[7]

The emphasis on authenticity thus becomes a matter of utmost importance. If the film fails to convince on any of these levels, it will most likely be a failure, both commercially as well as critically. I argue, however, that what these attempts at authenticity ultimately achieve (or in some cases, fail to achieve) is a sense of *emotional authenticity*.[8] Emotional authenticity appeals to our senses more than to our minds. If a film feels true, if the audience identifies with the team, if it is disappointed in their losses, if it celebrates their wins, in short, if the film draws the audience in and gets them to emotionally invest in the characters and the story, it has achieved emotional authenticity. This sense of emotional authenticity is not only necessary in order to involve the audience, but, more importantly, because it allows the filmmakers to deviate from the real events, and turn real events into an engaging, cohesive film narrative. Because of the framework of technical authenticity (of style, music, ticks, sports action, etc.) that has functioned to build emotional authenticity, the narrative can be shaped and dramatized to best capitalize on this framework. Since the ultimate truth about a certain event will always remain elusive, these films aim at emotional truthfulness to draw in their audience.

Emotional Authenticity and the American Dream

Audience's strong identification with the characters and the events displayed, which in turn helps to strengthen their belief in the American Dream as put forward by the film. The American Dream as a concept seems to resist a steadfast and hard definition. Jim Cullen argues that it is precisely this ambiguity and flexibility that is the secret to both its power and longevity, and Wilber Caldwell concurs when he points out that the "right kind of dream must be promising without being a promise."[9] Only then can it be a motivational force for the dreamer, and lead him/her to a successful outcome of that dream. Paradoxically, for the American Dream to work, it needs a certain chance of failure. Within the genre of the sports film, not only do the sporting contests themselves hold significant potential to invoke the American Dream, they also function on another level as a symbol or metaphor for the dreams of the protagonists. Usually, winning the game means 'winning'—i.e. achieving—one's dreams.

While the films in question here vary in their depiction of team sports and individual achievement, they keep the crucial balance between what Walter Fisher has called the "materialistic" and "moralistic myth" of the American Dream.[10] While the materialistic side of the dream caters to individual success, most commonly expressed in a rags-to-riches story, the moralistic myth invokes "values of tolerance, charity, compassion, and true regard for the dignity and worth of each individual."[11] Fisher's understanding of the American Dream as possessing two sides, a yin and yang of sorts, is useful as it sums up various competing definitions of the American Dream.[12] It also offers insight into the appeal of the American Dream for a wide variety of Americans, as it is an incredibly flexible and vague, yet immediately emotive idea.[13]

In *Invincible*, for example, the American Dream is bound to the personal achievement of the central character Vince Papale and his rise from substitute teacher and bartender to professional football player. The film is set against a backdrop off lay-offs and workers' strikes in Philadelphia in the 1970s, raising the stakes of Papale's struggle to achieve his dream of becoming a professional football player, as it will directly impact his financial livelihood. In typical rags-to-riches fashion, he overcomes difficult obstacles— such as the unlikely success in the open try-out of the Philadelphia Eagles and the lack of respect of the professional players—to become a regular player on the field. Yet, his success and his status as a member ofthe team remains precarious and indeed the film does not end with this achievement. instead, itsignals the instability of success by placing another obstacle in Papale's way:his less-than-glorious pro football debut, which nearly gets him kicked off the team. This setback reminds the audience that achieving one's dream is an ongoing process rather than and end in itself.

Driving through his old neighborhood and seeing kids play football with his Eagles number taped to their shirts, Papale realizes that, as a local "South Philly boy," the people of Philadelphia identify strongly with him. The final galvanizing moment for Papale comes during head coach Dick Vermeil's pep talk before Papale's second game, in which he refers to the working class battles of the time: "The people of Philadelphia have suffered. You are what they turn to in times like these! You are what gives them hope! Let's win one for them!" During this motivational speech, the camera closes in on Papale until he alone fills the screen. He is thus singled out as the potential saviour of both the team and the people of Philadelphia, representing their hopes and dreams through his example. Papale eventually wins the game for the Eagles after he forces a fumble on an opposing player. In doing so he reaffirms the possibilities of the American Dream as the sport becomes a metaphor for life in general. Audiences can relate to his plight not because they understand and know football, but because they can literally see the obstacles (e.g. the tackles of the opposing players) that he needs to overcome to achieve his dream of becoming an "Eagle." His training and playing visualize the hard work, determination and will power necessary to be successful.

Furthermore, Papale not only achieves the materialistic side of the American Dream by becoming a professional football player after having been laid off from his teaching job, but he does so decently and with respect for his fellow players and friends, whom he continuously helps, and who in turn come to respect him and, in the case of his teammates, welcome him into the professional football brotherhood. *Invincible* thus becomes a parable about the struggles of life and the American Dream.

The other Disney films follow *Invincible*'s example of balancing the two sides of the American Dream, despite their different narratives. The characters not only achieve significant financial improvement (if sometimes modest rather than over-the-top riches), but also achieve ongoing change for the better in society in general. *Glory Road* and *Remember the Titans* particularly foster the hope of social improvement in their narratives of "ending racism" and upward mobility for underprivileged black boys through sports. *The Rookie* highlights—in a similar vein to *Invincible*—the idea that it is never too late to fulfill your dream. Protagonist Jim Morris, high school teacher and baseball coach, becomes the second-oldest rookie in major league baseball history after losing a bet to his students and having to go to the open try-outs of the Tampa Bay Devil Rays. Once again, it is not excessive richness and fame that is portrayed as success—unlike what is promised by shows like *American Idol*—but a relatively short, modest as a relief pitcher.[14] This makes the American Dream achievable, as is shown by this exchange between Morris and a fan: "'Hey, Morris! Can I have your autograph?' I turned around and it was a big policeman. He said, 'You give guys like us a fighting chance.'"[15] Such relatively modest, "achievable" versions of success are likewise celebrated in the closing credits of each of these films, which outline the subsequent careers of the "real" athletes depicted beyond the timeline of the film. These "true life" conclusions build on the audience's emotional involvement to support the validity and accessibility of the American Dream.

Miracle differs slightly from the other films in that it is more concerned with the "moralistic myth of brotherhood" as Fisher calls it, then with the materialistic side of the American Dream. In *Miracle* the American Dream is bound up firmly with the "American way of life," which many Americans perceived—in the wake of the second Arab oil embargo, the Iranian hostage crisis, and the Soviet invasion of Afghanistan—to be under attack. This Cold War context cast the ferocious, quasi-professional Soviet team as symbols of renewed Soviet aggression. Legendary coach Herb Brooks' wife Patti reminds him that the semi-final against the Soviet Union is "more than a hockey game to a lot of people" when he complains about fans and reporters turning the game into a political event. Similarly, the film is much more than "just a movie," which is demonstrated not least by the war-laden rhetoric at the end of the film, when Coach Brooks describes the best moment of his career in a nostalgic voice-over over shots of a sea of American flags:

> Ah, it was here. The sight of twenty young men of such differing backgrounds, now standing as one. Young men willing to sacrifice so much of themselves, all for an unknown.

In post–9/11 America this could equally be said about the military's involvement in the "war on terror." However, the voice-over continues and refers directly to the importance of the American Dream in such trying times:

> A few years later the U.S. began using professional athletes at the Games—Dream Teams. I always found that term ironic, because now that we have Dream Teams, we seldom ever get to dream. But on one weekend, as America and the world watched, a group of remarkable young men gave the nation what it needed most—a chance, for one night, not only to dream, but a chance, once again, to believe.

The voice-over not only rejects the over-professionalization of sports today and thus conjures up the ideals of amateur sports and its rewards, but also asserts the significance of the American Dream in both the past and the present: the importance of every American having a chance to live their dream. Like the title of the film, it recalls the question that ABC-TV broadcaster Al Michaels shouted over the final buzzer: "Do you believe in miracles? Yes!"

Conclusion

The wave of "based-on-a-true-story" sports films produced by the Disney Company at the start of the new millennium served to revitalize the American Dream, in both its materialistic and moralistic embodiments, as a source of strength and vision in a nation beleaguered by war and economic recession. Building on careful attention to technical authenticity, the films created a sense of emotional authenticity that fostered the audience's identification with the characters depicted, and encouraged belief in their successes. Echoing the theme song of the classic Disney film *Pinocchio,* "When You Wish Upon A Star," the films demonstrated how both individual and social obstacles could be successfully overcome, and offered inspiration, reassurance, and hope that one's dreams could, indeed, become true.

Notes

1. See http://www.vincepapale.com/movie.html accessed 10/01/09.
2. As quoted in Calvin C. Jillson, *Pursuing the American Dream: Opportunity and Exclusion over Four Centuries*, American Political Thought (Lawrence: University Press of Kansas, 2004), 1.
3. See http://www.boxofficemojo.com/alltime/domestic.htm, accessed 22/12/2008 for a list of all time box office hits (domestic grosses). The top ten films of the new millennium so far are: *The Dark Knight* (2008), *Shrek 2* (2004), *Pirates of the Caribbean: Dead Man's Chest* (2006), *Spider-Man* (2002), *Star Wars: Episode III — Revenge of the Sith* (2005), *Lord of the Rings: The Return of the King* (2003), *Spider-Man 2* (2004), *The Passion of the Christ* (2004), *Lord of the Rings: The Two Towers* (2002), *Finding Nemo* (2003).
4. Kyle W. Kusz, "Remasculinizing American White Guys In/Through New Millenium Sports Dramas," *Sport in Society,* vol. 11, no. 2 & 3 (March 2008), 209–226, on p. 210.
5. See http://www.boxofficemojo.com/genres/chart/?id=sportsdrama.htm accessed 22 December 2008. The top ten sports dramas of the new millennium are: *Seabiscuit* (2003), *Remember the Titans* (2000), *Million Dollar Baby* (2004), *The Rookie* (2002), *Rocky Balboa* (2006), *Coach Carter* (2005), *Miracle* (2004), *Cinderella Man* (2005), *Friday Night Lights* (2004), and *Ali* (2001).
6. Basketball, for example has undergone dramatic changes in playing style since the 1960s. See for example: Aram Goudsouzian, *King of the Court: Bill Russell and the Basketball Revolution* (Berkeley and Los Angeles: University of California Press, 2010); and Jeffrey Lane, *Under the Boards: The Cultural Revolution in Basketball* (Lincoln, NE: Bison Books, 2007).
7. Quoted in Jones, "'Down on the floor and give me ten sit-ups': British Sports Feature Film," *Film & History*, vol. 35, no. 2 (Spring 2005), 29–40.

8. See Mikko Salmela, "What Is Emotional Authenticity?" *Journal for the Theory of Social Behaviour* vol. 35, no. 3 (2005):209–230.

9. Wilber W. Caldwell, *Cynicism and the Evolution of the American Dream* (Washington, DC: Potomac Books, 2006), 47.

10. Fisher builds his definition of myths on Joseph Campbell's, and he states that the "functions [of these two myths] are to provide meaning, identity, a comprehensive understandable image of the world, and to support the social order." Walter Fisher, "Reaffirmation and the Subversion of the American Dream." *Quarterly Journal of Speech* 59 (1973): 160–167, on p.161.

11. Fisher, 161.

12. See, for example: Jim Cullen, *The American Dream: A Short History of an Idea That Shaped a Nation* (New York: Oxford University Press, 2003); Cal Jillson, *Pursuing the American Dream: Opportunity & Exclusion over Four Centuries* (Lawrence: University Press of Kansas, 2004); and Jennifer Hochschild, *Facing Up to the American Dream* (Princeton: Princeton University Press, 1996).

13. See Cullen, *The American Dream.*

14. Morris played 20 games for the Rays over two seasons in which they were a struggling last-place team that finished 69–92 and 69–93.

15. As quoted in *Failure Magazine* http://www.failuremag.com/arch_sports_jim_morris.html, accessed 9 January 2009.

Bibliography

Caldwell, Wilber W. *Cynicism and the Evolution of the American Dream.* Washington, DC: Potomac Books, 2006.

Cullen, Jim. *The American Dream: A Short History of an Idea That Shaped a Nation.* New York: Oxford University Press, 2003.

Fisher, Walter. "Reaffirmation and the Subversion of the American Dream." *Quarterly Journal of Speech* 59 (1973): 160–167.

Goudsouzian, Aram. *King of the Court: Bill Russell and the Basketball Revolution.* Berkeley and Los Angeles: University of California Press, 2010.

Hochschild, Jennifer. *Facing Up to the American Dream.* Princeton: Princeton University Press, 1996.

"Invincible the Movie." Vince Papale: Speaker, Author, Spokesperson. http://vincepapale.com/meet-vince-papale/movie/

Jillson, Calvin. C. *Pursuing the American Dream: Opportunity and Exclusion over Four Centuries.* Lawrence: University Press of Kansas, 2004.

Jones, Glen. "Down on the floor and give me ten sit-ups.': British Sports Feature Film." *Film & History* 35, no. 2 (Spring 2005): 29–40.

Kusz, Kyle W. "Remasculinizing American White Guys In/Through New Millenium Sports Dramas" *Sport in Society* 11, no. 2 & 3 (March 2008): 209–226.

Lane, Jeffrey. *Under the Boards: The Cultural Revolution in Basketball.* Lincoln, NE: Bison Books, 2007.

Salmela, Mikko. "What Is Emotional Authenticity?" *Journal for the Theory of Social Behaviour* 35, no. 3 (2005):209–230.

Zasky, Jason. "The Unnatural." Failure Magazine. http://failuremag.com/index.php/feature/article/the_unnatural/

14

Beyond the *Ratoncito*

Disney's Idea of Latin America

BERNICE NUHFER-HALTEN

Walt Disney's perception of Latin America and its citizens is no different from his perception of the United States. A trip to one of his theme parks will testify that his idea of the U. S. is just that — an idea, not a reality, and a reflection of what Disney wanted the U. S. to be, rather than what it really is. Disney's manipulation of cultural reality into idealized fantasy was not limited to his own country, however; it extended to depictions of the rest of the world. *Saludos Amigos!* (1942) and *Three Caballeros* (1944)—films designed to interpret Latin America for wartime U. S. audiences—were among the earliest remakings of other cultures, presenting Latin America and Latin Americans not as they were but as Walt Disney thought they ought to be.

Disney's role in U. S. attempts to *literally* remake Latin America in its own image is well-documented. Wartime health education films for the Latin American market lectured their audiences on nutrition, sanitation, and disease control (holding up the farms of the Midwestern U. S. as a model). Disney comic books served — as Ariel Dorfman demonstrated in *How to Read Donald Duck* (1971)— as vehicles to promote U. S. political agendas: glorifying capitalism, normalizing social and economic inequality, and trivializing protest and dissent. Dorfman, in his discussion of one such comic book, describes an incident in which Donald offers a group of protestors free lemonade, causing them to drop their signs (and their ideals) and rush to him to slake their thirst:

> This strategy, by which protest is converted into imposture is called dilution: Analyze an unusual phenomenon of the social body and symptom of a cancer, in such a way that it appears as an isolated incident, removed from its social context, so that it can be then automatically rejected by "public opinion" as a passing itch. Just give yourself a scratch, and be done with it. Disney, did not, of course, get this little light bulb all on its own. It is part of the metabolism of the system, which reacts to the facts of the situation by trying to absorb and eliminate them. It is part of a strategy, consciously or unconsciously orchestrated."[1]

These techniques are, as Dorfman observes, indicative of Disney's larger strategy: seeking to absorb Latin America by diluting its identity, reducing it from being the "other" to being "just like us." It was an approach that Disney would return to, a decade later, in its *People & Places* series of documentaries (1954–1960) and — in more benign fashion — in the theme park attraction "It's A Small World."

Good Neighbors and Wartime Diplomacy

Saludos, Amigos! and *The Three Caballeros* are best understood in the context of World War II. Walt Disney and his company signed on to the war effort more emphatically than any other Hollywood studio. In fact, the Disney studio complex, unlike any other in Tinsel Town, was protected by sand bags and anti-aircraft guns during the war, because it was considered an enemy target.[2] Disney's contributions to the war effort included hundreds of training films and dozens of propaganda shorts, as well as *Victory Through Air Power* (1943): a feature-length lecture on the military value of strategic bombing that climaxed with the obliteration of Japan from the air.

Disney's fervent support of the war effort extended beyond military affairs, however, and into the realm of wartime diplomacy, specifically the "Good Neighbor Policy" toward Latin America.[3] Begun under the Hoover administration and expanded by the Roosevelt administration, it repudiated armed intervention in favor of engagement with strong, pro–U.S. local leaders and aggressive exports of American culture. The public face of the Good Neighbor Policy emphasized collective security. The Conference for the Maintenance of Peace, held in Buenos Aries in 1936, produced pledges of mutual consultation in the event of an external threat. Two years later, in Lima, nations participating the 8th Pan-American Conference agreed to present a united front against possible Axis aggression in the Western Hemisphere. Orchestrated by U. S. Secretary of State Cordell Hull, the agreement was a significant diplomatic achievement, signed by a number of governments whose leaders admired Hitler and Mussolini. When war came, all countries in Latin America did declare war on the Axis powers, and Mexico and Brazil even sent forces to fight. Argentina, which had leaned toward the Axis early in the war, was the last to endorse the conflict, finally declaring war at the last possible moment — March of 1945 — two months before the end of hostilities in Europe.

The value of such agreements for the United States ultimately went well beyond lining up allies. They prevented the Axis from opening a diplomatic or military "second front" in Latin America, and encouraged a steady flow of agricultural products and raw materials even in wartime. The Office of the Coordinator of Inter-American Affairs (CIAA) — a bureau of the U.S. government established in 1940 — was the focal point of such efforts within the government.

Its mission was to promote increased cooperation between the U.S. and other American states, and reinforce the "One For All and All for One" message of the Good Neighbor Policy. The CIAA was short-lived (abolished in 1946, its functions transferred to the Department of State), but it was active throughout World War II, with Nelson A. Rockefeller as the first Coordinator.

John Hay Whitney, the head of the CIAA's Motion Picture Division, asked Disney and members of his creative team to make a "goodwill tour" of Central and South America in 1941. The tour, aside from its inherent publicity value, was intended to gather material for a series of up to a dozen short, animated films. Each film would highlight a different country, simultaneously educating American audiences and building goodwill toward the United States in Latin America.[4] Four of the shorts were packaged into *Saludos Amigos!* and three more into *The Three Caballeros.* A planned third compilation, to be titled *Cuban Carnival,* was never completed.[5]

Saludos Amigos!

The shortest of all of Disney's feature films—a mere 42 minutes in length—*Saludos Amigos!* was first released in Brazil in August of 1942, fully six months before its U.S. premiere in February 1943.[6] It consists of four separate cartoons that highlight Peru ("Lake Titicaca"), Chile ("Pedro"), Argentina ("El Gaucho Goofy"), and Brazil ("Aquarella do Brasil"). The production mixes classic Disney animation, with comedy and musical numbers, interspersed with live action scenes of the actual Disney artists on their goodwill tour of Latin America. The presence of familiar Disney characters like Donald Duck and Goofy, as well as new ones like the hero of "Pedro," make the film feel like lighthearted family entertainment. It is marketed that way on DVD, listed (despite its brief length) with the studio's classic animated features like *Bambi* and *Cinderella.* The original, educational purpose of the film is clear both in the individual cartoons and especially in the material that links them.

The last words in the opening titles (which are themselves backed by a song, "Saludos Amigos," extolling brotherhood among nations) express: "Sincere appreciation for the courtesy and cooperation shown to us by the artists, musicians and our many friends in Latin America." The first scenes afterward show Disney artists flying to South America in order to *be* educated: to learn about local peoples and their cultures and find, in them, inspiration for new cartoons. The live-action image dissolves into an animated plane flying across an animated map, tracing the Disney group's journey from Brazil to "the Argentine" to Chile, Bolivia, and Peru. When live action returns, with the next scene, it shows a Peruvian marketplace along the shores of Lake Titicaca. The audience has thus been drawn from *seeing* the animators to standing alongside them and seeing *what* they see. The narrator's voiceover supplies information that is, implicitly their thoughts: that, for example, local tastes "run to bright-colored clothes, and conservative hats." A Peruvian woman passes, carrying a small child on her back in a sling, and the narrator (the animators' thoughts) refers to the sling as "a rumble seat for the baby." This is, the narrator explains, "just what the artists are after," and the camera shows an artist's hands sketching the woman and baby on a pad — the artist's interpretation of what artist and audience have implicitly "seen" together.

The transition from seeing alongside the artists to seeing *through* their work is repeated several times. A live-action scene of a man playing a flute for three children kids becomes a close-up of woman's hand drawing a picture of a boy with a flute (accompanied by the narrator's commentary about "strange and exotic" Peruvian music handed down from "Inca ancestors." A live action sequence of burros and llamas used as pack animals is accompanied by a voiceover comparing llamas to "aristocrats" whose cooperation (and tolerance for heavy loads) is limited, compared to that of the ever-willing burros ("peasants?"). Artists' hands then sketch the llamas' portraits, adding eyeglasses that, along with their haughty expressions, give the impression they are too good to carry heavy loads like the less-intelligent burros. The camera shows a series of still pictures— studies of rural, agricultural Peruvian scenes in stylized illustration by Disney artists—and then introduces the result: a "little travelogue" of Peru as seen through the eyes of "a celebrated American tourist." The tourist, Donald Duck, then appears in a pith helmet and safari jacket, binoculars in hand and baggage close by, sitting on a sign that says "Lake Titicaca."

The long sequence that follows—"Lake Titicaca," the first of the four cartoons that make up the core of the film — shows Donald Duck exploring Peru. It appears on the surface appears to be purely entertainment with no underlying message, but fragments of factual information are woven through it as the basis for gags. The narrator, for example, describes the symptoms of the altitude sickness that Peru induces in tourists, and Donald (who scoffs at first) suffers each in turn in comically exaggerated form. The film also strives to connect the Latin and Anglo cultures. One of its longest sequences involves Donald's encounter with a young Peruvian boy and his llama. The two try on each other's clothes, take each other's picture, and listen to each other play native music (Donald's is a jazz tune) on the boy's flute. Cross-cultural friendship between Americans— whether Latin or Anglo— is as easy as saying hello, the film suggests.

The second cartoon begins with live-action scenes that purports to depict its origin. A Disney team, flying across the Andes, is inspired by the scenery and the memory of mail planes that fly through the mountain passes. From this comes the sketches of little airplane named Pedro that represents Chile, and the scene (in a now-familiar pattern) shifts from live-action scenes of the mountains, to artists' drawings of mountains and a hand drawing the little plane. Before the actual airliner sets down at Santiago, the character has taken shape, and the opening words of the narration are show on a page rolled into a typewriter: "Once upon a time at a small airport near Santiago, Chile, lived three airplanes. A papa plane (a mail plane), a mama plane, and a baby plane named Pedro." The animated sequence tells the story of how Pedro is called on, when his parents are sick, to fly the mail route to Mendoza, Argentina. It takes the form of a typical Disney adventure. On the trip he comes eye-to-eye with a menacing condor — a character that Disney could have developed, but did not — a storm, and the tallest peak in the Andes: Aconcagua. Struggling to climb high enough to clear the mountains, Pedro disappears and his parents, back at the airfield, think he is gone. Disney's trademark optimism prevails, however, and it all ends happily as Pedro limps home — bouncing along the runway — with the mail.

"Pedro" is, except for a few incidental geographic details, strictly entertainment. "El Gaucho Goofy," the third cartoon, shifts the balance back toward education. It is introduced by a transition to a map of the Andes and live-action shots of the Disney crew flying into Buenos Aires. Scenes of the city — shots of prominent buildings, with factual, travelogue-style narration —follow. Then the location shifts from the city to the Pampas, and film shifts to the familiar pairing of live-action scenes and artist's hands interpreting them. The theme is life of the *gauchos*, and the images are rural and traditional. We see demonstrations of riding prowess; an *asado* (or Argentine open-air barbecue), and folk dances: not the modern tango of Buenos Aires, but the country dances of the Argentines. "Notice how closely these steps resemble the old time square dances of North America," narrator says, reducing Latin America to another version of Anglo America.

The reduction of the Pampas to an extension of the U. S. West continues in the cartoon itself, with a further comparison between the two cattle cultures. "We couldn't help compare the life of the Argentine gaucho to that of our own cowboy," the film says, presenting Goofy as the latter. Carried from Texas to Argentina by a magical wind, Goofy is outfitted with a *gaucho*'s clothing and equipment — each item given its Spanish name, by the narrator and in onscreen text — and turned loose in a series of slapstick encounters with an his dinner (at an *asado*), an ostrich, and his own horse. Like other Goofy shorts of the 1940s, "El Gaucho Goofy" contrasts the narrator's calm, authoritative voice with Goofy's wild, flailing on-screen actions. The narrator delivers education, while Goofy provides entertainment.

The fourth and final cartoon of *Saludos, Amigos!* splits education and entertainment more sharply. The introductory sequence follows a now-familiar pattern of travelogue-style tourist scenery, images of artists sketching, and close-ups of their work, including a new animated character: parrot José Carioca, Disney's characterization of the typical Brazilian. Crowd scenes, of Rio streets and of Carnival, are prominent, but Disney chooses to show only light-skinned Brazilians. This clearly a white-washed view of multi-cultured Brazil continues through the segment; eventually a few darker-complected people are shown, but none of African descent, despite their major presence in Brazil. In the pre-integration U. S., this view of Latin America would have been more palatable — less threatening — than Brazil's multiracial reality.

The cartoon itself, "Aquarella do Brasil" ("Watercolor of Brazil") features something that was missing in the animated sequences of other countries: identifiable music. The songs "Brazil" and "Tika Tika," composed and (in the first case) sung by Brazilians, provide the soundtrack to a mostly formless story. The first half shows an animated paintbrush sketching animated watercolor-style images of Brazilian nature, which turns into flora and fauna dancing to the music in a fantasy reminiscent of the "Nutcracker" sequence of *Fantasia* (1940).[7] The second half introduces Donald Duck and José Carioca, who hit it off and explore the nightlife of Rio together. They share a drink at a sidewalk café and Jose sings "Brazil" while Donald learns to dance the samba. Jose speaks to him mostly in rapid-fire Portuguese, with occasional lines in English, but Donald (who finds a stack of dictionaries no help) somehow grasps his meaning anyway. Cross-cultural understanding, the film implies, is requires only a face-to-face meeting and good intentions.

The Three Caballeros

The Three Caballeros, the second feature-length film Disney made at the request of the CIAA, uses the same structure as *Saludos, Amigos!*, joining together four cartoons that would later be able to be shown separately in order to generate more income to amortize the studio's costly feature-length productions. These cartoons, like those in the earlier film, each highlight different parts of Latin America: the Pacific Coast and Galapagos Islands ("The Cold Penguin"), Argentina ("The Gauchito"), Brazil ("Have You Been to Bahia?"), and "Mexico." The framework of the film, however, reflects its homogenization of Latin American cultures with one another and with Anglo culture. The title song begins with a song whose lyrics indicate this dilution of cultures on the part of Disney, introducing the three title characters as happy adventurers in "snappy serapes" and sombreros. The fact that one of the characters— the parrot José Carioca — is from Brazil, where Portuguese is spoken and Mexican-styled sombreros are not worn, is glossed over by Disney, seemingly implying that all Latinos are the same.[8] The opening sequence shows Donald Duck opening a large, wrapped package whose tag reads, in Spanish: "Congratulations to Donald Duck on his birthday, Friday the 13th, from his friends in Latin America." The date is meant to resonate with the bad luck that Donald repeatedly suffers onscreen, but in Hispanic cultures Friday the 13th is not considered unlucky–Tuesday the 13th is. The tag changes into English as Donald reads it, but the date remains the same, implying that the Anglo superstition about Friday the 13th must be universal.

The large box, once opened, reveals several smaller boxes, the first of which yields a movie projector and film. The film proves to be a nature documentary, on the birds of South America—Donald's "feathered cousins," the narrator says—that is narrated by a "Professor Holloway."[9] The "documentary," which combines visual gags with serious narration briefly describing (and giving the common Spanish names of) real South American birds, frames *The Three Caballeros'* first two cartoon segments, each of which thus becomes a film-within-a-film-within-a-film. The documentary's panorama of native Latin American birds—relatives of Donald's—including flamingos and other tropical birds, presents a good cross section of Latin America. It also stands out because it does a better job of synthesizing the disjointed sequences than in *Saludos Amigos!* with its series of clumsy transitions.

The first two cartoon shorts are, like the "Pedro" segment of *Saludos Amigos!,* essentially light-hearted entertainment with little educational content. The title character of "The Cold Penguin," for example, lives at "the South Pole" in an igloo and wears snowshoes (penguins are from Antarctica, though not the South Pole; snowshoes are from the Arctic). As usual, it's all the same to Disney). Disney thus squanders an opportunity toe educate viewers about South America by choosing to produce a vignette on penguins at the South Pole who live in North Pole igloos. Only the fact that Pablo the penguin leaves the frozen South Pole and sails past cities on the West coast like Santiago and Lima keeps the segment from being a total non-sequitur. The second cartoon, "Gauchito," features an old *gaucho* narrating an adventure (or telling a tall tale?) featuring himself as a boy. He sets out to capture a condor, discovers a flying donkey instead, and dreams of becoming wealthy by racing it against men on horses. Details of Argentine culture are slipped in around the edges of the story. The boy is shown (like Goofy) dressing in a *gaucho*'s traditional clothing, each item of which is given its Spanish name. During a fiesta scene, the revelers in the background are dancing the traditional Argentine dance called Zamba, and playing traditional games. The boy wins the horse race (described in the rapid speech of a U. S. track announcer), but before he can claim his prize of 1000 pesos, the donkey spots a *hornero* bird and flies after it, dragging him along. "We were never heard from again," says the narrator of his younger self, ending the film firmly in the realm of classic Disney fantasy.

The Three Caballeros cuts back to Donald who extracts a second present from the large package: a book, titled *Brasil,* whose pop-up pages become the framing device for the film's third cartoon segment: "Have You Been to Bahia?" The cartoon itself, in which José (now "Joe") Carioca from *Saludos, Amigos!* is once again Donald's friend and guide, is (even more than "Gauchito") an exercise in pure fantasy. Initially the fantasy is romantic. Joe sings the song "Bahia" over profuse, pulsating animation (derivative of *Fantasia*) depicting his memories of the seacoast city: lush jungles, a white bird in flight, ornate buildings, colorful water, and moonlight. Then it turns stylized surreal, with simple animation (derivative of Disney's *Alice in Wonderland*) showing Joe multiplying into four smaller characters, Donald shrinking to their size, and the two of them embarking on a journey through the pages of the book: psychedelia, with a Latin twist. These production techniques served to portray the Latin Americans and their cultures as palatable, yet exotic. The scenes (visually the most elaborate in either film) are clearly of an Other place—not the United States—and yet are (compared to earlier segments and to *Saludos Amigos*) oddly unspecific. Except for the tropical foliage, they could have been anywhere, and even with it they could be almost any tropical paradise. Is this another dilution?

Transported into the world of the book, Joe and Donald are on a street in Bahia. A shadow comes around the corner: a live-action image of a woman with cookies on her head, superimposed over the animated background. She is portrayed by Aurora Miranda, whose sister Carmen represented Hollywood's image of Latina exoticism. The live-action woman greets the cartoon birds and, joined by other live-action Brazilians (all male) they walk through an animated street scene of Bahia. The woman's song segues into another, sung by a man selling oranges. Donald—clearly attracted to the woman—is jealous of the citrus salesman, who she just as clearly prefers. Eventually, she kisses Donald and his eyes undulate to the music. Colors pulse, multi-hued confetti rains down, inanimate objects come to life, and live humans become animations. The line between "reality" and fantasy is crossed and re-crossed, leaving the audience to wonder what is real, what is not.

Stereotyped images are the Bahia segment's primary, regrettable "lesson" for the audience. It presents Latinas as superficial, sexual seductress—sirens who speak in double entendres—and turns Donald Duck, the film's representative of the U. S., into a sex-starved, horny individual whose only thought is to copulate with this enchanting seductress. Latin men fare little better. At one point two who are dancing with the woman face off (in silhouette) in an intensely competitive dance. Their kicks and arm thrusts suggest a stylized knife fight, and they morph (still in silhouette) into animated fighting cocks, then back into dancing men. The woman is clearly implied to be the object of their competition and her (sexual?) favor the prize to the winner. Donald, unable to compete with such hot-blooded men, returns to his own world with Joe, his memories of Bahia accompanied by a cardboard moon dangled from above on a rope, and centered around "beautiful girls." End of sequence/end of seduction.

The fourth and final segment of *The Three Caballeros,* which takes Donald and Joe to Mexico, appears at first to recreate their experience in Brazil. Donald opens his third present and the screen explodes into psychedelia reminiscent of the 1970s in design and behavior—wild colors swirl, and instruments play themselves. Donald is pulled in different directions like the image in a kaleidoscope, then inflates into a piñata that Joe explodes with a touch of his cigar. A rooster emerges wearing a Charro hat and pistols, which he proceeds to fire off thus representing the stereotypical Mexican *bandolero*. He shakes Donald and Joe's hands so vigorously that all their money and belongings shake out on the ground: a literal Mexican shakedown, reinforcing Anglo stereotypes of Mexicans as thieves. The long psychedelic scene ends, however, with the three birds locking arms and reprising the title song. Keeping with the film's political mission, they declare undying friendship for one another, but tellingly make one exception: If a woman is involved, it's "every man for himself."

The central section of the "Mexico" segment is the most openly didactic of the entire film. Panchito, the Mexican rooster, describes Mexican Christmas customs to Donald, and narrates a brief history of how Mexico City was founded. Xochimilco is portrayed by an illustration of the rafts in the garden waters that endure to this day. Other scenes include Mexican women, boats full of couples and flowers. The illustrations—drawn, but not animated—resemble those in children's books: realistic, but stylized. The cultural details are also stylized. The music accompanying the Mexico City segment, for example, is tropical, and not the Mexican music of that region. Mexico, it appears, is all the same to Disney.

Panchito invites Donald and Joe to fly on a magic serape—Disney's image of a Mexican flying carpet—and turns the illustration of Xochimilco into a photograph that the three birds enter. In Brazil, Donald and Joe interacted with live human figures in an animated landscape; in Mexico, the pattern is reversed. The three friends and their magic serape are the only animated elements in live action scenes. They fly over a 1940s-era car driving by beautiful green fields; over mountains and a river; and past fishing boats with large nets like insect wings. Flying out of and into the book several times, they visit several regions of Mexico, each time observing people and events that, because they are live humans, are meant to be taken as representative of Mexico as it is.

The air of realism is, to some extent, earned. Disney makes an effort to show the geography of the country and some of the local differences among Mexican states and regions. There are also pervasive distortions, however. The Mexicans shown in the crowd scenes often appear to be of European descent, and sometimes appear to be *mestizo*, but are never indigenous. Like the Caucasian-dominated Brazilian crowds in *Saludos Amigos!*, this "whitewashing" of Mexican made Latin America's multiracial reality more palatable to U. S. audiences still used to racial segregation but it undercuts the film's claims to reality. The irony is particularly strong when the trio visits Vera Cruz and dances the Lilongo, a local dance, with noticeably European-looking dancers.

The dance in Vera Cruz also reiterates Disney's conviction that all American culture—Latin or Anglo—is, at some basic level, interchangeable. Donald dances with one of the women, he music transitions from the local dance to jitterbug, and Donald dances wildly. It is something he recognizes. When Joe Carioca joins in, the music takes on a bit of Brazilian rhythm. U. S. viewers are thus invited to lean back and smile at the confirmation of their fondest hopes:

"They *are* the same as us, aren't they?" The film suggests that Americans can travel abroad, but remain in a hermetically sealed capsule of familiar cultural artifacts, with no fear of "contamination" by the Other they have come to see. Today, U. S. tourists can experience can achieve such results by eating at a McDonald´s when they go abroad, but Disney's films hinted that they could do so even in the 1940s.

The final realistic scene places the serape and its three passengers over live-action shots meant to represent the beach in Acapulco. Donald, even more aroused by Mexican women than he had been by Brazilian ones, dives toward the sand and spends the remainder of the film in the grip of frustrated sexual desire.[10] He chases (European-looking) women on the beach, swoons over a (European-looking) woman singing "You Belong to My Heart," the classic "*Solamente una vez.*" Donald floats along, entranced by the music. The singer's face is replaced by several guitars, the guitars turn into lips and they all kiss Donald. He goes shooting off like a rocket through a surreal landscape of flowers. Donald's rocket contrail is lush flowers and his behavior is nothing short of orgasmic. The film's images grow increasingly surreal as Donald appears to grow increasingly sex-crazed. He swoons over women engaged in a Busby Berkeley-style water ballet, becomes part of a three-bird chorus line in which his animated legs (along with Joe's and Panchito's) are replaced by live-action women's legs), and deliriously imagines himself dancing with and kissing women who morph into flowers and cactuses.

Mexican women are clearly and unambiguously the instigators of Donald´s uncontrollable sexual behavior. They make him delirious, uncontrollable, and irrational — turn him, in other words, into a slave to passion. The film does not emerge from its surreal final sequences, but ends in an explosion of fireworks that spell out "The End" in Spanish, Portuguese, and English in turn. It thus leaves Donald in the grip of his sexual insanity, and U. S. viewers with the none-to-subtle message Latins in general and Latin women particular are hypersexual, seductive, and dangerous.

Conclusion

Disney Studios responded to the call of the U.S. Government foster mutual understanding between the United States and Latin America by using the simplest of techniques — stereotyping. Elsewhere, they attempted to reduce the differences between Anglo and Latino America by diluting Latino culture so that it could be assimilated by the Anglo-American world. These efforts could have been much more effective had Disney made the effort to understand the Latino cultures. Instead, it took the most superficial cultural aspects and combined them with the vaguest of U.S. notions of what Latino culture is, and produced two very uneven short feature films. In fact, the very structure of them — each with almost independent constituent parts that could be later cannibalized for the purpose of recuperating the expense of their production—contributed to the problem. Given only a brief time to capture an entire national culture, Disney artists focused on the vivid and recognizable ... and then exaggerated them. The resulting films, though they implicitly and explicitly framed their images and stories as educational, were more successful at reinforcing what U. S. viewers already believed about Latin America.

Did Disney, in the end, contribute to the U. S. Government´s goal of convincing Latin America to join its war effort? It probably helped, but the stereotypes and garish oversimplifications it helped to perpetuate probably had a greater and more lasting impact upon the United States.

Notes

1. Ariel Dorfman, "From the Vaults: Donald Duck." http://www.adorfman.duke.edu/vaults/donald_duck/inner_pages/excerpts_lemonade.htm

2. Thomas Doherty, *Projections of War: Hollywood, American Culture, and World War II* (New York: Columbia University Press, 1993).

3. On the Good Neighbor Policy, see Irvin F. Gellman, *Good Neighbor Diplomacy: United States Politics in Latin America* (Baltimore: Johns Hopkins University Press, 1979) and Frederick B. Pike, *FDR's Good Neighbor Policy: Sixty Years of Generally Gentle Chaos* (Austin: University of Texas Press, 2005). On its cinematic dimension, see: Dale Adams, "Saludos Amigos: Hollywood and FDR's Good Neighbor Policy," *Quarterly Review of Film and Video* vol. 24, no. 3 (2007), 289–295.

4. The definitive history of the Latin American tour and the making of the films is: J. B. Kauffman, *South of the Border with Disney: Walt Disney and the Good Neighbor Program, 1941–48* (New York: Disney Editions, 2009). Footage of Disney and his artists in Latin America was edited into a short documentary, also titled *South of the Border with Disney*, available on the DVD edition of *Saludos Amigos* and *The Three Caballeros.* The contemporary documentary *Walt and El Grupo* (dir. Theodore Thomas, 2009) tells the same story with the benefit of hindsight. On the unproduced *Cuban Carnival* project, see Wade Sampson, "The Lost Caballero," *Wade's Wayback Machine*; accessed 21 June 2010 at http://www.mouseplanet.com/8154/The_Lost_Caballero .

5. The Latin American films were Disney's first attempts to construct feature films by combining short originally designed to be seen separately. See David Scott Diffrient, "Cabinets of Curiosities: A Critical History of the Animated 'Package Feature,' from *Fantasia* to *Memories.*" *Historical Journal of Film, Radio, and Television*, vol. 26, no. 4 (2006), 505–535, on pp. 511–513.

6. Ironically, the set-up of the *Saludos, Amigos*! DVD includes English and Spanish only, not Portuguese. This was odd because of the fact the film debuted in Brazil.

7. The animated paintbrush motif would reappear, later in the decade, as the opening to Disney's True-Life Adventure nature documentaries.

8. On Hollywood stereotypes of Latinos generally, see: Alfred Charles Richard, Jr. *Censorship and Hollywood's Hispanic Image: An Interpretive Filmography, 1936–1955* (Westport, CT: Greenwood, 2003).

9. The voice of "Professor Holloway" is that of actor Sterling Holloway, who went on to voice Disney's version of Winnie the Pooh.

10. Donald's hypersexuality in *The Three Caballeros* has attracted more critical attention than any other aspects of the two films. See, for example: Julianne Burton, "Don

Juan(ita) Donald and the Imperial Patriarchal Discourse," in *Reframing Latin America*, ed. Eric Kristofer Ching, et al. (Austin: University of Texas Press, 2007), 228–236; Jose Piedra, "Pato Donald's Gender Ducking," *Jump Cut*, no. 39 (June 1994), 72–82, 112; Douglas Brode, *Multiculturalism and the Mouse* (Austin: University of Texas Press, 2006), 231–233; and Julianne Burton-Carvajal, "'Surprise Package': Looking South with Disney," in *Disney Discourse: Producing the Magic Kingdom*, ed. Eric L. Smoodin (London: Routledge, 1992), 131–146.

Bibliography

Adams, Dale. "Saludos Amigos: Hollywood and FDR's Good Neighbor Policy," *Quarterly Review of Film and Video* 24, no. 3 (2007): 289–295.

Brode, Douglas. *Multiculturalism and the Mouse*. Austin: University of Texas Press, 2006.

Burton-Carvajal, Julianne."'Surprise Package': Looking South with Disney." In *Disney Discourse: Producing the Magic Kingdom*, edited by Eric L. Smoodin. London: Routledge, 1992.

Burton, Julianne. "Don Juan(ita) Donald and the Imperial Patriarchal Discourse." In *Reframing Latin America*, edited by Eric Kristofer Ching, et al., 228–236. Austin: University of Texas Press, 2007.

Diffrient, David Scott. "Cabinets of Curiosities: A Critical History of the Animated 'Package Feature,' from *Fantasia* to *Memories*" *Historical Journal of Film, Radio, and Television* 26, no. 4 (2006): 505–535.

Doherty, Thomas. *Projections of War: Hollywood, American Culture, and World War II*. New York: Columbia University Press, 1993.

Dorfman, Ariel. "From the Vaults: Donald Duck." http://www.adorfman.duke.edu/vaults/donald_duck/inner_pages/excerpts_lemonade.htm

Gellman, Irvin F. *Good Neighbor Diplomacy: United States Politics in Latin America*. Baltimore: Johns Hopkins University Press, 1979.

Kauffman, J. B. *South of the Border with Disney: Walt Disney and the Good Neighbor Program, 1941–48*. New York: Disney Editions, 2009.

Piedra, Jose. "Pato Donald's Gender Ducking" *Jump Cut*, no. 39 (June 1994): 72–82, 112.

Pike, Frederick B. *FDR's Good Neighbor Policy: Sixty Years of Generally Gentle Chaos*. Austin: University of Texas Press, 2005.

Richard, Alfred Charles, Jr. *Censorship and Hollywood's Hispanic Image: An Interpretive Filmography, 1936–1955*. Westport, CT: Greenwood, 2003.

Sampson, Wade. "The Lost Caballero," *Wade's Wayback Machine*. http://www.mouseplanet.com/8154/The_Lost_Caballero

15

Locating the Magic Kingdom

Spectacle and Similarity in People and Places

CYNTHIA J. MILLER

Introduction

History tells us that Disney's Magic Kingdom can be found in central Florida, that it came into existence in 1971, and that Walt himself never lived to see that happen. But in reality, Disney brought his magic kingdom into being more than a decade before. It was expansive, spectacular, and vibrant; brimming over with color and drama, and untouched by time. It was the world, seen through the lens of a camera; a camera held by many hands, but by aimed and focused by the vision of Walt Disney. One by one — Samoa, Morocco, Switzerland, Japan — all were drawn together beneath the kingdom's banner, to create the magical landscape of Disney's *People and Places*.

As an anthology series, Disney's *People and Places* delivered culture-as-spectacle into the viewing lives of American audiences for over half a decade, beginning with the Academy Award-winning title *The Alaskan Eskimo* in 1953, and concluding with *The Danube* in 1960. The years in between saw the production of fifteen additional short films, covering a range of cultural groups and locations, from Lapland to the Antarctic, and the lifeways from which they ostensibly derive their shared identities. In these short films, which typically run no more than 30 minutes, viewers are ushered into segments of daily life, contextualized by voiceover narration, that make the strange familiar, and highlight the beauty, rather than the challenge, in difference.

Cornerstones in Disney's efforts at edutainment, the films produced under the *People and Places* series' name were created to grant audiences in the United States a glimpse of the cultural wonders of the world beyond the country's borders. In 1959, Disney observed that "Most of the world's people will never travel to strange and faraway lands..."[1] and that belief was, undoubtedly, one of the motivators that led to the creation of the *People and Places* series. With each new episode, the magic kingdom's influence was extended. True to the series' title, the films situate people in their places, and those places, in turn, serve as the narrative's primary orientation. Affective, spiritual, economic, and cultural ties to landscape are often framed as defining characteristics, even in a Western culture such as Wales, where, to illustrate the persistence of artisanal skills, viewers are told: "Give a Welshman a witch-hazel wand and he's apt to weave a bit of magic." This framework automatically primitivizes these cultural Others in an era in which American culture draws its identity from scientific and technological innovation. The rest of the world is cast, by comparison, as "children of nature," frozen in time, and defined by traditional occupations rather than progress.

In this way, *People and Places* celebrates, commemorates, and seeks to retain echoes of the past in the rapidly-changing present. Although a noted innovator in the entertainment industry, Disney's lament of social and cultural progress is clear: In an era where modernity threatens to create fundamental change in gender roles, the family, and the economy, the past, with its wealth of "ancient lore" stands as a golden age that, once lost, will never return. *People and Places* wraps the cultures it represents in a rhetoric of primitivism, where customs are "unchanged by time, undisturbed by the march of progress," and rural lifeways are cast as "old ways ... carefully preserved by people who cherish ancestral cultures and ancient legacies." The series seeks to "capture and preserve these stories before they become only dim memories," as a remedy for the anxiety of change.

People and Places addresses another set of social anxieties, as well. From the midst of an apprehensive Cold War America, these films speak in reassuring tones to both the fearful and the curious, reminding viewers that, regardless of the superficial cultural differences in costume, food, crafts, and dwellings, human universals exist that create common bonds and "basic human problems of hopes, aspirations, and ambitions." Everywhere the camera looks, children cause mischief, girls fret about their appearances, family is a primary bond, and success is achieved through hard work. Disney offers these reminders of similarities with the hope of "strengthening the bonds of good will and understanding by which all men can exist together in peace"—suggesting that within these short films lie Cold War morality tales for America's internal and foreign relations.

The American Worldview

Emerging from the midst of the Cold War, Disney's *People and Places* series spoke to the uncertain social and ideological landscape of American audiences in uncharacteristically subtle, and perhaps unintended, ways, working in a curious tension with—and against—policies and initiatives of the postwar era. While much has been written about Walt Disney's political orientation, affiliations, and activities during the war and the postwar years, the *People and Places* series suggests degrees of complexity not always fully considered in discussions of Disney's cultural production. The series presented positive, outward-focused messages about cultural Others, but those messages were still produced in the midst of a broad, and often conflicting, array of ideas about the representation of cultural groups and their natural and social worlds that were influenced as much by American economics and industry as by politics and ideology.

The first half of the twentieth century had been dominated by the See America First campaign, designed to promote national tourism as "a ritual of citizenship."[2] The campaign, which originated in the interwar years, encouraged Americans to refocus their cultural, recreational, and environmental lenses on domestic sights, rather than investing in European or other foreign travel. First by train, then by automobile, Americans were offered "authentic" experiences of their country's own people and places, casting tourists as pioneers and explorers in their own land. Through the creation of a canon of national tourist sites that included national parks such as Yellowstone and the Grand Canyon, and casting Native Americans, Chinese, Mormons, and other groups as accessible cultural others, the campaign "mapped an idealized American history and tradition across the American landscape, defining an organic nationalism that linked national identity to a shared territory and history."[3]

These efforts to firmly ground Americans' national identity in the country's natural and cultural landscape, as well as to keep American dollars at home, also functioned as an effective means of keeping the cultural and touristic interests of middle-class Americans focused close to home, while people and places farther afield became the purview of adventurers, explorers, and anthropologists.

Americans' resulting disconnection from foreign cultures was reinforced by fears of communism, espionage, and subversion, along with the anxieties accompanying the Atomic Age. The anti-communist activities of J. Edgar Hoover and Senator Joseph McCarthy, along with related investigative committees formed in both the Senate and the House of Representatives kept the American public's fears and suspicions simmering, always ready to erupt into a boil with each new escalation of political "heat." With scandals of alleged infiltration and sympathy animating the news, Americans were mistrustful of difference and, heeding the warnings that abounded in the country's civic culture and popular culture alike, fearful of outsiders. Adding to these fears was uncertainty about the wisdom and outcomes of large-scale scientific progress, particularly developments related to the atomic bomb, and the potential for that progress to overreach collective morality and social controls.[4]

Disney's numerous armed forces films, along with the studio's wartime propaganda cartoons, had already firmly situated the studio in the political landscape of the times, with tongue-in-cheek offerings like *Donald Gets Drafted* (1942) and the classic *Der Fuehrer's Face* (1943), the blatantly anti–Nazi *Education for Death* (1943), as well as war bond promotions emphasizing the war effort on the homefront, such as the 1942 productions of *Donald's Decision* and *All Together Now*, both made for the National Film Board of Canada. Taken together, these productions not only supported the country's wartime interests, but served to reinforce the climate of fear, mistrust, and ethnocentrism that pervaded World War II America. By 1953, however, Disney's contributions to postwar popular culture grew more complex than they had been when the oppositions of war seemed to make mapping ideologies of good and evil so clear. With the *People and Places* anthology series, the studio put forth images of individuals and groups outside the country's borders that urged middle-class American audiences to reconsider these cultural Others, casting them as the objects of fascination, rather than fear.

The series' primitivizing framework diminished audiences' Atomic Age fears by freezing its subjects in a non-industrial moment in time, and by so doing, offering unspoken reassurances of American technological supremacy. Only Switzerland, a nation of legendary neutrality, is portrayed through the use of any urban images at all. Progress and innovation are recast here, from sources of Atomic Age anxiety to reminders of traditional American national identity and cultural dominance, making Cold War angst unnecessary — a message that was reinforced by the studio's 1957 film *Our Friend the Atom*, along with its Tomorrowland theme park exhibit and companion book. The book reminds readers that this converging set of media include "a picture of the future life of man as it would be shaped by the fabulous achievements of science."[5] Science, of course, that was not found in the cultures represented in *People and Places*.

Disney's subtle, or perhaps unintentional, reassurances, present throughout the series, along with his stated hope that the anthology's films would broaden cultural understandings leading to peace for "all men," prefigured the corporation's adoption of the "It's a small world" theme by over a decade.[6] They also marked a distinct departure from the country's Cold War environment of suspicion, paranoia, and isolationism, emphasizing human universals over superficial cultural differences.

Learning About People and Places

Following the model established in the wildlife-focused *True-Life Adventures*, *People and Places* brought then-rare glimpses of the world to Disney audiences, infusing the cultural and natural worlds with wonder, while at the same time making those wonders comprehensible and familiar. With these two series, Disney took his place among a constellation of travel-focused entertainers and educators in the United States whose lineage reached back into the nineteenth century. The *People and Places* series, in particular, was situated, though perhaps uneasily, amidst the evolving traditions of both travelogues and ethnographic films, borrowing elements from each, yet never realizing the potential of either.

The travel genre was one of the most popular and developed genres in early film, and the competition for upper and middle-class movie-goers' imaginations was steady and fierce.[7] Images and tales of Jack London's 1907 voyage on his yacht *Snark* thrilled traveling show audiences, as they chronicled his encounters with Solomon Islanders and other Pacific tribal groups.[8] The American Museum of Natural History sponsored and filmed a number of Asiatic ethnographic and zoological expeditions from 1916 through 1930; films of Arctic and Antarctic journeys were even more plentiful, such as those carried out by Amundsen (1910), Scott (1910), Lerner (1914), and Shackleton (1914–1917); Albert Blinkhorn offered *Hunting Wild Game in the South Pacific* (1914), while the Amazon was "captured" by J. Campbell Besley (1915). Later, travelers such as Burton Holmes, Lewis Cotlow, Martin and Osa Johnson, and Lowell Thomas were familiar figures who brought the world's exotic locales to life for Americans as they ventured into the twentieth century.

While these films shared locations and subjects with ethnographic films—cinematic documentations of cultural groups that were typically the products of anthropological research—their impulses to film the world's "primitive," wild, or exotic people and places had very different origins, processes, and generally, results. Early ethnographic films, such as Edward Curtis's *In the Land of the Headhunters* (1916), Robert J. Flaherty's *Nanook of the North: A Story of Life and Love in the Actual Arctic* (1922), and Merian C. Cooper and Ernest B. Schoedsack's, *Grass* (1925) focused not only on "difference," but on investigating its meaning, as well.[9] Considered to be the first commercially successful feature-length documentary, Flaherty's film was a hybrid of narrative and documentary that included staged or steered "actuality" scenes integrated with the filmmaker's documentary footage. The film was later critiqued for its manipulation of the subjects' lived reality in order to illustrate traditional lifeways.[10] Flaherty, a self-defined "explorer artist," claimed that a filmmaker must often distort a thing to catch its true spirit—a philosophy that spoke to the heart of the adventure travelogue genre.[11]

As the process of ethnographic filmmaking became institutionalized, standardized rules for film documentation were established: logs of activities (much like an anthropologist's fieldnotes) were required. Seizing on the problems of "truth" raised by cinéma vérité in the 1920s, restrictions were placed on dramatic angles or movement, and editing was permitted *only* for representativeness, rather than for narrative effect.[12] In this way, ethnographic film diverged sharply from travelogues and adventure films, seeking different truths, in different ways.

Following the Lumiere tradition of "placing the world within one's reach,"[13] these travelers, adventurers, and cultural educators explored, and exploited, cinema's power of exhibition — the power of "making images seen."[14] As travelogues, their films harkened back to what Tom Gunning has called the "cinema of attractions" of the early 1900s — presenting images that directly addressed spectators, and were, in and of themselves, the objects of curiosity, attention, and fascination — spectacles in their own right, rather than images in search of a narrative. For Gunning, the combination of "actuality" — in the form of undramatized individuals and events — and "novelty" — in the form of new cinematic technology like the Biograph or Vitascope — created the attraction of early cinema. As cinema became narrativized, beginning in 1907 and culminating in the appearance of feature films, moving picture images shifted from self-contained attractions to elements of dramatic expression, changing both uses and expectations of images in film.

While travelogues continued to place an emphasis on the exotic well into the mid-twentieth century, by the 1930s these popular shorts and feature films were joined by a strong new wave of films influenced by the increasing prominence of the automobile in American culture and its enhancement of the See America First campaign. While travel lecturers such as Burton Holmes had occasionally included footage of New York, Chicago, and other cities in their presentations, these new travelogues focused on and celebrated the cities of the United States and Canada, along with well-known foreign destination spots of the "rich and famous," such as Cuba and the Riviera. Emphasizing these locations' advances in transportation, social, economic, and industrial progress, and increasing popularity, these new additions to the genre greeted audiences with a message far different from their more exotic counterparts. They were designed to encourage tourism. Rather than addressing audiences as spectators of people and places that were strikingly foreign, these new travelogues spoke to audiences as potential tourists, minimizing difference, or framing it as superficial. They reassured viewers of the comfort and safety of these locales, supported by images of people just like them, enjoying familiar food, engaging in familiar forms of recreation, and creating relationships with locals who were not really all that different from themselves. Increasingly, in the post-war era, the non-fiction filming of "difference" and the exotic fell to ethnographic filmmakers, as popular culture in the Cold War United States focused its lens toward home.

While not produced until the following decade, Disney's anthology films — part natural history and part ethnography, part documentary and part staged action — demonstrate clear roots in these earlier traditions. However, they neither sought to create the air of adventure of early travelogues nor did they replicate ethnographic film's efforts toward unadorned truth. Instead, the *People and Places* series relied heavily on a careful crafting of "difference" that was vibrant and compelling, yet non-threatening. This and other elements of visual spectacle helped to blur whatever boundaries might have existed between the cinema of attractions and later, narrative cinema, combining elements of both to colonize people and places from around the world as wondrous subjects of the Magic Kingdom.

Creating Cultural Edutainment

The *People and Places* series is part of a long tradition of American edutainment focused on the marvels and mysteries of the world outside the country's borders. The decades leading up to the twentieth century were the heyday of the traveling show, as tent shows, Wild West extravaganzas, lectures, circuses, vaudeville troupes, and Chautauqua all traveled from town-to-town in good, barnstorming fashion. Between 1870–1920, one of the most popular among these traveling shows was the travel lecture or travelogue presentation, which brought the wonders of the world to audiences in both cities and rural areas, first via hand-painted glass slides, illuminated by the light of a magic lantern, and later, through the new medium of film, a spectacle in itself.

But these early silent cinema portrayals were by no means the only, or even the most spectacular, of culture-focused edutainment at the turn of the century. Dime museums—inexpensive urban edutainment venues that combined knowledge with spectacle—boasted collections of the bizarre and exotic that included artifacts and memorabilia from remote regions of the world, along with historical wax tableau and oddities of nature. On a much larger scale, the 1893 World's Columbian Exposition (or Chicago World's Fair), a celebration of American exceptionalism and technological progress, was conceptualized as a "veritable encyclopedia of civilization."[15] And for the fair's over 27 million spectators, "civilization" was defined by the juxtaposition of scientific and technological progress, on one hand, and the ethnographic villages found on the Midway Plaisance. These "realistic" village exhibits showcased foreign and exotic people and lifeways, and were designed to "afford visitors the opportunity to measure the progress of humanity toward the ideal of civilization presented in the White City."[16] The exposition would join the continuing traditions of travelogues, adventure writing and photography, ethnographic museums and films, and exploration films, in serving as a template for the representation of strange and exotic cultures into the twentieth century, and for decades to come.[17]

Disney Studios entered into the business of cultural representation a bit more opportunistically, from the worlds of animation and nature films. The story of Disney's animated cartoon *Bambi* setting the studio on the path to the *True-Life Adventure* series is well known, but the next chapter in the tale, a bit less so, as the footage that brought the first *True-Life Adventure*, *Seal Island* (1948), into being would also serve as Disney's inspiration for the *People and Places* series. Alaskan filmmakers and conservationists Alfred and Elma Milotte had already been contributors to the landscape of North American nature travelogues when they were hired by Disney to film the Alaskan wilderness. The pair, amateur naturalists who had been lecturing and showing films on the area, submitted footage not only of the natural environment, but of human interaction with it. Chronicles of hunting and other subsistence activities, creating a built environment, enacting rituals and celebrations, and carrying out family life were all included as part of a holistic representation of wilderness life. The Academy Award-winning featurette, *The Alaskan Eskimo* drew its life, not from the impulse to document the lifeways of a vanishing cultural group, but from the cutting room floor, created from footage deemed unsuitable for *Seal Island* when Disney insisted that the wildlife film not include the presence of humans. Both films launched successful series that ran until 1960, sharing the voice of narrator Winston Hibler and the guiding hand of producer Ben Sharpsteen, down their respective paths to success. Under Sharpsteen's guidance, the two anthology series brought eleven Academy Awards to Disney Studios, with eight of the thirteen *True-Life Adventures* and three of the seventeen *People and Places* series being honored.

But the two series shared something even more profound: Disney's trademark interpretive framework. In good documentary fashion, the *People and Places* series promised audiences its own version of true-life adventure. Each installment of the anthology opened with an on-screen affirmation of the film's value as a chronicle of culture, and assuring audiences that what they were about to see was authentic:

> This film is one in a series presenting interesting people and the places in which they live. All the scenes are authentic and the stories are factual.

But in both *People and Places* and the *True-Life* anthology, we find the natural and cultural worlds drawn into the magic kingdom and recast to entertain, educate, and promote a worldview compatible with Disney's vision. In that vision, colors splashed across the screen a bit brighter, challenges were met and overcome a bit easier, and both hard work and mischievous antics were carried out with the best of intentions. Musical scores, from the jaunty and satirical to the sweeping and romantic, were the unified voice with which Disney spoke, regardless of time, geography, or subject. Mocking horns, swelling strings, and the clatter of clumsy percussion crafted comedy, drama, and intentionality in the worlds of humans and animals alike. If it can be said that Disney's live-action animal features engaged in anthropomorphizing—attributing human motivation, emotion, and personality to animals—then a similar process can be observed in *People and Places*' treatment of children in Portugal, the elderly in Lapland, women in Japan, and men in Morocco. Lives are choreographed, personalities set to music, and all are reinterpreted through the lens of middle class American norms, values, and expectations. And while *The Alaskan Eskimo* and all of the culture-focused films that followed it in the series were created with an eye toward chronicling unique, traditional, non-industrial cultural production, they also shared a number of common themes that spoke directly to these American values and expectations, reinforcing audience's beliefs in their own day-to-day lived realities as they portrayed the lives of others across the globe.

American Values, Around the World

Glistening shores, lush green valleys, billowing deserts, and "highways made of ice"—all are interwoven with the lifeways they shape, and by which they are, in turn, shaped. The *People and Places* series takes its audiences from Alaska to Thailand in the 1954 *Siam*, and onward, to Europe [*Switzerland* (1955), *Sardinia* (1956), *Portugal* (1957), *The Danube* (1960)], the United Kingdom [*Scotland* (1958), *Wales* (1958)], Asia [*Japan* (1960), *The Ama Girls* (1958)], the Pacific and South Pacific [*Cruise of the Eagle* (1959), *Samoa* (1956)], Fennoscandia [*Lapland* (1957)], North Africa [*Morocco* (1957)], the polar regions [*Men Against the Arctic* (1955), *Seven Cities of Antarctica* (1958)] and at home to the then-heart of the magic kingdom itself, *Disneyland, U.S.A.* (1956). Place plays a significant role in these films, in part, for the audience appeal of breathtaking natural environments, but more importantly, for the its impact on subsistence activities, occupations, foodways, transportation, recreation, the structure of social relationships, and the production and use of material culture. The emphasis of Disney's edutainment here is squarely on cultural geography, setting the issue of global politics carefully aside. Brief glosses are offered for the complex political status of places such as Wales ("Not a nation, in the accepted sense, since she pays allegiance to the British crown") and Lapland ("A place, but not a nation"), but no additional mention of political or ideological orientation is made. In each case, place is treated locally, rather than as part of a larger whole; as the foundation, over time, for each group's distinctive and unique culture.

These close ties to place-as-landscape serve to create a "rustic" demeanor for each of the anthology's featured groups, framing them as close to, if not embedded in, nature, even when, as audiences are shown in the cases of Samoans and the Alaskan Eskimo, those groups are forced to battle the elements. In a telling scene from *Lapland*, audiences are informed that "In his kinship with nature, the Lap finds little to be desired. He has a fine, free life in a land of crisp air and clean water" while Samoa's elaborate customs and ceremonies are explained as arising as a remedy to boredom: "Providing for their simple needs takes up only part of their time, so they have developed elaborate customs and ceremonies to make their tranquil existence more exciting." Even in the case of Switzerland, where the fingerprints of progress are more apparent than in any other of *People and Places* culturally-focused films, Disney ushers viewers into life in a small village, advising that the Swiss have two indestructible bonds: Democracy and the mountains.

"Simple," "primitive," and "isolated," the portrayals of these groups resonate with descriptions of non-industrialized cultures throughout the history of Western cultures, as members of "civilized" societies crafted categories of "self" and "other" that privileged prevailing notions of progress. These frameworks often constructed romantic, or at least sympathetic, portrayals of the "noble savage," as found in Charles Dickens' nineteenth century description of the Alaskan Eskimo as "loving children of the North" who are "forever happy with their lot."[18] Disney's portrayals, just over a century later, are not all that far from those of Dickens, both creating images that stood in stark contrast to the cultures of industrialized progress of their respective audiences.[19]

Ties to nature are nowhere more evident than in the anthology's treatment of subsistence activities and occupations. Lives are intertwined with the natural landscape as the skills to herd, fish, gather, farm, build, and create are learned and perfected over the lifecourse. It is often these skills that define an individual's role in the family or community, and bring meaning to the chores and tasks of daily life. For the Morocco's Blue Men, or Tuaregs, livelihood, domestic labor and even social relationships are all centered on the camel. According to the Tuareg proverb, "He who has no milk in his home has nothing. He who has no milk has no friends."[20] In *Wales*, an 80-year-old woman gathers cockles in much the same way as she learned at age eight, while a young housewife practices baking scones ("A Welsh girl's reputation as a housewife depends on her skill with a scone"). A group of young boys in *Portugal* dream of one day becoming *toureiros*— bullfighters— and use young heifers as "sparring partners," while others apprentice as oarsmen on sturdy, but graceful, fishing boats. Their Samoan counterparts learn to participate in making copra, spreading the tender coconut meat to dry in the sun, the little ones earnestly standing watch against marauding chickens. From Alaska, where women sew communally as groups of men build, to Japan, where a long "drumline" is formed on the beach as community members pound seaweed to remove impurities, nature provides challenges— and raw materials— that create links to the past, shape visions of the future, and order the lived realities of Disney's subjects.

And whether in Siam or Samoa, the family is the element around which those day-to-day realities turn. As the basic economic and social unit, the family structure informs all daily activities. Women oversee the domestic chores, while men serve as the public face of the family, and viewers are instructed that "cooperation in the key to success."[21] Even *The Blue Men of Morocco,* which follows the journey of nomadic Tuaregs across a sea of sand to bring their camels to market in distant Marrakech, illustrates this division, with the women's side of the family tent reserved for cooking, weaving, and other homemaking chores, while the men's side is designated for hospitality. Only in the award-winning *Ama Girls*, Disney's thirteenth *People and Places* offering, are women featured working in a paid occupation, rather than in a family or community-centered subsistence activity (such as farming, horticulture, or animal husbandry). The film features young women of the Japanese seacoast who are trained to dive for shellfish and a mineral-rich seaweed known as "heaven grass." American viewers, grappling with the place of women in their own workforce are reassured that the Ama girls, who are of "superior stamina and exceptional physique" also "neglect no opportunity to look their prettiest," and only dive because they are better able than men to stand the icy waters. When families in *Portugal*, the tenth *People and Places* film, are seen industriously transforming grapes into wine, it is the women toil in the vineyards, harvesting the fruit, after which the men cheerfully roll up their shorts, lock arms, and stomp the grapes until their legs are blue — all choreographed, of course, to a playful, soundtrack that seeks to transform communal labor into vaudeville-like comedy.

The timelessness of these customs, skills, and ceremonies is central to the portrayals in *People and Places*. The "capture" and preservation of "old ways" that are "unchanged by time, undisturbed by the march of progress" was Disney's focus throughout the anthology. The series contains footage of lifeways, craftsmanship, ceremonies, costumes, and indeed, even landscapes, that have, undoubtedly, given way to the pressures of progress and globalization, making them invaluable visual records of cultural traditions. It can also be argued that the anthology represents an equally valuable window into the global outlook and cultural identity of America in the 1950s and 1960s— even more so given the iconic status of Walt Disney, and the studio's pivotal role in cultural production in the postwar era. However, that impulse to preserve is a double-edged sword, and in *People and Places*, it has also led to a tendency to primitivize and essentialize the groups it seeks to celebrate. The series' films repeatedly cast local knowledge and non-industrial production as "primitive," whether in reference to handcrafts, harvesting, or habitats, in Sardinia or Scotland. Even in *The Danube*, where villagers' explicit connection to history is illustrated through deliberate reenactment, designed to express cultural pride, those taking on historical roles are seamlessly visually integrated with scenes of present-day subjects in ways that blur the line between past and present. Narration suggests that the problems of the Atomic Age can be "drowned in the golden foam" of the scenic river that unites the villages on its banks in a shared history. With a similar focus on history, voiceover narration in *Wales* advises that the Welsh "cling to the old ways," focusing on hand-hewn water wheels, family factories, and women baking cakes over an open fire, without framing those traditions within the larger picture of the country's twentieth-century complexities.

Seen through the lens of Disney's cameras, these palpable links between present and past, whether visually inferred or made explicit through narration, distance the cultures of *People and Places* from the realities and anxieties of their audiences. They also create the need for a common language through which daily life can be understood across cultures, in order to assure American audiences that beneath the spectacle and strangeness of cultural detail, they and the individuals on the screen share a common humanity—common aspirations, and basic human problems, as Disney's own words assured them. For Disney, one strategy was the seemingly-universal language in which the studio was already fluent: comedy. Girls everywhere plot to snare boys; community food stores are framed as "the fish national bank"; and bullfight practice is glossed as the Portuguese equivalent of Little League, creating structures of meaning comprehensible to American audiences. Across the series' cultures, the antics of small children are framed in ways designed to elicit not only laughter, but nods of recognition from American parents. Japanese toddlers, playing at sailing tiny handmade boats in *The Ama Girls*, are cast as "Nautical Nippers of Nippon," while in *Lapland*, when a small boy, full of determination, struggles to cut himself a snack with a knife that would elicit gasps of panic from American adults, Hibler's narration observes that it is "customary to eat with fingers and forego forks, but this little lad may soon forego fingers!" And of course, these youngsters confirm what all parents in Disney's audiences suspected: "Children all over the world hate to go to bed."

The elderly have their role in this cultural comedy, as well, when the camera focuses on an elderly Lap woman drawing contentedly on her pipe. Framed as a parody of both age and gender, the image seeks to remind viewers that the "character" that comes with advanced age is also universal. Nearly thirty years earlier, however, when a parallel scene in the 1928 film *Simba*, depicted an elderly tribal woman, the "Queen of Lumbwa," puffing on a cigar, critics were outraged at the filmmakers' attempts to create vaudeville out of difference. Disney, whose animation and *True-Life Adventure* output in those intervening years had been trademarked by satire and the imposition of comedy, received no such criticism, raising unanswered questions about whether and in what ways the studio's history in cartoon animation affected the reception of Disney's edutainment efforts.

These questions are not the only complexities related to the ways in which the studio's history is interwoven in the *People and Places* series. In addition to the fourteen cultural groups represented in the anthology, it also includes three films focused on military projects in science and technology, continuing the studio's wartime relationship with the government, and making the series an uneasy combination of narrative essays on culture and progress. These curious additions, highlighting Coast Guard projects in the Arctic (*Men Against the Arctic)* and the Pacific Ocean (*The Cruise of the Eagle)*, and the creation of Naval bases in the Antarctic (*Seven Cities of Antarctica*) stand in sharp contrast to the majority of the series' depictions of primitive cultures, timelessly situated in nature. The anthology is further complicated by the inclusion of *Disneyland, U.S. A.*, the sixth film in the *People and Places* series. A study, in fact, of a "place" that wasn't. The film, like the theme park, celebrates American exceptionalism, innovation, and consumerism — or seeks, as Mitsuhiro Yashimoto observes in his essay on Tokyo Disneyland, "to equate the commodification of daily life ... with American nationalism."[22]

The inclusion of these films leads to questions about what constituted people or places meriting inclusion in the series. Despite Walt Disney's own journey to Latin America in the summer of 1941, and the studio's production of the features *Saludos Amigos* (1942) and *The Three Caballeros* (1944), no Latin American cultures received attention in *People and Places*. Neither did the Navajo, a group that was the focus of two Disney projects—*Navajo Adventure* (1957) and *The Navajo, Children of God* (1967). However, Navajo culture *is* included in a companion book of the same name, written by Jane Werner Watson, with a foreward by Walt Disney, in which only the cultural groups featured in the anthology appear. These Navajo films, created ten years apart, attest to the significant role played by cultural education themes in Disney's output, and yet, taken together, they demonstrate how severely the studio's perspective on what it meant to chronicle culture had fallen out of step with social progress in America. In 1966, the year before *Children of God* was released, anthropologists Sol Worth and John Adair were also working on Native American film. The pair facilitated the creation of *The Navajo Film Themselves*— an ethnographic project in which a small group of Navajo was asked to make 16 mm. black-and-white films about how they saw themselves, and how they *wanted* to be seen by outsiders.[23] Thus, both Disney productions share similar essentializing traits that marked adventure ethnography of the 1950s— effectively freezing the Navajo in time — while progress in fields like visual anthropology had moved the documenting of culture in directions that were more in-touch with subjects' lived realities.

Conclusion: The World as "Magic Kingdom"

But "reality," even in Disney's non-fiction productions, was a shifting term, and I would argue, not the primary motivator in the creation of the *People and Places* series. If "reality" had been at issue, there existed a range of continually-developing documentary methods that might have served as models. The work of the series, then, was about something more — something more fundamental to American national identity, to the country's Cold War ethos, and to solving the dissonance between valorizing progress, on the one hand, and maintaining a romantic nostalgia for a simpler, more certain time, on the other — about helping audiences locate themselves in a postwar world. Disney accomplished all of these through his films' portrayals of individuals and communities around the world, creating a multi-dimensional picture of America's place in the world that left its own people feeling safe, reassured, and confident about *their* place.

Through those portrayals, Disney both created structures of difference and collapsed them, narrating lives and landscapes that, while foreign and strange, contained values, characteristics, and relationships that mainstream

Americans recognized as part of themselves. Perhaps, more than that, those images contained values, characteristics, and relationships that audiences recognized as the *best* parts of themselves, creating nostalgia for a Golden Age that existed before the rapid social change brought about by war.

It is here, in the ability to simultaneously exoticize and familiarize Americans' cultural Others, that we find the true creation of Disney's magic kingdom. In *People and Places'* portrayal of cultural wonders—of bold, unique, colorful difference—lies the magic; in its reassurance that, despite those differences, there are human universals that make us all comprehensible—that the Cold War world really was a "small world after all"—lies the kingdom. Long before any physical representation of a "Magic Kingdom" came into being, Disney had already drawn Americans, and the rest of the world, inside.

Notes

1. Walt Disney, "Foreword" in Jane Werner Watson, *Walt Disney's People and Places* (New York: Golden Press, 1959), np.
2. Marguerite Schaffer, *See America First: Tourism and National Identity, 1880–1940.* (Washington, D.C.: Smithsonian Books, 2001), 4.
3. Schaffer, 122
4. For discussions of the range of responses to advances in technology, see Paul S. Boyer, *By the Bomb's Early Light: American Thought and Culture at the Dawn of the Atomic Age* (Chapel Hill: University of North Carolina Press, 1994; Stephen J. Whitfield, *The Culture of the Cold War* (Baltimore: Johns Hopkins University Press, 1991).
5. Dust jacket. *Our Friend the Atom* (New York: Simon and Schuster, 1956).
6. The Disney attraction "It's a Small World" originated with the Pepsi Pavilion at the 1964 World's Fair, themed after the eponymous song, commissioned by Disney. The attraction was transferred to Disneyland in 1966, where it grew into a key theme in the park's "Fantasyland." "It's a small world" includes representations from Europe, Asia, Africa, Latin America, the Arctic and Antarctic, the South Pacific, and the United States, emphasizing unity and interconnectedness.
7. Charles Musser, "American Vitagraph 1897–1901" in *Cinema Journal*, vol. 22 no. 3, Spring 1983, 47.
8. Martin Johnson, who accompanied London on his voyages, forged his early travelogue career using still images and footage from his voyages with London.
9. *Grass*, the least known of these, was set in the area then known as "Persia" (now, Iran). The film documents Bakhtiari herdsmen on their annual trek from winter to summer pastures.
10. It should be noted that this technique was common practice among documentaries of the day, though foreign to the goals of even early ethnographic film.
11. Richard Barsam, *Non-fiction Film: A Critical History* (Bloomington: Indiana University Press, 1973), 46–54.
12. Known as the "cinema of truth," one of cinéma vérité's hallmarks at the time was the use of stylized camera work and editing, along with staged action to "problematize" the notion of "truth."
13. Tom Gunning, "The Cinema of Attractions: Early Film, Its Spectator and the Avant-Garde" in Thomas Elsaesser (ed.), *Early Cinema: Space, Frame, Narrative* (London: British Film Institute, 1990), 56.
14. Fernand Leger, "A critical essay on the plastic qualities of Abel Gance's film *The*

Wheel," in Edward Fry (ed.), *Functions of Painting*, trans. Alexandra Anderson (New York: Viking, 1973), 21.

15. Rydell, np; see also Reid Badger. *The Great American Fair: The World's Columbian Exposition and American Culture* (Chicago: Nelson Hall, 1979).

16. Ibid.

17. In fact, Cleveland, Ohio, modeled its 1936 Great Lakes Exposition directly after the Columbian Exposition, including a "Streets of the World" exhibition.

18. Charles Dickens, "Our Phantom Ship on an Antediluvian Cruise" in *Household Words*, April 16, 1851.

19. In the case of the Alaskan Eskimo, narration observes that the Eskimo build their homes by instinct, and that, while they do not have many possessions, "their treasure is their way of life."

20. Jane Werner Watson, *Walt Disney's People and Places* (New York: Golden Press, 1959), 89.

21. Made explicit in this quote from *Ama Girls*.

22. Mitsuhiro Yoshimoto, "Images of Empire: Tokyo Disneyland and Japanese Cultural Imperialism" in Eric Smoodin (ed.), *Disney Discourse: Producing the Magic Kingdom*. AFI Film Readers Series (Oxford: Taylor and Francis, 2004), 192.

23. For more on this project and other early visual auto-ethnographies, see Sarah Pink's *Visual Interventions: Applied Visual Anthropology* (Oxford, UK: Berghahn Books, 2009), and Sol Worth and John Adair's *Through Navajo Eyes: An Exploration in Film Communication and Anthropology* (Bloomington: Indiana University Press, 1972).

Bibliography

Badger, Reid. *The Great American Fair: The World's Columbian Exposition and American Culture*. Chicago: Nelson Hall, 1979.

Barsam, Richard. *Non-fiction Film: A Critical History*. Bloomington: Indiana University Press, 1973.

Boyer, Paul S. *By the Bomb's Early Light: American Thought and Culture at the Dawn of the Atomic Age*. Chapel Hill: University of North Carolina Press, 1994.

Dickens, Charles. "Our Phantom Ship on an Antediluvian Cruise" in *Household Words*, April 16, 1851.

Disney, Walt. "Foreword" in *Walt Disney's People and Places*, written by Jane Werner Watson, np. New York: Golden Press, 1959.

Gunning, Tom. "The Cinema of Attractions: Early Film, Its Spectator and the Avant-Garde" in *Early Cinema: Space, Frame, Narrative*, edited by Thomas Elsaesser, 56 London: British Film Institute, 1990.

Leger, Fernand. "A critical essay on the plastic qualities of Abel Gance's film *The Wheel*," in *Functions of Painting*, edited by Edward Fry, translated by Alexandra Anderson, 21–27. New York: Viking, 1973.

Musser, Charles. "American Vitagraph 1897–1901" *Cinema Journal* 22 no. 3, (Spring 1983): 4–47.

Our Friend the Atom. "Dust Jacket." New York: Simon and Schuster, 1956.

Pink, Sarah. *Visual Interventions: Applied Visual Anthropology*. Oxford, UK: Berghahn Books, 2009.

Rydell, Robert. *All the World's a Fair: Visions of Empire at America's International Expositions, 1876–1916*. Chicago: University of Chicago Press, 1984.

Schaffer, Marguerite. *See America First: Tourism and National Identity, 1880–1940*. Washington, D.C.: Smithsonian Books, 2001.

Watson, Jane Werner. *Walt Disney's People and Places*. New York: Golden Press, 1959.

Whitfield, Stephen J. *The Culture of the Cold War.* Baltimore: Johns Hopkins University Press, 1991.

Worth, Sol, and John Adair. *Through Navajo Eyes: An Exploration in Film Communication and Anthropology.* Bloomington: Indiana University Press, 1972.

Yoshimoto, Mitsuhiro. "Images of Empire: Tokyo Disneyland and Japanese Cultural Imperialism" in *Disney Discourse: Producing the Magic Kingdom,* edited by Eric Smoodin. 181–199. AFI Film Readers Series. Oxford: Taylor and Francis, 2004.

16

America's Salesman
The USA in Circarama

SARAH NILSEN

The United States pavilion at the 1958 Brussels World's Fair was an ideological project constructed in order to push European visitors toward a positive outlook on the United States at a time when the nation's international reputation was being severely challenged by Soviet propaganda. President Dwight Eisenhower's second term was beset with concerns that his Administration was not dealing with its diplomatic, military, and domestic problems. Many Europeans feared the rapid militarization of the United States and its concomitant expansion of atomic power and additionally condemned its racial injustice. The Brussels World's Fair offered the U.S. government an opportunity to calm these fears and present an equitable image of the nation abroad. The fair exemplifies the type of soft psychological warfare developed in the Eisenhower administration in order to propagate a positive image of America throughout the world. The United States pavilion was constructed to create an actual space that would become America for its visitors, and this was an America demarcated by its ideological imperatives. Even though the fifties are often characterized as a time of the homogenization of American life and the solidification of traditional values against the onslaught of the communist threat, the difficulty on the part of both state and private entities to develop a coherent and stable national image to put on display for an European audience points to the inadequacy of the conception of American popular culture as a hegemonic force. This chapter, through the analysis of a film produced specifically to capture the image of America for an international audience, argues that Hollywood as a perceived hegemony in fact did not present a coherent and recognizable image of American national identity and that American propagandists struggled during this period to attempt to articulate and present an acceptable image of America for international consumption.

The exhibit that had the best success in attracting and selling the American way of life to Europeans at the Brussels World's Fair was created by Walt Disney. Housed in a separate theater attached to the American pavilion, the 360-degree travelogue film, *The USA in Circarama*, was projected continually for visitors throughout the day. As Walt Disney's first foray into building a world's fair attraction , the film proved to be a major hit for the Eisenhower administration mainly because Disney captured a saleable image of America that had eluded official American propagandists.

Disney as a Propagandist

Walt Disney saw himself as a producer of lighthearted popular entertainment. He shied away from overt messages, and even resisted the title of propagandist even after, at the government's request, he took on the role. Disney's transformation into an ambassador for the United States government and the American way of life was shaped by two significant events: a strike within the Disney Studios and the entry of the United States into the Second World War.

Firstly, the conversion of the Disney studio into wartime production marked Walt Disney's first direct involvement with the production of propaganda films for the government. Twenty eight percent of the Disney studio personnel were drafted into the war, and seventy five percent of the studio's output was targeted for the government. These films included animated instructional films for the armed forces, such as *Four Methods of Flush Riveting*, along with jingoistic cartoon shorts including *The New Spirit*, which had been commissioned by the Treasury Department to convince the general public to pay their income taxes in order to support the war effort. Additionally, Disney threw himself into producing two packages films, *Saludos Amigos!* and *The Three Caballeros*, for the Office of Coordinator of Inter-American Affairs, an office created in 1940 in order to promote relations between the United States and Latin America. By the war's end, Disney is estimated to have produced between 150 and 300 hours of government movies. These films kept the studio from bankruptcy and closure. Though Disney reportedly expressed to Treasury Department officials his fear of being labeled a propagandist in the public mind and the damage that it might cause to his reputation as a "whimsical, non-political artist," his extensive involvement in government backed, pro–American propaganda films provided Disney and the studio with the expertise in the production of effective political messages for a popular audience.[1]

Secondly, the bitter and divisive studio strike in 1941 convinced Disney of the existence of a communist conspiracy to destroy his studio. The strike converted Disney into an avowed anti-communist and directly led to his assumption of the position of the first vice president of the Motion Picture Alliance for the Preservation of American Ideals, an industry organization publicly opposed to leftist influences in the film industry. In September 1947, when the

House Un-American Activities Committee (HUAC) under Chair J. Parnell Thomas began its investigations of Communist influence in Hollywood, Disney's name was among a list of forty five "Possible Friendly Witnesses" compiled by the FBI. And Disney was also among the select group of friendly witnesses initially called to testify. In his testimony before the Committee, Disney claimed that the 1941 strike had been supported by "Commie front organizations" and that "throughout the world all the Commie groups began a smear campaign against [him] and [his] pictures."[2]

By the nineteen fifties, Walt Disney was viewed by American intelligence agencies as a singular figure in Hollywood who could be relied upon to spread the officially sanctioned message of the American way of life. Before the CIA backed overthrow the Iranian government in 1952, the American Embassy in Tehran sent a classified message to the Department of State suggesting that "if the Department is considering the production of films of more obvious propaganda type, that a short motion picture, probably of ten minutes duration, that pokes fun at the communist system without mentioning it as such, would find an appreciative audience in Iran. Further, if this film were done in the style of Disney, using his technique with the familiar Mickey Mouse, Donald Duck, Pluto, and so forth, the reception would be further enhanced."[3] By 1954, J. Edgar Hoover had made Disney into a special agent in charge contact for the FBI. In an office memorandum to Hoover, the Los Angeles special agent in charge wrote that "because of Mr. Disney's position as the foremost producer of cartoon films in the motion picture industry and his prominence and wide acquaintanceship in film production matters, it is believed that he can be of valuable assistance to this office and therefore it is my recommendation that he be approved as an SCA contact."[4]

Even with his stellar reputation as a spokesman for the American way of life, Disney had his work cut out for him. The HUAC investigations of Hollywood had significantly altered the tenor of the popular discourse and the perception of film as a form of escapist entertainment. Questions about the communist infiltration of American film production had transformed film, in the public mind, into a political medium capable of projecting ideologically potent images. Both the popular press and government officials debated and lamented the "distorted image of America" that Hollywood was popularizing abroad. Norman Cousins, the editor-in-chief of the *Saturday Review of Literature* and a well-known advocate of liberal causes including nuclear disarmament, wrote a well-publicized three-part editorial in the *Saturday Review* titled "The Free Ride" in 1950 in which he argued that "Soviet propaganda was not nearly as damaging as the grotesquely distorted view of the American people being created abroad by our own motion pictures."[5] The overriding complaint about the image that Hollywood was propagating was two-fold and linked. Firstly, Hollywood films created the impression that most Americans were excessively materialistic. As Cousins described, "We don't all live in plush duplex apartments with elaborate cocktail bars and retinues of servants. We don't all sleep in kingsize beds with silk topsheets nor do we all arise languidly at noon for breakfast in bed."[6] Coupled with the decadence and hedonism of American capitalism that Hollywood films broadcast internationally was the celebration of immorality and criminality. "We have more than our share of humanity's faults, but we by no means monopolize them," Cousins editorialized. "Nor are we predominantly a nation of murderers, gangsters, idlers, deadbeats, dipsomaniacs, touts, tarts, and swindlers, as Hollywood would have us appear."[7]

The assault by Cousins on Hollywood films and their detrimental effect on international perceptions of American society was reflective of widespread concerns about Hollywood within the government and elicited a heated response from Eric Johnston, the president of the Motion Picture Association of America who had replaced Will Hays in 1945. Unlike Hays, who had been hired to exercise his authority within and on the film industry, Johnston was, from the outset, designated as chief Washington lobbyist for the movie studios. Johnston found Cousins' arguments too reductive and he argued that American democracy was necessarily linked to consumerism and materialism, and it was something Hollywood films should flaunt as a means of selling the American way. "What would Mr. Cousins have us do?" Johnston asked. "Can we paint the American scene in film without showing our automobiles, our telephones, our bathtubs, our better clothes, better roads, higher buildings, refrigerators, radios, and household conveniences?... These 'dazzling gadgets' are products of a democracy, and we have them in such a multitude largely because we work and live by the rule of democracy."[8]

Walt Disney's extensive work for the government and his overt stance against Communism made Disney into the one of the few Hollywood executives that the Eisenhower government (and also most Americans) found to be a true American patriot who could be trusted to effectively present the American message abroad. Walt Disney was the only Hollywood studio executive chosen by the Cambridge Study Group for the Brussels Universal and International Exhibition at MIT, along with a group of America's top business and cultural leaders, to help determine the thematic basis for the American pavilion at the fair. The study group was composed of the key members of the CIA-funded Center for International Studies (CENIS). CENIS was contracted by the State Department as the initial planning group for the Brussels World's Fair. The CENIS study group for the fair, in a series of meetings conducted between 1956 and 1958, attempted to articulate a comprehensive strategy for the exhibit that would present for European visitors "The Undiscovered Country." "Of all the nations, great and small," the study group argued, "the United States today is probably the most widely known — and also the most widely misunderstood. To this day, ours, to the foreigner, remains an undiscovered country. The fact is disquieting.... Thus beyond the efforts of our statesmen, our diplomats, our overseas information services, there is an urgent need to bring to ordinary men and women abroad the true picture of what we are and what we are after." The group struggled over the challenge of selling the free market system abroad through the use of soft power techniques, the fair planners needed to determine, "basically what has set our nation apart, enabling it to achieve in a relatively short span of years a pinnacle of economic and social supremacy and world leadership?"[9]

Because of his close governmental ties and his espousal of corporate capitalism as the American way, Walt Disney was ideally suited to manage the challenge that faced the Cambridge study group. The group's initial interview of Disney was conducted by Robert Warner, the Coordinator of U.S. Building Exhibits, along with John Hench, one of the designers of the Disneyland park, at the Burbank studio on January 8, 1957. The summary of the meeting stated that "these gentlemen came up with almost nothing" but that they had "asked for time to study the problem." Disney did suggest that "it was important that we emphasize the fact that we are a people who like to enjoy ourselves. He felt we should play down the idea that we only want money and said we must avoid bragging about money and leisure."[10]

Warner spent a day touring Disneyland during his visit and by the end of January began negotiations with Walt Disney for the production of a 360-degree film comparable to the park's Circarama attraction. With a proposed budget of a million dollars for the new film, the search began for an official sponsor of the exhibit. James Plaut, the Deputy Commissioner General of the Brussels Exhibition wrote Howard Cullman, the Commissioner General, that "after due consideration, we feel that this would be the ideal vehicle for Ford. This is based on the fact that General Motors will have a big show in the Belgian section and that Ford is very keen to do something spectacular for the Belgian market.... We are prepared to go so far as to call the undertaking 'Fordarama' which ought to interest them."[11] The selection of a major automobile company for sponsorship of the film was a logical choice since the original Disneyland attraction was paid for by American Motors and was shot with a camera mounted to a car.

Disney and Circarama

The development of Walt Disney's Circarama occurred at a time when movie attendance had significantly declined in the United States due to the marked increase of television viewership and other leisure activities. Disney had a hand in both, producing the television anthology series *Disneyland* for ABC beginning in 1954 and opening his Disneyland theme park in 1955. Through the use of television, Disney was able to market his park and his stockpile of films to a new and ready audience. In addition, he was able to develop a symbiotic relationship with corporate sponsors that would fund his projects in exchange for the promotion of their products. Disney's reliance on corporate backing for his theme park was unprecedented.

The future envisaged in the Tomorrowland area of the Disneyland park was based on the prosperity and progress offered by corporate capitalism. Similar to the New York World's Fair of 1939 and its theme of "Building the World of Tomorrow," its images of the future were dominated by a consumer culture that foregrounded the beneficent success of the free enterprise system. The three main exhibitions in Tomorrowland at the time of the opening of Disneyland were American Motors' "Circarama," the Richfield show called "The World Beneath Us," and TWA's "Flight to the Moon." All three exhibits emphasized film innovations that combined education and entertainment in order to showcase Disneyfied corporate promotions. Corporate involvement in sites of leisure activity was common throughout the early twentieth century especially at world's fairs. As Tom Gunning has noted, world's fairs "provided an image of the world wide power of capitalism; they transformed a market place into a symbolic landscape that not only celebrated but exemplified modernity; and they formed a spectacle in which commodity provided the entertainment, and the commodity form of entertainment itself was raised to a new technical perfection."[12] But Disney greatly expanded corporate involvement in his theme park by using other corporation's monetary investment in pavilions to create a distinctly Disney-based product that would serve as a source of public relations advertising masked by the lure of entertainment. Although the *Disneyland* television program proved to be an unexpected success, Disneyland itself was considered a risky investment before its opening. Therefore, companies that chose to enter into an agreement with Disney at the park were counting on the popularity of the Walt Disney name to provide them with a distinctly white, middle-class, suburban audience and clientele.

In order to understand the evolution of the Circarama phenomenon that proved so popular at the Brussels World's Fair of 1958, it is instructive to chart the history of the "ride" within the context of Disneyland itself. Circarama was designed for a multitude of reasons beyond standard film exhibition. It was part travelogue, part patriotic anthem to the American way, and predominantly an advertisement within a corporate sponsored playground. By the time Disney's Circarama reached Brussels, it had undergone significant development and refinement as a product of Disney's synergy. The Circarama technology was originally developed by Ub Iwerks, who had been with Walt Disney since the start of their animation careers, but had by the 1950s been consigned to the engineering barns because of interpersonal conflicts. The Circarama exhibition required considerable financial investment for its initial development. A contemporaneous article in *Business Film*, the industrial film journal, made special mention of the complexity and ingenuity involved in this new widescreen technology. Even considering Disney's well-known perfectionism, his extensive investment in the technological development of Circarama signaled his confidence in the ability of this one-of-a-kind experience to effectively reach crowds of consumers.

The format of the original Circarama film was that of a traditional travelogue, *A Tour of the West*, displayed on a new 360-degree screen. The selection of a travelogue as the source material for the film can be traced to the recent development of Disney's *True-Life* series of nature documentaries, which began with *Seal Island* in 1948. These documentaries became a regular feature of the original *Disneyland* television series, and in the 1950s Disney created another related documentary series, *People and Places*, which did for cultural geography what the *True-Life Adventures* did for natural history. As Margaret King has shown, these documentaries anthropomorphized nature by transforming animals and their environments into human scenarios. They also used the symbolic landscapes of the United States in order to create films flooded with American optimism and manifest destiny.[13] James Algar, who wrote five Academy-Award-winning pictures for Disney, including *Nature's Half Acre*, *The Living Desert* and *The Vanishing Praire* and also directed several wartime films produced by the studio for the U.S. Armed Forces, was the scriptwriter for *The USA in Circarama.*

Disney's interest in Circarama was a direct product of his desire to compete with the hugely successful widescreen formats that transformed film exhibition in the fifties. It also provided Disney with the opportunity to establish his own specialized exhibition spaces for his films. Television became one aspect of Disney's expanding role as an exhibitor. With the Circarama films, he was able to turn theaters themselves into attractions. The difference between Disney's widescreen developments and other popular widescreen technologies such as Cinerama, was that the film was only one element in an integrated theatrical experience that also included dioramas, narration, and the actual integration of products into the show.

Even with the considerable financial investment in the Circarama technology, and the enlistment of many of Disney's most talented Imagineers, the development of Circarama was not without its setbacks. The first prototype of the 360-degree camera consisted of eleven cameras that caused eyestrain and dizziness. In his quest for perfection, Disney challenged his crew to eliminate this visual defect. Engineers discovered that the problem was that because the entire camera lens faced outwards, they did not share exactly the same focal or nodal point. In order for the system to work properly, the cameras had to be aimed and focused at the same central nodal point. The engineers were able to quickly solve the problem and the second generation required only nine cameras, all focused into the same centralized focal point, which was a highly polished, angled mirror. The system worked flawlessly.

The financiers of the Circarama exhibit were American Motors and Kelvinator appliances (the producers of the durable goods par excellence of the fifties) who invested $350,000 into developing the show in order to "make friends who will eventually become customers for cars or appliances."[14] American Motors needed the potentially vast audience available at Disneyland probably more than Disney needed their investment. In 1955, American Motors had lost nearly seven million dollars, and it lost another twenty million in 1956. Even though the company was experiencing a financial crisis, American Motors recognized the potentially great economic returns that an investment in a ride at Disney's amusement park might mean. They eagerly invested their money into a project that was entirely under the control of Disney. The company would actually run out of money just as Disney was about to start shooting, and the film was completed in two weeks with most of the final footage made up of test shots that were run to see if the equipment worked.

Circarama, with its eleven projectors, showed audiences simultaneously "where you are, where you are going and where you have been." Like television, the film was one element in a broad display of consumer goods. The theater contained softly lit displays of Kelvinator appliances, and around the open portion of the screen was a sampling of automobiles. Kelvinator, as a manufacturer of home appliances, had devised a series of successful advertisements at the end of the war that showed the transformative powers of its appliances in bringing together the postwar family in their dream homes. By the time that Kelvinator was placing its appliances into the Circarama exhibit, the dream that its ads evoked as a possible future reality had indeed become true for many Americans. The newest refrigerators, stoves, and dishwashers were filling the homes of America, helping to build a strong and robust economy.

The Disneyland Circarama film opened with a "line of Kelvinator appliances presented: one on each screen" supposedly in order to "give the audience the feeling of the medium."[15] This was an audience that had already become familiar with Disney's method of combining entertainment with corporate sponsorship through his television show. The appliances and automobiles were recognizable friends for the fans of the television show who had been primed for months with regular updates about the building and opening of the park. And yet this blatant commercial placement, though typical of television, was not a standard experience for film viewers. Most Americans held the view that "the cinema was supposed to be a place where you could escape from all those annoying commercials seen on network television."[16] But the wonder of the new widescreen technology and the sensory overload that the experience created facilitated audience acceptance of the placement of products within the screen as yet another enchanting Disney creation. As *The New York Times* described two weeks after the park opened, "For the most startling innovation in movie presentation, one will have to visit Disneyland.... Walt Disney and the Eastman Kodak Company have hit upon the ultimate in audience participation or envelopment, via a 360-degree screen.... The effect of viewing a motion picture that is going on all around you is fantastic. Particularly overpowering is the sense of motion, or moving with the picture."[17] No mention or judgment was made concerning the fact that the film was part of a large advertising campaign directed to the ideal consumers—the nuclear family—that flooded the park grounds.

Circarama was targeting the predominantly middle-class, Southern Californian audience who arrived from the suburbs in their American Motors station wagons. As car travel became a favorite leisure activity for the postwar middle-class, Circarama provided a ready inducement to begin planning next summer's trip to all the great American sights. This tour of America's great parks and historical sites was a crucial rite of passage for most middle-class American families, and Disney knew how to market that desire to his audience through the *The Tour of the West* Circarama experience. Spectators were placed in the driver's seat of a Nash automobile providing them with a first person hypervisuality that opened up the visual field to a 360-degree panorama. The viewer's trip began with a leisurely tour of the shopper's paradise of Beverly Hills which then abruptly shifted to a police chase on Wilshire Boulevard accompanied by a loud siren screech. The journey continued on to Monument Valley, and the Grand Canyon. These families were already very familiar with the iconographic sites of the American West via the Western shows that dominated television screens in the fifties. The proliferation of narratives about the mythical Western frontier was key to the construction of American exceptionalism during the Cold War. *A Tour of the West* was a journey into the majestic landscape that gave birth to this nation. Disney transformed the miniaturized, black and white, television image of the West into a color saturated, 360-degree, sensory sensation. This was the ultimate road trip that provided the viewer access to the most awe inspiring sites, their beauty and splendor enhanced by the technological wonders of the newest cameras and film stock. Free of the tedium of the road, devoid of kitschy tourist sites, this family road trip was a patriotic journey into the mythical space of American national identity.

Disney's first Circarama film was a travelogue of America's most popular tourist destinations in the Western United States. Even though it was a main attraction in Tomorrowland, the only futuristic image provided by the exhibit was the film technology that Disney devised in order to out-do all other new widescreen formats. As *Business Screen* reported, "Bigger and wider screens are the unmistakable trend of movie presentation. The best way to predict the future of movie presentation then, was to go to the end of the line—the widest possible screen is a complete circle."[18] The technological imperative of the Circarama camera and projector demanded images that would exploit the grand scale that the medium provided. Therefore the cinematographers sought out scenic environments that would foreground the awe inspiring rather than the intimate or the personal. Spectators were meant to naturally align the products of corporate capitalism that surrounded them in the Circarama theater with the spectacular and iconographic images of America presented on screen thus directly linking consumption with national pride. The Circarama exhibit stood alongside other Tomorrowland theme park attractions that similarly incorporated film images with corporate slogans. Overall, Disney's world of the future in Tomorrowland was a corporate park fronted with the façade of a fairground. Disney's conception of the future looked back to the successes of the past in order to pave the way for the new glories of the American corporate future.

The USA in Circarama

Though many elites began to attack Disney for his sentimentality and anti-intellectualism in the fifties, he had become a symbol of postwar American society and its middle-class, All-American values. During this period, the Disney Studio was entering into a period of unprecedented integration and expansion into television, the Disneyland theme park, and live action films while maintaining its animated productions. Considering the high level of studio demands it is surprising that Walt Disney was eager to produce a Circarama film for the U.S. government. Yet at this time, Disney's live action films were regularly being shot in Europe and Walt Disney had become a frequent visitor. The Hollywood studios were rapidly expanding their markets into Europe as the U.S. film market plummeted and the development of *The USA in Circarama* provided an ideal opportunity for Disney to directly address the middle-class, mainstream European audiences that were already fans of Disney productions. Additionally, the funds provided by the corporate sponsors for the film would give the studio the monies needed to further develop the Circarama attraction at the park.

The Ford Motor Company was the only corporation solicited for sponsorship of *The USA in Circarama* and the funding negotiations were contentious. Andrews, the regional executive responsible for English, Canadian and German manufacturing for, believed that the "International Division couldn't hope to get a half million dollars worth out of it from an advertising point of view."[19] Eventually, the Ford Motor Company Fund offered $200,000 to be spent on the production and exhibition of the film with the understanding that Ford would have no rights to the equipment and the film after the fair. The United States government provided the rest of the $412,000 total budget with $100,000 allotted to Walt Disney for the production of the film. The film went into production in October of 1957, and a preview of an hour of raw footage was provided for Robert Warner and Walt Disney in November. The footage shot, per the requests of Ford, included a tour of the River Rouge plant including shots of their test track. Shooting continued through November, with the crew photographing aerial shots of San Francisco, the Grand Canyon, and the Southwest. The production was halted in December after the studio requested and failed to secure an additional $100,000 or more to complete the film. Bill Anderson, the executive vice president of Walt Disney Studios, wrote Warner that "this show would be delivered at a real financial loss to Walt Disney Productions but, as always the case, all of the money is put into brick, mortar and furnishings with little or nothing left for the entertainment portion." Warner attended a preview screening of the film in March and wrote to Cullman that he had been told by Anderson that "in addition to the $100,000 we paid them for the production, they have about $100,000 of their own money sunk into it. Off the record, I doubt it. However, the film is very good and I am sure this is going to be a tremendous attraction."[20] *The USA in Circamara* had been filmed across the United States to provide a "continuous panorama" of America. The cameramen traveled in a Lincoln Premier and a modified Ford station wagon, and their shooting schedule was broken into three parts. The first shots were of a wheat harvest in upper Montana which had a dynamic climax shot from on top of the station wagon as nine combines harvested in unison. After the wheat harvest, shooting occurred at Yellowstone National Park and then at the world's largest open pit copper mine in Utah. The second shooting segment went on to capture fall foliage in New England, the harbors and bridges of New York, and the bustle of Times Square. Then it was off to Rockefeller's newly restored Colonial Williamsburg in Virginia, now a mecca for tourists. Next came the steel mills of Pittsburgh, and the Santa Fe Railroad's vast freight yard in Kansas City. Mounted on top of a caboose, the speed of the cameras was undercranked in order to speed up the action in the yard. A major sequence of the film was shot at the Ford Motor Company's River Rouge plant. After this, it was off to a gigantic supermarket with acres of parked cars, then a modern-day cowboy cattle roundup, ending on a vignette of the oil industry near Tulsa. The last shooting segment required the assistance of a B-52 bomber. Since Disney insisted that no parts of the plane should be visible in the image, the Disney engineers devised a boom that would lower the camera seven feet beneath the plane. This segment was thematically a repeat of the Disneyland attraction. The aerial shots captured the stunning grandeur of the American West,tarting with Monument Valley, including several trips through the Grand Canyon, and culminating with Hoover Dam and a sunset over the Golden Gate Bridge. Then itt was back to the station wagon for a few trips across the Bay bridges, running shots of the San Francisco cable cars, and night shots in Chinatown. In all, more than one-hundred thousand feet of 16-millimeter Kodachrome Commercial film was exposed during a year of shooting. This footage was edited to create the 18-minute film.

Structured as a visual journey across America, the film was a unique addition to the Disney oeuvre. Unlike the propaganda shorts produced for the U.S. government during the war, *The USA in Circarama* did not rely on the comedic antics of the Disney animated characters to present an overtly political message. And unlike the *True-Life Adventures* and their heavy reliance on the close-up shot to bring the viewer into the natural environment, this film was limited to the panoramic shot. But several aspects of the film do distinguish it as a Disney production. Firstly, Walt Disney was eager to appropriate the newest filmic technology to create a transformative cinematic experience. Similar to his pioneering work with sound and color film, Circarama was Disney's response to Cinerama. And Disney relied heavily on technical expertise of Ub Iwerks to develop the camera and projector for the process. Secondly, the film is framed within a capitalist discourse that reveals a clear faith in capitalism as the engine that drives the American Dream and provides Americans with the highest standard of living in the world. *The USA in Circarama* is an optimistic celebration of a country defined by growth, innovation, and success. And the reasons for American exceptionalism are linked by the film to hardworking pioneers who embodied the American ideals of faith, integrity, and individual initiative. Those traditional values, it suggests, are what sustains the nation and guarantees its continued dominance.

At the Brussels World's Fair, the film was presented in three languages—English, French, and Flemish—with live narrators who engaged in a round robin conversation and would adapt their comments to their respective middle-class, European audiences. Opening on a sunrise over the New York harbor to the tune of *America the Beautiful*, the narration is descriptive of the scenes being projected on the screen. "Welcome to America" the narrators begins and they continue to explain that "during the few brief moments of this film, we shall attempt to catch the essence of the American panorama." The film takes the viewer on a journey across the nation ending at dusk at the San Francisco bridge. At the end, the film cuts back to New York for a final image of the Statue of Liberty. The film is structured as a re-enactment of the emigrant journey into the Promised Land of American bounty and leisure in the midst of natural wonders. With its use of cameras positioned on airplanes and automobiles, America becomes in the film a land in constant motion. The engines of the American economy are rendered through images of colossal industrial plants that illustrate the manufacturing strength of the nation. This was the image of America that visitors understood and expected. There was no self-conscious pretense or cynical elitism in these images. America was a global industrial powerhouse that was still deeply rooted in its heritage as recreated in Williamsburg and its present day cowboys. The corporate forces behind Ford's River Rouge plant provided the workers there with the leisure to shop in immense modern supermarkets. These were the iconic images of America that were immediately recognizable to Europeans and it was based on combining America's modern corporate wonders with a nostalgic and sentimental presentation of the traditional values of small-town America.

The film was the smash hit of the fair. Surveys of top attractions at the American pavilion at the Brussels World's Fair consistently placed the Circarama as the number one attraction. Long lines formed outside the theater throughout the time of the fair, causing twenty people to pass out in the heat. Girl guides were pulled from the exhibit after getting hurt attempting to handle the crowds. Warner reported to Turner Shelton, the director of Motion Pictures for the USIA, that "this is the finest propaganda weapon I have ever seen."[21] George Allen, the director of the USIA, after viewing the exhibit was "quite prepared to take the equipment over on the spot" for use in later USIA exhibits and trade shows. Walt Disney spent four days at the fair, and was initially averse to letting the government use the film and the equipment following the show. "Happily," Warner wrote to the USIA, "Walt Disney is a tremendously public spirited person and he finally agreed, with the understanding that it would not be shown in North American and would only be used by the government."[22]

Descriptions of audience responses to the film emphasized the emotional and sensational impact that the experience provided rather than consideration of the political or ideological significance of the images. The *Atlantic Monthly* exclaimed, "The 19 minute movie, a masterpiece by Disney, sweeps its audience through the United States with one dramatic gesture. Americans walk out, heads high, tears in the eye, still hearing the strains of *America the Beautiful*. Visitors from abroad burst out with their favorite superlatives, Fantastique, magnifique, formidable!"[23] It seemed as there were no dry eyes after they saw Disney's vision images of America. *The Christian Century* reporter exclaimed that "Going back to The Hague, among all the hundreds I fell in with the elderly Dutch couple with whom I had shared a compartment coming down. They had had a fine but wearying day. The high point? Circarama! 'It was worth all the standing and waiting,' the wife told me. 'When it ended, I felt I had really seen America and met your people. And then the beautiful scenery, with "America the Beautiful" swelling up at the end—we both had tears in our eyes when the lights came on.'"[24] The actual scope of the screen enveloped the spectators and made them part of the vast vistas of a free, vibrant and productive society on the move. This was the image of a world leader that Europeans understood; technology and industry lead the American people forward into a divinely appointed land of liberty and abundance. After several years of testing Circarama before an American audience, Disney had perfected his technique in marketing the American corporate culture to a middle-class audience.

The visceral experience of the film that caused spectators to cover their eyes, and to sway along with the images, created within them a vicarious sensation of being part of the action. Through his application of the wide screen format, Disney was able to generate the feelings of sentimentalism and wholesomeness that the American pavilion failed to create. The wide screen technology created a new viewership experience for spectators that resulted in a "wow" effect. As *Variety* reported, "The auditors stand in the center and thus have the sense of complete audience-participation in the degree that one roller-coaster number had to be excised because of the equilibrium impact. The viewers would lean back so far, because of the overly realistic effect, as to fall on their backs. Almost the same thing happens in one scene as the auto-bus climbs a steep grade and then descends on the other side."[25] The technology made the film into a ride that was driven by the viewer's response to a visual onslaught. Circarama was a "cinema of attraction" that was new and unique for the spectators who were accustomed to the single screen theater with stationary seating.

As film screens were expanding due to the onslaught of television, Disney contrived to control both the medium of television and the advent of wide screen technology. As Tony Bennett shows in his discussion of the new 180-degree cinema shows at Blackpool Pleasure Beach that opened in the 1980s, "whereas thrill rides take the normally stationary body and hurtle it through space, [these rides] hurtle the vision through space whilst fixing the body as stationary."[26] Disney was able to make the particularity of local American culture, its supermarkets, cowboys, and New England churches, and transform them into a universally shared experience and moreover create within the spectator the desire to become part of that landscape and society that the Circarama presented. As the trade journal *Business Screen* explained, "The best product we have to sell to the people whose curiosity brings them to the World's Fair is American progress and our way of life. In fulfilling this assignment, movies tell a big story and tell it convincingly"[27] The best achievement overseas for the USIA was provided by Walt Disney, "whose Circarama tour of the United States seemed to surround the viewer with beautiful scenery and well-scrubbed faces. It was a hit in Casablanca, Moscow and Djkarta."[28] This may explain why an in-house Disney publication issued as part of educational programs for young people calls Circarama the culmination of film technology. A section titled "From the Silent Movies to Circle-Vision 360: The Art of Filmmaking" explained that "in the Main Street Cinema, the silent film tells a story. In Circle-Vision 360, film not only tells a story, but also communicates a sense of involvement, learning and a whole range of human feelings. Comparing the two films makes it easy to see how film is growing as a form of communication."[29]

Walt Disney was one of America's foremost cultural diplomats at the height of the Cold War. International exhibitions were considered particularly important events at which the State Department and the USIA could present a saleable image of American ideology to a waiting audience. But as the Brussels World's Fair illustrated, these government displays, created by panels of American experts, were incapable of moving their audiences. These tastemakers' lack of consensus and awareness translated into displays that alienated and confused their target audience. Walt Disney, with his years of experience as America's entertainer, was much better prepared to teach the world the supposed rightness of the American way of life. His combination of corporate skills and entertainment savvy moved the heartstrings of the middle-class, and his sentimental nationalism made his audiences weep in understanding. Disney's values were simple and straightforward, his message of a triumphant consumer culture easily sold to the European market. As he explained, "You don't build it for yourself. You know what the people want and you build it for them."[30] Disney's *USA in Circarama* clearly showed who was best equipped to sell America to the world; by the fifties, Walt Disney had become America's best salesman.

NOTES

1. Neal Gabler, *Walt Disney: The Triumph of the American Imagination* (New York: Knopf, 2006), 389
2. Steven Watts, *The Magic Kingdom: Walt Disney and the American Way of Life* (Boston: Houghton Mifflin, 1997), 284.
3. G. Edward Wells, "Motion Pictures–the Film Two Cities," in *Records of Department of State 1950–1954* (National Archives, 1950).
4. Eric Smoodin, *Animating Culture: Hollywood Cartoons from the Sound Era* (New Brunswick, NJ: Rutgers University Press, 1993), 161.
5. Norman Cousins, "The Free Ride, Part II," *The Saturday Review of Literature* 33, no. 4 (1950), 20.
6. _____, "The Free Ride," *The Saturday Review of Literature* 33, no. 3 (1950), 25.
7. Ibid., 25.
8. Eric Johnston, "Messengers from a Free Country," *The Saturday Review of Literature* 33, no. 9 (1950), 11.
9. "Theme Development Staff Discussions," in Max Frank Millikan Papers (Cambridge: MIT Institute Archives, 1956).
10. "Interview with Walt Disney and John Hench," in Max Frank Millikan Papers (Cambridge: MIT Institute Archives MC 188, 1957).
11. James Plaut, "Letter to Cullman," in *Records of Minor Congressional Commissions* (National Archives 1957).
12. Tom Gunning, "The World as Object Lesson: Cinema Audiences, Visual Culture and the St. Louis World's Fair, 1904 " *Film History* 6, no. 4 (1994), 423–434.
13. Margaret King, "The Audience in the Wilderness: The Disney Nature Films," *Journal of Popular Film and Television* 24, no. 2 (1996) .
14. David Gonzales, *The Rockefellers at Williamsburg: Backstage with the Founders, Restorers and World-Renowed Guests* (McLean, VA: EPM Publications, 1991), 110.
15. "Techniques at Disney's Tomorrowland," *Business Screen* 16, no. 4 (1955), 38–39.
16. Jon Bigness, "Coming to a Theater near You, More TV-Like Commercial " *Northwestern*, September 5 1999., D1.
17. "Techniques at Disney's Tomorrowland," *Business Screen* 1955., 37–38.
18. Ibid., 37.
19. Thurston Davies, "Letter to Robert Warner," in *Records of Minor Congressional Commissions* (National Archives, 1957).
20. Robert Warner, "Letter to Howard Cullman," in *Records of Minor Congressional Commissions* (National Archives 1958).
21. _____, "Letter to Turner Shelton," in *Records of Minor Congressional Commissions* (National Archives, 1958).
22. _____, "Letter to Robert Sivard," in *Records of Minor Congressional Commissions* (National Archives 1958).
23. Madeleine May, "Overheard at the Fair," *Atlantic Monthly*, August 1958., 70.
24. Margaret Frakes, "One Day at Brussels," *Christian Century*, October 1 1958, 1109.

25. "Disneyland Circarama Is Wow as Transported to Brussels' Big Expo," *Variety*, April 30 1958.
26. Tony Bennett, *Formations of Pleasure* (London: Routledge, 1983), 151.
27. "Film at Brussels," *Business Screen* 19, no. 4 (1958), 32.
28. Richard Dyer MacCann, "Film and Foreign Policy: The USIA, 1962–67," *Cinema Journal*, vol. 9, no. 1 (1969), 179.
29. *The Walt Disney World of Entertainment*, (Burbank, CA: Walt Disney Publications, 1984), 31.
30. Ibid., 171.

Bibliography

Bennett, Tony. *Formations of Pleasure*. London: Routledge, 1983.
Bigness, Jon. "Coming to a Theater near You, More TV-Like Commercial " *Northwestern*, September 5 1999, D1D4.
Cousins, Norman "The Free Ride." *The Saturday Review of Literature* 33, no. 3 (1950): 24–25.
_____. "The Free Ride, Part II." *The Saturday Review of Literature* 33, no. 4 (1950): 20–21.
Davies, Thurston. "Letter to Robert Warner." In *Records of Minor Congressional Commissions*: National Archives, 1957.
"Disneyland Circarama Is Wow as Transported to Brussels' Big Expo." *Variety*, April 30 1958.
"Film at Brussels." *Business Screen* 19, no. 4 (1958).
Frakes, Margaret. "One Day at Brussels." *Christian Century*, October 1 1958, 1109.
Gabler, Neal. *Walt Disney: The Triumph of the American Imagination*. New York: Alfred A. Knopf, 2006.
Gonzales, David. *The Rockefellers at Williamsburg: Backstage with the Founders, Restorers and World-Renowed Guests*. McLean, VA: EPM Publications, 1991.
Gunning, Tom. "The World as Object Lesson: Cinema Audiences, Visual Culture and the St. Louis World's Fair, 1904 " *Film History* 6, no. 4 (1994): 422–44.
"Interview with Walt Disney and John Hench." In *Max Frank Millikan Papers*. Cambridge: MIT Institute Archives MC 188, 1957.
Johnston, Eric. "Messengers from a Free Country." *The Saturday Review of Literature* 33, no. 9 (1950): 9–12.
King, Margaret. "The Audience in the Wilderness: The Disney Nature Films." *Journal of Popular Film and Television* 24, no. 2 (1996): 60–69.
MacCann, Richard Dyer. "Film and Foreign Policy: The Usia, 1962–67." *Cinema Journal* 9, no. 1 (1969): 23–42.
May, Madeleine. "Overheard at the Fair." *Atlantic Monthly*, August 1958, 69–70.
Plaut, James. "Letter to Cullman." In *Records of Minor Congressional Commissions*: National Archives 1957.
Smoodin, Eric. *Animating Culture: Hollywood Cartoons from the Sound Era*. New Brunswick, NJ: Rutgers University Press, 1993.
"Techniques at Disney's Tomorrowland." *Business Screen* 16, no. 4 (1955): 38–39.
"Techniques at Disney's Tomorrowland." *Business Screen* 1955, 38–39.
"Theme Development Staff Discussions." In *Max Frank Millikan Papers*. Cambridge: MIT Institute Archives, 1956.
The Walt Disney World of Entertainment. Burbank, CA: Walt Disney Publications, 1984.
Warner, Robert. "Letter to Howard Cullman." In *Records of Minor Congressional Commissions*: National Archives 1958.

_____. "Letter to Robert Sivard." In *Records of Minor Congressional Commissions*: National Archives 1958.
_____. "Letter to Turner Shelton." In *Records of Minor Congressional Commissions*: National Archives, 1958.
Watts, Steven. *The Magic Kingdom: Walt Disney and the American Way of Life*. Boston: Houghton Mifflin Company, 1997.
Wells, G. Edward. "Motion Pictures—the Film Two Cities." In *Records of Department of State 1950–1954*: National Archives, 1950.

About the Contributors

Katharina Bonzel holds an M.A. from the Humboldt Universität zu Berlin, and is currently completing her Ph.D. in the Cinema Studies program of the School of Culture and Communication at the University of Melbourne. Her research focuses on the representation of national identity in film, with particular emphasis on sports films. Her article "Soccer to the Rescue: How the Miracle of Bern Gave Germans Back Their Identity — Twice" appeared in the journal *Sporting Traditions*, and she has presented papers on sports, film, and national identity at international conferences in Australia, Europe, and the United States.

Bob Cruz, Jr., holds a degree in paleontology from Yale University. He is currently an MFA candidate in the Science and Natural History Filmmaking Program at Montana State University. His research analyzes the origins of the Disney *True-Life Adventures* series, their contested status as documentaries, and their impact on later wildlife filmmakers and the contemporary natural history film format. He has made films on earth science topics— particularly fossil birds and extinction events—for the National Park Service and Montana's Museum of the Rockies.

Douglas A. Cunningham is a major in the United States Air Force, and assistant professor of English at the U.S. Air Force Academy. He has published in *Screen*, *Cineaction*, *The Moving Image*, and *Critical Survey*, among other journals. He holds a Ph.D. in film studies from the University of California–Berkeley, where he wrote his dissertation on representations of masculinity in the World War II training films made by the First Motion Picture Unit of the United States Army Air Forces. He is editing a volume of essays on Alfred Hitchcock's classic psychological thriller *Vertigo* (1956) for Scarecrow Press.

Marianne Holdzkom holds a Ph.D. in early American history from Ohio State University. Her fields of specialization include the American Revolution, the history of religion and U.S. cultural history. Her interest in the depiction of history in popular culture began with her doctoral dissertation, "Parody and Pastiche: Images of the American Revolution in Popular Culture, 1765–1820." She published "An Inconvenient Founding Father: Adapting John Adams for Popular Culture" in the edited anthology *The Theme of Cultural Adaptation in American History Literature and Film: Cases When the Discourse Changed* (2009). She is currently an assistant professor of history at Southern Polytechnic State University in Marietta, Georgia.

Richard J. Leskosky recently retired from the University of Illinois at Urbana-Champaign, where he earned his Ph.D. in linguistics, and where he taught animation history courses in the Unit for Cinema Studies for more than twenty-five years. His work has appeared in *Animation Studies, Film History, The Velvet Light Trap,* as well as journals in the natural and social sciences. He continues to work on animated film genres, and on the nineteenth century optical devices that created the illusion of motion decades before the cinema.

Cynthia J. Miller is a cultural anthropologist, specializing in popular culture and visual media. She holds a Ph.D. from McGill University, teaches in the Institute for Interdisciplinary Studies at Emerson College, in Boston, and is an associate editor of *Film & History: An Interdisciplinary Journal of Film and Television Studies.* Her writing has appeared, most recently in *Why We Fought: War in Film, Television and History* (2008), *Heroes of Film, Comics, and American Culture* (2009); *Cultural Adaptation in American History, Literature, and Film* (2009); *Sounds of the Future: Essays on Music in Science Fiction Film* (2010). She is editing the volume *Too Bold for the Box Office: A Study in Mockumentary* for Wayne State University Press, and working on *The Encyclopedia of B Westerns* for Scarecrow Press.

Sarah Nilsen is assistant professor of film studies at the University of Vermont. She holds an MFA in screenwriting from the American Film Institute and an M.A. and Ph.D. in critical studies from the University of Southern California. Her areas of interest include Walt Disney, the popular culture of the Cold War, and cultural diplomacy. She has published articles on gender and ethnicity in *The Mickey Mouse Club* and the role of *Davy Crockett* in shaping American gun culture in the 1950s. Her book *Projecting America: Film and Cultural Diplomacy at the Brussels World's Fair of 1958,* is forthcoming from McFarland.

Martin F. Norden teaches and writes about film as a professor of communication at the University of Massachusetts–Amherst. He received his undergraduate and graduate degrees from the University of Missouri. He has written extensively on images of disability in film, and is the author of *The Cinema of Isolation: A History of Physical Disability in the Movies* (1994) and co-editor of the forthcoming *Making Differences: Images of Disability in Popular Culture.* He has also edited volumes on *The Changing Face of Evil in Film and Television* (2007) and *The Birth Control Films of Margaret Sanger and Lois Weber* (forthcoming).

Bernice Nuhfer-Halten is a Cuban-Polish-American veteran educator who teaches Spanish and French as foreign languages. She holds a Ph.D. in Spanish literature from Florida State University, and has been affiliated for almost a quarter of a century with the faculty of Southern Polytechnic State University, a branch of the University System of Georgia. Her research interests include film, deconstruction of poetry by computer application, the impact of study abroad on second language acquisition, and applied linguistics. She recently received a grant to imbue the entire campus with foreign language acquisition through the campus-wide use of Rosetta Stone software in several languages.

Bella Honess Roe is a lecturer in film studies at the University of Surrey in the United Kingdom. She holds a B.A. in philosophy from Cambridge University, and an M.A. and Ph.D. in critical studies from the University of Southern California. Her doctoral thesis ("Animating Documentary") was a study of the epistemological and phenomenological implications of the convergence of animation and documentary, and an investigation of the historical precedent for the hybridization of the two seemingly antithetical forms of media. Her work has appeared in *Film International*, *Animation: An Interdisciplinary Journal*, and the *British Journal of Film and Television*. She teaches courses on film analysis, cultural industries, and documentary history, and is currently at work on a monograph on animated documentaries.

John D. Thomas is a Ph.D. candidate in the Department of English at Rutgers, specializing in American literature. He holds degrees in English and history from the University of South Carolina and Baylor University. His work on the fiction of Edgar Allan Poe, F. Scott Fitzgerald, and Edith Wharton has appeared in *Critique: Studies in Contemporary Fiction*, the *F. Scott Fitzgerald Review*, the *Edith Wharton Review*, and *Notes on Contemporary Literature*. His work on *Victory Through Air Power* is rooted in a long-standing interest in wartime novels and films, and his presentation on the film at the 2006 Film and History Conference on "The Documentary Tradition" was one of those that created the impetus for this book.

Ronald Tobias, a natural history filmmaker, holds an MFA from Bowling Green State University. He is a founder of the MFA Program in Science and Natural History Filmmaking at Montana State University, where he teaches natural history and science filmmaking, screenwriting, and documentary production. He is the author of six books, including the *Insider's Guide to Writing for Screen and Television* (1997) and *20 Master Plots and How to Build Them* (1993). His screen credits as director, writer, and producer include more than 30 nature documentaries, which have aired on PBS, the Discovery Channel, the National Geographic Channel, and Animal Planet, as well as on networks in Germany, Sweden, and Japan.

A. Bowdoin Van Riper is a historian of science and technology who teaches in the Science, Technology, and Society program at Southern Polytechnic State University, a branch of the University System of Georgia. His work on the history of geology and archaeology, the history of aerospace technology, and images of science and technology in popular culture centers on the cultural impact of scientific and technological change. He is the author of *Men Among the Mammoths* (1993), *Science and Popular Culture* (2002), *Imagining Flight: Aviation and the Popular Imagination* (2003), and *Rockets and Missiles: The Life Story of a Technology* (2004; reprinted 2007), and is currently at work on *The Hollywood History of Science and Technology* (Scarecrow Press).

Eddy von Mueller is a lecturer in the Department of Film and Media Studies at Emory University in Atlanta, where he teaches courses in animation, Asian cinemas, film and television history, and filmmaking. His 2005 feature *The Lady from Sockholm*, co-directed with Evan Lieberman, has been screened in over 30 film festivals around the world. In addition to numerous reviews and commentaries for the popular press, he has published articles on the samurai films of Akira Kurosawa, police procedurals in print and on screen, and silent adaptations of Shakespeare. His first book, *Synthetic Cinema: Technology, Aesthetics and the Impact of Animation on Contemporary Filmmaking*, is currently being prepared for publication.

Index

The Absent-Minded Professor (1961) 7
Academy Awards 42, 44, 47, 57, 59, 113, 119, 145, 146, 149
advertising 41, 243–245
The African Lion (1955) 6, 148, 151, 152
agriculture 46–48, 247
Air Power and Armies (1945) 36
airplanes 18–19, 47, 50, 57, 64, 68, 73–77, 95, 212–213, 247
Alaska 64, 74, 75, 76, 227–228, 229
The Alaskan Eskimo (1953) 6, 221, 228, 229
Algar, James 149, 153, 243
"Alice" films 118–119
Alice in Wonderland (1950) 118–121, 137, 216
The Ama Girls (1957) 6, 229–231, 232
American Dream 201, 204–207
American exceptionalism 183–185
Andrews, James 192–193
animation 33, 35, 44, 90, 211–213, 215–216; caricatured 73, 139–140; life-like 1–2, 5, 17, 22–23, 29–30, 44–48, 54, 70–75, 92–93, 217–218; maps 29, 42, 45–48, 50, 75–76, 105, 130, 147, 151, 186, 184, 211, 213; schematic 21–24, 29–30, 43–44, 45, 93–94, 117–118, 135–136
Antarctica 7, 84, 85, 86–87, 92, 93, 95, 96, 215, 221, 229, 232
Antarctica: Operation Deep Freeze (1957) 85
Antarctica: Past and Present (1956) 85, 86, 93
anti-communism 238–241
Argentina 210, 211, 213
The Art of Skiing (1941) 108, 138
The Ascent of Man (television series) 175
Atomic Energy (unproduced film) 85
Attenborough, David 174, 175, 176
Australia 131, 151
Austria 7, 165
automobiles 8, 103–111, 240, 244, 248

Babes in Toyland (1961) 140
Bahia 215–216
Bakshi, Ralph 173
Bambi (1942) 1, 47, 90, 92, 106, 135, 149, 152, 158, 164–168, 169, 170, 180, 211, 227
The Band Concert (1935) 20
Banda, Milt 116, 119
Barks, Carl 116–154
Barnes, Howard 67
Battle of Dunkirk 75, 76
Bear Country (1953) 148
Beard, Charles 65
Beaver Valley (1950) 148, 152, 157
Bedknobs and Broomsticks (1971) 2
Berg, Bill 116
The Big Bad Wolf 18–19
Big Red (1962) 170
The Black Cauldron (1985) 150
Blue Men of Morocco (1957) 228, 229, 230
Bluth, Don 173
Bray, John Randolph 15
Brazil 210, 211, 213–214, 215–216, 217
Brooks, Herb 206–207
Bruns, George 140

Call of the Wild (book) 158
Canada 9, 15–24, 40, 43, 59, 131, 154, 224, 226
Capra, Frank 41, 47
Carioca, José (cartoon character) 214, 215–218
Carson, Rachel 158
Charlie, the Lonesome Cougar (1967) 8, 169
Chicken Little (1943) 57–58
Chile 211, 212–213
China 63, 74, 94
Churchill, Frank 18
Churchill, Winston 68
Cinderella (1950) 1, 128, 149, 211
Circarama 10, 237–251
Civil War 7, 184, 191–193, 194–195
The Civil War (television series) 175
Civilisation (television series) 174, 175
Clara Cleans Her Teeth (1926) 43, 128–130
Clark, Les 116, 118, 119

Cleanliness Brings Health (1945) 133–134
Clem, Johnny 191–192
Cleveland, Grover 196
Cold War 9, 10, 85–98; *passim* 114–115, 183–185, 186–188, 206–207, 222–224, 226, 233–234, 239–251
Collier's (magazine) 41, 89–90
comic books 2, 113, 114, 116, 120–121, 202, 209
Communications (unproduced film) 85
Cosmos (television series) 175
Cottrell, Bill 133
Cousins, Norman 239–240
Cruise of the Eagle (1958) 229, 232
Cutting, Jack 133

Dad, Can I Borrow the Car? (1970) 8, 104, 106–107, 110
The Danube (1960) 221, 229, 231
Darwin, Charles 157, 158, 178
Davis, Sid 138, 139, 142
Davy Crockett (1955–1956) 4, 7, 188–190, 195
De Bergerac, Cyrano 94
Defense Against Invasion (1943) 127, 132, 136, 139
dental hygiene 43, 128–130
Der Fuehrer's Face (1943) 5, 21, 52–54, 59, 64, 69, 119, 224
Dickens, Charles 230
Dinosaur (2000) 179
Disney, Roy 31–32, 68, 145
Disney, Walt 170–171, 173, 196–197; commitment to education 4, 114, 121–122, 136; involvement in production 24, 48–49, 133, 152–153; promotion of strategic bombing 65, 66–68; views of America 183–184, 237–241
Disney Channel 2, 98
Disneyland (television series) 2, 5, 117, 241, 242, 243; edutainment films broadcast on 6, 58–59, 113, 146; edutainment films produced for 6–7, 84–85, 90, 92–95, 98, 185–186, 188–190; unproduced episodes of, 85–86
Disneyland (theme park) 5–6, 121, 221, 241–245
Disneyland U.S.A. (1958) 229, 232
Donald Duck 1, 138, 239; in *Donald in Mathmagic Land* 113–122; in films about Latin America 209, 212, 214–218; in propaganda films 5, 19–20, 24, 41, 48–51, 52–54, 224
Donald in Mathmagic Land (1959) 4, 8, 9, 59, 86, 113–122
Donald in Nutziland *see* *Der Fuehrer's Face*
Donald's Better Self (1938) 19–20, 43
Donald's Decision (1941) 19–20, 43, 57, 59, 224
Dopey 17–18
Dumbo (1941) 1, 47, 53

Earth (2009) 8, 10, 157, 173–174, 177–180
Eden, Garden of 158, 159, 166
Education for Death (1943) 5, 21, 52, 54–55, 58, 59, 64, 69, 224
edutainment (definition) 2, 3–4
Edwards, Cliff 49, 53
Eiffel Tower 75
election of 1888 196–197
English Channel 74, 75
Escape to Witch Mountain (1975) 2
ethnographic film 225–227, 233
evolution 9, 47, 88, 92
exploration 194–195, 225
extraterrestrial life 89, 92–93, 94
Eyes in Outer Space (1959) 59, 86

Fadiman, Clifton 65
Fantasia (1940) 4–5, 8, 31, 42, 59, 90, 92–93, 106, 121, 130, 134, 135, 138, 139, 149, 150, 179
Farmyard Symphony (1938) 48
Felix the Cat 150
Ferdinand the Bull (1938) 42
The Fight (1969) 139
Fighting Prince of Donegal (1966) 7
Finding Nemo (2003) 180
First Motion Picture Unit (U.S. Army Air Forces) 27, 32–37
Flash, the Teenage Otter (1961) 164, 168–170, 171
Fleischer, Max 15, 55
Flowers and Trees (1932) 1
Fly with Von Drake (1963) 2, 98
food 46–48, 51–52, 53, 133–134
Food Will Win the War (1942) 46–47, 63
Foote, Shelby 175
Ford Motor Company 245–247
Four Methods of Flush Riveting (1940) 4, 16–17, 21, 22, 23, 42, 63, 116, 135
The Fox and the Hound (1981) 180
Frees, Paul 117
Freewayphobia (1965) 4, 8, 104, 107, 109–110
Der Fuehrer's Face (1943) 5, 21, 52–54, 59, 64, 69, 119, 224
Fuller, William 192–193

Gage, Gen. Thomas 187
The Game 139
Gannett, Lewis 65
gauchos 213, 215
Germany 5, 46, 53, 58, 66, 75, 78, 231
Geronimi, Clyde 54, 57
Ghana 141–142
Ghosts of the Abyss (2003) 8

Glory Road (2006) 201, 203
Goebbels, Josef 55
The Gold Coast *see* Ghana
Golden Eggs (1941) 46
Good Neighbor Policy 43, 46, 48, 58, 210–211
Goofy 8, 41–43, 44, 104, 107–110, 111, 138, 156, 211–213, 215
Goofy's Freeway Troubles (1965) 4, 8, 104, 107, 109–110
Göring, Hermann 53, 55
The Grain That Built a Hemisphere (1943) 47–48
Grand Canyon 245, 247
Grant, Joe 69
The Great Depression 19
The Great Locomotive Chase (1956) 7, 191–193, 195
The Greatest Game Ever Played (2005) 8
Grierson, John 16, 22

Haber, Heinz 89, 91–92, 98, 116
Harper, Brig. Gen. Robert W. 30–34
Harrison, Benjamin 196
Heath, Royal Vale 115
Helvering, Guy 48
Hibler, Winston 149, 150, 152, 228
High Level Precision Bombing (1944) 28–37
highways 104–106
Hirohito (Emperor of Japan) 46, 51, 53
Hitler, Adolf 21, 46, 51, 53–59, 74–75, 76, 77, 211
Hookworm (1945) 133, 141
How to Be a Sailor (1944) 117
How to Catch a Cold (1951) 59, 136–137
How to Fire a Lewis Gun (1917) 15
How to Have an Accident (1956, 1959) 138
How to Play Baseball (1942) 45
How to Play Golf (1944) 117, 138
How to Read an Army Map (1917) 15
How to Read Donald Duck (book) 209
How to Relax (1957) 108
How to Ride a Horse (1950) 117
Hubble, Edwin 86
Huemer, Dick 69
Huey, Dewey, and Louie (characters) 49, 121
The Human Body (1945) 134
Humboldt, Alexander von 157, 158

I'm No Fool (film series) 59, 137–138, 140, 141
IMAX 8
Indians 47–48, 188–191, 195, 233
Infant Care (1945) 133
International Geophysical Year 90, 97
Invincible (2005) 201, 202, 203
Ireland 7
Iron Will (1994) 8
Ising, Rudolf 32
Islands of the Sea (1960) 6
Iwerks, Ub 173, 242, 248

Jackson, Andrew 189
Jackson, Wilfred 50
Japan (1960) 221, 228, 229
Jiminy Cricket 49, 59, 137, 142
Johnny Shiloh (1963) 191–192, 193
Johnny Tremain (1957) 7, 10, 185–188
Jordan, David Starr 145, 158
The Jungle Book (1967) 1, 174
Jungle Cat (1959) 151, 152
Justin Morgan Had a Horse (1972) 8

Kimball, Ward 91, 104
King, Jack 51
Kinney, Jack 53
Krasna, Capt. Norm 34, 35

Lapland (1957) 6, 221, 229, 232
Latin America 5, 10, 40, 47–48, 130–134, 209–219, 233, 238
Latin names 109
laws of motion 87–88, 94
The Legend of Lobo (1962) 169, 170
lemmings 154–155
Leonardo da Vinci 86
Lessing, Gunther 130
Leventhal, Jack 15
Ley, Willy 89, 91, 98
Life (magazine) 41, 67
Lilo and Stitch (2002) 180
Lion King (1994) 2, 4, 156, 167, 169, 174, 180
The Little Mermaid 179
The Living Desert (1953) 4, 149, 150, 151, 152, 156, 157, 243
Lobo (book) 158
Lockheed Aircraft Corporation 16, 40, 42, 116
London, Jack 158
Los Angeles Examiner (newspaper) 71
The Love Bug (1968) 4
Lunch Money (1970) 139, 141
Luske, Hamilton 116–119, 121

Magic Highway USA (1958) 4, 85, 87, 91, 92, 93, 95, 97, 98, 103–105, 110–111
Maginot Line 75–76
Man and the Moon (1955) 59, 85, 88–90, 91, 92, 94, 96, 97
Man in Flight (1957) 2, 85, 87, 92, 93, 95, 97, 98
Man in Space (1955) 24, 59, 85, 87–88, 89, 90–95, 97
Marion, Francis 185–186
Mars and Beyond (1957) 4, 59, 85, 88–90, 91, 92, 93, 94, 95–96, 97

Mary Poppins (1964) 2
Matka and Kotik: A Tale of the Mist-Islands (book) 145, 158
McEvoy, J. P. 69
McLeish, John 117
Meador, Joshua 116, 119
Mein Kampf (book) 53, 54, 55, 57, 66
Men Against the Arctic (1955) 6, 232
Merrill, Lt. Col. Walt D. 31, 32–33
Mexico 210, 216–218
Michaels, Al 207
Mickey Mouse 1, 5, 20, 52, 116, 118, 121, 130, 150, 156, 239
The Mickey Mouse Club (television series) 59
military training films 15–16, 21–24, 27–37
Milotte, Albert and Elma 145, 148, 225
Minnie Mouse 24, 51–52
Miracle (2004) 4, 8, 10, 201, 202, 203, 206–207
Miracle of the White Stallions (1963) 7
Miranda, Aurora 216
Mississippi River 189–190
Mr. Walker & Mr. Wheeler (cartoon characters) 108–109
Mitchell, Brig. Gen. William 28–29, 30, 64–65, 71–73, 78
money 16–21, 43, 48–50, 121
Monument Valley 245, 247
Morganthau, Henry J. 48–49
Morris, Jim 206
Mosby's Marauders (1967) 191
Motor Mania (1948) 8, 104, 107–109, 110
Mulan (1998) 2, 8
multiplane camera 1, 44
music 4–5, 93, 140, 150, 178–179, 212, 214, 216–218, 228
Music Land (1935) 44
Mussolini, Benito 46, 53, 210

Napoleon and Samantha 169
narrative elements: authority figures 42–43, 52, 59 70–72, 84, 89–92, 98, 104–106, 114, 117, 134–137, 194–195; behavior modeling 17–20, 50–52, 106, 108–110, 128–130, 133–134, 137–139; comic relief 17–18, 19–20, 21, 22, 48, 49, 52–53, 93–94, 139–140, 209–218; familiar characters 17–21, 41–43, 49–53, 107–110, 112–122, 209–220
Nash, Clarence 116, 117
National Film Board of Canada 9, 15–17, 17–24; *passim* 224
Native Americans *see* Indians
Nature's Better Built Homes (1960) 2, 7
Nature's Half-Acre (1951) 148, 151
Navajo Adventure (1957) 233
The Navajo, Children of God (1967) 233
Naziism 5, 18–19, 50, 53–58, 59, 66, 75, 76, 224
Nehemkis, 1st Lt. Peter R. 31–33
The New Girl (1970) 139
The New Spirit (1942) 49–50, 115, 117
New York, NY 247, 248
New York Herald Tribune 65, 67
New York Times 30, 64–65, 244
The New Yorker (magazine) 65
Newton, Isaac 87, 93, 94, 96
Nielsen, Leslie 185
The Nine Lives of Elfego Baca (1958–1959) 7, 194
No Smoking (1951) 138
nuclear energy 88–90, 91–92, 95, 96

The Old Mill (1935) 44
Olivier, Laurence 175
The One and Only, Genuine, Original Family Band (1969) 10, 194, 195–197
Oscars *see* Academy Awards
Oswald the Rabbit 44
Our Friend the Atom (1957) 7, 59, 84, 85, 87, 88–89, 90, 91, 92, 95, 96, 97–98, 224
Out of the Frying Pan and into the Firing Line (1942) 24, 51–52

Panchito (character) 216–218
Papale, Vince 203, 204–205
Pearce, Perc 33–36
People and Places (film series) 6, 85, 86, 90, 221–234, 243
Perri (1957) 151, 152, 164–168, 170
Peru 211–212
Philadelphia Eagles 204–205
Physical Fitness and Good Health (1969) 138
Pickering, Ken 141–142
Pinocchio (1940) 1, 31, 130, 137, 149, 207
Planet Earth (television series) 174, 176–179, 181
Planning for Good Eating (1946) 133–134
Pluto (character) 20, 24, 41, 51, 52, 239
Pocahontas (1995) 4, 8, 197
Pocahontas II: Voyage to a New World (1998) 8
Potter, H. C. 68
Powell, John Wesley 194–195
Prescott, Orville 65
The Princess and the Frog (2009) 179
The Project (1970) 139
propaganda films 5, 9 15–21, 28–31, 41–45, 48–59, 58–59, 64–83, 70–78, 114, 146, 210–211, 223–224, 237–240, 247
Pryor, Thomas 67

race 188–191, 203, 205–206, 213–214, 216–218

Ravenscroft, Thurl 105
Reason and Emotion (1943) 52, 55–57, 59
Reitherman, Wolfgang 116, 119
Remember the Titans (2000) 8, 10, 201, 202, 203, 205
The Rescuers (1977) 179
Revere, Paul 186, 187
Revolutionary War 7, 183–188
RKO Pictures 145, 146
Rob Roy: The Highland Rogue (1954) 7
Roberts, Bill 47, 55
rockets 88–89, 91, 93–95, 97–98
Rolls, C. S. 74–75, 77
The Rookie (2002) 8, 201, 203, 206
Roosevelt, Franklin D. 19, 68, 210
Roving Mars (2006) 4, 8

Sagan, Carl 175
Saludos Amigos! (1942) 5, 130, 209–210, 211, 214, 215, 216, 217, 233, 238
Samoa (1956) 221, 229, 230
Saturday Review of Literature (magazine) 239–240
science 77–78, 84–86, 89, 94–95, 97–98
science fiction 94, 97, 98
Scotland 7, 229, 231
Scrooge McDuck (character) 51, 121
Scrooge McDuck and Money (1967) 121
Seal Island (1948) 6, 1457–147, 148, 149, 151, 152, 157, 227–228, 243
See America First 223, 226
Seton, Ernest Thompson 158
Seven Cities of Antarctica (1958) 7, 85, 229, 232
The Seven Dwarfs (characters) 131
Seven Wise Dwarfs (1941) 17–18
Seversky, Maj. Alexander de 5, 28–29, 59, 64–67, 70–72, 74–78
sexuality 134–136, 216–218
Sharpsteen, Ben 6, 46, 50, 141, 149, 153, 228
Shields, Fred 117
Siam (1954) 6, 229, 230
Siberia 74
Silly Symphonies (cartoon series) 17, 18, 42, 44, 52, 57, 59, 150, 159, 165, 173, 178
Skeleton Dance (1929) 178
Sleeping Beauty (1959) 1
Smith, Art 54
Snow White and the Seven Dwarfs (1938) 1, 17, 45, 130
Social Side of Health (1969) 138–139
Soviet Union 203, 206–207
space exploration *see Man in Space, Man and the Moon, Mars and Beyond*
The Spirit of '43 (1943) 50–51, 59, 115, 117
The Spirit of '76 (painting) 47
Sputnik 114–115
Squanto: A Warrior's Tale (1994) 8, 197
Steamboat Willie (1928) 1
Steel and America (1965) 8
Steps Toward Maturity and Health (1968) 138
Stop That Tank! (1942) 21–23, 24
The Story of Anyburg USA (1957) 104–106, 110
The Story of Menstruation (1946) 9, 127, 134–137, 140–142
The Story of Trains (unproduced film) 85
Stuhlinger, Ernst 89–90
The Swamp Fox (1959–1961) 4, 7, 185–188
swastika 19, 20, 53, 54, 55, 57, 75, 76, 119
Switzerland (1955) 6, 221, 224, 229
Sword and the Rose (1953) 7
Sword in the Stone (1963) 2

Tarzan (1999) 180
Taylor, Deems 59
Technicolor 1, 17, 21, 29, 30, 32, 156
technology 84–86, 95–97, 103, 105–106, 110–111
Ten Who Dared (1960) 4, 7, 194–195
Texas John Slaughter (1958–1961) 7, 194
This Week (magazine) 69
Thomas, Frank 32
Thompson, Bill 137
The Three Caballero (1945) 4, 5, 130, 209–211, 214–218
The Three Little Pigs (1933) 17–19, 42, 130, 152
Thrifty Pig (1941) 18–20, 63
A Tiger Walks (1964) 169, 170
Time (magazine) 66, 70, 188
To the South Pole for Science (1957) 4, 85, 87
Tommy Tucker's Tooth (1922) 9, 43, 128–130, 133
Tonka (1958) 194
travelogue 245–248
Treasure Island (1950) 4
Trouble on the Mountain (1970) 191
True-Life Adventures (film series) 2, 90, 146–159, 164–165, 167, 170, 178, 224, 228, 243, 247
True-Life Fantasies (film series) 10, 164–171
Tuberculosis (1945) 133
20,000 Leagues Under the Sea (1954) 6

Uganda 141–142
Under the Sea Wind (book) 158
Understanding Stresses and Strains (1968) 8, 138
United Artists 17, 18
United Productions of America (UPA) 93
United States Army Air Forces 27–37

United States Government: Central Intelligence Agency 240–241; Department of Agriculture 46–47; Department of the Interior 159; Department of the Navy 28; Department of State 211, 239–240, 250; Department of the Treasury 48–49, 238; National Park Service 159; Office of the Coordinator of Inter-American Affairs (CIAA) 47, 52, 131–134, 147, 211, 214; United States Information Agency 249–251
United States Navy 7, 28, 29, 63, 66, 67, 95, 97, 130; exploration of Antarctica by 86–87, 95
The USA in Circarama (1958) 238, 243, 246–248

V-for-Victory 50, 51
The Vanishing Prairie (1954) 151, 152, 159, 243
VD Attack Plan (1973) 9, 127, 139–141
Vermeil, Dick 205
Victory at Sea 174–175
Victory Through Air Power (1943) 2, 5, 9, 41, 59, 63; attitude toward science 76–78; footage reused 2, 85; impact on U.S. Army Air Force leaders 27–31, 33–34, 36–37; as propaganda 70–78; reception 66–70; visual style 72–76, 90, 92
Victory Through Air Power (book) 64–66
video recordings 2, 8, 70, 99, 204, 211
von Braun, Wernher 59, 89–92, 96–98

Wagner, Walter 67, 69
Wales (1958) 221, 229, 230, 231
Walt Disney Educational Media Company 139, 141
Walt Disney Presents (television series) *see Disneyland* (television series)
Walt Disney Studio: association with fantasy 1–2, 5; production of classroom films 115, 122, 134–136, 137–140, 146; repurposing of existing films 2, 6–7, 17, 20–21, 57–59, 98–99, 134; work with corporations 8, 138–139, 242–248; work with governments 17, 27–31, 33–34, 36, 40–41, 48–49, 65–66, 237–239; work with independent filmmakers 145–149;
Water — Friend or Enemy (1943) 131–132, 133
Watership Down (book) 158
The Way Disease Spreads (1945) 141
Westward Ho, the Wagons! (1956) 190–191
What Should I Do? (film series) 139
The Wheel (unproduced) 85
White Wilderness (1958) 154–156
Why We Fight (film series) 41, 45, 55, 146
The Wild Country (1970) 194
Winged Scourge (1943) 127, 131, 133, 141,
Winthrop, John 183
The Wonderful World of Color (television series) *see Disneyland* (television series)
The Wonderful World of Disney (television series) *see Disneyland* (television series)
The World at War (television series) 174–175
World War I 15–16
World's Fairs 227, 237–238, 240–241, 248–249
The Wright Brothers 75
Wynn, Keenan 139–140

Yellowstone Cubs (1963) 164, 169
Yellowstone National Park 247
You the Human Animal (film series) 137–138

Ziemer, Gregor 54